CRICKET
STATISTICS
YEAR BY YEAR
1946–1987

Reference books used in preparation of this book:

The Wisden Book of Test Cricket (1877–1984) – Bill Frindall (Queen Anne Press, 1979, 1985)

Who's Who of Cricketers – Philip Bailey, Philip Thorn, Peter Wynne-Thomas (Newnes Bookes, in association with the Association of Cricket Statisticians, 1984)

The Book of One-Day Internationals – David Lemmon (Stanley Paul, 1983)

Benson and Hedges Cricket Year – David Lemmon & Tony Lewis (Pelham Books, 1982, 1983, 1984, 1985)

Playfair Cricket Annual – Gordon Ross, later Bill Frindall (Queen Anne Press, various years)

Wisden Cricketers' Almanack (various years)

CRICKET STATISTICS YEAR BY YEAR 1946–1987

FRED TRUEMAN AND DON MOSEY

Statistics compiled by Wendy Wimbush

STANLEY PAUL
London Melbourne Auckland Johannesburg

Stanley Paul and Co. Ltd

An imprint of Century Hutchinson Ltd

Brookmount House, 62–65 Chandos Place
Covent Garden, London WC2N 4NW

Century Hutchinson Australia (Pty) Ltd
PO Box 496, 16–22 Church Street, Hawthorn,
Melbourne, Victoria 3122

Century Hutchinson New Zealand Limited
191 Archers Road, PO Box 40–086, Glenfield, Auckland 10

Century Hutchinson South Africa (Pty) Ltd
PO Box 337, Bergvlei 2012, South Africa

First published 1988

Copyright © Fred Trueman & Don Mosey 1988

Designed by Julian Holland

Set in 10/12pt Plantin Linotron 202

Photoset by Deltatype Lecru, Ellesmere Port, Cheshire

Printed and bound in Great Britain by
Butler and Tanner Ltd, Frome.

British Library Cataloguing in Publication Data

Trueman, Fred
    Cricket statistics year-by-year 1946–1987.
    1. Cricket — Statistics
    I. Title II. Mosey, Don
    796.35 '8' 021   GV925

ISBN 0 09 173667 6

Contents

Contents

Contents

Contents

Contents

Contents

Tests v India:

Lord's	England won by 10 wickets
Old Trafford	Match drawn
The Oval	Match drawn.

County Champions Yorkshire

TEST AVERAGES ENGLAND V INDIA 1946

	M	I	NO	HS	Runs	Av	100	50	Ct/St
J. Hardstaff	2	3	1	205*	210	105.00	1	–	–
D. C. S. Compton	3	4	2	71*	146	73.00	–	2	1
W. R. Hammond	3	4	1	69	119	39.66	–	1	2
C. Washbrook	3	5	1	52	146	36.50	–	1	1
L. Hutton	3	5	1	67	123	30.75	–	1	–
P. A. Gibb	2	3	0	60	84	28.00	–	1	2/1
J. T. Ikin	2	3	1	29*	47	23.50	–	–	5
A. V. Bedser	3	2	0	30	38	19.00	–	–	3
D. V. P. Wright	2	2	0	3	3	1.50	–	–	–

Also batted: W. E. Bowes (1 match) 2; L. B. Fishlock (1 match) 8; R. Pollard (1 match) 10*, 2ct; T. F. Smailes (1 match) 25; W. Voce (1 match) 0.
W. J. Edrich, T. G. Evans, A. R. Gover, J. Langridge and T. P. B. Smith played in one match but did not bat.

	Overs	M	Runs	Wkts	Av	5w	10w	BB
A. V. Bedser	144.2	33	298	24	12.41	2	2	7–49
R. Pollard	52	26	87	7	12.42	1	–	5–24

Also bowled: W. E. Bowes 29–8–73–1; D. C. S. Compton 12–1–38–0; W. J. Edrich 19.2–4–68–4; A. R. Gover 21–3–56–1; W. R. Hammond 1–0–3–0; J. T. Ikin 12–1–54–1; J. Langridge 29–9–64–0; T. E. Smailes 20–3–62–3; T. P. B. Smith 21–4–58–1; W. Voce 26–8–46–1; D. V. P. Wright 41–7–150–4.

CHAMPIONSHIP TABLE 1946

						First Inns Lead in Match		
	P	Won	Lost	D	NR	Lost	D	Pts
Points Awarded	–	12	–	–	–	4	4	–
YORKSHIRE (1)	26	17	1	5	3	0	5	216±
Middlesex (2)	26	16	5	5	0	1	2	204
Lancashire (6)	26	15	4	5	2	1	4	200
Somerset (14)	26	12	6	7	1	2	3	166*
Gloucestershire (3)	26	12	6	4	4	1	3	160
Glamorgan (13)	26	10	8	6	2	3	3	144
Kent (5)	26	11	8	7	0	0	3	144
Essex (4)	26	8	9	8	1	2	4	120
Worcestershire (7)	26	9	12	2	3	3	0	120
Hampshire (15)	26	8	15	3	0	2	2	112
Leicestershire (17)	26	7	13	4	2	2	2	100
Surrey (8)	26	6	11	7	2	3	4	100
Nottinghamshire (12)	26	6	8	11	1	1	5	96
Warwickshire (11)	26	7	15	3	1	1	1	92
Derbyshire (9)	26	5	12	8	1	3	4	88
Northamptonshire (16)	26	2	11	11	2	2	8	64
Sussex (10)	26	4	11	10	1	2	1	60

± includes eight points for win on first innings in one-day match.
*includes two points for tie on first innings in match lost.
1939 positions are shown in brackets.

FIRST CLASS AVERAGES 1946

	I	NO	HS	Runs	Av	100
W. R. Hammond (Gloucestershire)	26	5	214	1783	84.90	7
C. Washbrook (Lancashire)	43	8	182	2400	68.57	9
D. C. S. Compton (Middlesex)	45	6	235	2403	61.61	10
±M. P. Donnelly (Oxford Univ)	29	2	142	1425	52.77	6
M. M. Walford (Somerset)	10	1	141*	472	52.44	2
D. Brookes (Northamptonshire)	48	5	200	2191	50.95	7
±L. B. Fishlock (Surrey)	46	2	172	2221	50.47	5
H. Gimblett (Somerset)	41	2	231	1947	49.92	7
W. J. Edrich (Middlesex)	45	7	222*	1890	49.73	5
H. P. Crabtree (Essex)	17	1	146	793	49.56	3

Qualification throughout
10 wickets in 10 innings

	Overs	M	Runs	Wkts	Av	BB
±A. Booth (Yorkshire)	917.2	423	1289	111	11.61	6–21
J. C. Clay (Glamorgan)	812.2	204	1742	130	13.40	7–21
A. D. G. Matthews (Glamorgan)	693.2	215	1329	93	14.29	7–12
E. P. Robinson (Yorkshire)	1138.2	354	2498	167	14.95	8–76
W. E. Bowes (Yorkshire)	596.2	203	987	65	15.18	5–17
J. F. Parker (Surrey)	384.5	102	873	56	15.58	5–46
W. E. Hollies (Warwickshire)	1528	433	2871	184	15.60	10–49
±M. Leyland (Yorkshire)	86.5	23	250	16	15.62	4–30
J. A. Young (Middlesex)	1023.4	321	2036	122	16.68	8–31
±H. L. Hazell (Somerset)	430.4	124	940	54	17.40	6–18

The flowing off-drive of Joe Hardstaff, a handsome stroke-player

THE TESTS

Freddie Trueman: England's first Test side since 1939
was composed mainly of players who had lost six years of
their sporting lives during the war but there were three
new caps—Alec Bedser, Frank Smailes and Jack Ikin. Big
Al will certainly remember his first game for England
because he took 11 wickets for 145. India had six men new
to Test cricket but their captain, the Nawab of Pataudi,
had already played in three Tests—for England before the
war!

Don Mosey: I was in India myself at this time so my
reading of the first post-war series came through the
columns of the *Times of India*—and I mean *columns*.
Cricket-writing in those days was very largely about the
game and not the private lives of the players. Joe
Hardstaff, who made his highest score for England (205
not out) had been serving in India until very recently and
had played a lot of cricket there so his double century was
noted with a lot of personal interest. Rain interfered with

the Second and Third Tests during which England
introduced Dick Pollard (at Old Trafford) and Godfrey
Evans and Peter Smith, the Essex leg-spinner (The Oval).

COUNTY CHAMPIONSHIP

FST: It was good to see Yorkshire carrying on where they
had left off seven years earlier by winning the championship again. As a 15-year-old lad with, already, a burning
ambition to bowl for Yorkshire, I was thrilled to see them
score one more win than Middlesex which gave them a
12-point lead at the end of the season. Most of our players
had been through the war and men like Bill Bowes had
seen their health ruined through spending years in prison
camps; but the most remarkable of the lot had to be
Arthur Booth, born 3 November 1902. He was 43 when
the season started and had spent the 1930s waiting in the

shadow of Hedley Verity, only rarely getting a first-team chance, while he played most of his cricket in the leagues. To take 111 wickets at 11.61 was an achievement in itself. To do it at over 40 years of age with only very limited first-class experience makes you sit up a bit.

DM: If anyone ever doubted that it's bowlers who win championships, a glance at the bowling averages should dispel most of them—four Yorkshiremen in the top ten and three of them spinners. It's interesting, too, to see Austin Matthews up there. He had played most of his cricket (fast-medium bowler who batted a bit) with Northants, but joined Glamorgan in 1937 and had two post-war seasons with them as well. His best season with either county was in 1946 and like many an other Welsh-man he was a noted all-round sportsman, playing rugby for Northampton and East Midlands as well as his native Penarth. He also had a Welsh trial and represented his country at table tennis.

FST: What really surprises one is to see Eric Hollies, a leg spinner, taking 184 wickets in a season and seven of the top ten bowlers were spinners, too. I doubt whether Bill Bowes could have been much above medium pace when he came back after the war and together with Matthews and that fine all-rounder, John Parker of Surrey, he makes up a trio of non-spinners: but none of them was a *fast* bowler. Times have changed a bit since then.

DM: Some of the bowling figures are really good when you look at the wealth of really high-class batting around. The incomparable Hammond led the order and Cyril Washbrook and Denis Compton both scored nearly 2,500 runs. Martin Donnelly, that high-class left-hander from New Zealand, was up at Oxford where he won two Blues before joining Warwickshire and he won a cap for England at Rugby, too.

FST: It's good to see the name of Dennis Brookes there, too. What a marvellous servant he has been to North-amptonshire as player (for 20 seasons) and then as

Eric Hollies (Warwickshire and England), who took more wickets (2,323) than he scored runs (1,673)

Michael Walford, the schoolmaster who put his summer holidays to such good use with Somerset

Committee man. He scored 30,874 runs and got 1,000 in a season 17 times but only played once for England! Competition was a bit tougher in those days.

DM: And we have two other amateurs (apart from Hammond) in the top ten as well—Harry Crabtree, whose appearances for Essex were limited by his teaching duties and another schoolmaster, Michael Walford, who played for Somerset during the summer holidays from Sherborne School. He was a triple Blue at Oxford (cricket, rugby and hockey).

ATTENDANCES

FST: The only county matches I saw in those days were at Bramall Lane (it cost a bit too much for my family to start going off to Headingley or Bradford), but I remember the crowds being huge and the atmosphere at Sheffield was always something special. The Roses Match used to get crowds as big as any Test, especially on Bank Holiday Monday.

DM: I suppose a first-class cricket match was the most marvellous escapism from the war and from the years of austerity which followed it. Remember that rationing of things like food and clothing was still with us and was to continue for several years yet. If you could get away from it all for six hours a day it was the perfect way of forgetting for a time what everyone had gone through in the past six years.

FST: With no television, all I saw of the Tests of 1946 was on cinema newsreels in black and white and they only provided snippets. But Lord's was jam-packed for the first two days of the first post-war Test and it was great to see that—even if the newsreel came round a week later. Cameras weren't as good as they became later on and everything seemed to be speeded up, I remember—especially the bowling! One thing I can recall quite vividly was Compton running out Vijay Merchant at The Oval by kicking the ball onto his stumps. As Denis was as well known at that time for his football with Arsenal as his cricket for Middlesex he at once became every youngster's hero in both games. His picture was on every advertising hoarding, too, with his hair glossy with Brylcreem. He was our first sporting folk hero, I suppose, in a way which would have been a bit unusual before the war.

DM: True, but his best years were still to come. So were Alec Bedser's but he had taken his 100th first-class wicket of the season by 22 July and he took 24 in the rain-interrupted, three-Test series.

Tests in Australia (1946–47):

Brisbane	Australia won by an innings and 332 runs
Sydney	Australia won by an innings and 33 runs
Melbourne	Match drawn
Adelaide	Match drawn
Sydney	Australia won by five wickets.

One Test in New Zealand:

Christchurch	Match drawn.

Tests v South Africa:

Trent Bridge	Match drawn
Lord's	England won by ten wickets
Old Trafford	England won by seven wickets
Headingley	England won by ten wickets
The Oval	Match drawn.

County Champions Middlesex

TEST AVERAGES ENGLAND V AUSTRALIA 1946–47

	M	I	NO	HS	Runs	Av	100	50	Ct/St
L. Hutton	5	9	1	122*	417	52.12	1	2	1
D. C. S. Compton	5	10	1	147	459	51.00	2	2	4
W. J. Edrich	5	10	0	119	462	46.20	1	3	1
C. Washbrook	5	10	0	112	363	36.30	1	2	2
N. W. D. Yardley	5	10	2	61	252	31.50	–	2	3
W. R. Hammond	4	8	0	37	168	21.00	–	–	6
J. T. Ikin	5	10	0	60	184	18.40	–	1	4
A. V. Bedser	5	10	3	27*	106	15.14	–	–	3
T. G. Evans	4	8	2	29	90	15.00	–	–	9/–
W. Voce	2	3	1	18	19	9.50	–	–	1
D. V. P. Wright	5	8	3	15*	47	9.40	–	–	2
T. P. B. Smith	2	4	0	24	32	8.00	–	–	1

Also batted: L. B. Fishlock (1 match) 14, 0, 1ct; P. A. Gibb (1 match) 13, 11, 1ct; J. Hardstaff (1 match) 67, 9.

	Overs	M	Runs	Wkts	Av	5w	10w	BB
N. W. D. Yardley	114	15	372	10	37.20	–	–	3–67
D. V. P. Wright	240.2	23	990	23	43.04	2	–	7–105
W. J. Edrich	115.3	12	483	9	53.66	–	–	3–50
A. V. Bedser	246.3	34	876	16	54.75	–	–	3–97

Also bowled: D. C. S. Compton 16.2–0–78–0; L. Hutton 3–0–28–0; J. T. Ikin 7–0–48–0; T. P. B. Smith 47–1–218–2; W. Voce 44–12–161–0.

TEST AVERAGES ENGLAND V SOUTH AFRICA 1947

	M	I	NO	HS	Runs	Av	100	50	Ct/St
W. J. Edrich	4	6	1	191	552	110.40	2	2	5
D. C. S. Compton	5	8	0	208	753	94.12	4	2	2
C. Washbrook	5	10	2	75	396	49.50	–	3	–
L. Hutton	5	10	2	100	344	43.00	1	1	5
T. G. Evans	5	7	2	74	209	41.80	–	1	9/4
N. W. D. Yardley	5	7	0	99	273	39.00	–	2	7
C. J. Barnett	3	4	1	33	63	21.00	–	–	2
K. Cranston	3	4	0	45	71	17.75	–	–	1

Also batted: A. V. Bedser (2 matches) 7, 2, 0, 1ct; C. Cook (1 match) 0, 4; W. H. Copson (1 match) 6; H. E. Dollery (1 match) 9, 17; C. Gladwin (2 matches) 16, 51*, 1ct; W. E. Hollies (3 matches) 0, 18*, 5, 1ct; R. Howorth (1 match) 23, 45*, 2ct; J. W. Martin (1 match) 0, 26; G. H. Pope (1 match) 8*; J. D. B. Robertson (1 match) 4, 30; D. V. P. Wright (4 matches) 4*, 14; J. A. Young (1 match) 0*, 1ct. H. J. Butler played in one match but did not bat.

	Overs	M	Runs	Wkts	Av	5w	10w	BB
H. J. Butler	52	24	66	7	9.42	–	–	4–34
K. Cranston	82.1	23	186	11	16.90	–	–	4–12
W. J. Edrich	134.5	33	370	16	23.12	–	–	4–77
R. Howorth	76	24	149	6	24.83	–	–	3–64
D. V. P. Wright	183.2	50	484	19	25.47	2	1	5–80
W. E. Hollies	149.2	46	331	9	36.77	1	–	5–123
D. C. S. Compton	104	29	263	5	52.60	–	–	2–32

Also bowled: C. J. Barnett 13–4–23–0; A. V. Bedser 112–24–233–4; C. Cook 30–4–127–0; W. H. Copson 57–24–112–3; C. Gladwin 98–37–158–3; L. Hutton 4–0–29–0; J. W. Martin 45–6–129–1; G. H. Pope 36.2–12–85–1; N. W. D. Yardley 6–0–25–0; J. A. Young 36–12–85–2.

CHAMPIONSHIP TABLE 1947

							First Inns Lead in Match		
	P	Won	Lost	D	Tied	NR	Lost	D	Pts
Points Awarded	–	12	–	–	6	–	4	4	–
MIDDLESEX (2)	26	19	5	2	0	0	1	1	236
Gloucestershire (5)	26	17	4	5	0	0	1	2	216
Lancashire (3)	26	13	1	10	1	1	0	6	186
Kent (7)	26	12	8	6	0	0	2	5	172
Derbyshire (15)	26	11	9	5	0	1	3	4	160
Surrey (12)	26	10	7	8	0	1	0	5	140
Worcestershire (9)	26	7	11	8	0	0	4	5	120
Yorkshire (1)	26	8	7	10	0	1	1	5	120
Glamorgan (6)	26	8	8	8	0	2	3	2	116
Sussex (17)	26	9	12	5	0	0	1	1	116
Essex (8)	26	6	9	10	1	0	1	4	100*
Nottinghamshire (13)	26	6	6	13	0	1	1	6	100
Somerset (4)	26	8	12	6	0	0	0	1	100
Leicestershire (11)	26	6	14	5	0	1	2	3	92
Warwickshire (14)	26	6	12	7	0	1	2	1	84
Hampshire (10)	26	4	11	8	1	2	0	6	78
Northamptonshire (16)	26	2	16	6	1	1	2	4	54

*includes two points for tie on first innings in match lost
1946 positions are shown in brackets

FIRST CLASS AVERAGES 1947

	I	NO	HS	Runs	Av	100
D. C. S. Compton (Middlesex)	50	8	246	3816	90.85	18
W. J. Edrich (Middlesex)	52	8	267*	3539	80.43	12
E. Lester (Yorkshire)	11	2	142	657	73.00	3
C. Washbrook (Lancashire)	47	8	251*	2662	68.25	11
L. E. G. Ames (Kent)	42	7	212*	2272	64.91	7
J. Hardstaff (Nottinghamshire)	44	7	221*	2396	64.75	7
L. Hutton (Yorkshire)	44	4	270*	2585	64.62	11
W. Place (Lancashire)	47	7	266*	2501	62.52	10
±M. P. Donnelly (Oxford Univ)	30	6	162*	1488	62.00	5
M. M. Walford (Somerset)	18	2	264	971	60.68	2

*denotes not out
±denotes left-hand batsman

	Overs	M	Runs	Wkts	Av	BB
J. C. Clay (Glamorgan)	495.3	126	1069	65	16.44	7–32
T. W. Goddard (Gloucestershire)	1451.2	344	4119	238	17.30	9–41
±J. A. Young (Middlesex)	1291.1	416	2765	159	17.38	7–46
W. E. Bowes (Yorkshire)	789.5	270	1277	73	17.49	6–23
± R. Howorth (Worcestershire)	1254	375	2929	164	17.85	7–50
J. C. Laker (Surrey)	575.5	135	1420	79	17.97	8–69
G. H. Pope (Derbyshire)	786.1	186	2096	114	18.38	7–16
C. J. Barnett (Gloucestershire)	359	102	937	50	18.74	6–46
B. L. Muncer (Glamorgan)	802.2	206	2018	107	18.85	9–97
R. Aspinall (Yorkshire)	225	37	692	36	19.22	8–42

±denotes left-arm bowler

The Middlesex twins—Edrich and Compton in their golden summer of 1947

THE MIDDLESEX TWINS

Don Mosey: This was a sunny summer following just about the worst winter in living memory and the sun shone even more brightly on the Middlesex 'twins', Denis Compton and Bill Edrich, who both scored more than 3,000 runs.

Freddie Trueman: Yes, I remember when I joined the first-class circuit, two years later, the tale used to be that they scored 3,000 runs, drank 6,000 drinks and said, 'How d'you do' to 12,000 girls that season. It was a marvellous summer for them; there's never been anything to match it. They were both men who lived life to the full and how they must have enjoyed themselves.

WINTER TOUR

DM: Let's start with the winter tour, however. That wasn't nearly such good news for England cricket although when the sides got together at The Gabba for the First Test there would be a fair gathering of players who had known each other during the war. Bradman showed he was going to take over where he had left off in 1938 by hitting 187 and Australia totalled a massive 645. The Don

had not forgotten The Oval, 1938, and was ready to make our tourists pay for that humiliation (903 for seven declared). England were bowled out for 141 (Miller seven for 60) and 172 (Toshack, with his left-arm medium pacers, six for 82). It was Arthur Morris's first Test and England's bowlers were to see rather a lot of him in the future as well.

FST: In the first of the two Tests played in Sydney (Perth was not on the Test ground list then), Bradman got 234 and Sid Barnes hit exactly the same figure so England were out of that one fairly quickly. The batting was better in Melbourne and Adelaide (where Compton got two hundreds in the Test, one not out), and Alec Bedser achieved the notable feat of bowling Bradman for none—only Bill Bowes and Eric Hollies managed that in Bradman's other Tests against England. Back in Sydney for the Final Test, we might have saved it if Hutton had not been taken to bed with tonsillitis after scoring 122 and he couldn't bat in the second innings. Doug Wright's seven for 105 was his best analysis in 34 Tests for England but the Aussies won in the last over of the penultimate day.

William Ashdown batting during his benefit match against Cranfield of Gloucestershire

Doug Wright (Kent and England), the leg-spinner with the fast bowler's approach

HOME TESTS

DM: I had come home for demobilisation from 110 Oriental degrees to the blizzard which snowed up Britain for more than two months, so by the time June arrived I was more than ready for a bit of Test cricket in the sun. I had never seen a South African side play so I wasn't prepared for their score of 533 at Trent Bridge (Alan Melville 189 and Dudley Nourse 149) but that pitch was a notorious featherbed and it was to remain so for some years to come. At least I saw a lot of cricket to remember— 163 from Compton, Melville's second century in the match and Tufty Mann starting his Test career with eight consecutive maiden overs of slow left-arm bowling.

FST: It's interesting that that was JW Martin's only Test match. He opened the bowling with Alec Bedser and his only Test wicket was Melville's—when he had scored 189. It's interesting, too, to see how much reliance sides placed on their spinners in those days. Eric Hollies bowled more than 60 overs of leg spin in the match though Sam Cook, in *his* first Test, was called on for only 30 overs of left-arm spin and didn't take a wicket. I'm not really surprised when I remember what Trent Bridge was like at that time.

DM: It was a bit of a treat for those who saw Compton and Edrich play at Lord's in the Second Test. Denis got 208 and Bill 189 in a third wicket partnership of 370 and Edrich was also Alec Bedser's new ball partner. He got three wickets and Compton four with his Chinamen so I think one can say the 'twins' earned their match fees in that particular Test. At Old Trafford the pair were at it again, Compton scoring 115 and Edrich 191 as well as being England's No. 1 fast bowler this time (eight for 172 in the match). At Headingley, naturally enough, it was Len Hutton's turn with 132 runs for once out (and that was a run out) and Harold Butler, of Notts, in his first Test, taking seven wickets in the match for 66.

FST: And it may surprise one or two people to learn that that was Leonard's first Test appearance at Headingley— more than ten years since his England debut! The last Test, at The Oval, was drawn largely because Bruce Mitchell got 120 in the first innings and 189 not out in the second. He wasn't the fastest of scorers at the best of times and I remember the newspapers (who were much more polite in their cricket-writing than they are today) seeming a bit irritated about the amount of time he was on view. In fact Mitchell was on the field for all but eight minutes of the match. And another thing worth remembering about the game is that Dick Howorth, that fine Worcestershire all-rounder, took a wicket with his first ball in Tests.

MORE TALENT AROUND

DM: Writing this at the end of the 1987 season when the black joke was that it was easier to get into the England side than out of it, it is fascinating to see how ruthless Selectors were with players—bowlers in particular—who did not deliver the goods. Three of Derbyshire's seamers were employed during the series—George Pope, Cliff Gladwin and Bill Copson—but Edrich was one of the two main strike bowlers in three of the Tests and he missed the final game because of injury. Doug Wright was the main spinner with another leg-break bowler, Eric Hollies, in support in three Tests while three slow left-armers came and went—Sam Cook, Jack Young and Dick Howorth. And this was a series England won easily. Contrast it with the appearances during the losing series of 1987 against Pakistan, and you are left with the inescapable fact that there was infinitely more talent around than 40 years earlier.

COUNTY CHAMPIONSHIP

FST: Middlesex won 19 of their 26 championship matches, lost five and drew two. Even in a sunny summer, Old Trafford's weather was not so good because Lancashire, who finished third, drew ten of their matches and so did Yorkshire so the age-old complaint of Northerners that they were always handicapped by days lost to rain would seem to be justified. Compton scored 3,816 runs and hit 18 hundreds; Edrich piled up 3,539 runs, with 12 centuries and the most successful of their bowlers, Jack Young, had a haul of 159 wickets at 17.38. But just look at the figures of Tom Goddard—238 wickets at 17.30. No wonder Gloucestershire finished second in the county championship! The top two bowlers in the country were both off-spinners who had started their careers as fast-medium merchants—JC Clay and Goddard. Then came Young (slow left-arm) in third place, Howorth (SLA) fifth, Jim Laker (off-spin and quite the best I ever saw) sixth and Len Muncer (who switched to off-breaks from leg-spinning that season) ninth. Only four of the top ten were medium pace or medium fast—Bill Bowes (4th), George Pope (7th), Charlie Barnett (8th) and Ron Aspinall (10th).

DM: Hammond had now retired from playing regular first-class cricket but Edrich became an amateur in 1947 to provide three unpaid batsmen in the top ten, Martin Donnelly and Michael Walford once again appearing in the list. Walford averaged 60.68 (tenth of our leading batsmen!) from just 18 innings. There was obviously

Tom Goddard—238 wickets in 1947 when he was 46 years old

something to be said for schoolmastering until mid-July and then playing full-time cricket through the summer holidays. Leslie Ames totalled 2,272 runs—what a man to have as your wicket-keeper! And Lancashire's third place in the table was due to Cyril Washbrook and Winston Place topping the 2,500 run mark. WH (Bill) Ashdown, of Kent, played his final first-class game for Maurice Leyland's XI at Harrogate in 1947. As he had made his debut for GJV Weigall's XI v Oxford in 1914, Ashdown is the only man to have played first-class cricket *before* the First World War and *after* the Second. He was 15 when he played for Weigall (Wellington and Cambridge) who was coach to Kent in the 1920s and 48 when he played his last match. In between Ashdown played 482 matches for Kent, scored 22,589 runs and took 602 wickets.

1948

Winter Tour to West Indies (1947–48):

Bridgetown	Match drawn
Port of Spain, Trinidad	Match drawn
Georgetown, British Guiana	West Indies won by 7 wickets
Kingston, Jamaica	West Indies won by 10 wickets

Summer Series with Australia:

Trent Bridge	Australia won by 8 wickets
Lord's	Australia won by 409 runs
Old Trafford	Match drawn
Headingley	Australia won by 7 wickets
The Oval	Australia won by an innings and 149 runs

County Champions Glamorgan

TEST AVERAGES ENGLAND V WEST INDIES 1947–48

	M	I	NO	HS	Runs	Av	100	50	Ct/St
J. D. B. Robertson	4	8	1	133	390	55.71	1	3	3
L. Hutton	2	4	0	60	171	42.75	–	2	3
J. Hardstaff	3	6	0	98	237	39.50	–	3	2
W. Place	3	6	1	107	144	28.80	1	–	–
G. A. Smithson	2	3	0	35	70	23.33	–	–	–
G. O. B. Allen	3	6	1	36	94	18.80	–	–	3
T. G. Evans	4	7	0	37	128	18.28	–	–	6/1
J. C. Laker	4	7	1	55	109	18.16	–	1	1
K. Cranston	4	8	0	36	123	15.37	–	–	–
J. T. Ikin	4	7	0	24	82	11.71	–	–	5
R. Howorth	4	8	1	16	77	11.00	–	–	–
M. F. Tremlett	3	5	2	18*	20	6.66	–	–	–

Also batted: D. Brookes (1 match) 10, 7, 1ct; H. J. Butler (1 match) 15*, 0, 1ct; S. C. Griffith (1 match) 140, 4; J. H. Wardle (1 match) 4, 2*.

	Overs	M	Runs	Wkts	Av	5w	10w	BB
H. J. Butler	40	6	149	5	29.80	–	–	3–122
J. C. Laker	186.4	47	548	18	30.44	1	–	7–103
K. Cranston	65	13	196	6	32.66	–	–	4–78
R. Howorth	180	33	486	13	37.38	1	–	6–124
G. O. B. Allen	45	1	205	5	41.00	–	–	2–82

Also bowled: J. T. Ikin 74–11–252–2; M. F. Tremlett 82–13–226–4; J. H. Wardle 3–0–9–0.

TEST AVERAGES ENGLAND V AUSTRALIA 1948

	M	I	NO	HS	Runs	Av	100	50	Ct/St
D. C. S. Compton	5	10	1	184	562	62.44	2	2	2
C. Washbrook	4	8	1	143	356	50.85	1	2	3
L. Hutton	4	8	0	81	342	42.75	–	4	5
W. J. Edrich	5	10	0	111	319	31.90	1	2	5
T. G. Evans	5	9	2	50	188	26.85	–	1	8/4
J. C. Laker	3	6	1	63	114	22.80	–	1	–
A. V. Bedser	5	9	1	79	176	22.00	–	1	1
J. F. Crapp	3	6	1	37	88	17.60	–	–	6
N. W. D. Yardley	5	9	0	44	150	16.66	–	–	1
H. E. Dollery	2	3	0	37	38	12.66	–	–	–
J. A. Young	3	5	2	9	17	5.66	–	–	2

Also batted: C. J. Barnett (1 match) 8, 6; A. Coxon (1 match) 19, 0; K. Cranston (1 match) 10, 0, 2ct; J. G. Dewes (1 match) 1, 10; G. M. Emmett (1 match) 10, 0; J. Hardstaff (1 match) 0, 43; W. E. Hollies (1 match) 0*, 0; R. Pollard (2 matches) 3, 0*, 1ct; A. J. Watkins (1 match) 0, 2; D. V. P. Wright (1 match) 13*, 4.

	Overs	M	Runs	Wkts	Av	5w	10w	BB
N. W. D. Yardley	84	22	204	9	22.66	–	–	2–32
W. E. Hollies	56	14	131	5	26.20	1	–	5–131
A. V. Bedser	274.3	75	688	18	38.22	–	–	4–81
J. C. Laker	155.2	42	472	9	52.44	–	–	4–138
R. Pollard	102	29	218	5	43.60	–	–	3–53
J. A. Young	156	64	292	5	58.40	–	–	2–35

Also bowled: C. J. Barnett 17–5–36–0; D. C. S. Compton 37–6–156–1; A. Coxon 63–13–172–3; K. Cranston 21.1–1–79–1; W. J. Edrich 53–4–238–3; L. Hutton 4–1–30–0; A. J. Watkins 4–1–19–0; D. V. P. Wright 40.3–12–123–2.

CHAMPIONSHIP TABLE 1948

					First Inns Lead in Match			
	P	Won	Lost	D	NR Lost	D	Pts
Points Awarded	–	12	–	–	– 4	4	–
GLAMORGAN (9)	26	13	5	6	2 1	3	172
Surrey (6)	26	13	9	4	0 1	3	168±
Middlesex (1)	26	13	4	8	1 0	1	160
Yorkshire (8)	26	11	4	10	1 3	3	156
Lancashire (3)	26	8	2	15	1 0	14	152
Derbyshire (5)	26	11	6	7	2 0	4	148
Warwickshire (15)	26	9	7	8	2 1	5	132
Gloucestershire (2)	26	9	7	9	1 1	4	128
Hampshire (16)	26	9	8	8	1 2	1	120
Worcestershire (7)	26	6	8	11	1 1	7	104
Leicestershire (14)	26	6	11	8	1 1	5	96
Somerset (13)	26	5	14	6	1 4	4	92
Essex (11)	26	5	8	11*	2 2	4	90
Nottinghamshire (12)	26	5	10	9*	2 1	3	82
Kent (4)	26	4	11	10	1 0	7	76
Sussex (10)	26	4	11	10	1 1	5	72
Northamptonshire (17)	26	3	9	14	0 1	3	52

± includes eight points for a win on first innings in one-day match
*Essex and Nottinghamshire six points each for equal aggregate scores
1947 positions are shown in brackets

FIRST CLASS AVERAGES 1948

	I	NO	HS	Runs	Av	100
G. O. Allen (Middlesex)	8	3	180	384	76.80	1
C. Washbrook (Lancashire)	31	4	200	1900	70.37	7
L. Hutton (Yorkshire)	48	7	176*	2654	64.73	10
D. C. S. Compton (Middlesex)	47	7	252*	2451	61.27	9
A. E. Fagg (Kent)	48	3	203	2423	53.84	8
J. D. B. Robertson (Middlesex)	54	7	154	2366	50.34	7
W. J. Edrich (Middlesex)	55	6	168*	2428	49.55	8
T. N. Pearce (Essex)	44	7	211*	1826	49.35	4
±J. F. Crapp (Gloucestershire)	45	6	127	1872	48.00	5
±J. T. Ikin (Lancashire)	37	5	106	1493	46.65	2

	Overs	M	Runs	Wkts	Av	BB
J. C. Clay (Glamorgan)	259.5	61	581	41	14.17	5–15
P. A. Whitcombe (Oxford Univ)	391.3	112	749	47	15.93	7–51
C. Gladwin (Derbyshire)	960.3	266	2174	128	16.98	8–56
G. H. Pope (Derbyshire)	699	171	1724	100	17.24	8–38
B. L. Muncer (Glamorgan)	1289.2	381	2758	159	17.34	9–62
N. G. Hever (Glamorgan)	633.5	150	1493	84	17.77	5–34
±J. Bailey (Hampshire)	1118.3	375	2194	121	18.13	7–39
W. E. Hollies (Warwickshire)	1270	357	2697	147	18.34	8–107
±J. A. Young (Middlesex)	1149.4	432	2165	118	18.34	7–25
E. P. Robinson (Yorkshire)	589.3	222	1148	62	18.51	6–25

THE GREATEST TOURING SIDE?

Freddie Trueman: This was one of the vintage years of international cricket. All everyone could talk about in the summer of '48 was that it was to be Bradman's last tour of England, and what a marvellous side he brought with him! People who were better able to judge at that time than I was have always said it was the greatest side ever to tour this country and I am not going to argue with them.

Don Mosey: Most decidedly it was the greatest I have ever seen in terms of individual ability, of collective effort and of balance in all the skills of the game. First, I suppose, we should have a quick look at the winter tour to the West Indies who had yet to develop as a real force in the game. Traditionally, England sides on tour there were below the strength of those which turned out against Australia; they included men who might be regarded as being on the fringe of the Test side and one or two others who had never made it and were being rewarded for service to the game by a pleasant sea voyage to the Caribbean and to two or three months in the sun. The

Sir Donald Bradman, the greatest of them all—but an anti-climax for his farewell

development of West Indian cricket had been under-estimated in the winter of 1947–48 and Gubby Allen, captain at the age of 45, found himself overwhelmed in both British Guiana (as Guyana then was) and Jamaica, by seven wickets and ten wickets respectively, with the Barbados and Trinidad Tests drawn. It was a bit of a shock but no one worried too much about it—the important thing was the summer series against the ancient enemy.

THE BOWLING

FST: The bowling was spear-headed by the great Ray Lindwall with Keith Miller and Bill Johnston in support. Miller was the Denis Compton of Australian cricket—small wonder that they were great pals off the field—and I believe Bradman didn't always approve of Miller's life-style or his relaxed approach to playing cricket. The game was a very serious business indeed to The Don; to Miller, as to Compton, it was a game to be savoured and enjoyed like all other aspects of life—but what a fine player he was!

DM: He startled everyone on that tour by his pace off a fairly relaxed approach which quite often varied from 25 yards to five. He was just as capable of bowling a back-of-the-hand leg break as a swirling out-swinger in the opening overs and no one had ever seen anything like it. He was a great catcher of the ball and a hugely talented batsman in the middle order. A superb entertainer. Most people who saw him at his peak and are still around today rate him as highly as, if not more highly than, the great

all-rounders of the modern era—Botham, Imran Khan, Kapil Dev and Hadlee.

FST: Yes, and it's very important to remember that when Miller was over here there were more *great* players around and very many more *good* ones.

DM: Backing up the opening pair was the left-arm quick stuff of Johnston, who could do a great deal with the ball both in the air and off the seam when conditions were right. There was Ernie Toshack as the perfect stock bowler, left arm medium pace, whose line and length could tie down and frustrate the most patient of bats-men. Ian Johnson was perhaps not the best off-spinner of all time but he provided the balance the attack needed, and Doug Ring, the leg break bowler, only got in for the last match of the series, and he was hardly required.

FST: Let's look at the batting, now—Sid Barnes and Arthur Morris to open, Bradman at No. 3, Lindsay Hassett at No. 4, Miller at 5 and either Bill Brown or Sam Loxton at 6 (and remember Loxton was a pretty good fast bowler, too).

DM: And to go with all this talent, Don Tallon behind the stumps, the best Australian wicket-keeper I think I have seen.

FST: I'd go for Wally Grout myself but certainly it was a marvellous side. And what marvellous cricket the series

Keith Miller—in the first rank of world-class all-rounders

produced—Australia won by eight wickets, 409 runs, seven wickets and an innings and 149 runs with a draw only at Old Trafford where it rained for a change! And this was against a very good England line-up.

A GREAT TEST

DM: But the series as a whole has so much very good cricket—Compton's 184 at Trent Bridge where he had to start or restart his innings no fewer than nine times. In what was Australia's summer, Compton's innings was nevertheless one of the great pieces of Test batting. And then there was the Headingley Test—surely one of the most fascinating of all time. It had just about everything, with England scoring 496 (Washbrook 143, Edrich 111, Hutton 81 and Bedser reaching 79, after going in as nightwatchman). The Aussies replied with 458—a century for Neil Harvey in his first Test against England, Loxton hitting five sixes in his 93, and that wonderful bowler, Ray Lindwall, proving (not for the first, or last, time) that he was also an accomplished batsman, with 77. England declared their second innings at 356 for eight setting Australia a target (404) which no side had ever reached in the fourth innings to win a Test. The pitch was taking spin and England must have felt confident that even if they didn't win, they couldn't lose.

But they were a spinner short. They had gone in with five seam bowlers and the only partners for Jim Laker had to be either Compton or Hutton. Bradman was magnificent—173 not out. Morris, in his own way, was just as majestic—182. And Australia got the runs with time to spare. That was one of the best Tests I have ever seen. The final match—at The Oval—was entirely different because once England had been bowled out for 52 (Hutton, last out, got 30 of them) it was no contest. But it was a massively sentimental occasion because when Bradman came out to play his last Test innings in England the whole crowd, and the England team, gave him an overwhelming reception. Nothing will ever convince me that Eric Hollies' second ball, a googly, would have bowled the great man if he had not been thinking about the occasion and that reception. There was no chance for him to bat a second time and he left The Oval knowing that a four, instead of that duck, would have given him a Test average of 100. That would have been just for he was a uniquely great batsman.

NEW CHAMPIONS

FST: In 1948, Glamorgan won the first of the only two county championship titles to their name. As they had no batsman in the top ten, it will come as no surprise to find three bowlers there—JC Clay, Len Muncer and Norman Hever, a fast-medium bowler who had joined them from

Wilf Wooller—a great competitor and a great character

Middlesex at the start of the season. And the three of them, I am sure, would agree that brilliant close-to-the-wicket catching was a major factor in their success. Len Hutton was the country's leading run-scorer with 2,654 and Len Muncer took more wickets (159) than anyone else, but three not outs in his eight innings saw Gubby Allen top the first-class batting averages in a season in which he reached the age of 46 on 31 July. He gave Middlesex four batsmen in the top ten (Compton, Edrich and that most under-rated of openers, Jack Robertson were the others) and there were three amateurs there—Allen, Edrich and TN Pearce, of Essex.

DM: Glamorgan were renowned for many years for the quality of their close catching. Alan Watkins would be foremost in this respect—a brilliant short leg—and their captain, the redoubtable Wilfred Wooller not far behind. A great all-round sportsman, he played rugby for Cambridge University and Wales but perhaps he is best remembered as one of the all-time great *competitors* in everything he did. Stories of his uncompromising leadership of Glamorgan form a major part of the folklore of cricket, and they did not dry up when he retired as a player and became secretary of the county club. He played 400 matches for Glamorgan and, like so many others, had six years of his playing life stolen by the war.

Winter Tour to South Africa (1948–49):

Durban	England won by two wickets
Johannesburg	Match drawn
Cape Town	Match drawn
Johannesburg	Match drawn
Port Elizabeth	England won by three wickets

Summer Series with New Zealand:

Headingley	Match drawn
Lord's	Match drawn
Old Trafford	Match drawn
The Oval	Match drawn

County Champions (joint)   Middlesex/Yorkshire

TEST AVERAGES ENGLAND V SOUTH AFRICA 1948–49

	M	I	NO	HS	Runs	Av	100	50	Ct/St
L. Hutton	5	9	0	158	577	64.11	2	2	2
C. Washbrook	5	9	0	195	542	60.22	1	2	–
D. C. S. Compton	5	9	1	114	406	50.75	1	2	9
J. F. Crapp	4	7	1	56	231	38.50	–	3	1
F. G. Mann	5	8	1	136*	254	36.28	1	–	3
A. J. Watkins	5	9	2	111	251	35.85	1	1	6
C. Gladwin	5	8	4	23	98	24.50	–	–	1
R. O. Jenkins	5	6	0	29	86	14.33	–	–	1
A. V. Bedser	5	8	1	33	94	13.42	–	–	3
T. G. Evans	3	4	0	27	49	12.25	–	–	5/5
D. V. P. Wright	3	3	1	11	12	6.00	–	–	–
S. C. Griffith	2	3	0	8	13	4.33	–	–	5

Also batted: R. T. Simpson (1 match) 5, 0; J. A. Young (2 matches) 10*, 0.

	Overs	M	Runs	Wkts	Av	5w	10w	BB
R. O. Jenkins	132.7	21	495	16	30.93	–	–	4–48
C. Gladwin	171.5	47	346	11	31.45	–	–	3–21
A. V. Bedser	206.5	37	554	16	34.62	–	–	4–39
D. V. P. Wright	86	11	316	9	35.11	–	–	4–72
D. C. S. Compton	98.2	20	308	7	44.00	1	–	5–70

Also bowled: A. J. Watkins 40–4–149–4; J. A. Young 105–30–222–4.

TEST AVERAGES ENGLAND V NEW ZEALAND 1949

	M	I	NO	HS	Runs	Av	100	50	Ct/St
C. Washbrook	2	3	1	103*	157	78.50	1	–	2
L. Hutton	4	6	0	206	469	78.16	2	2	2
T. E. Bailey	4	5	2	93	219	73.00	–	2	–
W. J. Edrich	4	6	0	100	324	54.00	1	2	9
D. C. S. Compton	4	6	0	116	300	50.00	2	–	3
F. G. Mann	2	4	1	49*	122	40.66	–	–	–
T. G. Evans	4	4	0	27	61	15.25	–	–	8/4
W. E. Hollies	4	3	2	1*	1	1.00	–	–	–

Also batted: A. V. Bedser (2 matches) 20, 0, 4ct; F. R. Brown (2 matches) 22, 21, 4ct; D. B. Close (1 match) 0; C. Gladwin (1 match) 5; H. L. Jackson (1 match) 7*; J. C. Laker (1 match) 0; J. D. B. Robertson (1 match) 26, 121, 1ct; R. T. Simpson (2 matches) 103, 68; A. J. Watkins (1 match) 6, 49*, 1ct; A. Wharton (1 match) 7, 13; D. V. P. Wright (1 match) 0, 2ct; J. A. Young (2 matches) 0, 1*, 2ct.

	Overs	M	Runs	Wkts	Av	5w	10w	BB
D. C. S. Compton	33	2	126	5	25.20	–	–	1–6
J. A. Young	62.4	13	158	6	26.33	–	–	3–65
A. V. Bedser	85	19	215	7	30.71	–	–	4–74
T. E. Bailey	158	22	599	16	37.43	2	–	6–84
W. E. Hollies	175	54	385	10	38.50	1	–	5–133

Also bowled: F. R. Brown 54–8–157–2; D. B. Close 42–14–85–1; W. J. Edrich 27–3–97–2; C. Gladwin 28–5–67–1; L. Hutton 4–1–23–0; H. L. Jackson 39–14–72–3; J. C. Laker 32–6–89–4; R. T. Simpson 2–1–9–0; C. Washbrook 2–0–8–0; A. J. Watkins 3–1–11–0; D. V. P. Wright 28–1–114–1.

CHAMPIONSHIP TABLE 1949

						First Inns Lead in Match		
	P	Won	Lost	D	NR	Lost	D	Pts
Points Awarded	—	12	—	—	—	4	4	—
Middlesex (3)	26	14	3	9	0	1	5	192
Yorkshire (4)	26	14	2	10	0	0	6	192
Worcestershire (10)	26	12	7	7	0	2	5	172
Warwickshire (7)	26	12	5	8	1	0	6	168
Surrey (2)	26	11	8	6	1	2	4	156
Northants (17)	26	10	7	9	0	2	3	140
Gloucestershire (8)	26	10	7	7	2	0	3	132
Glamorgan (1)	26	7	6	12	1	2	7	120
Essex (13)	26	7	9	10	0	0	6	108
Somerset (12)	26	8	15	3	0	2	1	108
Lancashire (5)	26	6	7	13	0	0	7	100
Nottinghamshire (14)	26	6	5	13	2	0	7	100
Kent (15)	26	7	15	4	0	1	2	96
Sussex (16)	26	7	10	7	2	1	2	96
Derbyshire (6)	26	6	13	6	1	2	2	88
Hampshire (9)	26	6	13	6	1	2	1	84
Leicestershire (11)	26	3	14	8	1	3	2	56

1948 positions are shown in brackets

FIRST-CLASS AVERAGES 1949

	I	NO	HS	Runs	Av	100
J. Hardstaff (Nottinghamshire)	40	9	162*	2251	72.61	8
L. Hutton (Yorkshire)	56	6	269*	3429	68.58	12
P. B. H. May (Combined Services)	12	1	175	695	63.18	1
R. T. Simpson (Nottinghamshire)	46	6	238	2525	63.12	6
J. R. Thompson (Warwickshire)	12	2	103	609	60.90	2
John Langridge (Sussex)	53	5	234*	2914	60.70	12
W. W. Keeton (Nottinghamshire)	38	1	210	2049	55.37	6
D. J. Insole (Camb Univ/Essex)	39	9	219*	1640	54.66	4
C. Washbrook (Lancashire)	27	1	141	1419	54.57	5
M. M. Walford (Somerset)	16	2	120	763	54.50	1

*denotes not out
±denotes left-hand batsman

	Overs	M	Runs	Wkts	Av	BB
T. W. Goddard (Gloucestershire)	1187.2	326	3069	160	19.18	9–61
±A. H. Kardar (Ox Univ/Warwicks)	922.5	366	1777	92	19.31	7–33
±R. Howorth (Worcestershire)	1113.4	386	2278	117	19.47	7–18
±H. L. Hazell (Somerset)	923.1	303	2065	106	19.48	8–27
±J. A. Young (Middlesex)	1453.3	526	2948	150	19.65	7–47
J. C. Laker (Surrey)	1191.1	419	2422	122	19.85	8–42
H. L. Jackson (Derbyshire)	1030.1	256	2450	120	20.41	7–51
W. E. Hollies (Warwickshire)	1626.4	584	3413	166	20.56	8–54
A. Coxon (Yorkshire)	920.2	238	2100	101	20.79	6–36
M. H. Wrigley (Oxford Univ)	314.4	75	792	38	20.84	5–75

±denotes left-arm bowler

Whoops! Where's deep square leg? Reg Simpson of Notts and England

'COMETH THE HOUR . . .'

Don Mosey: The winter tour of South Africa enriched the folklore of cricket when Cliff Gladwin, that genial Derbyshire bowler, aimed an enormous heave at the last ball of the First Test (Durban), missed, and was called for a leg-bye by his partner, Alec Bedser. England had won by two wickets and Gladwin modestly dismissed congratulations with the comment, 'Cometh the hour, cometh the man.' The next three Tests were drawn, with Hutton and Washbrook scoring 359 in just over five hours on the first day of international cricket to be played at Ellis Park, Johannesburg (Second Test). At the end of the third day's play, the South African Selectors announced their team for the Third Test and Eric Rowan, currently playing in the Second, was dropped. He responded, with typical impishness, by scoring 156 not out, batting right through the day and pretty certainly saving South Africa from defeat. The Final Test was won with one minute to spare, Jack Crapp, the Gloucestershire left-hand batsman, hitting ten off three successive balls of the last over. Their target had been 172 in 95 minutes.

Freddie Trueman: Declarations like that are certainly not generous but you don't see much like that happening these days. South Africa could have made it impossible for England to win but they preferred to go for a result. It's interesting to see Roley Jenkins leading the Test wicket-takers. He was on his first tour and took a wicket with his third ball in Test cricket. That was in the First Test and it was the first for Reg Simpson as well as George Mann, the captain. Cuan McCarthy started playing Test cricket in the game at Kingsmead as well. His action caused a few raised eyebrows, and before long 'chucking' became a big issue for the first time, really, since the 1860s.

NEW FACES

DM: Back home in the summer of 1949, first-class cricket was enlivened by the first appearance of two young Yorkshiremen called Freddie Trueman and Brian Close! ***FST***: Don't forget Frank Lowson. He played his first game with the two of us at Cambridge and went on to become a very good opening partner for Len Hutton. It was a pity he retired as early as he did.

DM: It was one of the peak years in Hutton's career. He topped the run-scorers in South Africa, averaging 64.11 and again in England against the New Zealanders, though he was pipped for the averages by Cyril Washbrook—by .34 of a run. He scored 1,294 runs in the month of June and 1,050 in August. In all he totalled 3,429 runs in the season.

FST: So it's not surprising that we were up on top again, though Yorkshire shared the championship title with Middlesex. I think I am right in saying Middlesex had to win on the last day of the season to tie with us. I didn't make much of an impact in that first season but Brian Close certainly did . . . youngest man to do the double of 1,000 runs and 100 wickets, youngest player to be picked by England. He certainly was a great all-round cricketer. He bowled seamers, mostly, in his early days and then could switch to off-spin bowling. As a middle-order batsman he hit the ball very hard indeed. He developed a habit in some of his early games for Yorkshire of getting off the mark with a six, but he came unstuck when he tried it in his first Test against New Zealand at Old Trafford. He tried to hit Tommy Burtt, the slow left-armer, over the fence and complained (after he was out for a duck): 'If he hadn't had the tallest man in the team fielding at long on (Geoff Rabone) I would have done it, too.' A typical bit of Closey thinking!

DM: The New Zealanders did well to get four draws from the four Tests and they did it principally because of the depth of their batting in games of three days' duration. The brilliant young left-hander, Bert Sutcliffe, scored well throughout the series and they had Walter Hadlee, Merv Wallace and Martin Donnelly in the middle order. George Mann created a bit of a sensation—and at Lord's, too—by declaring at 313 for nine on the first day only to find that the experimental law which allowed a first-day declaration in a three-day match did not apply in that Test rubber. Donnelly, who scored 206 in that match, completed a remarkable treble of three-figure innings at Lord's in a Test, the University match and the Gentlemen v Players game. Reg Simpson scored 103 at Old Trafford in his first home Test and was promoted to open at The Oval where he shared a first-wicket partnership of 147 with Hutton (206). There were two specially interesting first appearances for England in that series.

FST: That's right. One was Trevor Bailey who was to be with us for a long time to come, I'm very glad to say, and the other was Les Jackson, a marvellous Derbyshire bowler, who played at Old Trafford in 1949 and his next (and last) Test was at Headingley in 1961. Any batsman around in the fifties and sixties could have told the Selectors that, day in, day out, he was one of the most respected bowlers in cricket. I have *never* understood why he didn't play more Tests.

ENTER PETER MAY

DM: Joe Hardstaff topped the first-class averages that year though Nottinghamshire finished well inside the bottom half of the championship table and a young man called PBH May made his first appearance in the top ten, averaging 63.18 in 12 first-class innings. He was then doing National Service after a brilliant record as a schoolboy at Charterhouse and before going up to Cambridge to establish himself as the most polished batsman of his era. But in 1949 his club was listed as Combined Services.

FST: At least two batsmen who had reached the veteran stage had an outstanding season in 1949. Walter Keeton, of Nottinghamshire, was 44 when he scored 2,049 runs and John Langridge was just 86 runs short of 3,000 in his 40th year. And he hit 12 hundreds, as well. Then there was our old friend Michael Walford, back again from Sherborne School to play 16 innings for Somerset and average 54.50. The bowling was topped by Tom Goddard—another 160 wickets for him—and next came four left-armers: AH Kardar (Oxford University and Warwickshire), Dick Howorth, of Worcestershire, Horace Hazell, of Somerset and Jack Young, of Middlesex. An interesting character, AH Kardar. He was born in Lahore when it was still part of India, and played in all three Tests for India in England in 1946. He was then known as Abdul Hafeez. On his next trip, in 1954, he was playing for Pakistan and by this time he had become AH Kardar! In fact he captained Pakistan in that new country's first 23 Tests. He later became President of the Board of Control for Cricket in Pakistan and is still a major behind-the-scenes influence there.

DM: It's good to see the name of Horace Hazell up there, too. He was so much a part of the Somerset scene when I was a boy and the scoreline 'st Luckes, b Hazell,' used somehow to leap out of the pages of a newspaper. He played 350 games for Somerset until his retirement in 1952 and in the year under review at the moment (1949) he got into the newspapers again by bowling 17 overs and three balls in succession against Gloucestershire without conceding a run. That would have made an interesting spell to be commentating on! Seven out of the top ten bowlers were spinners. The only exceptions were Les Jackson, Alec Coxon, who got 101 wickets for Yorkshire, and a young gentleman called Michael Harold Wrigley, who had reached Oxford University by way of Harrow School. I wonder whatever became of him?

POSTSCRIPT

FST: I would like to add one footnote to the Test series against New Zealand. It finally became obvious that three days were not long enough for a Test against a side then regarded as probably the weakest in the world when at Old Trafford England used ten bowlers in the second innings and at The Oval they used eight in the first. In two of the

Jack Young, bowling for Middlesex during his last season of 1952 (163 wickets)

others, at least seven men got a chance to turn their arm over so (a) New Zealand's batting was stronger than had been expected; (b) the pitches were pretty good; and (c) three days were clearly not long enough to get a result.

Tests v West Indies:

Old Trafford	England won by 202 runs
Lord's	West Indies won by 326 runs
Trent Bridge	West Indies won by ten wickets
Oval	West Indies won by an innings & 56 runs

County Champions (joint)   Lancashire/Surrey

TEST AVERAGES ENGLAND V WEST INDIES 1950

	M	I	NO	HS	Runs	Av	100	50	Ct/St
L. Hutton	3	6	1	202*	333	66.60	1	–	2
C. Washbrook	2	4	0	114	255	63.75	2	–	–
T. E. Bailey	2	4	1	82*	145	48.33	–	1	1
T. G. Evans	3	6	0	104	224	37.33	1	1	3/6
W. G. A. Parkhouse	2	4	0	69	130	32.50	–	1	–
R. T. Simpson	3	6	0	94	171	28.50	–	1	–
W. J. Edrich	2	4	0	71	94	23.50	–	1	1
J. G. Dewes	2	4	0	67	87	21.75	–	1	–
G. H. G. Doggart	2	4	0	29	76	19.00	–	–	3
N. W. D. Yardley	3	6	0	41	108	18.00	–	–	3
R. O. Jenkins	2	4	1	39	53	17.66	–	–	2
A. V. Bedser	3	6	0	13	20	3.33	–	–	–
R. Berry	2	4	2	4*	6	3.00	–	–	2
W. E. Hollies	2	4	1	3	5	1.66	–	–	1

Also batted: F. R. Brown (1 match) 0, 15; D. C. S. Compton (1 match) 44, 11; H. E. Dollery (1 match) 8, 0, 1ct; M. J. Hilton (1 match) 3, 0; D. J. Insole (1 match) 21, 0, 1ct; J. C. Laker (1 match) 4, 40; A. J. McIntyre (1 match) 4, 0, 3ct; D. Shackleton (1 match) 42, 1; D. S. Sheppard (1 match) 11, 29; J. H. Wardle (1 match) 33*, 21; D. V. P. Wright (1 match) 4, 6*.

	Overs	M	Runs	Wkts	Av	5w	10w	BB
R. Berry	108.5	47	228	9	25.33	1	–	5–63
W. E. Hollies	119	38	268	10	26.80	1	–	5–63
D. V. P. Wright	53	16	141	5	28.20	1	–	5–141
A. V. Bedser	181	49	377	11	34.27	1	–	5–127
R. O. Jenkins	118.2	20	409	10	40.90	1	–	5–116

Also bowled: T. E. Bailey 47.2–12–121–3; F. R. Brown 21–4–74–1; D. C. S. Compton 7–2–21–0; W. J. Edrich 34–8–81–0; M. J. Hilton 41–12–91–0; J. C. Laker 31–9–86–1; D. Shackleton 49–9–135–1; R. T. Simpson 1.3–0–9–0; J. H. Wardle 47–16–104–2; N. W. D. Yardley 31–4–94–1.

CHAMPIONSHIP TABLE 1950

						First Inns Lead in Match					
	P	Won	Lost	D	Tied	NR	Lost	D	Pts
Points Awarded	–	12	–	–	8/4	–	4	4	–
} LANCASHIRE									
} (11)	28	16	2	10	0	0	1	6	220
} SURREY (5)	28	17	4	6	0	1	0	4	220
Yorkshire (1)	28	14	2	10	0	2	0	8	200
Warwickshire (4)	28	8	6	13	0	1	1	8	132
Derbyshire (15)	28	8	9	9	0	2	3	4	124
Worcestershire (3)	28	7	9	9	0	3	0	7	114*
} Gloucestershire									
} (7)	28	6	6	16	0	0	2	9	112±
} Somerset (9)	28	8	8	10	0	2	1	3	112
Kent (13)	28	6	12	8	1	1	3	5	108$
Northamptonshire (6)	28	6	4	15	0	3	2	6	104
Glamorgan (8)	28	6	4	9	0	9	0	7	100
Hampshire (16)	28	7	9	9	1	2	0	2	96±@
Sussex (13)	28	5	11	11	0	1	6	2	92
Middlesex (1)	28	5	12	8	0	3	2	4	84
Nottinghamshire (11)	28	3	6	17	0	2	0	8	68
Leicestershire (17)	28	3	13	11	0	1	2	5	64
Essex (9)	28	4	12	11	0	1	0	3	60

± includes eight points for win on first innings in one-day match
@ includes eight points for first innings lead in match tied
$ includes four points for tie without first innings lead
* includes two points for tie on first innings in match lost
1949 positions are shown in brackets

FIRST-CLASS AVERAGES 1950

	I	NO	HS	Runs	Av	100
±W. Watson (Yorkshire)	12	2	132	684	68.40	3
R. T. Simpson (Nottinghamshire)	47	6	243*	2576	62.82	8
±J. G. Dewes (Camb Univ/ Middlesex)	45	4	212	2432	59.31	9
L. Hutton (Yorkshire)	40	3	202*	2128	57.51	6
M. B. Hofmeyr (Oxford Univ)	21	2	161	1063	55.94	4
C. Washbrook (Lancashire)	36	3	114	1807	54.75	4
J. Hardstaff (Nottinghamshire)	30	4	149*	1383	53.19	5
D. Brookes (Northamptonshire)	45	6	171	2000	51.28	5
G. Cox (Sussex)	55	7	165*	2369	49.35	6
±L. Livingston (Northamptonshire)	47	5	123	1966	46.80	2

*denotes not out
± denotes left-hand batsman

	Overs	M	Runs	Wkts	Av	BB
R. Tattersall (Lancashire)	1404.4	501	2623	193	13.59	8–60
A. Hamer (Derbyshire)	82.3	14	220	15	14.66	4–27
J. C. Laker (Surrey)	1409.5	522	2544	166	15.32	8–2
±E. Davies (Glamorgan)	413	132	923	57	16.19	5–20
J. B. Statham (Lancashire)	300.5	82	613	37	16.56	5–18
±J. H. Wardle (Yorkshire)	1627.5	741	2909	174	16.71	8–26
±M. J. Hilton (Lancashire)	1169.3	484	2267	135	16.79	6–32
±R. T. Weeks (Warwickshire)	146	49	275	16	17.18	5–42
C. Gladwin (Derbyshire)	752.4	223	1682	94	17.89	7–73
A. Coxon (Yorkshire)	1155.5	299	2437	131	18.60	7–51

TEST SHOCK

Freddie Trueman: Just beginning to make my way as a Yorkshire bowler, I was *really* interested in the series against West Indies for all kinds of reasons: the three Ws playing together in England for the first time; the spin twins, Ramadhin and Valentine, having a rare old series, tying the England batsmen in knots; and Leonard's (Hutton) double century at The Oval which broke all kinds of records. How he must have loved that ground! I was to have one or two differences of opinion with Len a little later in my career but never for one moment have I ceased to admire his batting. He has always been the greatest for me and his 202 not out in the Final Test—carrying his bat right through the first innings—remains one of the outstanding feats in the England/West Indies series. Compared with what was to happen in the future, the England Selectors called on a remarkable number of players in that series—25 in all.

Don Mosey: But all those changes couldn't prevent West Indies taking the rubber by three Tests to one, even after England had won the First by a resounding 202 runs at Old Trafford. Bob Berry, the Lancashire slow left-armer, had nine wickets in the match which was his first Test, and Alf Valentine in *his* Test debut, took eight for 104 in the first innings and 11 for 204 in the match.

FST: It was a remarkable Test in every way. Clyde Walcott was the wicket-keeper on that tour, but in the second innings at Old Trafford he actually opened the bowling because Hines Johnson had pulled a muscle in his side. How many times has that been done?

DM: And Godfrey Evans scored his first century in first-class cricket in this country. In fact it was his sixth-wicket partnership with Trevor Bailey (161) which put England in a position to win. Without their runs, England might well have lost all four Tests.

FST: Well, they certainly lost the next three and if Valentine had caused all the bother in Manchester, it was little Sonny Ramadhin who did the damage at Lord's—11 for 152 and no one could sort him out. He turned the ball both ways but as a *finger*-spinner. I suppose his leg break

The ever-spectacular Godfrey Evans

was really a flipper but no one could work out when it was coming. Basically, you had to play him as an off-spinner who would occasionally slip one in which went the other way. He was only about five ft six or five ft seven and his combination with the tall, gangling Alf Valentine bowling slow left arm at the other end had everyone in a flap. But at least we had something to cheer about in the Yorkshire dressing-room when Johnny Wardle took a wicket with his first Test delivery in England—he dismissed Jeff Stollmeyer. I remember Johnny coming back to tell the tale of West Indian supporters singing and dancing on the pitch at Lord's at the end of the game. They'd never seen anything like it at HQ.

DM: They wouldn't be so happy in Glamorgan, though. Gilbert Parkhouse joined the list of batsmen who failed to score in his first Test innings and then Walcott (back behind the stumps again) hit 168 not out in West Indies' second innings. But it was the other two Ws (Worrell and Weekes) who mangled England in the next Test at Trent Bridge. By this time I was working in Nottingham and I sat enthralled, right through their partnership of 283 at far better than a run a minute. I can still see Everton Weekes stepping back outside his leg stump to *cut* the two leg-spinners, Hollies and Jenkins, to the third man boundary. He was always one of the great cutters but if he ever enjoyed himself more than in that innings of 129 I wish I had been there to see it. And as for Frankie Worrell's 261–it was simply fantastic. For the first time I was seeing West Indies batting which set the pattern for the future: 'Where can I hit *this* ball for four?'

FST: He got another 'ton' in the last Test as well (138) and even Leonard's 202 not out in a total of 344 couldn't save England. That's when they wrote that calypso in Trinidad, 'Those two little pals of mine, Ramadhin and Valentine,' and soon it seemed to be on the wireless every day in this country. I got sick of the sound of it. I never like to see England beaten in a Test series, especially at home.

DM: Well, they had earned their place in the charts, I suppose. Alf took 33 wickets in the series and Sonny 26. And they arrived here having played just *two* first-class matches each. We were never to look at West Indies cricket in a patronising way again.

JOINT TITLE-WINNERS

FST: For the second year in succession the championship title was shared, this time by Lancashire and Surrey, so naturally enough we expect to see bowlers from those two counties doing well. Roy Tattersall (Lancashire) headed the first-class averages with 193 at 13.59—marvellous figures—and Jim Laker was third in the list with 166 at 15.32.

The two little pals—of whom? Not England in 1950

DM: That was the year Jim took eight wickets for two runs in the so-called Test trial at Bradford. I say 'so-called' because he wrecked the game with that analysis of 14–12–2–8 and it gave rise to one of the best stories of cricket journalism. In the middle of an interview, Jim was asked by the *Daily Express* representative, 'Was this your best performance?' With that dry, tongue-in-cheek humour which was very much his trade mark he replied, 'Well, I haven't done it right often.' So with Arnold Hamer nipping into the averages that year we had three off-spinners and four slow left-armers in the top ten.

WARDLE AND LOCK

FST: Johnny Wardle took 174 wickets; he was a spendid bowler. I played a great deal of cricket with him and quite a lot with his great rival, Tony Lock. Johnny, in my view, was the better of the two because he was so much more a *complete* bowler.

Tony had a low trajectory which they do say was as a result of bowling so much in Alf Gover's school where there was a low roof. Wardle could bowl the high, flighted delivery in the classic slow left-armer's style and he had all kinds of variations. Tony Lock, I should add, was the best catcher of a ball I ever saw.

DM: The leading quick bowler that season was another old friend of yours, Brian Statham.

FST: That's right. He was up-and-coming then—just 300 overs that season, I notice. He had to bowl a lot more than that before his career was over, and so had I. We were a good team, I thought, 'George' and me.

DM: Back to the batting in 1950: Reg Simpson had a good season—2,576 runs in 47 innings—and he hit eight hundreds.

FST: Reg was a good player of quick bowling but of course it was never *quite* so quick at Trent Bridge and he would make a lot of his runs there. And then there's John Dewes who had a spectacular career as a batter when he was up at Cambridge but he never made it at Test level and his business commitments, I believe, limited the amount of cricket he could play for Middlesex when he finished at University. But good to see dear old Dennis Brookes there, scoring exactly 2,000 first-class runs.

Winter Tour to Australia (1950–51):

Brisbane	Australia won by 70 runs
Melbourne	Australia won by 28 runs
Sydney	Australia won by an innings & 13 runs
Adelaide	Australia won by 274 runs
Melbourne	England won by eight wickets

New Zealand:

Christchurch	Match drawn
Wellington	England won by six wickets

Summer Series with South Africa:

Trent Bridge	South Africa won by 71 runs
Lord's	England won by ten wickets
Old Trafford	England won by nine wickets
Headingley	Match drawn
Oval	England won by four wickets

County Champions   Warwickshire

TEST AVERAGES ENGLAND V AUSTRALIA 1950–51

	M	I	NO	HS	Runs	Av	100	50	Ct/St
L. Hutton	5	10	4	156*	533	88.83	1	4	9
R. T. Simpson	5	10	1	156*	349	38.77	1	1	4
F. R. Brown	5	8	0	79	210	26.25	–	2	4
W. G. A. Parkhouse	2	4	0	29	77	19.25	–	–	1
T. G. Evans	5	9	1	49	144	18.00	–	–	11/–
C. Washbrook	5	10	0	34	173	17.30	–	–	1
D. S. Sheppard	2	3	0	41	51	17.00	–	–	–
T. E. Bailey	4	7	2	15	40	8.00	–	–	4
D. C. S. Compton	4	8	1	23	53	7.57	–	–	3
A. V. Bedser	5	8	2	14*	43	7.16	–	–	5
J. G. Dewes	2	4	0	9	23	5.75	–	–	–
R. Tattersall	2	3	0	10	16	5.33	–	–	1
D. V. P. Wright	5	7	1	14	23	3.83	–	–	–
J. J. Warr	2	4	0	4	4	1.00	–	–	–

Also batted: D. B. Close (1 match) 0, 1, 1ct; A. J. McIntyre (1 match) 1, 7, 1ct.

	Overs	M	Runs	Wkts	Av	5w	10w	BB
T. E. Bailey	75.1	18	198	14	14.14	–	–	4–22
A. V. Bedser	195	34	482	30	16.06	2	1	5–46
F. R. Brown	109	12	389	18	21.61	1	–	5–49
D. V. P. Wright	103	6	500	11	45.45	–	–	4–99

Also bowled: D. B. Close 7–1–28–1; D. C. S. Compton 11.6–1–43–1; R. Tattersall 68.5–12–257–4; J. J. Warr 73–6–281–1.

TEST AVERAGES ENGLAND V NEW ZEALAND 1950–51

	M	I	NO	HS	Runs	Av	100	50	Ct/St
F. R. Brown	2	3	1	62	119	59.50	–	1	4
L. Hutton	2	3	0	57	114	38.00	–	1	–
D. C. S. Compton	2	3	0	79	107	35.66	–	1	1
R. T. Simpson	2	3	0	81	92	30.66	–	1	–

Also batted: T. E. Bailey (2 matches) 134*, 29, 1ct; A. V. Bedser (2 matches) 5, 28, 1ct; T. G. Evans (2 matches) 19, 13, 2ct/1st; W. G. A. Parkhouse (1 match) 2, 20, 1ct; D. S. Sheppard (1 match) 3, 4*, 1ct; J. B. Statham (1 match) 9; R. Tattersall (2 matches) 2, 1; C. Washbrook (1 match) 58; D. V. P. Wright (2 matches) 45, 9*, 1ct.

	Overs	M	Runs	Wkts	Av	5w	10w	BB
R. Tattersall	52	18	108	8	13.50	1	–	6–44
T. E. Bailey	55.2	12	112	7	16.00	–	–	3–43
D. V. P. Wright	58	7	179	7	25.57	1	–	5–48

Also bowled: A. V. Bedser 84–26–138–2; F. R. Brown 22.2–4–45–2; D. C. S. Compton 6–0–31–0; L. Hutton 3–0–7–0; R. T. Simpson 4–1–4–2; J. B. Statham 24–6–47–1; C. Washbrook 4–0–25–1.

TEST AVERAGES ENGLAND V SOUTH AFRICA 1951

	M	I	NO	HS	Runs	Av	100	50	Ct/St
P. B. H. May	2	3	0	138	171	57.00	1	–	1
L. Hutton	5	9	2	100	378	54.00	1	2	8
D. C. S. Compton	4	6	0	112	312	52.00	1	2	2
R. T. Simpson	3	5	1	137	185	46.25	1	–	–
T. E. Bailey	2	3	0	95	109	36.33	–	1	–
W. Watson	5	7	0	79	240	34.28	–	2	1
F. A. Lowson	2	3	0	58	95	31.66	–	1	2
J. T. Ikin	3	6	1	51	149	29.80	–	1	12
J. C. Laker	2	3	1	27	46	23.00	–	–	1
A. V. Bedser	5	6	3	30*	66	22.00	–	–	1
J. H. Wardle	2	3	0	30	53	17.66	–	–	–
F. R. Brown	5	7	0	42	122	17.42	–	–	6
R. Tattersall	5	5	2	4	6	2.00	–	–	4
T. G. Evans	3	4	0	5	7	1.75	–	–	4/1

Also batted: D. V. Brennan (2 matches) 16, 0 1st; T. W. Graveney (1 match) 15; M. J. Hilton (1 match) 9*, 1ct; D. Shackleton (1 match) 14, 5*; J. B. Statham (2 matches) 1, 1.

	Overs	M	Runs	Wkts	Av	5w	10w	BB
J. C. Laker	111	30	208	14	14.85	1	1	6–55
A. V. Bedser	275.5	84	517	30	17.23	2	1	7–58
R. Tattersall	261.2	99	439	21	20.90	1	1	7–52
J. H. Wardle	95.5	39	171	5	34.20	–	–	3–46
F. R. Brown	116	38	258	7	36.85	–	–	3–107

Also bowled: T. E. Bailey 65–17–168–0; D. C. S. Compton 13–1–45–0; M. J. Hilton 71.3–23–193–3; D. Shackleton 25–7–39–1; J. B. Statham 48–14–78–4.

CHAMPIONSHIP TABLE 1951

| | | | | | First Inns Lead in Match | | | |
Points Awarded	P –	Won 12	Lost –	D –	NR –	Lost 4	D 4	Pts –
WARWICKSHIRE (4)	28	16	2	10	0	0	6	216
Yorkshire (3)	28	12	3	11	2	0	10	184
Lancashire (1)	28	8	2	14	4	1	9	136
Worcestershire (6)	28	9	7	10	2	2	4	132
Glamorgan (11)	28	8	4	13	3	1	7	128
Surrey (1)	28	7	6	13	2	0	9	120
Middlesex (14)	28	7	6	13	2	1	7	116
Essex (17)	28	6	2	18	2	0	9	110*
Hampshire (12)	28	5	7	13	3	1	9	100
Sussex (13)	28	6	6	15	1	0	5	94*
Derbyshire (5)	28	5	6	16	1	2	6	92
Gloucestershire (7)	28	5	9	12	2	1	6	88
Northamptonshire (10)	28	4	4	17	3	1	7	80
Somerset (7)	28	5	15	6	2	3	1	76
Leicestershire (16)	28	4	7	16	1	0	4	64
Kent (9)	28	4	15	8	1	1	2	60
Nottinghamshire (15)	28	1	11	13	3	0	7	40

*includes two points for a tie on first innings in match drawn
1950 positions are shown in brackets

FIRST-CLASS AVERAGES 1951

	I	NO	HS	Runs	Av	100
P. B. H. May (Camb Univ/Surrey)	43	9	178*	2339	68.79	9
D. C. S. Compton (Middlesex)	40	6	172	2193	64.50	8
±J. G. Dewes (Middlesex)	10	2	116*	515	64.37	2
±F. Jakeman (Northamptonshire)	41	6	258*	1989	56.82	6
J. D. B. Robertson (Middlesex)	56	4	201*	2917	56.09	7
L. Hutton (Yorkshire)	47	8	194*	2145	55.00	7
J. K. Aitchison (Scotland)	8	0	108	435	54.37	1
D. S. Sheppard (Camb Univ/Sussex)	43	3	183*	2104	52.60	7
±J. T. Ikin (Lancashire)	35	7	192	1371	48.96	4
T. W. Graveney (Gloucestershire)	50	3	201	2291	48.74	8

*denotes not out
± denotes left-hand batsman

	Overs	M	Runs	Wkts	Av	BB
R. Appleyard (Yorkshire)	1313.1	391	2829	200	14.14	8–76
J. B. Statham (Lancashire)	714.2	178	1466	97	15.11	5–20
A. V. Bedser (Surrey)	1100	130	2024	130	15.56	7–58
J. E. McConnon (Glamorgan)	862.3	238	2186	136	16.07	7–30
J. J. Warr (Camb Un/Middlesex)	449.2	119	1011	59	17.13	6–28
W. E. Hollies (Warwickshire)	1393.2	500	2566	145	17.69	7–67
C. Gladwin (Derbyshire)	1065.1	297	2526	142	17.78	9–64
J. C. Laker (Surrey)	1301.3	400	2681	149	17.99	7–36
±R. Howorth (Worcestershire)	1066.2	326	2242	124	18.08	6–63
R. Tattersall (Lancashire)	1171.5	430	2236	121	18.47	8–51

±denotes left-arm bowler

YOUNG BRIAN CLOSE

Don Mosey: Warwickshire's first championship for 40 years, a magnificent tour of Australia for Len Hutton but a disaster for England, young Peter May arrives on the Test scene and Bob Appleyard takes 200 wickets in his first full season—quite an eventful year.

Freddie Trueman: Yes, but let's start with that terrible tour of Australia because I think it had a disastrous effect on Brian Close's career. He had been picked by England 15 months earlier, then discarded, and now was plucked from National Service with the Army to go on the greatest tour of all. He could scarcely have had a worse captain than Freddie Brown, who wasn't particularly interested in helping young players, and he didn't get much comfort from the senior players either. Close's description of it was 'a tour of misery' and while in many ways he had a remarkable career I think it would have been a good deal more successful but for going on a long tour as a young and impressionable player.

DM: Agreed, absolutely. Now let's look at Leonard's tour, starting with that remarkable game on the 'sticky dog' in Brisbane. Len has said his second innings 62 (out of 122) was one of the best he ever played.

FST: It must have been. He was a truly great player on bad wickets and he batted at No. 6 in the first innings and

A boyish Brian Close, with Len Hutton, setting off for Australia 1950–51

was 8 not out when England declared at 68 for seven—160 runs behind. The idea was to get at the Aussies while the pitch was like something out of a nightmare and hope it eased out later. Lindsay Hassett countered (when Bedser and Bailey started to go through them) by declaring at 32 for seven, leaving England to get 193 to win. I wish I had had a chance to bowl on a pitch like that! Leonard went in at No. 8, when the score was 46 for six and was 62 not out when England lost by 71 runs. He batted at No. 4 in the second Test but was back as an opener for the last three, scoring 62, 9, 156 not out (the second time he had carried his bat through an innings in six months!); 45, 79 and 60 not out.

DM: One set of figures will interest you from that tour, Fred— JJ Warr, two Tests, 73–6–281–1.

FST: Well, he's renowned as the great humorist. I suppose you've got to be with figures like that.

DM: One of the remarkable things about the tour was the decline of Denis Compton who had gone as Brown's vice-captain. It's astonishing to think he totalled only 53 runs in eight Test innings. Hutton, who might well have been appointed vice-captain but was not surprised by the Selectors' preference for Compton, averaged 88.83 in Tests, 50 runs an innings better than his nearest challenger, Reg Simpson.

ENTER JB STATHAM

FST: The tour finished off with two games in New Zealand where Brian Statham took his first Test wicket and Trevor Bailey got his only Test hundred. That might surprise a lot of people—only one century for Trevor. He batted long enough to have made a hundred of them! Seriously, he was a really great all-rounder and he used to love playing against the Australians in particular. He nearly drove them mad on occasions when they couldn't get him out, like the time in Brisbane in 1958 when he batted for over 7½ hours. It was the first Test to be televised in Australia—I wonder how many people got rid of their sets after that?

AT HOME TO SOUTH AFRICA

DM: Jackie McGlew played his first Test for South Africa at Trent Bridge and for the first time (on his dismissal) we see 'st. Evans, b Bedser.' Godfrey had a high proportion of stumpings—46 against 173 catches in his 91 Tests as wicket-keeper—and to see him standing up to Bedser was one of the great sights of cricket. In that first Test, Reg Simpson became the first Notts batsman to make a century for England on his own ground which seems quite remarkable when you think of the Gunns and the Hardstaffs who had played there before him, but South

Brian ('George') Statham, a fast bowler with a big heart and pin-point accuracy

Africa won for the first time in 28 Tests. The series was squared at Lord's where Tattersall achieved the best figures of his Test career (12 for 101), and England won again at Old Trafford and The Oval.

FST: And at Old Trafford, Hutton was 98 not out when England won by nine wickets. If he and Reg Simpson had staged-managed it a bit better, Leonard would have been the first man to score his 100th hundred in a Test match. At Headingley, PBH May got 138 on his first appearance for England and my old friend Don Brennan was also turning out for his country for the first time. He was a bit of a rarity, an amateur wicket-keeper, and when in the 1980s he turned out under my captaincy for the Courage Old England XI, for a fee of £100, he laughed: 'It's a bit daft to lose your amateur status at 63.' He still brought off a few smart stumpings, just the same. He had a beautiful pair of hands.

DM: We just can't get away from Len Hutton. At The Oval he became the first man for more than 50 years to be given out 'obstructing the field'. After getting a top edge to the off-spinner, Athol Rowan, he hit the ball again to prevent it falling onto the stumps but in doing so prevented Russell Endean, the wicket-keeper, from catching the ball. Compton was back to form, averaging

52 in the Tests and Bedser claimed 30 wickets in the series.

FST: Warwickshire were clear winners of the county championship with 16 wins, four more than Yorkshire, the runners-up. This was the product of a lot of solid teamwork under the captaincy of Tom Dollery, a professional skipper which was something of an innovation in modern cricket. David Sheppard, shortly to become the Rev and later the Bishop of Liverpool, topped 2,000 runs, dividing his cricket between Cambridge University and Sussex. He was joined in the top ten by another parson, the Rev James Aitchison, who averaged 54.37 in eight first-class innings for Scotland.

DM: I know you were a great admirer of Jack Robertson, Fred. He's there again, hammering out nearly 3,000 runs for Middlesex.

FST: Jack was another of those fine players who lost so many good years because of the war. He scored 1,000 runs in a season 14 times, just the same, and 2,000 or more nine times. He hit three double centuries and 331 not out against Worcestershire in 1949. And he averaged 46.36 in 11 Tests. Why he didn't play in more than that, I don't know. It can only have been because Hutton, Washbrook and Simpson were around at the time. But it was Peter May who topped the averages.

DM: He was in his middle year at Cambridge at probably the vintage period for cricket there.

FST: I can tell you this: the word around the dressing-rooms at that time was, 'Have you come up against this kid, May, yet? *What* a fine player.' He was the best on-driver I think I have ever seen and that's a quality shot.

DM: Robert Appleyard was one of the most remarkable bowlers Yorkshire has produced, yet he was 26 before he came on the scene. What had he been doing until then? Playing for Bowling Old Lane in the Bradford League where he was primarily a medium-fast bowler. I believe he developed the off-spinning in the Yorkshire Colts side.

FST: He could use the new ball, swinging it a lot, and then switch to off-breaks but not the Laker variety; Bob bowled his at nearer medium pace. Sometimes it was unbelievable to watch him in action, especially in 1951 which was his first full season in the game—200 wickets at 14.14. Incredible! Ray Illingworth thinks he can pin down the origins of the off-spinning to a particular game— Yorkshire II v Staffordshire at Knypersley.

DM: Well, Staffordshire has produced a lot of fine cricketers but this is the first time I have heard of the connection with Bob Appleyard's career.

Top right: *The Rev. David Sheppard's cover drive*

Walter Hammond, superb stroke-player, a most complete cricketer

Winter Tour to India (1951–52):

Delhi	Match drawn
Bombay	Match drawn
Calcutta	Match drawn
Kanpur	England won by eight wickets
Madras	India won by an innings & 8 runs

Summer Series with India:

Headingley	England won by seven wickets
Lord's	England won by eight wickets
Old Trafford	England won by an innings & 207 runs
Oval	Match drawn

County Champions Surrey

TEST AVERAGES ENGLAND V INDIA 1951–52

	M	I	NO	HS	Runs	Av	100	50	Ct/St
A. J. Watkins	5	8	1	138*	451	64.42	1	3	4
T. W. Graveney	4	8	2	175	363	60.50	1	–	1
C. J. Poole	3	5	1	69*	161	40.25	–	2	1
J. D. B. Robertson	5	9	1	77	310	38.75	–	3	2
R. T. Spooner	5	10	1	92	319	35.44	–	3	8/2
D. B. Carr	2	4	0	76	135	33.75	–	1	–
R. Tattersall	5	6	5	10*	23	23.00	–	–	1
F. A. Lowson	4	8	0	68	145	18.12	–	1	2
N. D. Howard	4	6	1	23	86	17.20	–	–	4
J. B. Statham	5	6	1	27	59	11.80	–	–	1
D. Kenyon	3	6	0	35	67	11.16	–	–	1
M. J. Hilton	2	3	0	15	25	8.33	–	–	–
F. Ridgway	5	6	0	24	49	8.16	–	–	3

	Overs	M	Runs	Wkts	Av	5w	10w	BB
M. J. Hilton	93.5	34	187	11	17.00	1	–	5–61
R. Tattersall	247.5	65	595	21	28.33	1	–	6–48
J. B. Statham	126	36	293	8	36.62	–	–	4–96
F. Ridgway	132.1	23	379	7	54.14	–	–	4–83

Also bowled: D. B. Carr 35–6–140–2; T. W. Graveney 1–0–9–0; E. Leadbeater 48.1–8–218–2; C. J. Poole 5–1–9–0; J. D. B. Robertson 23–4–58–2; D. Shackleton 29–7–76–1; A. J. Watkins 116–26–264–4.

Also batted: E. Leadbeater (2 matches) 2, 38, 3ct; D. Shackleton (1 match) 10, 20*.

TEST AVERAGES ENGLAND V INDIA 1952

	M	I	NO	HS	Runs	Av	100	50	Ct/St
L. Hutton	4	6	1	150	399	79.80	2	1	3
T. G. Evans	4	4	0	104	242	60.50	1	2	4/4
T. W. Graveney	4	5	1	73	191	47.75	–	2	2
P. B. H. May	4	6	0	74	206	34.33	–	2	3
R. T. Simpson	2	4	0	53	129	32.25	–	2	–
D. C. S Compton	2	4	2	35*	59	29.50	–	–	2
J. C. Laker	4	4	2	23*	44	22.00	–	–	3
A. J. Watkins	3	3	0	48	52	17.33	–	–	6
A. V. Bedser	4	3	0	17	27	9.00	–	–	1

Also batted: J. T. Ikin (2 matches) 29, 53, 4ct; R. O. Jenkins (2 matches) 38, 21, 1ct; G. A. R. Lock (2 matches) 1*, 3ct; D. S. Sheppard (2 matches) 34, 119, 1ct; F. S. Trueman (4 matches) 0*, 17, 1ct; W. Watson (1 match) 18*.

	Overs	M	Runs	Wkts	Av	5w	10w	BB
F. S. Trueman	119.4	25	386	29	13.31	2	–	8–31
A. V. Bedser	163.5	57	279	20	13.95	2	–	5–27
J. C. Laker	90.3	33	189	8	23.62	–	–	4–39
R. O. Jenkins	57.3	10	194	6	32.33	–	–	4–50

Also bowled: D. C. S. Compton 9–1–30–0; G. A. R. Lock 15.3–7–37–4; A. J. Watkins 51–13–111–3.

CHAMPIONSHIP TABLE 1952

							First Inns Lead in Match			
Points Awarded	P	Won	Lost	D	Tied	NR	Lost	D	Pts
	—	12	—	—	8/4		4	4	—
SURREY (6)	28	20	3	5	0	0	0	4	256
Yorkshire (2)	28	17	2	8	0	1	0	5	224
Lancashire (3)	28	12	3	11	1	1	1	8	188±
Derbyshire (11)	28	11	8	9	0	0	2	6	164
Middlesex (7)	28	11	12	4	0	1	0	1	136
Leicestershire (15)	28	9	9	9	0	1	1	5	132
Glamorgan (5)	28	8	7	13	0	0	2	6	130▲
Northamptonshire (13)	28	7	8	12	0	1	3	8	128
Gloucestershire (12)	28	7	10	11	0	0	4	6	124
Essex (8)	28	8	4	13	1	2	1	4	120$
Warwickshire (1)	28	8	10	8	1	1	0	4	120±
Hampshire (9)	28	7	11	9	0	1	4	3	112
Sussex (10)	28	7	12	6	1	2	0	2	96$
Worcestershire (4)	28	6	11	10	0	1	1	3	90*
Kent (16)	28	5	15	8	0	2	4		84
Nottinghamshire (17)	28	3	11	13	0	1	2	7	72
Somerset (14)	28	2	12	13	0	1	1	4	44

± includes eight points for first innings lead in match tied
$ includes four points for tie without first innings lead
* includes two points for tie on first innings in match drawn
1951 positions are shown in brackets

FIRST-CLASS AVERAGES 1952

	I	NO	HS	Runs	Av	100
D. S. Sheppard (Camb Univ/ Sussex)	39	4	239*	2262	64.62	10
P. B. H. May (Camb Univ/Surrey)	47	7	197	2498	62.45	10
L. Hutton (Yorkshire)	45	3	189	2567	61.11	11
E. Lester (Yorkshire)	42	6	178	1786	49.61	6
±W. Watson (Yorkshire)	43	9	114	1651	48.55	3
T. W. Graveney (Gloucestershire)	50	7	171	2066	48.04	6
D. Brookes (Northamptonshire)	54	7	204*	2229	47.42	6
J. Hardstaff (Nottinghamshire)	39	5	144*	1597	46.97	6
±J. T. Ikin (Lancashire)	46	4	154	1912	45.52	4
C. A. Milton (Gloucestershire)	55	11	146*	1922	43.68	3

	Overs	M	Runs	Wkts	Av	BB
F. S. Trueman (Yorkshire)	282.4	57	841	61	13.78	8–31
A. V. Bedser (Surrey)	1184.4	296	2530	154	16.42	8–18
±G. A. R. Lock (Surrey)	1109.4	416	2237	131	17.07	6–15
C. W. Grove (Warwickshire)	945.3	238	2022	118	17.13	9–39
B. L. Muncer (Glamorgan)	862.2	259	1816	105	17.29	7–35
A. Townsend (Warwickshire)	508.2	101	1310	74	17.70	6–76
R. Tattersall (Lancashire)	1165.5	409	2586	146	17.71	8–28
J. C. Laker (Surrey)	1072	342	2219	125	17.75	7–57
J. B. Statham (Lancashire)	881.5	186	1989	110	18.08	5–32
D. Shackleton (Hampshire)	1156.1	351	2479	135	18.36	6–22

'Fiery Fred' Trueman, with the perfect cartwheel action

A NEW ERA

Don Mosey: This was so much of a new era in so many ways that I think we should leave our review of the winter tour until the end of this chapter. What happened in England during the summer of 1952 was of far greater significance, starting with the appointment of Hutton as England's first professional captain, and the arrival on the Test scene for the first time of a young fast bowler then doing National Service in the RAF. . . .

Freddie Trueman: Aircraftman Trueman, FS, was working in the stores at RAF Hemswell, in Lincolnshire, when the Station Commander, Group Captain Warfield, sent for him to say Norman Yardley had been on the 'phone to ask for his release to play in the First Test against India at Headingley. The group captain said he would release me on condition he got two tickets for his wife and himself to watch the game. He got them.

DM: Trueman, bowling up the hill from the football end (which was unfamiliar territory to him as a *Yorkshire* bowler) had the unremarkable figures of three for 89 in India's first innings which reached 293, but when they batted a second time he changed ends and, bowling at a pace no Indian batsman had yet experienced, he took three wickets in eight balls for no runs. Bedser took another and the most photographed scoreboard in the history of cricket read: India 0 for 4 wickets at close of play on the Saturday. His final figures of four for 27 in India's defeat by seven wickets, ensured his inclusion in the side for the Second Test at Lord's.

FST: I had four wickets in each innings at Lord's where the Indians batted a lot better. I seem to remember they called up Vinoo Mankad from the Lancashire League where he was playing for Haslingden. He opened the innings, scored 72 in the first innings, 184 in the second and bowled 97 overs in the match (five for 231) so he'd think it was a harder way of making his money than playing on Saturday afternoon. Leonard got 189 for once out and what a match for Godfrey Evans—his 100th dismissal in Tests and 104 runs, 98 of them before lunch on the third day.

DM: And then Old Trafford. That's certainly your story, Fred. . . .

FST: Well, let's talk about Tony Lock first because it was his debut and the first time he touched the ball was to bring off a blinding catch at leg slip off Bedser to get rid of Mankad. As I've said already, he had the best pair of hands I've ever seen in the game and he started as he meant to go on. Mankad had hit the first ball for four and he played a genuine leg glance off the last ball of Alec's over, expecting it to go for another four, but there was Lockie, scooping it up. Leonard set me a field, from the Stretford end, of three slips, three gullies, silly point and two short legs and it was one of those days when all the catches stuck. The fielding was marvellous and the Indian batting wasn't as tough as it was to become later with players like Gavaskar, Viswanath and Vengsarkar around. All the same, Roy, Hazare, Umrigar and Manjrekar were national heroes at home in India and I certainly didn't expect to see them back away as some of them did. Panic spread through the ranks and Dattu Phadkar actually charged down the pitch to me and carved it to gully. Great catch, David Sheppard! I could actually see Lock, at leg slip, between the stumps and the batsman as I ran in to bowl to Polly Umrigar.

DM: Fred's figures were eight for 31 and England won by an innings and 207 runs. The Trueman story had now really begun. Hutton got 104 at Old Trafford and Sheppard got 119 at The Oval where only ten hours play was possible because of rain. It must have been a terrible disappointment of a tour for India because only the previous February they had won their first Test against England in nearly 20 years—by an innings and eight runs at Madras where Roy scored 111 and Umrigar 130 not out, and Mankad bowled beautifully to take eight first-innings wickets for 55. But England's team wasn't anything like what would have been regarded as a full-strength side in England. Eddie Leadbeater, the leg-spinner, actually played for England in Bombay (Second Test) before he had been capped by either of the two English counties he played for, Yorkshire and Warwickshire.

SURREY'S REIGN

FST: That summer saw the start of Surrey's seven-year reign as county champions. It drove us mad in Yorkshire at the time because we always regarded ourselves as a better side. We finished runners-up to them four times and were third once but we couldn't get that top place.

DM: To be fair, Fred, Surrey were a great team. Strong batting, good close-catching and Laker and Lock, the Bedser twins, Peter Loader and Surridge as back-up bowler and captain—it was a very well balanced side.

FST: And, don't forget, they played all their home matches at The Oval so they knew what they were doing. Our batting wasn't so bad with Hutton, Watson, Wilson,

Tony Lock—'the best catcher of a ball I ever saw'

Lester, Close and what about the bowling? Appleyard, Close, Illingworth, Trueman, Wardle—not bad?

DM: Surridge had a side in which all the players pulled together for the common good; it is now generally accepted that Yorkshire didn't always give the same 100 per cent backing to either Norman Yardley or Billy Sutcliffe in that period.

FST: It was a side of great players, all the same. We *should* have been winning.

GREAT BATSMEN, GREAT BOWLERS

DM. There were an awful lot of good bowlers around in the early fifties and I know a lot more first-class matches were played but 2,000 runs or more in a season was a regular thing with a remarkable number of batsmen, and many more got over 1,500. The first-class batting averages were led in 1952 by two young men at Cambridge University—David Sheppard (2,262 at 64.62 with ten centuries) and Peter May (2,498 at 62.45, also with ten hundreds). Why did things change so much later on?

FST: Because of one-day cricket, of course. It cut down the number of first-class innings a batsman could play— but that's not the whole answer. It changed batting techniques completely. But we'll look at that a bit later. Sheppard and May were fine players, even as quite young men. Counties didn't send seriously weakened sides to play at the Universities: one, or perhaps two youngsters who were being given a chance, but that was all. The Universities faced good sides of top-class players so the runs the students made were genuine first-class runs. When you talk about declining standards all round, you have to include the Universities as well. In the fifties, and right up to the sixties, Oxford and Cambridge turned out players who were very obviously first-class players in every sense. Just as one-day cricket changed the county sides, so the educational system in schools changed the intake into the Universities.

DM: Looking at the first-class averages, it makes you think just how many players were around who made the game so delightful to watch—players whose batting evoked adjectives like 'graceful' and 'elegant'. You immediately associate such descriptions with men like Hardstaff, Graveney, Watson and Sheppard. Hutton and May could play like that too, but overall they were more ruthless in their approach to batting.

QUICK MEN TO THE FORE

FST: And with the bowling. The spinners are still there—Laker, Lock, and Muncer—but we now begin to see some of the quicker men coming more to the fore. Appleyard missed nearly all the 1952 and 1953 seasons, but my 29 Test wickets helped me top the first-class averages with Alec Bedser second. Then there was Charlie Grove who had such a great partnership with Tom Pritchard at Warwickshire and we see Alan Townsend there from Warwickshire as well. He was a genuine all-rounder who batted well in the middle order and was a good medium pacer. And now we see possibly the best medium-pacer of the lot apart, perhaps, from Tom Cartwright a bit later—the great Shack.

DM: Derek Shackleton, of Hampshire (though he was Yorkshire born, I don't think he knew that Todmorden was in Yorkshire at the time!) took at least 100 wickets in a season for 20 consecutive years from 1949 and I know batsmen used to pray there was no moisture in the pitch when they came up against him.

Derek Shackleton—perpetual motion and deadly on a seamer's wicket

FST: Shack could swing it and move it off the seam, and he had mastered consistent line and length so you never got a chance to relax when he was bowling. If a batter was able to offer no stroke at him Shack regarded it as a major disaster—he had wasted a ball. His record, year in, year out, forced the Selectors to call him up for England from time to time, but on firm Test pitches he was not so effective. But around the counties, everyone respected Shack.

1953

Tests v Australia:

Trent Bridge	Match drawn
Lord's	Match drawn
Old Trafford	Match drawn
Headingley	Match drawn
Oval	England won by eight wickets

County Champions Surrey

TEST AVERAGES ENGLAND V AUSTRALIA 1953

	M	I	NO	HS	Runs	Av	100	50	Ct/St
L. Hutton	5	9	1	145	443	55.37	1	3	4
W. J. Edrich	3	5	1	64	156	39.00	–	2	6
W. Watson	3	5	0	109	168	33.60	1	–	1
D. C. S. Compton	5	8	1	61	234	33.42	–	2	4
T. E. Bailey	5	7	0	71	222	31.71	–	2	3
J. H. Wardle	3	4	2	29*	57	28.50	–	–	–
P. B. H. May	2	3	0	39	85	28.33	–	–	–
T. W. Graveney	5	7	0	78	169	24.14	–	2	4
T. G. Evans	5	7	2	44*	117	23.40	–	–	11/5
R. T. Simpson	3	5	1	31	74	18.50	–	–	1
J. C. Laker	3	4	0	48	64	16.00	–	–	–
A. V. Bedser	5	6	3	22*	38	12.66	–	–	1
D. Kenyon	2	4	0	16	29	7.25	–	–	1
G. A. R. Lock	2	3	0	9	21	7.00	–	–	3

Also batted: F. R. Brown (1 match) 22, 28, 1ct; J. B. Statham (1 match) 17*, 2ct; R. Tattersall (1 match) 2, 2ct; F. S. Trueman (1 match) 10, 2ct.

	Overs	M	Runs	Wkts	Av	5w	10w	BB
A. V. Bedser	265.1	58	682	39	17.48	5	1	7–44
G. A. R. Lock	61	21	165	8	20.62	1	–	5–45
J. C. Laker	58.5	11	212	9	23.55	–	–	4–75
J. H. Wardle	155.3	57	344	13	26.46	–	–	4–7
T. E. Bailey	143	33	387	8	48.37	–	–	3–71

Also bowled: F. R. Brown 52–11–135–4; D. C. S. Compton 3–0–21–1; J. B. Statham 43–10–88–2; R. Tattersall 28–5–81–3; F. S. Trueman 26.3–4–90–4.

CHAMPIONSHIP TABLE 1953

							First Inns Lead in Match		
	P	Won	Lost	D	Tied	NR	Lost	D	Pts
Points Awarded	–	12	–	–	6	–	4	4	–
SURREY (1)	28	13	4	10	0	1	0	7	184
Sussex (13)	28	11	3	13	0	1	1	8	168
Lancashire (3)	28	10	4	10	0	4	1	8	156
Leicestershire (6)	28	10	7	11	0	0	3	6	156
Middlesex (5)	28	10	5	11	1	1	1	5	150
Derbyshire (4)	28	9	7	9	0	3	2	5	136
Gloucestershire (9)	28	9	7	10	0	2	2	5	136
Nottinghamshire (16)	28	9	10	8	0	1	4	1	128
Warwickshire (10)	28	6	7	14	0	1	2	11	124
Glamorgan (7)	28	8	4	14	0	2	0	6	120
Northamptonshire (8)	28	6	3	15	1	3	2	7	114
Essex (10)	28	6	7	13	0	2	1	6	100
Yorkshire (2)	28	6	6	13	0	3	1	6	100
Hampshire (12)	28	6	11	11	0	0	2	4	96
Worcestershire (14)	28	5	12	10	0	1	1	2	72
Kent (15)	28	4	14	8	0	2	1	3	64
Somerset (17)	28	2	19	6	0	1	0	3	36

1952 positions are shown in brackets

FIRST-CLASS AVERAGES 1953

	I	NO	HS	Runs	Av	100
±James Langridge (Sussex)	10	5	104*	358	71.60	1
L. Hutton (Yorkshire)	44	5	241	2458	63.02	8
±L. Livingston (Northamptonshire)	36	6	140	1710	57.00	7
P. B. H. May (Surrey)	59	9	159	2554	51.08	8
±R. Subba Row (Camb Univ/ Surrey)	46	10	146*	1823	50.63	4
D. W. Barrick (Northamptonshire)	38	7	166*	1530	49.35	3
W. J. Edrich (Middlesex)	60	6	211	2557	47.35	5
R. T. Simpson (Nottinghamshire)	60	5	157	2505	45.54	7
D. S. Sheppard (Sussex)	57	7	186*	2270	45.40	7
±W. Watson (Yorkshire)	48	9	162*	1769	45.35	3

*denotes not out
±denotes left-hand batsman

	Overs	M	Runs	Wkts	Av	BB
C. J. Knott (Hampshire)	223	65	521	38	13.71	6–114
H. L. Jackson (Derbyshire)	741.4	229	1574	103	15.28	5–23
±G. A. R. Lock (Surrey)	732.1	282	1590	100	15.90	8–23
T. W. Graveney (Gloucestershire)	94.3	19	324	20	16.20	5–28
J. B. Statham (Lancashire)	723.5	229	1650	101	16.33	6–49
B. Dooland (Nottinghamshire)	1332.3	461	2852	172	16.58	7–19
A. V. Bedser (Surrey)	1253	340	2702	162	16.67	8–18
G. Smith (Kent)	226.5	89	536	31	17.29	6–63
J. C. Laker (Surrey)	1165.5	383	2366	135	17.52	6–25
R. Tattersall (Lancashire)	1186	345	2974	164	18.13	9–40

ASHES REGAINED

Don Mosey: With South Africa in Australia, and New Zealand and India touring West Indies in the winter of 1952–53, England enjoyed a 'free' close season to get ready for the visit of the 1953 Australians, now led by Lindsay Hassett, with Bradman accompanying the party as an expert comments man for the *Daily Mail*! For Len Hutton it was a winter of mental preparation for what he had come to regard as a personal crusade—the regaining of the Ashes.

Freddie Trueman: The Aussies had had them for nearly 19 years and Leonard didn't like that one little bit. Tests against Australia were something very special to him all his playing life and when he became captain he wanted more than anything else to win back the Ashes. We didn't manage it until the final game of the series but I was very happy to be in the side when it came. Leonard lost the toss in all five games.

DM: It was very much Alec Bedser's series with the ball, in a summer in which we had a lot of rain. I saw him bowl marvellously at Trent Bridge where Australia reached 237 for three and were then 249 all out. He took 39 wickets in the series, and at Lord's became the first bowler to take 200 Test wickets for England.

FST: Just like Bradman, in very much the Australian style, Hassett led by personal example and got centuried at Trent Bridge and Lord's but if Big Al had a great series with the ball, let's not forget Leonard with the bat. *He wanted those Ashes back*, and he could lead by example as well: 43 and 60 not out at Trent Bridge, 145 and 5 at Lord's, 66 at Old Trafford, 82 and 17 at The Oval. We'll draw a veil over his innings at Headingley where Ray Lindwall bowled him with the second ball of the innings and the ten-year-old Richard Hutton, sitting with his mother, disgraced himself by bursting into tears.

DM: Well, I burst into tears myself when he beat Bradman's 334 at The Oval in 1938 so I entirely sympathise with Richard.

FST: I think a lot of people might have been in tears at the batting of our mutual friend Trevor Bailey in that series, but they'd be mostly Aussies. Do you remember his stand with Willie Watson at Lord's?

DM: Who could forget it? They batted from long before lunch until the last hour of the game to save England—Watson 109 in 5¾ hrs, Bailey 71 in 4¼ hrs. And all round the country people were asking each other anxiously, 'Are they still together?' To a generation now used to limited-

Willie Watson well caught by Stewart off Lock at The Oval

overs cricket it might sound like a big yawn but in 1953, and in the context of England–Australia Tests, it was a rearguard action of heroic proportions. It saved England from defeat and that was what mattered.

FST: In the Fourth Test, Bedser passed Clarrie Grimmett's record of 216 Test wickets and it seemed that pace, swing and seam had taken over from spin but it was still the spinners who decided the rubber in the end—Lock five for 45 in the second innings and Laker four for 75, at The Oval. I told you they knew their way around there!

DM: More than half a million people watched the five Tests in a rather miserable summer. England v Australia was still the greatest attraction in the game in 1953.

FST: Yet even in that successful summer I found myself wondering what Selectors think about sometimes. At Old Trafford, Johnny Wardle turned in a marvellous spell of bowling, 5–2–7–4, absolute perfection of slow left-arm spinning on a helpful pitch, and they dropped him for the next match! There was absolutely no sense or reason to some of the selections.

COUNTY CHAMPIONSHIP

DM: Surrey's championship again, but it was a bit strange to see Sussex in the runner-up spot while Yorkshire plummeted down to joint-twelfth.

FST: It was one of those seasons when nothing went right for us. Appleyard was still poorly and neither Wardle nor I got into the top part of the first-class bowling averages. Jim Langridge played his last season for Sussex and topped the batting averages in the country with 71.60. His figures were helped by five not outs in ten innings but it was a marvellous way to sign off for a man who was 47 years old at the end of the season and who had played 622 games for Sussex. He was a very good county all-rounder and of course, along with the Parks, the Cornfords and the Oakes, very much a part of the family affair which was the Sussex team of the 1930s.

LEG-SPINNERS

DM: The leading wicket-taker in the country was Bruce Dooland, the Australian leg-spinner who played for Notts—172 at 16.58. They are remarkable figures for a bowler of his type.

FST: A truly wonderful bowler. I have to rate Gupte, the Indian, as the best bowler of that type I ever faced but Dooland must be up there as well. He had a tremendous repertoire. They used to say he had six different stock deliveries and there wouldn't be many batsmen on the circuit who could pick one from the other. Charlie Knott, the Hampshire off-spinner, is up there at the top of the list; he'd be getting close to 40 years of age in 1953 but he

Bruce Dooland, a leg-spinning genius

was a great trouper and one of John Arlott's favourite cricketers. Les Jackson second in the averages, and once again I have to marvel that he played only two Tests. It's impossible to think of Les without remembering days at Chesterfield when there was a bit of green in the wicket and one batsman after another would come back looking anxiously at bruised fingers and rubbing aching parts of their ribs.

DM: And your friend 'George' Statham—101 wickets for him and 164 for Roy Tattersall. . . .

FST: We would shortly be starting our international partnership in the West Indies but in the summer of 1953, 'George' had a much better season than I had and when you see Bedser, Laker and Lock taking 397 wickets between them it's not hard to see why Surrey were still winning the championship, especially with Peter May now a full time player.

DM: And a new name in the top-ten batters—DW Barrick?

FST: Desmond was one of those league cricketers in Yorkshire like Arnold Hamer (Derbyshire) and Freddie Jakeman (Northamptonshire), who couldn't find a place in the Yorkshire side at that time and went off to try their luck with other counties. He did a very good job for Northamptonshire for ten or 11 seasons.

DM: And we now see Raman Subba Row coming through, in his third year at Cambridge, to give us (with May, Edrich, Simpson and Sheppard) five amateurs in the top ten batsmen. He was later to become one of the game's top administrators as manager of the 1981–82 England tour to India and Sri Lanka (during the first Test ever played there), chairman of Surrey and of the Test and County Cricket Board.

FST: And also there in the top ten is 'Jock' Livingston, that gutsy little Australian who had eight good seasons with Northamptonshire. He was an excellent fielder who could also keep wicket—a good cricketer to have in any county side. But wait a minute—who is this G Smith, of Kent, who turns up at No. 8 in the bowling averages?

DM: Another Yorkshireman, Fred—didn't you know? Geoffrey Smith, a medium fast bowler and an amateur who had a few matches spread over seven years. Most of them must have been played in 1953.

FST: An amateur from Huddersfield? There haven't been many of them!

1954

Winter Tour to West Indies (1953–54):

Kingston	West Indies won by 140 runs
Bridgetown	West Indies won by 181 runs
Georgetown	England won by nine wickets
Port-of-Spain	Match drawn
Kingston	England won by nine wickets

Summer Series with Pakistan:

Lord's	Match drawn
Trent Bridge	England won by an innings & 129 runs
Old Trafford	Match drawn
Oval	Pakistan won by 24 runs

County Champions Surrey

TEST AVERAGES ENGLAND V WEST INDIES 1953–54

	M	I	NO	HS	Runs	Av	100	50	Ct/St
L. Hutton	5	8	1	205	677	96.71	2	3	1
D. C. S. Compton	5	7	0	133	348	49.71	12	4	–
P. B. H. May	5	10	1	135	414	46.00	1	2	–
T. E. Bailey	5	7	2	49	193	38.60	–	–	2
T. W. Graveney	5	10	3	92	265	37.85	–	2	8
W. Watson	5	10	2	116	224	28.00	1	–	3
F. S. Trueman	3	4	1	19	38	12.66	–	–	–
T. G. Evans	4	6	0	28	72	12.00	–	–	5/1
J. C. Laker	4	5	1	27	44	11.00	–	–	3
J. B. Statham	4	6	2	10*	28	7.00	–	–	1
G. A. R. Lock	5	7	1	13	31	5.16	–	–	4

Also batted: A. E. Moss (1 match) 0, 16; C. H. Palmer (1 match) 22, 0; R. T. Spooner (1 match) 19, 16; J. H. Wardle (2 matches) 38, 66, 2ct.

	Overs	M	Runs	Wkts	Av	5w	10w	BB
J. B. Statham	153	24	460	16	28.75	–	–	4–64
T. E. Bailey	182	51	459	14	32.78	1	–	7–34
J. C. Laker	221.1	84	469	14	33.50	–	–	4–71
F. S. Trueman	133.2	27	420	9	46.66	–	–	3–88
G. A. R. Lock	296.5	87	718	14	51.28	–	–	3–76

Also bowled: D. C. S. Compton 26.4–3–144–2; T. W. Graveney 8–0–59–0; L. Hutton 6–0–43–0; A. E. Moss 36–5–114–2; C. H. Palmer 5–1–15–0; J. H. Wardle 83.3–23–187–4.

TEST AVERAGES ENGLAND V PAKISTAN 1954

	M	I	NO	HS	Runs	Av	100	50	Ct/St
D. C. S. Compton	4	5	0	278	453	90.60	1	2	5
R. T. Simpson	3	4	0	101	170	42.50	1	–	–
T. E. Bailey	3	3	1	42	81	40.50	–	–	–
T. W. Graveney	3	4	0	84	150	37.50	–	–	2
P. B. H. May	4	5	0	53	120	24.00	–	1	3
J. H. Wardle	4	5	1	54	88	22.00	–	–	6
T. G. Evans	4	5	0	31	63	12.60	–	–	6/1
J. E. McConnon	2	3	1	11	18	9.00	–	–	4
L. Hutton	2	3	0	14	19	6.33	–	–	–
J. B. Statham	4	3	1	2*	3	1.50	–	–	–

Also batted: A. V. Bedser (2 matches) 22*; W. J. Edrich (1 match) 4, 1ct; J. C. Laker (1 match) 13*; P. J. Loader (1 match) 8*, 5; J. M. Parks (1 match) 15, 1ct; D. S. Sheppard (2 matches) 37, 13, 4ct; F. H. Tyson (1 match) 3, 3. R. Appleyard and R. Tattersall played in one match but did not bat.

	Overs	M	Runs	Wkts	Av	5w	10w	BB
J. H. Wardle	142.5	82	176	20	8.80	1	–	7–56
F. H. Tyson	22.4	5	57	5	11.40	–	–	4–35
A. V. Bedser	74.5	28	158	10	15.80	–	–	3–9
R. Appleyard	47.4	13	123	7	17.57	1	–	5–51
J. B. Statham	89	26	213	11	19.36	–	–	4–18

Also bowled: T. E. Bailey 12–4–32–1; D. C. S. Compton 13–2–36–1; J. C. Laker 32.2–17–39–2; P. J. Loader 34–13–61–3; J. E. McConnon 36–12–74–4; R. Tattersall 25–9–39–1.

CHAMPIONSHIP TABLE 1954

							First Inns Lead in Match		
	P	Won	Lost	D	Tied	NR	Lost	D	Pts
Points Awarded	–	12	–	–	6	–	4	4	–
SURREY (1)	28	15	3	8	0	2	1	6	208
Yorkshire (12)	28	13	3	8	1	3	0	5	186*
Derbyshire (6)	28	11	6	9	0	2	3	6	168
Glamorgan (10)	28	11	5	10	0	2	0	4	148
Nottinghamshire (8)	28	10	6	8	0	4	2	4	144
Warwickshire (9)	28	10	5	10	0	3	1	4	140
} Middlesex (5)	28	10	5	10	0	3	1	3	136
} Northamptonshire (11)	28	9	9	9	0	1	3	4	136
Sussex (2)	28	8	7	12	0	1	1	5	120
Lancashire (3)	28	6	3	12	0	7	1	8	108
} Kent (16)	28	5	7	15	0	1	3	7	100
∫ Worcestershire (15)	28	5	12	9	0	2	2	7	100*
Gloucestershire (6)	28	5	11	10	0	2	4	5	96
Hampshire (14)	28	4	10	13	0	1	1	7	80
Essex (12)	28	3	11	12	0	2	2	5	64
Leicestershire (3)	28	3	9	11	1	4	0	5	62
Somerset (17)	28	2	18	8	0	0	2	2	40

*includes eight points for first innings lead in drawn matches restricted to last day
1953 positions are shown in brackets

FIRST-CLASS AVERAGES 1954

	I	NO	HS	Runs	Av	100
D. C. S. Compton (Middlesex)	28	2	278	1524	58.61	4
T. W. Graveney (Gloucestershire)	38	4	222	1950	57.35	5
±L. Livingston (Northamptonshire)	48	7	207*	2269	55.34	6
D. Kenyon (Worcestershire)	58	7	253*	2636	51.68	6
±G. G. Tordoff (Comb Serv/ Somerset)	11	1	156*	512	51.20	2
P. B. H. May (Surrey)	41	7	211*	1702	50.05	6
±P. E. Richardson (Worcestershire)	23	2	185	1010	48.09	2
D. S. Sheppard (Sussex)	37	4	120	1398	42.36	3
A. V. Wolton (Warwickshire)	49	6	165	1770	41.16	3
D. J. Insole (Essex)	51	6	172*	1841	40.91	4

	Overs	M	Runs	Wkts	Av	BB
J. B. Statham (Lancashire)	615.3	194	1300	92	14.13	6–76
R. Appleyard (Yorkshire)	1026.3	315	2221	154	14.42	7–16
P. J. Loader (Surrey)	699.2	167	1589	109	14.57	8–79
H. L. Jackson (Derbyshire)	949.4	296	1851	125	14.80	7–64
A. V. Bedser (Surrey)	957.4	299	1828	121	15.10	7–38
J. C. Laker (Surrey)	966.2	315	2048	135	15.17	8–51
J. E. McConnon (Glamorgan)	730.2	233	1680	109	15.41	7–23
B. Dooland (Nottinghamshire)	1287.1	408	3035	196	15.48	8–39
F. S. Trueman (Yorkshire)	808.2	187	2085	134	15.55	8–28
±J. H. Wardle (Yorkshire)	1262	520	2449	155	15.80	9–25

MATTING WICKET

Freddie Trueman: When I die, they might as well cover the grave with a bit of jute matting because I'll swear that's what cut down my life by a year or two on the tour to West Indies in the first three months of 1954. It started with a sensation: Tony Lock 'called' for throwing—the first time it had happened in a Test for 55 years—in Jamaica where the family of one of the umpires where threatened because he had given JK Holt out lbw when he was on 94. I had got two wickets for 139 at Sabina Park and didn't play at Barbados where (as in Kingston) West Indies won, and as I missed out on the Third Test, in Georgetown, which we won, I was thinking that touring wasn't all that much fun by the time we reached Port of Spain, Trinidad. By the time we left I was convinced that serving a term of hard labour would be a lot *more* fun. The Fourth Test was played on a jute matting wicket, the first I had ever seen, and by the time West Indies had declared at 681 for eight I had decided that this form of batting surface had been invented by a panel consisting of WG Grace, Don Bradman, George Headley, 'Slasher' Mackay and Geoff Boycott. After nine overs Brian Statham pulled a muscle

in his side and could not bowl again on the tour. Everton Weekes got an edge three times without being given out and when he finally went for 206 I grinned at him, 'Well played. Not bad, 206, for four innings'. 'Five,' said Everton, 'I got another nick in the sixties but nobody appealed.' I was too tired to respond: 'Are you surprised?' Thirty-three overs in that heat and humidity represented donkey-work in the highest degree.

Don Mosey: Never mind, Fred. At least the tour ended on an heroic note when England won the final Test in Kingston—not bad to come back after being two down in the series?

FST: We owed it first of all to Leonard, who got 205 in the first innings and to Trevor Bailey whose seven for 34 represented magnificent bowling. And we had our first glimpse of the man who was to become the world's best all-rounder, Gary Sobers; but he was playing there mainly as a bowler. His first Test wicket was Trevor—the man who would later write his biography. I wonder if either of them thought about that on their first meeting? It wasn't a happy tour for me but I have at least one fond memory. In that huge score in Trinidad just one man missed out— Bruce Pairaudeau. Before he had even got off the mark he was run out by my throw from a 70-yard boundary. Well, it seemed the best way of getting anybody out on that pitch.

NEW TEST VISITORS

DM: The English summer saw a visit from cricket's newest Test-playing nation—Pakistan. They had had a series against India 18 months earlier when Hanif Mohammad had opened the batting (and kept wicket) before he was 18 years old. That started a marvellous family connection with Pakistan Test cricket. The tourists got a poor reception from the English weather with no play possible on the first three days at Lord's, and they were bowled out for 87 by Statham (four for 18) and Wardle (four for 33—from 30.5 overs!). Then Khan Mohammad, who had been called out of Lancashire League cricket to join the party, bowled Len Hutton with his first delivery and clean bowled May, Edrich, Bailey and Evans as well. Not a bad little haul!

FST: Didn't they have someone even younger than Hanif playing in the Second Test?

DM: They did—Khalid Hassan, a leg-spinner, who was a fortnight or so short of his 17th birthday when he played at Trent Bridge.

FST: Compton got 278 there and Bob Appleyard took a wicket with his second ball in Test cricket. He was back in the game after a couple of seasons of illness and his first Test analysis was five for 51. England won and Appleyard

Fazal Mahmood in action at The Oval where his bowling helped Pakistan to their first win over England

addition to Brian Statham—Peter Loader and Frank Tyson. There was a lot of useful opposition around in those days. You were as good as your last performance and sometimes not even as good as that if Appleyard's experience was anything to go by!

SURREY AGAIN

FST: Surrey's championship again, of course with Loader, Bedser and Laker taking 365 wickets between them and Yorkshire were runners-up with an even better striking rate by the bowlers—Appleyard, Wardle and I took 443.

DM: And your eight for 28 against Kent at Dover, all before lunch on the first day, remained your best figures to the end of your playing career.

FST: I can think of a lot of times I bowled better and got worse figures. There was a bit of help that morning, you might say. What really fascinates me about the bowling averages of 1954 is Bruce Dooland's 196 wickets for Nottinghamshire. A leg spinner! It shows you just what a marvellous bowler he was. Les Jackson's there again with 125 wickets and Derby wasn't the best pitch in the world

Les Jackson, respected by batsmen everywhere, yet only two Tests

didn't play in the next Test!

DM: Another of those mysteries, Fred. Three days were washed out in the Third Test at Old Trafford. That really was a bad summer.

FST: It was, and the rain affected the pitch at The Oval to give England the shock defeat of their lives. When you think of all the runs that were to be scored there in the future the totals are worth recording: Pakistan 133 and 164; England 130 and 143.

DM: Fazal Mahmood was the match-winner, with six for 53 and six for 46—marvellous figures for a man on his first tour of England. I became very friendly with Fazal on two later tours of Pakistan when he had become a senior police officer in Lahore. A big, jolly man and a splendid bowler of the Alec Bedser type. He was, in fact, a great admirer of Alec.

FST: I think Al might have been an admirer of his, as well, if he had been playing. I missed out in that series and at The Oval England played two new fast bowlers in

to bowl on, but still the Selectors never bothered to consider him and the old off-spinning tradition of Glamorgan saw Jim McConnon taking 109 wickets for them.

DM: A grand chap, Jim. He came from the same Durham village as Colin Milburn (Burnopfield) and when he retired from cricket he worked with Brian Statham as a Guinness salesman. Like many cricketers at that time, he was a useful soccer player, too. Now, what about the batsmen, Fred—still five amateurs there, I see?

FST: Including Geoffrey Tordoff, a Yorkshire gentleman who later skippered Somerset. He was a Royal Navy officer. That was Don Kenyon's best season. He was a prolific batsman, usually the first to 1,000 runs in a season and often first to 2,000 as well but one of those—there have been quite a few of them—who didn't seem to be able to do it at Test level. He had a number of chances in the early part of the 1950s but he just couldn't score anything like as heavily as he did for Worcestershire. Compton tops the list and he's now 36 years of age and, after Graveney, there's Jock Livingston again. And one new name creeps in, Albert Victor George Wolton, who was a very useful middle order batsman for Warwickshire. Now that's one of those names (alongside many in these pages which belong to immortals) that makes you blink and ask, 'Who?' But I remember Wolton could be an extremely difficult man to shift at times. He had a couple of very good seasons in the first half of the fifties.

DM: And finally, Doug Insole, another product of that great cricketing period at Cambridge, who also became one of the game's most influential figures in administration at Lord's. Noticeably, in 1954, the top batsmen scored fewer runs and the best bowlers took more wickets—a wet summer.

Don Kenyon loses his middle stump to A. V. Bedser at the start of the match between Surrey and Worcestershire at The Oval

1955

Winter Tour to Australia (1954–55):

Brisbane	Australia won by an innings & 154 runs
Sydney	England won by 38 runs
Melbourne	England won by 128 runs
Adelaide	England won by five wickets
Sydney	Match drawn

New Zealand

Dunedin	England won by eight wickets
Auckland	England won by an innings & 20 runs

Summer Series with South Africa:

Trent Bridge	England won by an innings & 5 runs
Lord's	England won by 71 runs
Old Trafford	South Africa won by three wickets
Headingley	South Africa won by 224 runs
Oval	England won by 92 runs

County Champions Surrey

TEST AVERAGES ENGLAND V AUSTRALIA 1954–55

	M	I	NO	HS	Runs	Av	100	50	Ct/St
T. W. Graveney	2	3	0	111	132	44.00	1	–	4
P. B. H. May	5	9	0	104	351	39.00	1	2	6
D. C. S. Compton	4	7	2	84	191	38.20	–	1	–
T. E. Bailey	5	9	1	88	296	37.00	–	2	2
M. C. Cowdrey	5	9	0	102	319	35.44	1	2	4
L. Hutton	5	9	0	80	220	24.44	–	1	2
W. J. Edrich	4	8	0	88	180	22.50	–	1	3
R. Appleyard	4	5	3	19*	44	22.00	–	–	4
J. H. Wardle	4	6	1	38	109	21.80	–	–	1
T. G. Evans	4	7	1	37	102	17.00	–	–	13/–
J. B. Statham	5	7	1	25	67	11.16	–	–	1
F. H. Tyson	5	7	1	37*	66	11.00	–	–	2

Also batted: K. V. Andrew (1 match) 6, 5; A. V. Bedser (1 match) 5, 5, 1ct; R. T. Simpson (1 match) 2, 9.

	Overs	M	Runs	Wkts	Av	5w	10w	BB
R. Appleyard	79	22	224	11	20.36	–	–	3–13
F. H. Tyson	151	16	583	28	20.82	2	1	7–27
J. H. Wardle	70.6	15	229	10	22.90	1	–	5–79
J. B. Statham	143.3	16	499	18	27.72	1	–	5–60
T. E. Bailey	73.4	8	306	10	30.60	–	–	4–59

Also bowled: A. V. Bedser 37–4–131–1; W. J. Edrich 3–0–28–0; T. W. Graveney 6–0–34–1; L. Hutton 0.6–0–2–1.

TEST AVERAGES ENGLAND V NEW ZEALAND 1954–55

	M	I	NO	HS	Runs	Av	100	50	Ct/St
T. W. Graveney	2	3	1	41	86	43.00	–	–	2
M. C. Cowdrey	2	3	1	42	64	32.00	–	–	1
P. B. H. May	2	3	0	48	71	23.66	–	–	1
L. Hutton	2	3	0	53	67	22.33	–	1	1

Also batted: R. Appleyard (2 matches) 0*, 6; T. E. Bailey (2 matches) 0, 18, 2ct; T. G. Evans (2 matches) 0, 0 3ct/1st; R. T. Simpson (2 matches) 21, 23; J. B. Statham (2 matches) 13, 2ct; F. H. Tyson (2 matches) 16, 27*; J. H. Wardle (2 matches) 32*, 0.

	Overs	M	Runs	Wkts	Av	5w	10w	BB
J. B. Statham	58.4	24	91	12	7.58	–	–	4–24
F. H. Tyson	49	17	90	11	8.18	–	–	4–16
R. Appleyard	36	12	80	9	8.88	–	–	4–7
J. H. Wardle	76.3	43	116	5	23.20	–	–	2–41

Also bowled: T. E. Bailey 33.2–12–62–2.

TEST AVERAGES ENGLAND V SOUTH AFRICA 1955

	M	I	NO	HS	Runs	Av	100	50	Ct/St
P. B. H. May	5	9	1	117	582	72.75	2	3	7
D. C. S. Compton	5	9	0	158	492	54.66	1	3	1
T. W. Graveney	5	9	0	60	219	24.33	–	1	9
T. E. Bailey	5	9	1	49	184	23.00	–	–	1
D. Kenyon	3	5	0	87	96	19.20	–	1	3
K. F. Barrington	2	3	0	34	52	17.33	–	–	–
T. G. Evans	3	5	0	36	82	16.40	–	–	9/1
G. A. R. Lock	3	6	1	19*	79	15.80	–	–	2
J. H. Wardle	3	5	0	24	71	14.20	–	–	–
F. J. Titmus	2	4	0	19	39	9.75	–	–	2
J. B. Statham	4	7	1	20	42	7.00	–	–	–
F. H. Tyson	2	3	0	8	10	3.33	–	–	–

Also batted: R. Appleyard (1 match) 0*; A. V. Bedser (1 match) 1, 3; D. B. Close (1 match) 32, 15; M. C. Cowdrey (1 match) 1, 50; J. T. Ikin (1 match) 17, 0, 1ct; D. J. Insole (1 match) 3, 47; J. C. Laker (1 match) 2, 12; P. J. Loader (1 match) 0*, 0*; F. A. Lowson (1 match) 5, 0, 1ct; A. J. McIntyre (1 match) 3, 4, 4ct; R. T. Spooner (1 match) 0, 0, 2ct; F. S. Trueman (1 match) 2*, 6*; W. Watson (1 match) 25, 3, 1ct.

	Overs	M	Runs	Wkts	Av	5w	10w	BB
J. C. Laker	60.4	31	84	7	12.00	1	–	5–56
J. H. Wardle	165.4	77	273	15	18.20	–	–	4–24
F. H. Tyson	103	19	258	14	18.42	1	–	6–28
J. B. Statham	177.2	54	363	17	21.35	1	–	7–39
G. A. R. Lock	174	65	353	13	27.15	–	–	4–39
T. E. Bailey	142.5	40	328	9	36.44	–	–	3–97

Also bowled: R. Appleyard 47–13–78–2; A. V. Bedser 41–3–153–4; P. J. Loader 48 16–119–4; F. J. Titmus 33–10–101 1; F. S Trueman 35–4–112–2.

CHAMPIONSHIP TABLE 1955

						First Inns Lead in Match			
	P	Won	Lost	D	Tied	NR	Lost	D	Pts
Points Awarded	–	12	–	–	6	–	4	4	–
SURREY (1)	28	23	5	0	0	0	2	0	284
Yorkshire (2)	28	21	5	2	0	0	2	2	268
Hampshire (14)	28	16	5	6	1	0	0	3	210
Sussex (9)	28	13	8	6	1	0	3	5	196★
Middlesex (7)	28	14	12	2	0	0	6	0	192
Leicestershire (16)	28	11	10	7	0	0	3	2	154±
Northamptonshire (7)	28	9	10	9	0	0	3	7	148
Derbyshire (3)	28	9	10	9	0	0	2	7	146±
Lancashire (10)	28	10	9	8	0	1	2	3	140
Warwickshire (6)	28	10	9	9	0	0	2	3	140
Nottinghamshire (5)	28	10	11	7	0	0	1	2	132
Gloucestershire (13)	28	9	13	6	0	0	2	3	128
Kent (11)	28	8	13	7	0	0	0	2	104
Essex (15)	28	6	15	7	0	0	3	4	100
Worcestershire (11)	28	5	17	6	0	0	2	4	84
Glamorgan (4)	28	5	14	8	0	1	2	3	80
Somerset (17)	28	4	17	7	0	0	2	2	64

± includes two points for a tie on first innings in match drawn
★ includes two points for tie on first innings in match lost
1954 positions are shown in brackets

FIRST-CLASS AVERAGES 1955

	I	NO	HS	Runs	Av	100
P. B. H. May (Surrey)	42	5	125	1902	51.40	5
M. C. Cowdrey (Kent)	25	4	139	1038	49.42	4
±J. G. Dewes (Middlesex)	16	2	117	673	48.07	2
±W. Watson (Yorkshire)	48	14	214★	1623	47.73	4
T. W. Graveney (Gloucestershire)	51	2	159	2117	43.20	5
D. J. Insole (Essex)	62	5	142	2427	42.57	9
K. J. Grieves (Lancashire)	35	6	137	1232	42.48	2
J. M. Parks (Sussex)	63	8	205★	2314	42.07	5
±L. Livingston (Northamptonshire)	58	5	172★	2172	40.98	5
C. Washbrook (Lancashire)	46	3	170	1743	40.53	4

★denotes not out   ±denotes left-hand batsman

	Overs	M	Runs	Wkts	Av	BB
R. Appleyard (Yorkshire)	558	185	1106	85	13.01	7–29
D. Shackleton (Hampshire)	1220.2	438	2183	159	13.72	8–4
H. L. Jackson (Derbyshire)	469.1	151	914	64	14.28	6–40
±G. A. R. Lock (Surrey)	1407.4	497	3109	216	14.39	8–82
J. B. Statham (Lancashire)	754.5	216	1573	108	14.56	7–39
R. E. Marshall (Hampshire)	188.4	69	439	28	15.67	6–44
F. S. Trueman (Yorkshire)	996.5	214	2454	153	16.03	7–23
±J. H. Wardle (Yorkshire)	1486.4	572	3149	195	16.14	7–72
C. Gladwin (Derbyshire)	1163.5	434	2383	147	16.21	7–16
F. J. Titmus (Middlesex)	1449.5	522	3117	191	16.31	8–44

±denotes left-arm bowler

DISAPPOINTMENT

Freddie Trueman: I was bitterly disappointed to miss the 1954–55 tour to Australia, especially as England's emphasis was so much on pace bowling. I thought it was a few personal differences I had had with Leonard in the West Indies which kept me out of the party, but Leonard has said publicly that he wanted me there and was over-ruled by the Selectors. Tyson joined Statham and Bedser as the front-line attack and Bailey and Appleyard were there to back them up. Leonard seems to have made an enormous miscalculation in the First Test in Brisbane, putting Australia in to bat and seeing them pile up 601 for eight declared. We played without a spinner and lost by an innings and 154 runs.

Don Mosey: England won the next three, though, and Tyson, on those fast, bouncy Australian wickets, was obviously a tremendous force. Jim Laker used to say that Tyson's bowling in Melbourne (where he took seven for 27 in the second innings) was the fastest he ever saw, and he saw the West Indian quartets in the 1980s, of course, before his death.

FST: There was a bit of an outcry because it was said the pitch was illegally watered in Melbourne on the rest day but it worked against the Aussies more than us. It was another tremendous triumph for Leonard's captaincy— he had won the Ashes at home and retained them in Australia. It's difficult to think of many captains tough enough to come back from that mistake, and overwhelming defeat, in the First Test to win the series.

NEW ZEALAND

DM: The first of the two Tests in New Zealand was played at Carisbrook, Dunedin—the first Test cricket to be played there—and bedevilled by rain, but once again the quality of Bert Sutcliffe's batting shone through. He hit 74 out of a total of 125. The Second Test, in Auckland was historic. New Zealand were bowled out for 26, the lowest total in all Test cricket and yet four bowlers shared the wickets (Tyson 7–2–10–2, Statham 9–3–9–3, Appleyard 6–3–7–4, and Wardle 5–5–0–1). It was Len Hutton's last Test—what a way to go out! And he was England's top scorer with 53, as well. He would have carried on in the home series against South Africa but he was troubled by lumbago so he stood down. May took over and retained the captaincy for the next 41 Tests.

BARRINGTON'S FIRST TEST

FST: Ken Barrington started his international career in the First Test of 1955 at Trent Bridge. He didn't really get established until five or six years later but after getting a duck in his first Test innings he went away to develop his

*Barrington, a great batsman, gets nought on this occasion—
swept away by the Typhoon, Frank Tyson*

defensive technique which was so valuable to England later.

DM: South Africa had probably their most formidable opening attack of all time on that tour with Adcock and Heine, wouldn't you say?

FST: They were both pretty sharp and with Leonard missing England had an opening batting problem. In fact people began to realise that season just how much England had relied upon him for so long. Don Kenyon and Tom Graveney opened in the first three Tests, Bailey and Frank Lowson in the Fourth and Brian Close and Jack Ikin in the Fifth. Only Kenyon and Lowson were regular openers for their counties.

DM: Godfrey Evans claimed his 150th victim at Trent Bridge and Denis Compton reached 5,000 Test runs at Lord's where Statham bowled unchanged for 3¾ hours (29–12–39–7), but the game that sticks in my mind was at

Old Trafford where a whirlwind innings by Paul Winslow is still remembered there. He and John Waite, batting at seven and eight, both made centuries and I can still see Winslow reaching his first Test hundred with a straight six off Lock.

FST: And that was Alec Bedser's last Test. He finished with 236 wickets in 51 Tests when there were world-class batsmen in every Test side. That's a great record.

DM: At Headingley, Frank Chester stood for the last time in a Test Match. He'd umpired in 48 and was acknowledged as the best in the world.

FST: And England had to win the last match to take the series. Lock (eight for 101 in the match) and Laker (seven for 84) did it—at The Oval, needless to say! Oh ay, they knew that pitch.

DM: You only played in one match of that series, Fred. Were you out of form that season?

FST: I must have been. I only took 153 first-class wickets! No, I was a bit out of favour and there were, as we've seen, a lot of good fast bowlers about. Competition was tough, very tough. You've only got to look at the county averages to see that.

FAST BOWLERS

DM: Fast, or medium-fast bowlers took six of the top ten places that year with Appleyard (who didn't play a full season) in the lead. It would be interesting to know how many of his wickets were taken when he was swinging the new ball and how many came from his medium-paced off-breaks, but that's one statistic I've never seen. Derek Shackleton, Les Jackson, Brian Statham and Cliff Gladwin are all in the list with you, Fred, along with two off-spinners (Titmus and Marshall) and two slow left-armers.

FST: Wardle and Lock took 411 wickets between them

and both were really at the peak of their careers at that time. You don't really think of Roy Marshall as a bowler. He was a superb opening bat from Barbados who spent 20 years with Hampshire and skippered them in the last four or five. He was a great catcher of the ball, too—a really tremendous cricketer. He scored over 35,000 runs in his career.

DM: And then went to live in Somerset and joined the county committee there.

FST: We've already seen Jock Livingston, Bruce Dooland and Martin Donnelly as successful overseas players in English county sides. Now we've got Roy Marshall with Hampshire and Ken Grieves with Lancashire. Ken had been around for a few years, in fact, playing football at Bury and Bolton Wanderers while spending his summers with Lancashire. He was a good leg-spinner when he got a chance and a magnificent slip-catcher.

DM: So we have two overseas players in the top batting

Roy Marshall accumulating four of his 35,725 first-class runs

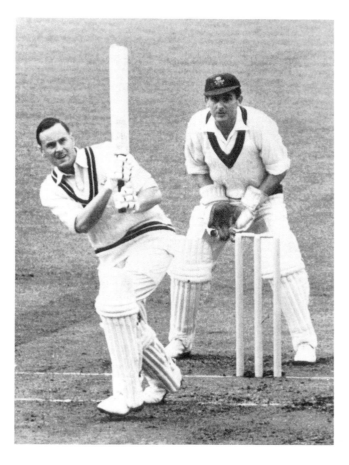

averages (Grieves and Livingston) and Marshall amongst the bowlers. It will be interesting to watch how this develops.

FST: The batting averages generally reflect the really class batsmen of the country at that time who were in form but most of them are middle-order men. With Len Hutton troubled by lumbago, only his old (and favourite) opening partner for England, Cyril Washbrook figures in the top ten as a regular opening batsman. Jim Parks (later England's wicket-keeper) got his career-best score in that season, 205 not out against Somerset at Hove, and he had not started keeping wicket at that stage. He was, in fact, known as one of the best cover-point fieldsmen in the game.

COUNTY CHAMPIONSHIP

DM: A fourth successive title for Surrey and one astonishing feature of their record was that not a single game was drawn. In an England summer, that's staggering, but it also indicates a very positive attitude to their cricket. Yorkshire second again; a slump for Derbyshire and a big jump up the table for Hampshire.

Left: *May, the great on-driver (wicket-keeper Jimmy Binks, Yorkshire)*

1956

Tests v Australia:

Trent Bridge	Match drawn
Lord's	Australia won by 185 runs
Headingley	England won by an innings & 42 runs
Old Trafford	England won by an innings & 170 runs
Oval	Match drawn

County Champions Surrey

TEST AVERAGES ENGLAND V AUSTRALIA 1956

	M	I	NO	HS	Runs	Av	100	50	Ct/St
P. B. H. May	5	7	2	101	453	90.60	1	4	3
Rev D. S. Sheppard	2	3	0	113	199	66.33	1	1	–
P. E. Richardson	5	8	0	104	364	45.50	1	2	1
C. Washbrook	3	3	0	98	104	34.66	–	1	2
M. C. Cowdrey	5	8	0	80	244	30.50	–	2	3
T. E. Bailey	4	5	1	33★	117	29.25	–	–	6
T. G. Evans	5	7	1	47	115	19.16	–	–	7/2
G. A. R. Lock	4	4	1	25★	46	15.33	–	–	10
T. W. Graveney	2	4	1	18	41	13.66	–	–	1
W. Watson	2	4	0	18	32	8.00	–	–	–
J. C. Laker	5	6	1	12	37	7.40	–	–	–
F. S. Trueman	2	3	0	7	9	3.00	–	–	4

	Overs	M	Runs	Wkts	Av	5w	10w	BB
J. C. Laker	283.5	127	442	46	9.60	4	2	10–53
F. S. Trueman	75	13	184	9	20.44	1	–	5–90
G. A. R. Lock	237.2	115	337	15	22.46	–	–	4–41
J. B. Statham	106	35	184	7	26.28	–	–	3–33
T. E. Bailey	108.5	39	223	6	37.16	–	–	4–64

Also bowled: R. Appleyard 30–10–49–2; T. W. Graveney 6–3–6–0; A. E. Moss 4–3–1–0; A. S. M. Oakman 8–3–21–0; F. H. Tyson 14–5–34–1; J. H. Wardle 27–9–59–1.

Also batted: R. Appleyard (1 match) 1★; D. C. S. Compton (1 match) 94, 35★; D. J. Insole (1 match) 5; A. S. M. Oakman (2 matches) 4, 10, 7ct; J. B. Statham (3 matches) 0★, 0★, 0, 0, 2ct; F. H. Tyson (1 match) 3, 1ct; J. H. Wardle (1 match) 0, 0. A. E. Moss played in one match but did not bat.

CHAMPIONSHIP TABLE 1956

						First Inns Lead in Match		
	P	Won	Lost	D	NR	Lost	D	Pts
Points Awarded	–	12	–	–	–	4	4	–
SURREY (1)	28	15	5	6	2	1	4	200
Lancashire (9)	28	12	2	12	2	0	9	180
Gloucestershire (12)	28	14	7	5	2	1	1	176
Northamptonshire (7)	28	8	5	15	0	2	11	148
Middlesex (5)	28	11	9	7	1	1	2	144
Hampshire (3)	28	9	6	10	3	1	7	140
Yorkshire (2)	28	8	7	10	3	4	6	136
Nottinghamshire (11)	28	7	4	15	2	1	9	128±
Sussex (4)	28	7	10	9	2	2	5	112
Worcestershire (15)	28	8	4	14	2	0	4	112
Essex (14)	28	6	10	9	3	5	4	110★
Derbyshire (8)	28	7	6	11	4	0	4	102★
Glamorgan (16)	28	6	9	9	4	2	5	100
Warwickshire (9)	28	5	11	9	3	3	2	80
Somerset (17)	28	4	15	8	1	3	4	76
Kent (13)	28	4	12	10	2	1	2	60
Leicestershire (6)	28	3	12	9	4	1	4	76

± includes eight points for first innings lead in drawn match restricted to last day
★ includes two points for tie on first innings in drawn match
1955 positions are shown in brackets

FIRST-CLASS AVERAGES 1956

	I	NO	HS	Runs	Av	100
T. W. Graveney (Gloucestershire)	54	6	200	2397	49.93	9
±L. Livingston (Northamptonshire)	47	6	188★	2006	48.92	2
T. E. Bailey (Essex)	38	11	141★	1186	43.92	3
D. Brookes (Northamptonshire)	52	7	203★	1916	42.57	4
M. A. Eagar (Oxford Univ)	21	4	125	713	41.94	1
Rev D. S. Sheppard (Sussex)	17	1	113	670	41.87	1
J. M. Parks (Sussex)	51	6	129	1884	41.86	4
D. J. Insole (Essex)	51	3	162	1988	41.41	4
±A. Wharton (Lancashire)	48	6	137	1738	41.38	4
D. Kenyon (Worcestershire)	52	3	259	1994	40.69	4

	Overs	M	Runs	Wkts	Av	BB
±G. A. R. Lock (Surrey)	1058.2	437	1932	155	12.46	10–54
R. Illingworth (Yorkshire)	620.4	206	348	103	13.08	6–15
±M. J. Hilton (Lancashire)	1199.5	558	2207	158	13.96	8–39
±C. Cook (Gloucestershire)	1195.1	475	2111	149	14.16	7–27
R. K. Platt (Yorkshire/RAF)	269	78	584	41	14.24	7–40
J. C. Laker (Surrey)	959.3	353	1906	132	14.43	10–53
R. Tattersall (Lancashire)	955.4	387	1722	117	14.71	8–43
J. B. Statham (Lancashire)	679.3	210	1351	91	14.84	6–27
D. J. Shepherd (Glamorgan)	1226.5	433	2719	177	15.36	8–33
P. J. Loader (Surrey)	893.2	227	1946	124	15.69	8–50

SPINNERS' YEAR

Don Mosey: The summer of 1956 was dominated by slow bowlers. They led the Test and first-class averages and the Old Trafford Test saw history turned upside down by Jim Laker's unforgettable performance in taking 19 Australian wickets for 90 runs.

Freddie Trueman: Spinners took six of the top seven places in the first-class bowling averages and five out of the top six Test batsmen were amateurs.

DM: England still had problems in finding the right opening pair and for the First Test against Ian Johnson's tourists Peter Richardson was called up for the first time to partner Colin Cowdrey who was not an opener by nature or personal preference. Richardson made an excellent start, scoring 81 and 73, but with 12 hours lost to rain no result was possible at Trent Bridge. At Lord's, however, where we saw 'Slasher' Mackay—so called because of his obdurate batting—for the first time, Australia won despite losing one of their opening pair of bowlers, Pat Crawford when he pulled a muscle in his fifth over.

FST: Keith Miller should really have been skippering Australia on that tour, of course, and he made up for Crawford's absence by taking ten wickets in the match. But it was an innings of 97 by the young Richie Benaud which put the Aussies in a position to win. I got a recall in that game but not for long. I had seven wickets at Lord's and got the No. 1 batsman, Colin McDonald, in both innings at Headingley where it was very much a spinner's pitch (all the other 18 wickets were taken by Laker and Lock) and I went out into the cold once again.

DM: That Headingley match (Third Test) was the one in which Cyril Washbrook's co-Selectors persuaded him to play for England again five-and-a-half years after his previous Test. He went in at 17 for three and was out for 98 at 204 for four. England won by an innings.

FST: The Old Trafford pitch for the Fourth Test looked fine when England were scoring 459. Peter Richardson got 104, David Sheppard (now the Rev) 113 and Colin Cowdrey 80 and Johnson's off-breaks gave him four wickets which cost 151 runs. It was a different tale when England's spinners took over. Lock took the wicket of Jimmy Burke—the third to fall in Australia's first innings—and Jim Laker took the rest (nine for 37 and ten for 53). Alan Oakman, who had made his Test debut in the previous match at Headingley, held five close-to-the-wicket catches.

DM: Denis Compton was recalled for the Final Test at The Oval after having his right knee-cap removed. It was an old football injury, a legacy of his playing days with Arsenal, and he got the top score of 94. More than 12 hours were lost to rain which was as well for the Aussies.

They were in desperate trouble to Laker again at 27 for five when the match was drawn. Laker had taken 46 wickets in the series at 9.6 apiece.

FST: Don't forget he took all ten for Surrey against the Aussies in that summer as well. He really had them mesmerised and was certainly the best off-spinner I ever saw.

SURREY'S STRENGTH

DM: And in the same season Tony Lock took all ten for Surrey against Kent at Blackheath—ten for 54. Lock, Laker and Loader shared 411 wickets that season so there is no need to ask how Surrey won the championship yet again. They really were a splendid all-round side and remember we haven't even seen the name of Alec Bedser's twin brother, Eric, in either batting or bowling averages. He could open the batting or go in the middle order and got 14,716 first-class runs in his career. Now with Laker around there would not seem to be much call for another off-spinner but that was Eric Bedser's trade and it brought him 833 wickets. He also got 1,000 runs in a season six times so when you put him there with May, Subba Row,

A young Ray Illingworth (at Yorkshire), who was to become a fine Leicestershire and England captain

David Fletcher, Bernie Constable and Tom Clark it becomes clear why Surrey were such a solid outfit.

FST: Raymond Illingworth comes into the picture for the first time. He had started as a batsman who bowled medium-pace seamers but, as illness affected Bob Appleyard more and more, Raymond began to develop off-spin bowling. He was 24 when he got 100 wickets for the first time and it got him second place in the first-class averages. Next came two slow left-armers, Malcolm Hilton and Sam Cook, and in fifth place we find another of the 40-odd opening partners I had during my career—Bob Platt. He divided his time between RAF cricket while doing his National Service and bowling in-swingers for Yorkshire.

DM: In-swingers were a bit unfashionable in Yorkshire, weren't they? Right back to George Hirst and beyond it was held that the ball which left the bat was the one most likely to bring success.

FST: That's right. We haven't really seen many right-arm in-swingers over the years but Bob Platt bowled his stuff really well and there was as much of a search going on in Yorkshire to find an opening partner for me as there was

One off-spinner observing another—Roy Tattersall watches Jim Laker in action

at England level to find the right sort of opening batsmen.

DM: Illingworth, Laker, Tattersall and Don Shepherd of Glamorgan make four bowlers in the top ten who moved the ball from the off.

FST: Shepherd bowled a bit quicker in his younger days but he really became a wily old bird, especially with variations of pace. He played until he was 45—647 matches—and was a tremendous servant to Glamorgan. In all he took 2,218 wickets and that's an awful lot of scalps for a man who never got a Test Match in his career.

DM: And the only two really quick bowlers in the list are Brian Statham and Peter Loader. It really was a spinners' summer.

FST: Once again we see fewer batsmen topping the 2,000 mark; even Don Kenyon missed it by six. But it was a good season for Alan Wharton, a bit of a character in that Lancashire side which finished second in the championship. He played Rugby League with Salford, one of the very few people who have combined these two games at top level. He loved a good argument and he'd have made a good mate for Phil Edmonds if they had played at the same time.

DM: They might have been on different sides politically?

FST: No doubt at all about that but it would have been good to hear them arguing with each other.

DM: David Sheppard was unable to play full time for Sussex but his form earned him a recall to the England

Don Shepherd, 647 matches in 23 seasons for Glamorgan

Tom Graveney, as graceful and elegant as ever

side, as we've seen, and what about that other amateur name in the list, MA Eagar?

FST: Never heard of him!

DM: It was his first year up at Oxford, Michael Anthony Eagar, and he got four Blues (between 1956 and 1959) which not too many people have done. He also played hockey for Ireland. But looking at the championship table, Fred, we see Northamptonshire a bit higher up than they had been for a long time?

FST: Well, they had Tyson and Nobby Clarke to open the bowling and they must have been the quickest *pair* around. We see Livingston and Brookes well up in the batting, getting nearly 4,000 runs between them. And then they had George Tribe, that marvellous Aussie bowler of left-arm 'funny stuff,' and he was, in fact, an excellent all-rounder. He did the double six times. He had taken nine against us at Bradford the previous year and we had a healthy respect for George Tribe, I can tell you.

DM: And Gloucestershire in third place. They drew only five games, fewer than anybody else so they either had better weather in the West Country than anywhere else or Gloucestershire were playing positive cricket.

FST: Graveney got more runs than anyone else in the country and Sam Cook had 149 wickets—that's positive enough.

Winter Tour to South Africa (1956–57):

Johannesburg	England won by 131 runs
Cape Town	England won by 312 runs
Durban	Match drawn
Johannesburg	South Africa won by 17 runs
Port Elizabeth	South Africa won by 58 runs

Summer Series with West Indies:

Edgbaston	Match drawn
Lord's	England won by an innings & 36 runs
Trent Bridge	Match drawn
Headingley	England won by an innings & 5 runs
Oval	England won by an innings & 237 runs

County Champions Surrey

TEST AVERAGES ENGLAND V SOUTH AFRICA 1956–57

	M	I	NO	HS	Runs	Av	100	50	Ct/St
D. J. Insole	5	10	2	110*	312	39.00	1	1	7
P. E. Richardson	5	10	0	117	369	36.90	1	1	–
M. C. Cowdrey	5	10	0	101	331	33.10	1	3	10
T. E. Bailey	5	10	0	80	259	25.90	–	1	3
D. C. S. Compton	5	10	0	64	242	24.20	–	2	–
T. G. Evans	5	10	0	62	164	16.40	–	1	18/2
P. B. H. May	5	10	0	61	153	15.30	–	1	2
F. H. Tyson	2	4	0	23	48	12.00	–	–	1
J. H. Wardle	4	7	1	22	68	11.33	–	–	3
J. B. Statham	4	7	3	12*	35	8.75	–	–	1
J. C. Laker	5	9	3	17	40	6.66	–	–	1
P. J. Loader	4	7	1	13	34	5.66	–	–	–

Also batted: G. A. R. Lock (1 match) 14, 12.

	Overs	M	Runs	Wkts	Av	5w	10w	BB
T. E. Bailey	142.3	43	232	19	12.21	1	–	5–20
F. H. Tyson	49	14	100	8	12.50	1	–	6–40
J. H. Wardle	139.6	37	359	26	13.80	3	1	7–36
J. B. Statham	130.1	20	349	14	24.92	–	–	3–37
J. C. Laker	145.1	46	324	11	29.45	–	–	2–7
P. J. Loader	121	27	291	9	32.33	–	–	3–35

Also bowled: D. C. S. Compton 3–1–8–0; G. A. R. Lock 26–11–38–2.

TEST AVERAGES ENGLAND V WEST INDIES 1957

	M	I	NO	HS	Runs	Av	100	50	Ct/St
T. W. Graveney	4	5	1	258	472	118.00	2	–	1
P. B. H. May	5	6	1	285*	489	97.80	2	1	5
F. S. Trueman	5	4	3	36*	89	89.00	–	–	7
M. C. Cowdrey	5	6	0	154	435	72.50	2	2	8
P. E. Richardson	5	7	0	126	411	58.71	2	1	–
T. G. Evans	5	6	2	82	201	50.25	–	1	14/1
D. B. Close	2	3	0	42	89	29.66	–	–	2
G. A. R. Lock	3	3	0	20	37	12.33	–	–	4
J. C. Laker	4	3	1	10*	18	9.00	–	–	1
D. V. Smith	3	4	1	16*	25	8.33	–	–	–
T. E. Bailey	4	4	1	3*	5	1.66	–	–	3

Also batted: D. J. Insole (1 match) 20, 0; P. J. Loader (2 matches) 1, 0, 1ct; D. W. Richardson (1 match) 33, 1ct; Rev D. S. Sheppard (2 matches) 68, 40, 2ct; J. B. Statham (3 matches) 13, 7, 2ct; J. H. Wardle (1 match) 11.

	Overs	M	Runs	Wkts	Av	5w	10w	BB
P. J. Loader	44.3	17	100	10	10.00	1	–	6–36
G. A. R. Lock	114.2	59	163	15	10.86	2	1	6–20
F. S. Trueman	173.3	34	455	22	20.68	1	–	5–63
T. E. Bailey	117	37	277	12	23.08	1	1	7–44
J. C. Laker	246.2	99	448	18	24.88	–	–	4–119
J. B. Statham	158.1	37	433	13	33.30	1	–	5–118

Also bowled: D. B. Close 2–1–8–0; T. W. Graveney 5–2–14–0; D. V. Smith 45–13–97–1; J. H. Wardle 22–5–53–1.

CHAMPIONSHIP TABLE 1957

						First Inns Lead in Match		
							Bonus	
	P	Won	Lost	D	NR	Lost D	Pts	Pts
Points Awarded	–	12	–	–	–	2	2	–
SURREY (1)	28	21	3	3 1	3	3	48	312
Northamptonshire (4)	28	15	2	10 1	0	8	22	218
Yorkshire (7)	28	13	4	11 0	0	5	24	190
Derbyshire (12)	28	10	8	9 1	2	4	30	162
Essex (11)	28	11	6	10 1	0	5	16	158
Lancashire (2)	28	10	8	8 2	2	4	24	156
Middlesex (5)	28	10	12	3 3	2	1	22	148
Somerset (15)	28	9	14	5 0	3	2	20	138
Glamorgan (13)	28	10	9	8 1	0	2	12	136
Sussex (9)	28	8	9	9 2	2	6	24	136
Warwickshire (14)	28	9	7	11 1	0	6	16	134
Gloucestershire (3)	28	8	13	6 1	1	5	24	132
Hampshire (6)	28	7	12	8 1	1	5	20	116
Kent (16)	28	6	13	9 0	2	3	8	90
Nottinghamshire (8)	28	5	13	9 1	3	4	14	88
Worcestershire (9)	28	4	9	14 1	1	4	8	72±
Leicestershire (17)	28	2	16	9 1	2	5	2	40

±includes six points for fourth innings of drawn match with Sussex when the final scores were equal

1956 positions are shown in brackets

FIRST-CLASS AVERAGES 1957

	I	NO	HS	Runs	Av	100
P. B. H. May (Surrey)	41	3	285*	2347	61.76	7
M. C. Cowdrey (Kent)	43	6	165	1917	51.81	5
T. W. Graveney (Gloucestershire)	53	5	258	2361	49.18	8
J. M. Parks (Sussex)	55	6	132*	2171	44.30	4
F. A. Lowson (Yorkshire)	19	2	154	752	44.23	3
C. A. Milton (Gloucestershire)	31	9	89	943	42.86	–
±D. V. Smith (Sussex)	54	5	166	2088	42.61	5
D. R. W. Silk (Camb Univ/Somerset)	16	3	79	526	40.46	–
±W. Watson (Yorkshire)	39	2	162	1462	39.51	4
D. J. Insole (Essex)	49	5	150*	1725	39.20	4

*denotes not out
±denotes left-hand batsman

	Overs	M	Runs	Wkts	Av	BB
±G. A. R. Lock (Surrey)	1194.1	449	2550	212	12.02	7–49
±V. H. Broderick (Northamptonshire)	130.3	52	236	17	13.88	5–29
J. B. Statham (Lancashire)	896.4	251	1895	126	15.03	8–34
J. C. Laker (Surrey)	1016.5	393	1921	126	15.24	7–16
E. A. Bedser (Surrey)	548.5	178	1188	77	15.42	7–53
P. J. Loader (Surrey)	878.2	215	2058	133	15.47	7–30
D. Shackleton (Hampshire)	1217.3	447	2429	155	15.67	7–51
±C. W. Leach (Warwickshire)	155.2	58	305	19	16.05	3–19
G. Smith (Kent)	389.1	109	923	57	16.19	8–110
H. L. Jackson (Derbyshire)	1014.2	362	2295	141	16.27	7–27

±denotes left-arm bowler

Peter Loader in action for Surrey against Kent

OUT IN THE COLD

Freddie Trueman: The winter tour was another I missed and it was a bitter disappointment that I actually ended my career without having played a Test in South Africa. Peter Loader got the place I thought I had earned during the previous summer but as things turned out the dominant bowlers of the Test were two spinners—Johnny Wardle and 'Tooey' Tayfield who got a record 37 wickets.

Don Mosey: He came over to play in Lancashire League cricket and didn't have the same sort of success. But the fascinating thing about that series was the coincidence of having the first dismissal in Tests for 'handling the ball'. This came in the Second Test at Newlands where Russell Endean prevented a ball hitting the stumps by deflecting it with his hand after padding off a delivery from Laker. Endean was the man waiting to make the catch when Hutton was out for obstructing the field at The Oval six years earlier.

FST: Peter Richardson started the tour with the slowest century in Test history up to that point (488 minutes). England still hadn't replaced Hutton satisfactorily and

Trevor Bailey went in first with Richardson throughout that tour. Trevor did well with the ball in the First Test (the first on that fine new ground at the Wanderers Club in Johannesburg)—five for 20 as South Africa were all out for 72 in their second innings.

DM: And here's coincidence again: in the Second, apart from the 'handled the ball' incident, their second innings total in Cape Town was also 72, this time with Wardle returning seven for 36 (12 for 89 in the match). Bailey broke a bone in his right hand but he finished his innings with the hand in plaster and played in all the three remaining Tests as well. It was a poor first tour as captain for Peter May. He played magnificently in the opening games but couldn't find his touch at all in the Tests. South Africa were very happy with a tied rubber.

TWINS BACK AGAIN

FST: Ramadhin and Valentine were with us once more for the summer of '57 but their dominance ended in the

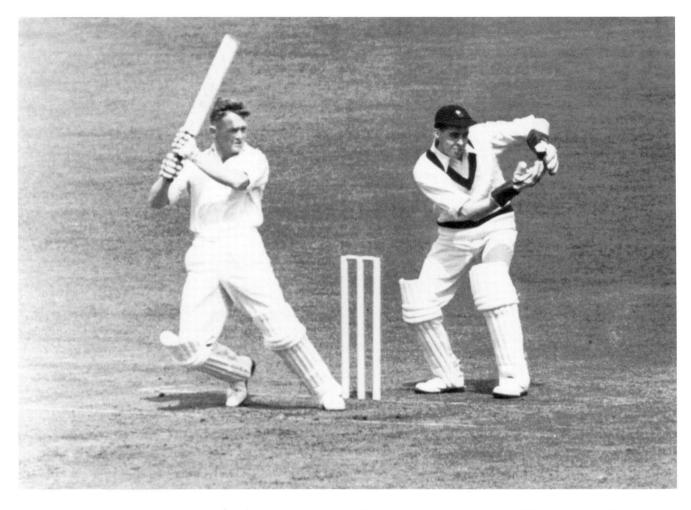

'Pakistan Pete' Richardson of Worcestershire, Kent and England

second innings of the First Test, the first to be played at Edgbaston since 1929. Ramadhin (seven for 49) mesmerised England in the first innings as he had done seven years earlier, but May and Cowdrey killed him off in the second by extensive use of their pads. ('Kicked me to bloody death', is Sonny's own description of the experience.) His final figures were 98–35–179–2—that's 11 more overs than Fleetwood-Smith bowled in England's 1938 innings of 903–7 dec. May scored 285 not out, Cowdrey 154, and the Ramadhin/Valentine partnership was never the same again. I was back in favour that season and I remember we gave the Windies a bit of a scare at Edgbaston. Their first innings lead was 288, but by the time May and Cowdrey had finished we were 295 ahead and we had them in a right old state at 72 for seven at close of play. Brian Close, I notice, was Richardson's opening partner in that Test. He scored 15 and 42, and was promptly dropped as an opener but batted at No. 7 at Lord's. The Selectors then brought in a specialist opener, Don Smith, of Sussex. He lasted for three Tests, totalling

25 runs, and then made way for another recall for the Rev David Sheppard. At Lord's, Bailey took seven for 44 bowling as third seamer. What a great competitor he was in every way.

DM: The Third Test, at Trent Bridge, was drawn but it was one to remember in many ways. Dick Richardson, of Worcestershire, was picked to play alongside his brother—the first instance of this since the Hearnes in 1892—and Tom Graveney scored a superb 258. But as I recall the game, Fred, you had reason to be proud of yourself.

FST: Yes, well five for 63 from 30 overs on that featherbed wasn't bad and my mate Statham had five for 118 in the second innings. In fact we took nine between us in the second. I couldn't help feeling a bit sorry for Don Smith—he was caught behind for one in a total of 619 for six declared!

HAT-TRICK

DM: And at Headingley I saw the first hat-trick to be taken in a home Test for over half a century. . . .

FST: And I saw it from closer quarters because I caught Sonny Ramadhin, the second of Loader's three victims. In one way I was a bit sorry when he bowled Gilchrist first ball. He had let me have a bouncer at Lord's and I had promised to pin him to the sightscreen when I had the chance. . . .

DM: But you'd already had a warning at Headingley for bowling four bouncers in an over at Rohan Kanhai. . . .

FST: Well, that was the non-striker, Clyde Walcott, winding up the umpire, Dai Davies, a bit. He was a great old boy, Dai. I'm sure he warned me with a twinkle in his eye.

DM: At The Oval Lock had match figures of 11 for 48 and Everton Weekes bagged a pair. That didn't happen too often in his career and you had gone through a five-Test series playing in every match. Did you think you were now established at last?

FST: Well, it did occur to me that if they didn't think my bowling was good enough I might get in as a batter. I was

Trevor Bailey leads England off the field after his seven West Indian wickets at Lord's, 1957

third in the averages!

DM: At least you were now established as a short leg catcher—seven in the series.

RUNAWAY CHAMPIONSHIP

FST: It was a runaway success for Surrey in the county championship—94 points ahead of Northamptonshire—so it's not surprising to see them with four bowlers in the top ten. With Laker involved in four Tests there was a bit more chance for Eric Bedser as an off-spinner and 77 wickets at 15.42 was a good performance, especially when you think how valuable his batting was.

DM: Two slow left-armers at the top of the list. Vince Broderick was probably past his best at that time but he had done a good job for Northamptonshire as an all-rounder for a long time. He played one pre-war season and did the double in 1948. And Clive Leach, of Warwickshire, bowled slow left arm as well although one thinks of him primarily as a batsman.

FST: And there's 'Shack' again, churning out the overs. He had a marvellously economical action and he always seemed as if he could go on all day. Sometimes he did! Les Jackson as usual up there and our amateur friend from Huddersfield, Geoffrey Smith, appears again.

PROLIFIC BATSMEN

DM: As we have seen from the Tests it was a good season for May and Graveney with the bat but while Peter Richardson averaged 58 in the Tests he couldn't match that in all first-class games. A new amateur name in the list and one that makes a colourful entry in any reference book: Dennis Raoul Whitehall Silk, born Eureka, California. He was one of what we might call the second wave of Cambridge cricketers. He didn't play a lot of county cricket (for Somerset) but played a good deal for MCC sides. He was a man of great charm and made a first-class cricketing ambassador, notably in East Africa, America and New Zealand. He is one of four amateurs in the top ten with Doug Insole there again, now in steady partnership with Trevor Bailey for Essex. And in this Cambridge-dominated age perhaps we should make it clear that Cowdrey (No. 2 in the averages) was an *Oxford* man.

FST: I suppose the most dramatic change in county fortunes was Gloucestershire's drop from third to 12th place in the table. Since Tom Goddard's retirement, Sam Cook had not found wicket-taking quite so easy as when bowling at the opposite end to such a great player and the opening attack was never very frightening in those days. Then, of course, they lost Graveney's batting while he played in four Tests but it's good to see Arthur Milton there in the averages. One of the nicest men ever to play first-class cricket, a fine batsman and a brilliant close-to-the-wicket catcher. And a double international—six Tests and an England soccer player while with Arsenal.

Geoff Smith, the amateur from Huddersfield who got into the first-class averages as a Kent player

Tests v New Zealand:

Edgbaston	England won by 205 runs
Lord's	England won by an innings & 148 runs
Headingley	England won by an innings & 71 runs
Old Trafford	England won by an innings & 13 runs
Oval	Match drawn

County Champions Surrey

TEST AVERAGES ENGLAND V NEW ZEALAND 1958

	M	I	NO	HS	Runs	Av	100	50	Ct/St
P. B. H. May	5	6	1	113*	337	67.40	2	1	4
M. C. Cowdrey	4	4	0	81	241	60.25	–	3	7
P. E. Richardson	4	5	0	100	242	48.40	1	1	–
T. W. Graveney	4	5	0	37	119	23.80	–	–	2
G. A. R. Lock	5	4	1	25	59	19.66	–	–	6
F. S. Trueman	5	4	1	39*	52	17.33	–	–	6
M. J. K. Smith	3	4	0	47	57	14.25	–	–	3
J. C. Laker	4	3	1	15	27	13.50	–	–	2
T. E. Bailey	4	4	1	17	39	13.00	–	–	3
T. G. Evans	5	5	0	12	28	5.60	–	–	7/–

Also batted: E. R. Dexter (1 match) 52; R. Illingworth (1 match) 3*; P. J. Loader (3 matches) 17, 4, 1ct; C. A. Milton (2 matches) 104*, 36, 4ct; R. Subba Row (1 match) 9, 1ct; W. Watson (2 matches) 66, 10, 2ct. J. B. Statham (2ct) played in two matches but did not bat.

	Overs	M	Runs	Wkts	Av	5w	10w	BB
G. A. R. Lock	176	93	254	34	7.47	3	1	7–35
J. C. Laker	131	67	173	17	10.17	1	–	5–17
T. E. Bailey	66	24	93	7	13.28	–	–	2–17
F. S. Trueman	131.5	44	256	15	17.06	1	–	5–31
J. B. Statham	67	20	130	7	18.57	–	–	4–71
P. J. Loader	75.3	34	114	6	19.00	–	–	3–40

Also bowled: E. R. Dexter 5–0–23–0; R. Illingworth 45–18–59–3; C. A. Milton 4–2–12–0.

CHAMPIONSHIP TABLE 1958

						First Inns Lead in Match		
							Bonus	
	P	Won	Lost	D	NR	Lost D	Pts	Pts
Points Awarded	–	12	–	–	–	2	2	–	–
SURREY (1)	28	14	5	8	1	0	6 32	212
Hampshire (13)	28	12	6	10	0	3	4 28	186
Somerset (8)	28	12	9	7	0	2	3 20	174
Northamptonshire (2)	28	11	6	6	5	0	5 18	160
Derbyshire (4)	29	9	9	8	2	4	5 24	151*
Essex (5)	28	9	7	7	5	4	3 24	146
Lancashire (6)	28	9	7	8	4	3	5 18	142
Kent (14)	28	9	10	7	2	1	4 20	139@
Worcestershire (16)	28	9	7	8	4	1	2 20	134
Middlesex (7)	28	7	4	16	1	1	10 18	130±
Yorkshire (3)	28	7	5	10	6	2	6 14	126±±
Leicestershire (17)	28	7	13	6	2	3	1 12	104
Sussex (9)	28	6	7	11	4	2	4 18	102
Gloucestershire (12)	28	5	9	11	3	3	4 14	89@
Glamorgan (9)	28	5	11	11	1	1	5 10	82
Warwickshire (11)	28	3	7	14	4	2	6 16	68
Nottinghamshire (15)	28	3	15	8	2	1	4 4	50

±± includes sixteen points for first innings lead in two matches restricted by rain to last third of time allotted
± includes eight points for first innings lead in match restricted by rain to last third of time allotted
* includes one point for tie on first innings in match lost
@ includes one point for tie on first innings in match drawn
1957 positions are shown in brackets

FIRST-CLASS AVERAGES 1958

	I	NO	HS	Runs	Av	100
P. B. H. May (Surrey)	41	6	174	2231	63.74	8
±W. Watson (Leicestershire)	44	9	141	1632	46.62	3
±R. Subba Row (Northamptonshire)	48	9	300	1810	46.41	5
M. J. K. Smith (Warwickshire)	51	3	160	2126	44.29	3
R. E. Marshall (Hampshire)	57	3	193	2118	39.22	5
M. C. Cowdrey (Kent)	41	4	139	1437	38.83	3
P. T. Marner (Lancashire)	50	6	110	1685	38.29	1
D. M. Young (Gloucestershire)	57	5	194	1914	36.80	5
±W. B. Stott (Yorkshire)	30	1	141	1036	35.72	2
T. W. Graveney (Gloucestershire)	47	6	156	1459	35.58	2

	Overs	M	Runs	Wkts	Av	BB
H. L. Jackson (Derbyshire)	829	295	1572	143	10.99	7–18
±G. A. R. Lock (Surrey)	1014.4	382	2055	170	12.08	8–99
J. B. Statham (Lancashire)	894.2	275	1648	134	12.29	7–29
F. S. Trueman (Yorkshire)	637.5	176	1414	106	13.33	6–23
D. M. Sayer (Oxford Univ/ Kent)	552.2	155	1206	89	13.55	7–37
J. C. Laker (Surrey)	882.5	330	1651	116	14.23	8–46
F. Ridgway (Kent)	649.5	181	1454	98	14.83	7–42
±J. H. Wardle (Yorkshire)	716.4	281	1401	91	15.39	6–28
D. Shackleton (Hampshire)	1320.2	505	2549	165	15.44	9–59
B. D. Wells (Gloucestershire)	276.5	105	572	37	15.45	5–29

UNIQUE DEBUT

Freddie Trueman: Let's carry on where we left off in 1957 by talking about Arthur Milton. He made his Test debut against New Zealand at Headingley by batting right through the innings, and as we bowled out the opposition twice to win by an innings and 71 runs 'Milt' was on the field for the whole of his first Test match. As he opened the batting with MJK Smith, our innings was started by a soccer and a rugby international. That was the Third Test. Mike Smith had started a brilliant international career two matches earlier, at Edgbaston, where he skippered Warwickshire from 1957 to 1967. He was another Oxford man, let it be noted. It was a spinners' year in the Tests but in contrast fast bowlers largely dominated the first-class averages.

Don Mosey: Tony Lock certainly had a great summer once again—34 wickets in the five-Test series which was badly affected by rain. England won by mid-afternoon on the fourth day at Edgbaston, in three days at Lord's, three days at Headingley, while eight hours were lost at Old Trafford to take the game into the fifth day. At The Oval, only 12 hours play was possible over the five days and that wasn't enough to allow England to win all five matches in a rubber for the first time. New Zealand were in something of a transitional stage and were never a match for a full-strength England side (whatever form it took). They were bowled out for 94 (Edgbaston), 47 and 74 (Lord's), 67 (Headingley), 85 (Old Trafford) and only at The Oval did they avoid a double-figure dismissal. And you were devastating with the bat again, Fred—three sixes off Alex Moir, the leg-spinner, at The Oval?

FST: Yes, I enjoyed that 39 not out but I think some of the New Zealanders might remember my bowling as well. I hit Noel Harford in the face at Edgbaston, Eric Petrie had to go off after trying to hook me at Old Trafford and Jack Sparling ducked into a bouncer which didn't bounce so much at The Oval.

DM: There were three notable debutants at Old Trafford—Ted Dexter, Raman Subba Row and Raymond Illingworth—and Lock took his 100th Test wicket in the same match. The Selectors' main pre-occupation in that series was to find a couple of opening batsmen to go with Richardson on the following winter's tour of Australia. Having decided that Milton had passed the test at Headingley (but Mike Smith hadn't) they tried out Willie Watson at Old Trafford and he made 66 in his only innings. He had gone to Leicestershire as captain that season, but he wasn't by nature an opener. There were a few problems for the Selectors around that time. When they went for the most free-scoring county openers, like Kenyon, they found he couldn't come good in Tests.

TURMOIL IN YORKSHIRE

DM: It was not an easy time to be a Yorkshire player because there had been no championship success now since the joint effort with Middlesex in 1949—the longest period the county had gone without a title in the 20th century! Norman Yardley had been succeeded as captain by Bill Sutcliffe and in 1958 the committee had appointed Ronnie Burnet, 39 years old and with no experience at all of first-class cricket. There had been a major clash of temperaments with Johnny Wardle towards the end of the season and as a result, Yorkshire had dispensed with Wardle's services. He had taken 102 wickets in 28 Tests and had been picked to go to Australia that winter. At 35, he had some good years ahead of him to add to his 1,846 first-class wickets. It was a tragic end to a career of superb slow bowling and colourful big hitting. And yet it led to a

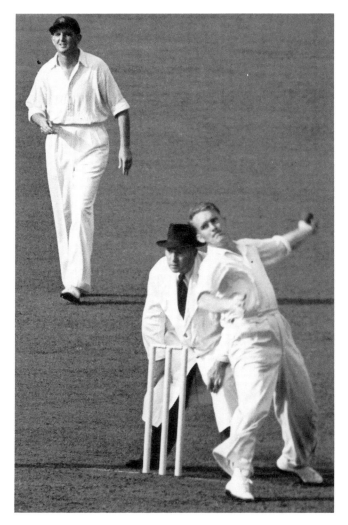

Johnny Wardle, a marvellous dual-purpose slow left-armer

complete change in Yorkshire's fortunes the following season.

FST: Yes, it was a tragedy all right. Johnny expressed some of the bitterness he felt in a series of articles in the *Daily Mail* and that cost him his place in the tour party to Australia. The whole business really shook up the dressing-room and we knew we were going to feel the terrible loss of Johnny's bowling. At the same time, the whole side got right behind Ronnie after that. Just for the moment, in 1958, we were slipping down the championship table to 11th place, while Surrey sailed home again with two more wins than either of their nearest challengers, Hampshire and—what's this?—Somerset? There were a couple of real turn-ups for the book. Somerset had neither a batsman nor a bowler (Hampshire had only Marshall) in the leading averages but they managed 12 wins apiece as a result of some solid team-work. Bill Alley, the big Australian all-rounder, had left League cricket in the North to join Somerset at the age of 38 and was to give them 12 wonderful seasons. Colin Ingleby-Mackenzie was in his first season as captain of Hampshire with a tongue-in-cheek claim that his policy was one of rigid team-discipline: 'I insist that everyone is in bed before breakfast.'

DM: Les Jackson was still knocking over the wickets without being noticed by the Selectors—143 at fewer than ten runs apiece and a striking rate of better than a wicket every six overs. Lock, in one of his outstanding seasons, had 170 victims but after him came three quick men, Statham, Trueman and David Sayer. He was in his first year at Oxford (the balance had swung noticeably from Cambridge in recent years) and for one who spent half his season bowling at The Parks he was distinctly lively. He had good shoulders and could get quite a lot of bounce, predictably earning himself the nickname 'Slayer'. His opening partner with Kent was Fred Ridgway, then in his 35th year and generally supposed to be slightly over the hill. Ridgway was one of the great post-war troupers of the county scene, his efforts recognised only at international level by a tour of India in 1951–52 with what was virtually a 'B' side. And stepping in at No. 10 we find one Bryan Douglas Wells but known universally as 'Bomber', one of the great characters of the game. He was as unlikely-looking a first-class cricketer as it was possible to imagine, with his roly-poly figure—once described in a newspaper as bearing more resemblance to a Chipping Sodbury postman—but he was a good off-spinner in 141 matches for Gloucestershire and 151 for Nottinghamshire. His batting defied description. . . .

FST: He was known to hit me for six over backward point while standing on the toes of the square leg

B. D. 'Bomber' Wells in action for Gloucestershire

umpire. . . .

DM: And it was a considerable task for any captain to hide him in the field. His lovely West Country burr made him a raconteur par excellence and in retirement he has become a renowned after-dinner speaker. His repertoire of runout mix-up stories is the very stuff of cricket folklore.

FST: And please note 'Shack' wheeling down another 1,320 overs of pin-point accuracy to take 165 more wickets. He was born in Yorkshire and I don't know how he got away but I'd have given a lot to have had him pinning down batsmen at the other end from me. Some new names in the batting top ten: Mike Smith topping 2,000 runs; Peter Marner, that beefy Lancashire batsman and medium-pace bowler who later went to Leicestershire; Martin Young, born in Leicestershire, learned his trade with Worcestershire and then had a good career with Gloucestershire; and Bryan Stott, capped by Yorkshire the previous season and one of the new crop of young players stepping up to take the places of those who had given service since just after the war. Subba Row was in his first season as skipper of Northamptonshire where he had moved from Surrey in 1955.

Winter Tour to Australia (1958–59):

Brisbane	Australia won by eight wickets
Melbourne	Australia won by eight wickets
Sydney	Match drawn
Adelaide	Australia won by ten wickets
Melbourne	Australia won by nine wickets

New Zealand:

Christchurch	England won by an innings & 99 runs
Auckland	Match drawn

Summer Series with India:

Trent Bridge	England won by an innings & 59 runs
Lord's	England won by eight wickets
Headingley	England won by an innings & 173 runs
Old Trafford	England won by 171 runs
Oval	England won by an innings & 27 runs

County Champions Yorkshire

TEST AVERAGES ENGLAND V AUSTRALIA 1958–59

	M	I	NO	HS	Runs	Av	100	50	Ct/St
M. C. Cowdrey	5	10	1	100*	391	43.44	1	1	6
P. B. H. May	5	10	0	113	405	40.50	1	2	1
T. W. Graveney	5	10	1	54	280	31.11	–	2	5
P. E. Richardson	4	8	0	68	162	20.25	–	1	–
T. E. Bailey	5	10	0	68	200	20.00	–	1	1
W. Watson	2	4	0	40	72	18.00	–	–	–
J. B. Statham	4	7	3	36*	64	16.00	–	–	2
R. Swetman	2	4	0	41	56	14.00	–	–	3/–
F. S. Trueman	3	6	0	36	75	12.50	–	–	3
J. C. Laker	4	7	2	22*	62	12.40	–	–	–
F. H. Tyson	2	4	0	33	48	12.00	–	–	–
C. A. Milton	2	4	0	17	38	9.50	–	–	1
G. A. R. Lock	4	8	1	21	60	8.57	–	–	1
E. R. Dexter	2	4	0	11	18	4.50	–	–	–
T. G. Evans	3	6	0	11	27	4.50	–	–	5/1
P. J. Loader	2	4	2	6*	7	3.50	–	–	–

Also batted: J. B. Mortimore (1 match) 44*, 11.

	Overs	M	Runs	Wkts	Av	5w	10w	BB
J. C. Laker	127.6	24	318	15	21.20	1	–	5–107
J. B. Statham	104	12	286	12	23.83	1	–	7–57
P. J. Loader	60.2	10	193	7	27.57	–	–	4–56
F. S. Trueman	87	11	276	9	30.66	–	–	4–90
G. A. R. Lock	126.2	25	376	5	75.20	–	–	4–130

Also bowled: T. E. Bailey 75–7–259–4; M. C. Cowdrey 1.3–0–9–0; J. B. Mortimore 11–1–41–1; F. H. Tyson 54–2–193–3.

TEST AVERAGES ENGLAND V INDIA 1959

	M	I	NO	HS	Runs	Av	100	50	Ct/St
J. B. Statham	3	3	2	38	70	70.00	–	–	–
M. J. K. Smith	2	3	0	100	207	69.00	1	1	1
G. Pullar	3	4	0	131	242	60.50	1	1	–
K. F. Barrington	5	6	0	87	357	59.50	–	4	5
R. Illingworth	2	3	1	50	118	59.00	–	1	5
M. C. Cowdrey	5	7	1	160	344	57.33	1	2	7
R. Swetman	3	4	2	65	114	57.00	–	1	11/–
P. B. H. May	3	4	1	106	150	50.00	1	–	5
W. G. A. Parkhouse	2	3	0	78	144	48.00	–	1	1
E. R. Dexter	2	3	0	45	58	19.33	–	–	–
J. B. Mortimore	2	3	0	29	43	14.33	–	–	–
K. Taylor	2	3	0	24	33	11.00	–	–	1
F. S. Trueman	5	6	0	28	61	10.16	–	–	5
C. A. Milton	2	3	0	14	26	8.66	–	–	–
T. Greenhough	3	3	1	2	2	1.00	–	–	1

Also batted: D. B. Close (1 match) 27, 4ct; T. G. Evans (2 matches) 74, 0, 3ct/1st; M. J. Horton (2 matches) 58, 2, 2ct; A. E. Moss (3 matches) 11, 26, 1ct; H. J. Rhodes (2 matches) 0*; R. Subba Row (1 match) 94.

	Overs	M	Runs	Wkts	Av	5w	10w	BB
D. B. Close	16	1	53	5	10.60	–	–	4–35
J. B. Statham	112.2	44	223	17	13.11	1	–	5–31
F. S. Trueman	177.4	53	401	24	16.70	–	–	4–24
T. Greenhough	139.1	47	255	14	18.21	1	–	5–35
A. E. Moss	101	47	147	7	21.00	–	–	2–30
K. F. Barrington	47	7	135	5	27.00	–	–	3–36
H. J. Rhodes	74.5	10	244	9	27.11	–	–	4–50

Also bowled: E. R. Dexter 38–10–71–3; M. J. Horton 39.4–18–59–2; R. Illingworth 85–33–124–4; J. B. Mortimore 55.4–21–135–4.

CHAMPIONSHIP TABLE 1959

							First Inns Lead in Match			
									Bonus	
Points Awarded	P	Won	Lost	D	Tied	NR	Lost	D	Pts	Pts
	–	12	–	–	6	–	2	2	–	–
YORKSHIRE (11)	28	14	7	7	0	0	0	5	26	204
Gloucestershire (14)	28	12	11	4	1	0	1	3	28	186
Surrey (1)	28	12	5	11	0	0	0	8	26	186
Warwickshire (16)	28	13	10	5	0	0	2	1	22	184
Lancashire (7)	28	12	7	9	0	0	1	5	28	184
Glamorgan (15)	28	12	8	7	0	1	3	4	20	178
Derbyshire (5)	28	12	6	10	0	0	3	2	20	174
Hampshire (2)	28	11	10	7	0	0	1	4	26	168
Essex (6)	28	11	7	9	1	0	0	4	22	168
Middlesex (10)	28	10	9	9	0	0	3	3	24	157±
Northamptonshire (4)	28	8	10	10	0	0	4	9	24	146
Somerset (3)	28	8	13	7	0	0	4	3	20	130
Kent (8)	28	8	12	8	0	0	2	5	18	128
Worcestershire (9)	28	6	8	13	0	1	1	7	18	106
Sussex (13)	28	6	11	10	0	1	3	3	18	102
Leicestershire (12)	28	5	16	7	0	0	0	2	8	72
Nottinghamshire (17)	28	4	14	9	0	1	1	3	6	62

±includes one point for tie on first innings in match lost
1958 positions are shown in brackets
Where points are equal, the side with most wins shall have priority. If the points and matches won are equal, the side with the greater number of bonus points takes precedence. (This was first year for this so no longer possible to have equal placings. This will be re-introduced later)

FIRST-CLASS AVERAGES 1959

	I	NO	HS	Runs	Av	100
M. J. K. Smith (Warwickshire)	67	11	200*	3245	57.94	8
±W. Watson (Leicestershire)	50	10	173	2212	55.30	7
±G. Pullar (Lancashire)	55	7	161	2647	55.14	8
K. F. Barrington (Surrey)	52	6	186	2499	54.32	6
P. B. Wight (Somerset)	39	3	222*	1930	53.61	6
±J. H. Edrich (Surrey)	45	11	126	1799	52.91	7
J. M. Parks (Sussex)	56	11	157*	2313	51.40	6
M. C. Cowdrey (Kent)	44	4	250	2008	50.20	6
W. G. A. Parkhouse (Glamorgan)	49	3	154	2243	48.76	6
H. Horton (Hampshire)	59	8	140*	2428	47.60	4

* denotes not out
± denotes left-hand batsman

	Overs	M	Runs	Wkts	Av	BB
J. B. Statham (Lancashire)	977.4	267	2087	139	15.01	8–44
D. A. Allen (Gloucestershire)	635.5	286	1322	84	15.73	7–66
±D. A. D. Sydenham (Surrey)	174.4	41	399	25	15.96	7–61
J. J. Warr (Middlesex)	804.5	218	1798	109	16.49	7–38
H. L. Jackson (Derbyshire)	1168.5	349	2461	140	17.57	9–17
R. G. Thompson (Warwickshire)	789.1	207	1743	97	17.96	8–40
J. E. McConnon (Glamorgan)	789.1	202	2059	113	18.22	8–62
J. B. Mortimore (Gloucestershire)	1091.3	472	2066	113	18.28	8–59
±C. Cook (Gloucestershire)	932.4	404	1850	101	18.31	6–76
A. E. Moss (Middlesex)	785.5	228	1796	96	18.70	7–78

±denotes left-arm bowler

ASHES LOST

Freddie Trueman: The winter tour to Australia started badly when we were beaten by eight wickets in both of the first two Tests (Brisbane and Melbourne). The First Test was interesting because Trevor Bailey established the sort of record he enjoyed—batting for just under six hours (357 minutes) before he reached 50 and that's still a record! In all, he got 68 in our second innings in seven hours 38 minutes but even that couldn't save us. It might not have been pretty to watch but it was a marvellous attempt to stave off defeat.

Don Mosey: I felt sure I was going to see that beaten in Madras in 1982 by Chris Tavaré but in fact he was out for 35—after 5½ hours.

FST: It was a bit of an historic match for Peter May because he was skippering England in his 26th successive Test and that beat Woodfull's record for Australia. It was in the Brisbane game that Norman O'Neill made his debut. We were to become great mates but somehow I felt he never really fulfilled his potential as a batsman. He looked a world-beater at that time and he certainly seemed capable of scoring more than the six centuries he made in 42 Tests. In fact he looked like another Bradman when he first started.

DM: May's century at Melbourne was the first by an England captain in Australia since 1901–2 (AC MacLaren) and that does make you sit up a bit. You got into the side for the Third Test, Fred, but it was Laker and Lock who took most of the wickets. Some slow batting there, too, with Cowdrey taking more than six hours to make a century. Roy Swetman kept wicket in that match for the first time in a Test.

FST: Yes, Godfrey Evans had a bit of injury trouble on that tour. He came back in the Fourth Test in Adelaide and straightaway fractured his little finger again. He finished off the first day but Tom Graveney went behind the stumps after that—he let through only two byes in a total of 476, as well. But we lost by ten wickets and the Aussies had the Ashes back. We just couldn't get started in any innings. Richardson lost his form and neither Bailey nor Milton, who were his partners, ever really got going. The umpiring wasn't always very good, either. We were certain Colin McDonald should have been out hit wicket in the Fifth Test when he was 12 and he went on to get 133. Ray Lindwall was getting past his best by this time but he still managed to top Grimmett's record of 216 Test wickets.

FIVE WINS AGAINST INDIA

FST: The home series against India promised to be a bit easier and in fact we won all five Tests. It seemed that the Selectors took the opportunity to do a certain amount of experimenting. Tommy Greenhough, the Lancashire leg-spinner, made his debut at Trent Bridge (First Test) along with Ken Taylor from Yorkshire and Martin Horton (Worcestershire) and Geoff Pullar and Harold Rhodes at Headingley (Third). But I couldn't help feeling sorry for Brian Close. He played at Headingley, got 27 in his only innings, held four catches and took five wickets for 53—and was dropped!

DM: India's batting was still not strong enough on English wickets.

FST: No, they still didn't like really fast bowling and I suppose we softened them up a bit in the First Test. I broke Borde's little finger and Brian Statham bruised Nadkarni's hand so badly that he couldn't bowl—but 'George' did it with the bat! Nadkarni was bowling to him at the time. He tried to stop a return drive and he couldn't even complete the over.

DM: Peter May got his last Test century and Ken Barrington averaged 59 in the series without scoring a century. So did Ray Illingworth. The Indian opening attack, Desai and Surendranath, was really pretty friendly but Gupte, as you've already said, was a fine leg-spinner. Nadkarni was not a bad slow left-armer and he played a lot of League cricket in England in his time. Chandu Borde on that tour was a good all-rounder; he hit 1,060 runs and took 72 wickets so the League clubs were soon after him, as well. Another leg-break bowler. Brian Statham got his 150th Test wicket at Lord's and Godfrey Evans played his final Test before retiring with 219 Test victims, including 46 stumpings . . .

FST: A great player and a great tourist. There was never a dull minute with 'Godders' around, either on or off the field and, bless him, he hasn't changed a bit. We see him every day of the home Tests, bringing round Ladbroke's betting odds. At Old Trafford, Geoff Pullar became the

David Allen (Gloucestershire and England)

first Lancashire player to score a hundred on that ground, and that seems just as astonishing as Reg Simpson being the first Nottinghamshire man to get a Test century at Trent Bridge. Gupte ended with 17 wickets in the series and he had impressed everyone.

NEW COUNTY CHAMPIONS

FST: I was happy with 24 Test wickets but the great thing about that season for me was Yorkshire winning the championship at last. We had to wait until the last day of the season to do it and we had to get 215 runs in 95 minutes to beat Sussex at Hove. It was Ronnie Burnet's second (and last) season as county captain and in view of the problems he had had in his first year we were just as delighted to do it for him as for ourselves. Three of the side were still Colts—Don Wilson, Jackie Birkenshaw and Brian Bolus.

DM: And yet not one Yorkshire player figures in the top ten of the first-class batting and bowling averages?

FST: Well, team-work is a bit of an overworked phrase but you can't describe it any other way. We used 19

Geoff ('Noddy') Pullar, Lancashire and England

players during that season, many of them completely inexperienced. Five players got more than 1,000 runs and five bowlers took 50 wickets or more.

DM: We see a few new names in the batting averages like Pullar; Peter Wight, of Somerset; John Edrich, of Surrey; Gilbert Parkhouse, of Glamorgan and Henry Horton, of Hampshire.

FST: 'Noddy' Pullar got his nickname because of a tendency to nod off in the outfield but he was a damn good left-hand bat. He started in the middle order and it was really England's still-desperate need for reliable openers that started him going in first. He was just starting a very good run in Roses matches at this time and at one stage he was averaging 70 against us. We had a healthy respect for Geoff Pullar. Henry Horton had perhaps the ugliest stance at the wicket of any batsman in modern cricket ('like a man sitting on a shooting-stick,' was Brian Johnston's description) but he was a very difficult man to shift. It was Gilbert Parkhouse's best season although he got over 1,000 runs 15 times in his career.

DM: And the bowling—six quick men up there but no Laker or Lock?

FST: Jim was becoming a bit disenchanted with various aspects of the game at this stage and in fact he finished with Surrey at the end of the 1959 season. This obviously affected Lockie in some ways. The new off-spinner in the list is David Allen, of Gloucestershire, who was to provide Test competition for Ray Illingworth and Fred Titmus (as well as his county colleague John Mortimore) over the next few years.

DM: In 1959 an amendment to the system of points-scoring in the county championship brought a bonus of two points to the side achieving a first innings lead if the side also had a faster scoring rate (in runs per over) at the time of gaining the lead.

1960

Winter Tour to West Indies (1959–60):

Bridgetown	Match drawn
Port-of-Spain	England won by 256 runs
Kingston	Match drawn
Georgetown	Match drawn
Port-of-Spain	Match drawn

Summer Series with South Africa:

Edgbaston	England won by 100 runs
Lord's	England won by an innings & 73 runs
Trent Bridge	England won by eight wickets
Old Trafford	Match drawn
Oval	Match drawn

County Champions Yorkshire

TEST AVERAGES ENGLAND V WEST INDIES 1959–60

	M	I	NO	HS	Runs	Av	100	50	Ct/St
E. R. Dexter	5	9	1	136*	526	65.75	2	2	1
M. C. Cowdrey	5	10	1	119	491	54.55	2	2	1
K. F. Barrington	5	9	0	128	420	46.66	2	1	2
G. Pullar	5	10	1	66	385	42.77	–	3	–
R. Subba Row	2	4	0	100	162	40.50	1	–	–
M. J. K. Smith	5	9	0	108	308	34.22	1	1	3
D. A. Allen	5	9	4	55	171	34.20	–	1	1
P. B. H. May	3	5	0	45	83	16.60	–	–	–
J. B. Statham	3	4	1	20*	46	15.33	–	–	1
F. S. Trueman	5	8	2	37	86	14.33	–	–	6
R. Illingworth	5	8	1	41*	92	13.14	–	–	1
R. Swetman	4	7	0	45	58	8.28	–	–	6/1

Also batted: A. E. Moss (2 matches) 4, 1; J. M. Parks (1 match) 43, 101*, 1ct/2st.

	Overs	M	Runs	Wkts	Av	5w	10w	BB
F. S. Trueman	220.3	62	549	21	26.14	1	–	5–35
J. B. Statham	130.4	42	286	10	28.60	–	–	3–42
E. R. Dexter	64.4	18	170	5	34.00	–	–	2–7
K. F. Barrington	106.5	41	217	5	43.40	–	–	2–34
D. A. Allen	197	53	417	9	46.33	–	–	3–57

Also bowled: M. C. Cowdrey 2–0–19–0; R. Illingworth 196–61–383–4; A. E. Moss 85–17–226–3; G. Pullar 1–0–1–1; M. J. K. Smith 1–0–15–0; R. Subba Row 1–0–2–0.

TEST AVERAGES ENGLAND V SOUTH AFRICA 1960

	M	I	NO	HS	Runs	Av	100	50	Ct/St
G. Pullar	3	6	1	175	293	58.60	1	1	–
R. Subba Row	4	6	1	90	251	50.20	–	2	2
K. F. Barrington	4	7	1	80	227	37.83	–	2	–
M. C. Cowdrey	5	9	0	155	312	34.66	1	1	7
M. J. K. Smith	4	6	0	99	192	32.00	–	2	4
P. M. Walker	3	4	0	52	128	32.00	–	1	5
E. R. Dexter	5	9	0	56	241	26.77	–	2	–
R. Illingworth	4	6	2	37	81	20.25	–	–	1
J. M. Parks	5	8	0	36	154	19.25	–	–	16/–
J. B. Statham	5	7	3	22	57	14.25	–	–	1
F. S. Trueman	5	8	1	25	99	14.14	–	–	4
D. A. Allen	2	4	2	14*	26	13.00	–	–	1
D. E. V. Padgett	2	4	0	31	51	12.75	–	–	–

Also batted: R. W. Barber (1 match) 5, 4; T. Greenough (1 match) 2; A. E. Moss (2 matches) 3*.

	Overs	M	Runs	Wkts	Av	5w	10w	BB
A. E. Moss	50.1	7	138	9	15.33	–	–	4–35
J. B. Statham	203	54	491	27	18.18	2	–	6–63
F. S. Trueman	180.3	31	508	25	20.32	1	–	5–27
R. Illingworth	77	32	146	6	24.33	–	–	3–15
E. R. Dexter	64.2	16	157	5	31.40	–	–	3–79

Also bowled: D. A. Allen 56.5–26–101–4; R. W. Barber 16–2–55–1; K. F. Barrington 3–1–5–0; M. C. Cowdrey 1–0–4–0; T. Greenough 49–19–102–2; D. E. V. Padgett 2–0–8–0; G. Pullar 1–0–6–0; P. M. Walker 13–3–34–0.

CHAMPIONSHIP TABLE 1960

| | | | | | | | | First Inns Lead in Match | | |
| | | | | | | | | | Bonus | |
	P	Won	Lost D	NR	Lost D	Pts	Pts	Av
Points Awarded	–	12	– – –	2 2	–	–	–
YORKSHIRE (1)	32	17	6 6 3	2 2	34	246	7.68
Lancashire (5)	32	13	8 10 1	3 9	34	214	6.68
Middlesex (10)	28	12	4 12 0	0 7	28	186	6.64
Sussex (15)	32	12	6 12 2	2 6	28	188	5.87
Derbyshire (7)	28	10	7 10 1	1 5	20	152	5.42
Essex (9)	28	9	3 14 2	1 7	28	152	5.42
Surrey (3)	28	9	6 10 3	2 3	20	138	4.92
Gloucestershire (2)	28	9	7 12 0	0 3	16	130	4.64
Northamptonshire (11)	28	8	6 13 1	1 6	16	126	4.50
Kent (13)	28	7	7 12 2	1 6	20	118	4.21
Glamorgan (6)	32	9	14 7 2	0 4	16	133±	4.15
Hampshire (8)	32	8	8 14 2	1 6	22	132	4.12
Worcestershire (14)	32	8	12 10 2	1 6	20	130	4.06
Somerset (12)	32	5	11 15 1	2 10	22	106	3.31
Warwickshire (4)	32	4	12 16 0	2 9	26	96	3.00
Nottinghamshire (17)	28	4	16 7 1	4 2	12	72	2.57
Leicestershire (16)	28	2	13 12 1	0 5	12	46	1.64

± includes one point for tie on first innings in match lost

1959 positions are shown in brackets

69

FIRST-CLASS AVERAGES 1960

	I	NO	HS	Runs	Av	100
±R. Subba Row (Northamptonshire)	32	5	147*	1503	55.66	4
Javed Burki (Oxford Univ)	22	4	144*	961	53.38	3
M. J. K. Smith (Warwickshire)	63	7	169*	2551	45.55	4
E. R. Dexter (Sussex)	53	2	157	2217	43.47	7
H. Horton (Hampshire)	59	9	131	2170	43.40	7
K. F. Barrington (Surrey)	53	9	126	1878	42.68	2
W. J. Stewart (Warwickshire)	45	3	129	1764	42.00	1
R. E. Marshall (Hampshire)	62	5	168	2380	41.75	5
P. B. Wight (Somerset)	62	5	155*	2375	41.66	7
M. J. Stewart (Surrey)	51	6	169*	1866	41.46	5

	Overs	M	Runs	Wkts	Av	BB
J. B. Statham (Lancashire)	844.1	274	1662	135	12.31	7–17
H. L. Jackson (Derbyshire)	1082.2	310	2179	160	13.61	8–44
A. E. Moss (Middlesex)	852	223	1866	136	13.72	8–31
F. S. Trueman (Yorkshire)	1068.4	274	2447	175	13.98	7–41
J. D. F. Larter (Northamptonshire)	325.2	108	750	46	16.30	6–26
H. J. Rhodes (Derbyshire)	722.2	184	1550	91	17.03	5–18
D. J. Shepherd (Glamorgan)	1130.4	358	2488	142	17.52	8–40
R. Illingworth (Yorkshire)	992.4	422	1914	109	17.55	8–70
D. Gibson (Surrey)	636.2	144	1584	90	17.60	7–26
D. Shackleton (Hampshire)	1271.5	503	2300	130	17.69	9–30

VICTORY IN WEST INDIES

Freddie Trueman: A winning series in the Windies didn't seem very likely when over 1,100 runs were scored in Barbados while only 18 wickets fell and, much as we admired them as players and liked them both as individuals, we saw just a little too much of Gary Sobers and Frankie Worrell before the First Test was finished. They came together at 102 for three and the score was 501 before they were parted. Sobers got 226, Worrell was 197 not out and I reckoned four for 93 from 47 overs wasn't bad going. It was all a bit different in the Second Test in Trinidad. A spinner called Charran Singh made his Test debut; he was a local lad and when he was run out for a duck in his first innings (and one of the only three he was destined to play) there was pandemonium. The crowd of 30,000 was the biggest there had ever been for a Test in the West Indies and it seemed as though most of them had got hold of half-a-dozen bottles to throw at us when that decision was given. I have never seen a ground in such a mess as the Queen's Park Oval was and play was abandoned for the day just after tea on the third day.

Don Mosey: But England won in the end after you and Statham had bowled out West Indies for 112 in their first

innings. Ken Barrington got his second consecutive hundred in the only two innings he had so far played against the Windies and he had two for 34 with his leg-breaks as well. There were three interesting debuts in that series—men who were to figure prominently in future tests and in League cricket in England as well—Chester Watson, Seymour Nurse and Charlie Griffith. You topped the England bowling, Fred, with 21 wickets at 26.14.

FST: I was pretty happy with those figures because the wickets certainly helped the batsmen. Six hundreds were scored by our side; Sobers got two big hundreds as well as his double-century and a 92 for good measure while Worrell and Kanhai also got tons. Weekes' Test career had finished but there was plenty of good batting about.

DM: And you held six catches in the series—as many as the No. 1 wicket-keeper, Roy Swetman, and more than any other fieldsman.

FST: Including the one which gave Noddy Pullar his only Test wicket!

THROWING

DM: The sixties were something of a 'throwing' decade and Geoff Griffin, who opened the bowling with Neil Adock on South Africa's tour of 1960, was called out of Test cricket in that series. In the Second Test, at Lord's, he was called for throwing 11 times by Frank Lee but he finished off England's first innings with a hat-trick. Do you remember who his victims were by any chance, Fred?

FST: You know perfectly well I do: Mike Smith was caught behind on 99 off the last ball of one over; Peter Walker was bowled by the first ball of his next and I was bowled by the second. One or two of us had rather strong views on the legality of Griffin's action, I can tell you.

DM: Bob Barber played his first Test at Trent Bridge (the first of the series) and 'Hooky' Walker made his debut in that match as well, and it's rather remarkable that England won the first two despite Griffin's hat-trick—and his throwing. After Lord's he didn't bowl again on the tour. Duggie Padgett played his only two Tests at Old Trafford and The Oval but couldn't find his Yorkshire form and John Waite completed the wicket-keeper's double (1,000 runs and 100 dismissals) in the last Test. In fact his 100th victim was Pullar who made 175 of an opening partnership of 290 with Cowdrey, and it gave Atholl McKinnon his first Test wicket. Twenty-five wickets in the series for you, Fred, and 27 for Brian Statham. That would be one of your outstanding seasons with 175 first-class wickets altogether?

FST: I suppose that was when my partnership with 'George' really blossomed. He had 135 wickets in the season and topped the first-class averages. Between us we bowled over 1,900 overs.

FAST BOWLERS' YEAR

Geoff Griffin, a Test hat-trick but 'called' out of the game for throwing

DM: It was a vintage year for quicker bowlers—nine out of the top ten were medium pace or above and the only full-time spinner in the list was Ray Illingworth. Don Shepherd was a mere lad of 33 in that season and he wouldn't have settled down to full-time off-spinning. And we see David Larter coming into the picture in his first season with Northamptonshire.

FST: He was a big lad, about six ft seven tall although he was only 20 and he was the man Northamptonshire were hoping would take over from Tyson. He did well for them but he was rather prone to injuries, perhaps because he *was* so tall.

DM: Dennis Brookes and George Tribe had retired and Subba Row was called up for four Tests so Northampton-shire had their problems that year but Subba Row finished top of the first-class batting averages just the same.

FST: Lancashire were runners up to Yorkshire in the county championship, largely because of Statham's great bowling and the support he was now getting from Ken Higgs. That was Higgs's best season, although he was

around for a long time, 132 wickets at 19.42—and Pullar was getting a lot of runs.

DM: Four amateurs topped the batting averages with Javed Burki second to Subba Row in his final year at Oxford. Burki was a cousin of Imran Khan and Majid Khan and obviously had a lot of talent but he was not very successful as a captain of Pakistan. Mike Smith was still scoring heavily for Warwickshire (and England) and Dexter was possibly at his most brilliant as a batsman that year. What an immense talent the man had.

FST: He was one of the finest strikers of the ball I have ever seen, an absolutely magnificent stroke player. He made everything look so easy that it seemed that half the time he was playing with only half his mind on the game. He was a fine golfer and when he became the England captain it was nothing to see him practising golf shots in the middle of a vital period of the Test. It drove us mad at times but no one doubted his ability. It was tremendous.

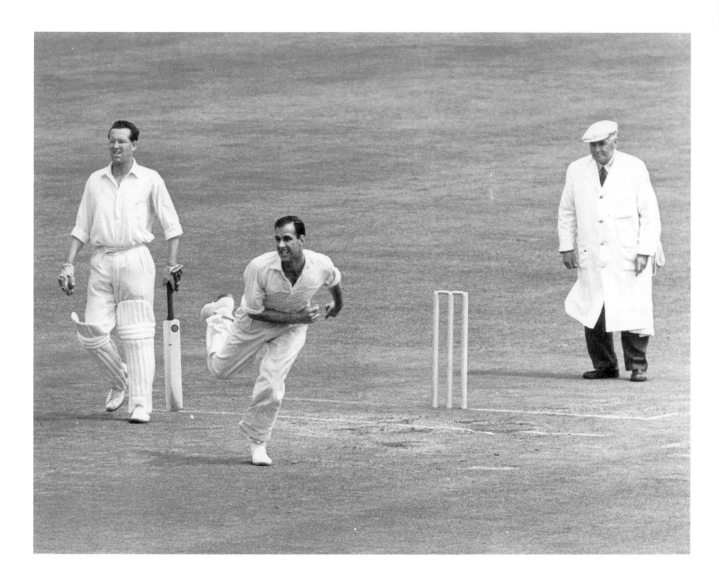

Alan Moss, service with a snarl. Roy Marshall looks on

DM. And what about Yorkshire's second successive championship?

FST: Well, I had 132 championship wickets and four other bowlers—Illingworth, Wilson, Mick Cowan and Brian Close took more than 60 apiece. That was the foundation of 17 wins; the batting was pretty settled and of the 19 players we used, most were extra bowlers when Ray Illingworth and I were away during the Tests. Close got his highest score, 198 against Surrey at The Oval.

DM: There was a changed format to the county championship in 1960. Eight of the counties (Yorkshire, Lancashire, Sussex, Glamorgan, Hampshire, Worcestershire, Somerset and Warwickshire) played all the other counties twice, making a total of 32 championship matches while the remaining nine counties played only 28 matches. For the purposes of the championship, therefore, the number of points gained was divided by the number of matches played and the title was decided on the average number of points (including bonus points) achieved. The top two sides both played 32 matches and the bottom two 28 but as the third-in-the-table played 28 and five of the bottom seven played 32 no clear conclusions can be drawn from that. The most dramatic change of fortunes fell to Warwickshire who dropped from fourth place to 15th while Sussex jumped from 15th to fourth.

1961

Tests v Australia:

Edgbaston	Match drawn
Lord's	Australia won by five wickets
Headingley	England won by eight wickets
Old Trafford	Australia won by 54 runs
Oval	Match drawn

County Champions   Hampshire

TEST AVERAGES ENGLAND V AUSTRALIA 1961

	M	I	NO	HS	Runs	Av	100	50	Ct/St
R. Subba Row	5	10	0	137	468	46.80	2	1	2
K. F. Barrington	5	9	1	83	364	45.50	–	4	4
D. A. Allen	4	6	3	42*	132	44.00	–	–	–
E. R. Dexter	5	9	0	180	378	42.00	1	1	2
P. B. H. May	4	8	1	95	272	38.85	–	2	–
G. Pullar	5	10	1	63	287	31.88	–	2	–
M. C. Cowdrey	4	8	0	93	168	21.00	–	1	4
J. T. Murray	5	8	0	40	160	20.00	–	–	17/1
J. B. Statham	4	7	4	18	59	19.66	–	–	1
J. A. Flavell	2	3	2	14	14	14.00	–	–	–
F. S. Trueman	4	6	0	25	60	10.00	–	–	2
R. Illingworth	2	3	0	15	28	9.33	–	–	5
G. A. R. Lock	3	5	0	30	39	7.80	–	–	1

Also batted: D. B. Close (1 match) 33, 8, 2ct; H. L. Jackson (1 match) 8, 1ct; M. J. K. Smith (1 match) 0, 1*.

	Overs	M	Runs	Wkts	Av	5w	10w	BB
E. R. Dexter	79.4	16	223	9	24.77	–	–	3–16
F. S. Trueman	164.4	21	529	20	26.45	2	1	6–30
D. A. Allen	134	53	354	13	27.23	–	–	4–58
J. B. Statham	201.4	41	501	17	29.47	1	–	5–53
J. A. Flavell	82.4	17	231	5	46.20	–	–	2–65

Also bowled: D. B. Close 8–1–33–0; H. L. Jackson 44–16–83–4; R. Illingworth 55.3–17–126–3; G. A. R. Lock 107–33–250–3.

CHAMPIONSHIP TABLE 1961

						First Inns Lead in Match Bonus			
	P	Won	Lost	D	NR	Lost D	Pts	Pts	Av
Points Awarded	–	12	–	–	–	2 2	–	–	–
HAMPSHIRE (12)	32	19	7	6	0	1 3	32	268	8.37
Yorkshire (1)	32	17	5	10	0	1 5	34	250	7.81
Middlesex (3)	28	15	6	6	1	3 1	26	214	7.64
Worcestershire (13)	32	16	9	7	0	2 3	24	226	7.06
Gloucestershire (8)	28	11	11	5	1	2 2	18	158	5.64
Essex (6)	28	10	8	10	0	2 4	26	158	5.64
Derbyshire (5)	28	10	9	9	0	3 3	22	154	5.50
Sussex (4)	32	11	10	11	0	1 8	20	170	5.31
Leicestershire (17)	28	9	13	5	1	2 4	26	146	5.21
Somerset (14)	32	10	15	7	0	6 3	24	162	5.06
Kent (10)	28	8	8	12	0	1 7	20	132	4.71
Warwickshire (15)	32	9	10	13	0	1 7	26	150	4.68
Lancashire (2)	32	9	7	15	1	1 7	18	142	4.43
Glamorgan (11)	32	9	12	11	0	1 4	10	128	4.00
Surrey (7)	28	4	13	11	0	6 8	24	100	3.57
Northamptonshire (9)	28	5	13	10	0	1 5	10	82	2.92
Nottinghamshire (16)	28	4	20	4	0	6 2	12	76	2.71

1960 positions are shown in brackets

FIRST-CLASS AVERAGES 1961

	I	NO	HS	Runs	Av	100
K. F. Barrington (Surrey)	42	7	163	2070	59.14	4
±W. E. Alley (Somerset)	64	11	221*	3019	56.96	11
Nawab of Pataudi (Oxford Univ)	24	2	144	1216	55.27	4
F. W. Neate (Oxford Univ)	19	6	112	712	54.76	1
M. C. Cowdrey (Kent)	34	1	156	1730	52.42	7
R. A. E. Tindall (Surrey)	22	5	100*	751	44.17	1
R. E. Marshall (Hampshire)	62	2	212	2607	43.45	5
±G. Pullar (Lancashire)	61	7	165*	2344	43.40	5
E. J. Craig (Camb Univ/Lancashire)	41	5	208*	1528	42.44	5
M. J. K. Smith (Warwickshire)	67	5	145	2587	41.72	5

*denotes not out
±denotes left-hand batsman

	Overs	M	Runs	Wkts	Av	BB
J. A Flavell (Worcestershire)	1245.2	300	3043	171	17.79	8–43
B. S. Boshier (Leicestershire)	800	193	1930	108	17.87	6–46
R. Illingworth (Yorkshire)	1104.3	437	2292	128	17.90	8–50
J. S. Savage (Leicestershire)	1013.3	378	2310	122	18.93	7–87
D. Shackleton (Hampshire)	1501.5	532	3017	158	19.09	6–36
L. J. Coldwell (Worcestershire)	1142.2	295	2696	140	19.25	8–41
F. S. Trueman (Yorkshire)	1190.1	302	3000	155	19.35	7–45
D. A. Allen (Gloucestershire)	907.1	315	2410	124	19.43	7–78
C. T. Spencer (Leicestershire)	999.4	247	2406	123	19.56	8–88
A. E. Moss (Middlesex)	922	282	2260	115	19.65	8–49

Ted Dexter, in lordly mood

CAPTAIN BENAUD

Freddie Trueman: Richie Benaud, who was to become a household name in Britain as a TV commentator, captained the 1961 Australians and proved a very shrewd leader, especially at Old Trafford where tactics played a great part in the game. A new opening batsman appeared on that tour, Bill Lawry, and he proved one of the most stubborn batsmen I've ever had to bowl at. When you think that 'Slasher' Mackay was in the side as well it was obviously going to be hard work to bowl the Aussies out twice.

Don Mosey: You didn't manage it even once in the First Test (Edgbaston), where they scored 516 for nine after bowling out England for 195.

FST: It was a typical Egbaston pitch, but we didn't bat very well in the first innings. Oddly enough, the only man in the game to get a duck was Mike Smith, who knew the pitch better than anyone else. But Ted Dexter played a brilliant innings of 180 second time round and Subba Row got a hundred in his first Test against Australia. Another new face appeared on the scene, another we were to see a lot of in the future—'Garth' McKenzie—in the Second Test where Statham took his two hundredth Test wicket.

DM: And it was at this time that popular newspapers, acting on information received (as they say) from certain batsmen, first reported the existence of a 'ridge' in the Lord's wicket. Since then, every conceivable kind of investigation and corrective measure has been carried out and there are those who refuse to accept the existence of a ridge. When a genuinely quick bowler is around in helpful conditions, however, batsmen will swear the most solemn oaths that the ball behaves strangely for no other accountable reason. Australia won at Lord's and Lawry in his second Test match got his first hundred against England. With Benaud suffering from an injured shoulder, Neil Harvey skippered Australia for the only time.

FST: Twelve years after his first Test, Les Jackson got his second chance to play for England. Year after year he had turned in 100 wickets a season for Derbyshire at a small cost but Old Trafford, 1949, and Headingley, 1961, were his only appearances in Tests. He was 40 years old when he was recalled because Statham was injured. When Australia started their second innings 62 behind, Les bowled Colin McDonald and Australia were four for one. Then there was a bit of a stand and Peter May asked me to bowl an over so he could switch round the spinners, Allen and Lock, and I decided to try a cutter. I had watched Alan Davidson bowling them with some success in the morning and the cutter was a delivery I had been experimenting with a bit in the nets. The first one bit and lifted and Harvey, who had been going well, skied it to cover. Peter May (who had taken back the captaincy from Colin Cowdrey) changed his mind about switching the spinners, told me to carry on and in 24 deliveries I took five wickets for no runs. Australia were all out for 120, we won by eight wickets and made it one Test each in the series.

DM: What a different story at Old Trafford: Jack Flavell making his Test debut as Jackson was dropped again (and forever) and England getting a first innings lead of 177. Solid batting by Australia in the second innings but England should still have won, Fred?

FST: It all went wrong on the last morning. Australia were 334 for nine and then Davidson and McKenzie were allowed to put on 98 for the last wicket. Still, we were in with a good chance when Dexter hit a brilliant 76 but then Richie Benaud decided to bowl his leg breaks round the wicket, aiming at the bowlers' rough—five for 12 in 25 balls and we had lost by 54 runs. It was good thinking by Richie and he put the ball on the right spot, but we shouldn't have lost. It cost us the rubber as well because the last Test at The Oval was drawn.

DM: John Murray, who took over from Jim Parks in that series, claimed 18 dismissals in the Tests. Subba Row scored a hundred in what was to be his last Test against

Australia, having hit one in his first. Peter May ended his Test career at The Oval.

NEW CHAMPIONS

FST: We had a bit of a shock in the county championships, finishing second to Hampshire who had never won the title before and have only won it once more since then (in 1973). What really upset us was that we beat them at Bournemouth and had much the better of a drawn match at Headingley. We felt that they did well on other sides' declarations while no one ever declared against Yorkshire.

DM: That's probably true, Fred, but Hampshire weren't a bad side by any means . . . Roy Marshall and Jimmy Gray to open the batting, Shack and 'Butch' White the bowling . . . a pretty solid middle order with men like Henry Horton, Mike Barnard and Danny Livingstone (who came from Antigua when Viv Richards was still only a nipper) . . . and Peter Sainsbury was a good all-rounder.

'No need to make such a song and dance about it, mate. I'm in.' Bill Alley to Derek Ufton (Kent)

Ingleby-Mackenzie was a dashing sort of captain with his everyone-in-bed-by-breakfast-time philosophy. The national Press loved him and gave him the title 'the gay cavalier of cricket'. He certainly had a refreshing approach to the game and to have a brand new champion county wasn't a bad thing for the game.

FST: That was not the unanimous view of the Yorkshire side.

DM: It was a bit sad to see Surrey down near the bottom of the table so recently after their seven-championships sequence. They had lost Laker but they still had the Bedsers, Loader and Lock, Stewart and John Edrich to open the batting, May and Barrington in the middle order. Yet they won only four games in the season. Leicestershire and Worcestershire (who had now been joined by

Graveney) made dramatic advances in the table but a fearful drop for Lancashire, from second to 13th.

ALLEY'S 3,000 RUNS

FST: A mutual friend of ours got over 3,000 runs in 1961—Bill Alley, now 42 years old. What a marvellous all-rounder he was. He had played with Colne in the Lancashire League and Blackpool in the Northern League before he joined Somerset. He was a fine seam bowler as well and not much got past him in the gulley. He hit 11 hundreds in that season including 155 not out against us at Taunton.

DM: Five amateurs amongst the top ten batsmen including the Nawab of Pataudi (known universally as The Noob). He had a serious car accident that year which badly affected his eyesight, yet he went on to have a distinguished cricket career at Oxford, with Sussex and as captain of India. The great improvement in Leicestershire's fortunes is reflected by three bowlers in the top ten—Brian Boshier, a big man who bowled big in-swingers, John Savage, the off-spinner (later coach at Lancashire) and Terry Spencer, who bowled pretty sharply down the hill at Grace Road.

FST: Jack Flavell and Len Coldwell were a great opening pair for Worcestershire and you can see why they finished fourth in the table. Shack had a major part in Hampshire's championship win and there are just three spin bowlers in the list—Illingworth, Savage and Allen.

DM: All off-spinners. Not a slow left-armer or a leg-spinner in sight.

FST: But every county had one or other—there were not quite so many leg-spinners now but they were still about. And no self-respecting side would have dreamed of taking the field without a slow left-arm bowler.

Winter Tour to India (1961–62):

Bombay	Match drawn
Kanpur	Match drawn
Delhi	Match drawn
Calcutta	India won by 187 runs
Madras	India won by 128 runs

Pakistan:

Lahore	England won by five wickets
Dacca	Match drawn
Karachi	Match drawn

Summer Series with Pakistan:

Edgbaston	England won by an innings & 24 runs
Lord's	England won by nine wickets
Headingley	England won by an innings & 117 runs
Trent Bridge	Match drawn
Oval	England won by ten wickets

County Champions   Yorkshire

TEST AVERAGES ENGLAND V INDIA 1961–62

	M	I	NO	HS	Runs	Av	100	50	Ct/St
K. F. Barrington	5	9	3	172	594	99.00	3	1	2
G. Pullar	3	4	0	119	337	84.25	1	2	1
E. R. Dexter	5	9	2	126*	409	58.42	1	3	2
P. E. Richardson	5	9	0	71	304	33.77	–	2	4
P. H. Parfitt	2	4	0	46	125	31.25	–	–	7
B. R. Knight	4	5	1	39*	115	28.75	–	–	1
R. W. Barber	5	8	1	69*	184	26.28	–	1	4
G. A. R. Lock	5	7	2	49	108	21.60	–	–	6
M. J. K. Smith	4	7	0	73	126	18.00	–	1	1
G. Millman	2	4	1	32*	50	16.66	–	–	6/2
D. A. Allen	5	6	0	34	89	14.83	–	–	3
D. R. Smith	5	5	1	34	38	9.50	–	–	2
J. T. Murray	3	4	1	9*	21	7.00	–	–	0/1

Also batted: W. E. Russell (1 match) 10, 9. A. Brown (1ct) played in one match but did not bat.

	Overs	M	Runs	Wkts	Av	5w	10w	BB
D. A. Allen	301.5	121	583	21	27.76	1	–	5–67
G. A. R. Lock	306.3	124	628	22	28.04	1	–	6–65
B. R. Knight	103.3	22	305	8	38.12	–	–	2–18
D. R. Smith	162	47	359	6	59.83	–	–	2–60

Also bowled: R. W. Barber 79–10–315–4; K. F. Barrington 12–1–57–0; A. Brown 24–2–79–0; E. R. Dexter 83–16–240–4; P. H. Parfitt 22–3–46–2; P. E. Richardson 6–3–10–2; W. E. Russell 5–0–19–0; M. J. K. Smith 8–3–10–1.

TEST AVERAGES ENGLAND V PAKISTAN 1961–62

	M	I	NO	HS	Runs	Av	100	50	Ct/St
E. R. Dexter	3	4	1	205	303	101.00	1	1	4
K. F. Barrington	2	3	0	139	229	76.33	1	1	1
G. Pullar	3	5	1	165	233	58.25	1	1	1
R. W. Barber	3	4	1	86	154	51.33	–	1	1
M. J. K. Smith	3	4	0	99	199	49.75	–	2	4
P. E. Richardson	3	5	1	48	118	29.50	–	–	1
D. A. Allen	3	3	0	40	41	13.66	–	–	2

Also batted: A. Brown (1 match) 3*; B. R. Knight (2 matches) 10, 6, 1ct; G. A. R. Lock (2 matches) 4, 0*, 4ct; G. Millman (2 matches) 3*, 0, 3ct; J. T. Murray (1 match) 4, 5ct; P. H. Parfitt (2 matches) 9, 111, 3ct; W. E. Russell (1 match) 34, 0; D. W. White (2 matches) 0, 0.

	Overs	M	Runs	Wkts	Av	5w	10w	BB
D. A. Allen	180.4	82	334	13	25.69	1	–	5–30
B. R. Knight	79	26	180	6	30.00	–	–	4–66
G. A. R. Lock	166	71	337	10	33.70	–	–	4–70
E. R. Dexter	97.2	32	205	6	34.16	–	–	3–86
R. W. Barber	126.5	26	351	10	35.10	–	–	3–54

Also bowled: K. F. Barrington 38–14–81–0; A. Brown 29.5–7–71–3; P. H. Parfitt 11–5–18–0; G. Pullar 9–3–30–0; P. E. Richardson 14–6–38–1; W. E. Russell 19–9–25–0; D. W. White 36.4–5–119–4.

TEST AVERAGES ENGLAND V PAKISTAN 1962

	M	I	NO	HS	Runs	Av	100	50	Ct/St
P. H. Parfitt	5	5	2	119	340	113.33	3	–	5
T. W. Graveney	4	4	0	153	401	100.25	2	1	8
E. R. Dexter	5	6	1	172	446	89.20	1	3	2
M. C. Cowdrey	4	5	0	182	409	81.80	2	–	9
M. J. Stewart	2	3	1	86	159	79.50	–	1	1
Rev D. S. Sheppard	2	3	1	83	149	74.50	–	2	–
D. A. Allen	4	3	1	79*	143	71.50	–	2	–
K. F. Barrington	4	4	1	50*	60	20.00	–	1	3

Also batted: L. J. Coldwell (2 matches) 0*; R. Illingworth (1 match) 2*; B. R. Knight (2 matches) 14, 3, 1ct; G. A. R. Lock (3 matches) 7, 2ct; G. Millman (2 matches) 7, 4ct; J. T. Murray (3 matches) 29, 14*, 10ct; G. Pullar (2 matches) 22, 5; J. B. Statham (3 matches) 26*, 3ct; F. J. Titmus (2 matches) 2, 11*, 2ct; F. S. Trueman (4 matches) 29, 20, 6ct. J. D. F. Larter played in one match but did not bat.

	Overs	M	Runs	Wkts	Av	5w	10w	BB
L. J. Coldwell	105	30	223	13	17.15	1	–	6–85
J. B. Statham	120.1	40	278	16	17.37	–	–	4–50
J. D. F. Larter	46.1	4	145	9	16.11	1	–	5–57
F. S. Trueman	164.5	37	439	22	19.95	1	–	6–31
B. R. Knight	58	15	130	6	21.66	–	–	4–38
E. R. Dexter	76.1	20	199	7	28.42	–	–	4–10
D. A. Allen	165	68	322	11	29.27	–	–	3–47
G. A. R. Lock	98	32	241	6	40.16	–	–	3–80

Also bowled: K. F. Barrington 6–2–22–0; M. C. Cowdrey 1–0–1–0; R. Illingworth 34–14–81–1; P. H. Parfitt 3–1–7–0; F. J. Titmus 44–12–74–3.

CHAMPIONSHIP TABLE 1962

							First Inns Lead in Match Bonus		
	P	Won	Lost D	NR	Lost D	Pts	Pts	Av
Points Awarded	–	12	– –	–	2 2	–	–	–
YORKSHIRE (2)	32	14	4 14	0	1	9 36	224	7.00
Worcestershire (4)	32	14	3 14	1	1	8 34	220	6.87
Warwickshire (12)	32	12	5 15	0	2	11 32	202	6.31
Gloucestershire (5)	28	11	11 6	0	5	4 24	174	6.21
Surrey (15)	28	10	3 14	1	2	9 32	174	6.21
Somerset (10)	32	12	7 13	0	1	7 30	190	5.93
Derbyshire (7)	28	8	6 13	1	2	8 28	144	5.14
Northamptonshire (16)	28	7	5 16	0	1	10 22	128	4.57
Essex (6)	28	8	6 13	1	2	7 12	126	4.50
Hampshire (1)	32	7	5 19	1	2	11 30	140	4.37
Kent (11)	28	7	9 10	2	2	3 16	110	3.92
Sussex (8)	32	7	12 13	0	4	6 18	122	3.81
Middlesex (3)	28	6	8 13	1	2	4 18	102	3.64
Glamorgan (14)	32	6	13 13	0	1	4 14	96	3.00
Nottinghamshire (17)	28	4	12 11	1	0	1 4	54	1.92
Lancashire (13)	32	2	16 14	0	6	5 14	60	1.87
Leicestershire (9)	28	2	12 13	1	2	5 12	50	1.78

1961 positions are shown in brackets

FIRST-CLASS AVERAGES 1962

	I	NO	HS	Runs	Av	100
R. T. Simpson (Nottinghamshire)	20	4	105	867	54.18	2
T. W. Graveney (Worcestershire)	48	6	164*	2269	54.02	9
E. R. Dexter (Sussex)	47	7	172	2148	53.70	5
M. C. Cowdrey (Kent)	38	3	182	1839	52.54	6
P. B. H. May (Surrey)	31	5	135	1352	52.00	3
±J. H. Edrich (Surrey)	55	7	216	2482	51.70	7
K. F. Barrington (Surrey)	46	8	146	1865	49.07	6
D. C. Morgan (Derbyshire)	51	15	124	1669	46.36	3
±P. H. Parfitt (Middlesex)	51	4	138	2121	45.12	8
M. J. Stewart (Surrey)	55	9	200*	2045	44.45	5

	Overs	M	Runs	Wkts	Av	BB
±C. Cook (Gloucestershire)	477.1	209	994	58	17.13	5–28
±D. A. D. Sydenham (Surrey)	985.2	295	2030	115	17.65	5–18
F. S. Trueman (Yorkshire)	1141.5	273	2717	153	17.75	8–84
L. J. Coldwell (Worcestershire)	1104	253	2722	152	17.90	8–64
P. J. Loader (Surrey)	991.4	236	2426	131	18.51	6–42
J. C. Laker (Essex)	379.5	96	962	51	18.86	7–37
J. D. F. Larter (Northamptonshire)	817.1	212	1924	101	19.04	7–48
H. L. Jackson (Derbyshire)	1018	326	2012	105	19.16	7–35
O. S. Wheatley (Glamorgan)	1202.2	355	2628	136	19.32	7–55
H. J. Rhodes (Derbyshire)	654.2	198	1321	68	19.42	6–30

LONG TOUR

Don Mosey: The winter tour to the Indian sub-continent was a long one by any standards, starting in mid-October and ending in mid-February. Taking into account that there were few hotels of western standards outside the merest handful of major cities and that most of the travelling of immense distances had to be undertaken by train, this was not an easy tour. It started in Pakistan with one Test, moved on to India for five, then finished off with two more in Pakistan—but more than 2,000 miles apart.

Freddie Trueman: The First Test in Lahore was the first between England and Pakistan in that country and it brought a win for England by five wickets. There haven't been many definite results in Pakistan/England series.

DM: In fact there wasn't another for 22 years, with a dreary catalogue of draws in between. There were Test debuts for Alan Brown, of Kent; Eric Russell, of Middlesex; and 'Butch' White, of Hampshire, who took the wickets of both openers—Hanif Mohammad and Imtiaz Ahmed, in his first three overs.

FST: Ken Barrington made 139 in Lahore, then 151 not out and 52 not out in Bombay in the First Test against

India, 172 in the Second, 113 not out in the Third. He obviously liked the wickets even though he wasn't so keen on the curry. The Fourth Test brought a debut for Geoff Millman, of Nottinghamshire, who took over behind the stumps from JT Murray, and for Peter Parfitt, of Middlesex.

DM: And, significantly, the Fifth Test saw the first appearance of Prasanna, the off-spinner, who was to be such a potent force in Indian Test cricket over the next two decades. Ken Barrington averaged 99 in the five Tests against India and was on the losing side. It was India's first rubber against England.

FST: And David Allen, the off-spinner, topped the bowling averages against both India and Pakistan. Even after he'd bowled nearly 500 overs and been away from home for four months, the tour still went on to Sri Lanka (then Ceylon and not yet a first-class cricketing country in ICC terms). A good cricketer, David Allen; he'd done the double the previous season at home and he was always a better-than-average batsman.

DM: One interesting point about the Pakistan series—in two of the Tests we see the name of Haseeb Ahsan who was to come to England as manager of the 1987 touring party and got himself into all kinds of controversial headlines.

FST: And Ted Dexter got his career-best score of 205 in Karachi, right at the end of the tour he skippered.

PAKISTAN AGAIN

DM: Pakistan were the summer visitors in 1962 and Parfitt, who had got his first Test century against them during the winter tour, started with another at Edgbaston, where England declared at 544 for five and won by an innings and 24. The Second Test (Lord's) had a special significance for you, Fred?

FST: Yes, my 200th Test wicket in 47 matches. My new opening partner was Len Coldwell, of Worcestershire, who took a wicket with his fifth ball in Test cricket but don't forget my batting—a partnership of 76 for the ninth wicket with Tom Graveney!

DM: Cowdrey took over from Dexter as captain in the Third Test while Dexter was restored for the Fourth and Fifth. The Selectors then decided to have a look at David Larter as a tour candidate for Australia. He took five for 57 and four for 88 which won him a place in the party for the winter trip.

DM: The Pakistan series was a good one for Parfitt, who topped the averages with 113.33 and he made three hundreds. While David Allen had done well in Pakistan it was the quicker men who were more effective on our own pitches—the first six in the Test averages were all above medium pace.

Above: *Worcestershire's bowling twins of the sixties—Jack Flavell meets the pre-war 'great', Frank Woolley, and* (below) *Len Coldwell bowls in his first Test match (umpire: Sid Buller)*

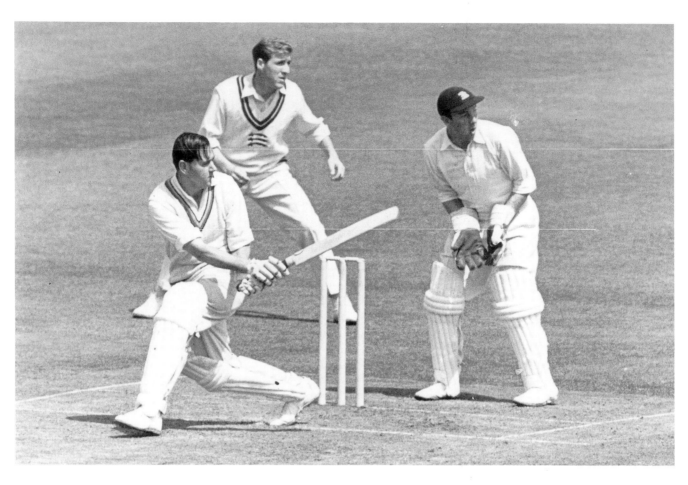

FAST BOWLERS' SUMMER

FST: It was a good summer all round for the quicker bowlers—eight out of ten in the first-class averages and neither of the two spinners in the list got anything like 100 wickets. Jim Laker came out of retirement to play for Essex and showed that he had lost none of his skill and Sam Cook's slow left arm bowling took him to the top of the averages. But the other eight were all quick men.

DM: It was David Sydenham's best season. He had a fairly short career with Surrey as a left-arm quickie but it was a pretty effective one. And Ossie Wheatley is there with 136 wickets—he had two years at Cambridge, then four seasons with Warwickshire before going to Glamorgan as captain. Les Jackson, now 41, takes 100 wickets yet again and now has a new Derbyshire opening partner in Harold Rhodes.

FST: 'Dusty' Rhodes had a bit of a chequered career. He was called for throwing in 1960 and 1961 but he didn't have any problems in 1962 although a lot of muttering went on round the circuit. It must have been terrible for his father, Bert, who was a first-class umpire himself at the time. He was loyal to Harold and was convinced there was

Colin Cowdrey v the Middlesex Mafia—Peter Parfitt at slip, J. T. Murray behind the stumps and Fred Titmus was the bowler. Result: Cowdrey 4, Mafia 0

nothing wrong with the lad's action but of course he had to share changing rooms with umpires who had called Harold.

DM: Reg Simpson was getting towards the end of his career but his 20 innings for Nottinghamshire enabled him to top the batting averages, and Tom Graveney had clearly settled in at Worcestershire. Now we see John Edrich beginning to blossom as Surrey's opener. His aggregate in 1962 was the best of his career but it was only one of 21 good seasons with the county, and for 12 years he was a consistently successful England opener. It was the best season of Derek Morgan's career with Derbyshire, too. I used to play rugby with him when he was qualifying for Derbyshire CCC so I knew him pretty well.

FST: It's a pity you couldn't have livened him up a bit, then, because if he decided to dig in it needed a stick of dynamite to shift him! He was a good county all-rounder, Derek—bowled a tidy medium pace and he was a good catcher close to the wicket. As captain (1965–69) he was a bit dour, didn't give much away.

DM: Surrey, with four leading batsmen and two bowlers, climbed ten places up the championship table but Lancashire slumped badly and so did Middlesex.

FST: They both had captaincy problems. Middlesex had recalled Ian Bedford, the amateur leg-break bowler, to skipper the side when he had been out of first-class cricket for 12 or 13 years and it didn't work. In Lancashire, it was Joe Blackledge's one season as captain and that didn't work either. He was a lovely man, Joe, and I suppose the Lancashire Committee were hoping he could do what Ronnie Burnet had done for Yorkshire three years before. There were one or two lively characters in the Lancashire side who needed a firm hand but Joe was too nice a chap to apply it.

DM: And Yorkshire won their second championship in three years under Vic Wilson's captaincy. In his other year they had been runners-up so he retired with an excellent record as Yorkshire's first modern professional captain. Vic was an East Yorkshire farmer, a rather phlegmatic character who was a dependable middle-order left-hand batsman with a superb pair of hands as a close-to-the-wicket catcher. Worcestershire were runners-up and beginning to look a very useful side indeed with bowlers like Coldwell, Flavell and Norman Gifford and the batting

headed by Kenyon, Martin Horton, Ron Headley and Graveney. In fact they were just pipped for the title that year by Yorkshire's victory over Glamorgan on a rain-affected pitch at Harrogate on the last day of the season. But there is one notable piece of cricket history for us to record, Fred, before we are finished with 1962. . . .

FST: Certainly. That was the year of the last Gentlemen v Players fixture at Lord's when I had the honour of leading the Players against Ted Dexter's Gentlemen. A total of 137 matches took place at Lord's of which the Players won 68, Gentlemen 41 and 28 were drawn. The fixture came to an end because after 1962 the distinction between amateurs and professionals was abolished by the MCC and all players became simply cricketers. This was to silence allegations of 'shamateurism' against players who were ostensibly unpaid for their cricket but who were salaried by their counties as secretaries or assistant secretaries or cushioned financially in other ways.

The last Gents v Players match. Tony Lewis batting, Keith Andrew keeps wicket, Philip Sharpe at slip

Winter Tour to Australia (1962–63):

Brisbane	Match drawn
Melbourne	England won by seven wickets
Sydney	Australia won by eight wickets
Adelaide	Match drawn
Sydney	Match drawn

New Zealand:

Auckland	England won by an innings & 215 runs
Wellington	England won by an innings & 47 runs
Christchurch	England won by seven wickets

Summer Series with West Indies:

Old Trafford	West Indies won by ten wickets
Lord's	Match drawn
Edgbaston	England won by 217 runs
Headingley	West Indies won by 221 runs
Oval	West Indies won by eight wickets

County Champions Yorkshire

Gillette Cup Sussex

TEST AVERAGES ENGLAND V AUSTRALIA 1962–63

	M	I	NO	HS	Runs	Av	100	50	Ct/St
K. F. Barrington	5	10	2	132*	582	72.75	2	3	6
E. R. Dexter	5	10	0	99	481	48.10	–	5	2
M. C. Cowdrey	5	10	1	113	394	43.77	1	3	5
F. J. Titmus	5	8	3	59*	182	36.40	–	1	3
Rev D. S. Sheppard	5	10	0	113	330	33.00	1	2	2
T. W. Graveney	3	5	1	41	116	29.00	–	–	6
P. H. Parfitt	2	4	0	80	112	28.00	–	1	–
G. Pullar	4	8	0	56	170	21.25	–	2	–
F. S. Trueman	5	7	0	38	142	20.28	–	–	7
R. Illingworth	2	3	0	27	57	19.00	–	–	–
A. C. Smith	4	5	1	21	47	11.75	–	–	13/–
J. B. Statham	5	6	2	17*	29	7.25	–	–	3
L. J. Coldwell	2	3	1	2*	3	1.50	–	–	–

Also batted: D. A. Allen (1 match) 14, 1ct; B. R. Knight (1 match) 0, 4*, 1ct; J. T. Murray (1 match) 0, 3*, 1ct.

	Overs	M	Runs	Wkts	Av	5w	10w	BB
F. S. Trueman	158.3	9	521	20	26.05	1	–	5–62
F. J. Titmus	236.3	54	616	21	29.33	2	–	7–79
E. R. Dexter	95.2	6	373	11	33.90	–	–	3–65
J. B. Statham	165.2	16	580	13	44.61	–	–	3–66
D. A. Allen	62	26	113	5	22.60	–	–	3–26

Also bowled: K. F. Barrington 39–6–154–1; L. J. Coldwell 57–5–159–3; T. W. Graveney 7–1–34–0; R. Illingworth 40–10–131–1; B. R. Knight 31.5–3–128–3.

TEST AVERAGES ENGLAND V NEW ZEALAND 1962–63

	M	I	NO	HS	Runs	Av	100	50	Ct/St
M. C. Cowdrey	3	4	2	128*	292	146.00	1	1	1
K. F. Barrington	3	4	0	126	294	73.50	1	1	5
B. R. Knight	3	4	1	125	208	69.33	1	–	2
P. H. Parfitt	3	4	1	131*	166	55.33	1	–	6
E. R. Dexter	3	3	0	46	84	28.00	–	–	3
R. Illingworth	3	3	0	46	68	22.66	–	–	4
Rev D. S. Sheppard	3	4	0	42	85	21.25	–	–	2
F. J. Titmus	3	3	0	33	63	21.00	–	–	1

Also batted: J. D. F. Larter (3 matches) 2, 2ct; J. T. Murray (1 match) 9*2ct; A. C. Smith (2 matches) 69*, 2*, 7ct; F. S. Trueman (2 matches) 3, 11. L. J. Coldwell (1ct) played in one match but did not bat.

	Overs	M	Runs	Wkts	Av	5w	10w	BB
F. S. Trueman	88	29	164	14	11.71	1	–	7–75
R. Illingworth	45	20	73	5	14.60	–	–	4–34
B. R. Knight	78.4	21	152	9	16.88	–	–	3–32
F. J. Titmus	132	54	227	13	17.46	–	–	4–46
J. D. F. Larter	105.1	31	238	10	23.80	–	–	4–26

Also bowled: K. F. Barrington 30.3–8–89–4; L. J. Coldwell 32–11–70–2; E. R. Dexter 29–9–48–0.

TEST AVERAGES ENGLAND V WEST INDIES 1963

	M	I	NO	HS	Runs	Av	100	50	Ct/St
P. J. Sharpe	3	6	1	85*	267	53.40	–	3	4
E. R. Dexter	5	10	0	73	340	34.00	–	3	1
D. B. Close	5	10	0	70	315	31.50	–	3	2
K. F. Barrington	5	10	0	80	275	27.50	–	2	3
M. J. Stewart	4	8	0	87	211	26.37	–	1	5
J. B. Bolus	2	4	0	43	105	26.25	–	–	1
J. M. Parks	4	8	0	57	190	23.75	–	1	10/–
F. J. Titmus	4	8	1	52*	145	20.71	–	1	2
G. A. R. Lock	3	6	0	56	115	19.16	–	2	7
J. H. Edrich	3	6	0	38	103	17.16	–	–	2
M. C. Cowdrey	2	4	1	19*	39	13.00	–	–	6
D. Shackleton	4	7	5	8	20	10.00	–	–	1
F. S. Trueman	5	10	1	29*	82	9.11	–	–	3
D. A. Allen	2	4	1	5	12	4.00	–	–	–
J. B. Statham	2	4	0	14	29	7.25	–	–	–

Also batted: K. V. Andrew (1 match) 3*, 15, 1ct; P. E. Richardson (1 match) 2, 14.

	Overs	M	Runs	Wkts	Av	5w	10w	BB
F. S. Trueman	236.4	53	594	34	17.47	4	2	7–44
E. R. Dexter	95	22	227	7	32.42	–	–	4–38
D. Shackleton	243.2	73	518	15	34.53	–	–	4–72
G. A. R. Lock	91.5	24	230	6	38.33	–	–	3–54
F. J. Titmus	101	23	256	6	42.66	–	–	4–44

Also bowled: D. A. Allen 88.1–32–208–4; D. B. Close 25–5–88–0; J. B. Statham 81–10–243–3.

CHAMPIONSHIP TABLE 1963

| | | | | | | First Inns Lead in Match | | |
Points Awarded	P –	Won 10	Lost –	D –	NR –	Lost 2	D 2	Pts –
YORKSHIRE (1)	28	13	3	11	1	1	6	144
Glamorgan (14)	28	11	8	8	1	1	6	124
Somerset (6)	28	10	6	11	1	2	7	118
Sussex (12)	28	10	6	12	0	1	7	116
Warwickshire (3)	28	10	3	14	1	1	7	116
Middlesex (13)	28	9	5	11	3	1	7	106
Northamptonshire (8)	28	9	8	11	0	1	5	105±
Gloucestershire (4)	28	9	7	11	1	2	3	100
Nottinghamshire (15)	28	6	8	13	1	4	7	82
Hampshire (10)	28	7	8	10	3	1	4	80
Surrey (50)	28	5	6	17	0	1	11	74
Essex (9)	28	6	4	17	1	0	5	70
Kent (11)	28	5	6	17	0	1	8	68
Worcestershire (2)	28	4	8	13	3	2	8	60
Lancashire (16)	28	4	10	13	1	2	7	58
Leicestershire (17)	28	3	13	10	2	2	3	40
Derbyshire (7)	28	2	14	9	3	1	3	28

± includes five points instead of two for fourth innings of drawn match when the final scores were level
1962 positions are shown in brackets

FIRST-CLASS AVERAGES 1963

	I	NO	HS	Runs	Av	100
M. J. K. Smith (Warwickshire)	39	6	144*	1566	47.45	3
G. Boycott (Yorkshire)	43	7	165*	1628	45.22	3
±C. C. Inman (Leicestershire)	51	11	120*	1708	42.70	1
J. B. Bolus (Nottinghamshire)	57	4	202*	2190	41.32	5
K. F. Barrington (Surrey)	45	7	110*	1568	41.26	2
±J. H. Edrich (Surrey)	55	7	125	1921	40.02	2
S. E. Leary (Kent)	38	5	158	1311	39.72	2
±P. E. Richardson (Kent)	56	2	172	2110	39.07	5
±P. H. Parfitt (Middlesex)	53	5	135*	1813	37.77	3
G. G. Atkinson (Somerset)	50	2	177	1797	37.43	3

*denotes not out
±denotes left-hand batsman

	Overs	M	Runs	Wkts	Av	BB
F. S. Trueman (Yorkshire)	844.3	206	1955	129	15.15	8–45
P. H. Parfitt (Middlesex)	105	31	286	18	15.88	5–33
K. E. Palmer (Somerset)	1018.5	289	2234	139	16.07	9–57
A. E. Moss (Middlesex)	642.5	249	1355	84	16.13	8–40
±D. A. D. Sydenham (Surrey)	819.1	239	1753	108	16.23	8–67
J. B. Statham (Lancashire)	791	168	1874	113	16.58	7–96
D. Shackleton (Hampshire)	1387.3	583	2446	146	16.75	7–30
J. D. F. Larter (Northamptonshire)	821.1	226	2028	121	16.76	8–41
A. G. Nicholson (Yorkshire)	589	180	1189	69	17.23	6–36
A. S. M. Oakman (Sussex)	408.2	136	953	55	17.32	6–53

±denotes left-arm bowler

ONE-DAY CRICKET BEGINS

Don Mosey: A momentous year . . . the first without amateurs . . . the beginning of limited-overs cricket for first-class cricketers . . . the centenary of Yorkshire County Cricket Club, and of *Wisden Cricketers' Almanack*.

Freddie Trueman: Ay, 100 years since we set up shop with a subscription of half-a-guinea a year and a couple of fixtures with Surrey. England had a great winter tour to Australia and New Zealand followed by a tremendous battle with the West Indies at home.

DM: Alan Smith of Warwickshire—today the Chief Executive of the Test and County Cricket Board—was England's wicket-keeper in four of the five Tests, making his debut in Brisbane. England won in Melbourne (Second Test), Australia in Sydney (Third) and the other three were drawn. Barrington topped the batting averages but Dexter, too, had a splendid tour. Harvey and Davidson ended their memorable Test careers for Australia, 'Davo' taking a wicket with his very last ball. Brian Statham overtook Alec Bedser's record of 236 wickets and ended the series with a total of 242, a fact which you noted

with personal interest, Fred. . . .

FST: Yes, my partner held the record for just under two months and I passed him in New Zealand. I thought it was fair enough because I had taken the catch which took 'George' past Bedser's record.

DM: All three Tests in New Zealand were won and you ended the tour with exactly 250 wickets in 56 Tests, now the leading wicket-taker in the world. Cowdrey averaged 146 in his four Test innings.

HALL AND GRIFFITH

FST: Keith Andrew, of Northamptonshire, was widely regarded as the outstanding wicket-keeper of his generation yet he only played twice in Tests—the first was in Australia in 1954 and the second was the First Test of 1963. There is no doubt at all that he was absolutely brilliant behind the stumps; in some ways his record is sadly like Les Jackson's. He kept at Old Trafford and the match was drawn and Jim Parks came back for the next four games. England won the Third Test, West Indies the

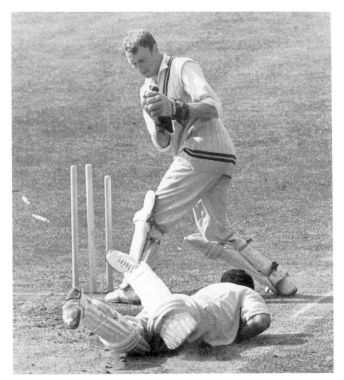

A. C. Smith, the wicket-keeper who took off his pads to bowl and did the hat-trick

Fourth and Fifth but most people remember the drawn Second at Lord's for its heroics. West Indies scored 301 and we replied with 297; in the second innings they made 229 so we needed 234 to win. Barrington followed his first innings 80 with another 60 but then came Brian Close's finest Test hour. As usual, he had worked out a theory of his own. Hall and Griffith, the most feared pair in world cricket at that time had given everybody trouble and Cowdrey had had his left forearm fractured when he had scored 19. Close decided to take on the fast bowling pair by walking down the pitch to meet them on the basis that (a) he couldn't be lbw and (b) it would put the bowlers off! He was absolutely black and blue the next day when we rejoined Yorkshire and the Press photographers filled the dressing-room to photograph him. But he got 70 of the bravest runs anybody will ever see and damn near won the game for England. But once he had been caught behind Hall took a couple of wickets and we ended with Cowdrey having to go out with his left arm in plaster to help us save it. Fortunately he didn't have to face a ball; we finished six runs short and the Windies couldn't take the last wicket (David Allen). It was a hell of a game.

DM: And modesty prevents Fred from pointing out that he took 11 for 152 in the match and 34 at 17.47 in the series. England had three new caps in the series—John

Edrich played in the first two Tests, Philip Sharpe in the last three and Brian Bolus in the last two. Sharpe had scored 1,872 runs for Yorkshire the previous season and held 71 slip catches. Bolus had joined Nottinghamshire from Yorkshire in 1963 and changed his previously rather painstaking style to one of a free-flowing bat. He on-drove his first ball in Test cricket for four! It was a tremendous series with great fast bowling on both sides and nearly half a million people watched it in spite of a lot of rain. To celebrate their centenary, *Wisden* awarded the Wisden Trophy for the winners of the England/West Indies series. I watched Fred bowl throughout the whole of his career and I can never remember him in more devastating form than the summer of 1963 when he was 32.

FST: It was a great year for the game of cricket. The Test series excited public interest to a greater extent than anything since Laker's 19 for 90. Frankie Worrell, the West Indies skipper, called it the greatest series he had ever played in. He was, for my money, by far the greatest skipper West Indies have ever had in terms of tactical skill *and* man-management. In the New Year's Honours List he became Sir Frank Worrell and at a reception for the West Indies the Lord Mayor of London (Sir Ralph Peering) said, 'A great gale of change has blown through the hallowed halls of cricket.' The series excited and stimulated me tremendously. Hall and Griffith, operating together, seemed to have provided an extra dimension to attacking cricket and somehow I was determined they weren't going to have all the limelight to themselves. You might say they inspired me. Everyone around the circuit was suspicious about the legality of Griffith's quicker ball and his yorker, but since no one called him we simply had to fight back with the weapons we had.

GILLETTE CUP

DM: The first games in the new knock-out competition were played on 1 May 1963 with Lancashire and Leicestershire (the two bottom championship sides of 1962) playing an eliminating match to reduce the number of teams involved to 16. The duration of each innings was 65 overs and as rain, inevitably, interfered at Old Trafford, the game went over into a second day. Lancashire (304 for nine) beat Leicestershire (203) by 101 runs. Lancashire went on to reach the semi-final but were beaten by Worcestershire who bowled them out for 59 and won by nine wickets. In the other semi-final, Sussex beat Northamptonshire by 105 runs with their captain, Ted Dexter, hitting 115. In the final Sussex beat Worcestershire by 14 runs watched by a full house at Lord's on 7 September and it is worth noting that the most economical bowlers were Gifford and Slade (slow left-arm) and Oakman (off-spin).

Surrey's M. D. Willett caught Sharpe bowled M. Ryan (Surrey v Yorkshire at The Oval)

Gifford, in fact, became the first Gillette Final 'Man of the Match', and he was on the losing side.

COUNTY CHAMPIONSHIP

FST: Because of the new competition it was impossible for counties to fit in 32 championship fixtures and the county championship reverted to a straightforward 28 games for each county. Bonus points were abolished and the methods of scoring became ten points for an outright win, two for first-innings lead in a match lost or drawn. Les Jackson was at last coming to the end of his fine career and Derbyshire plunged to the bottom of the table. Yorkshire scored their first success under Brian Close's captaincy and Glamorgan jumped 12 places into the runners-up position. Tony Lewis was now available after coming down from Cambridge and they had some work-manlike cricketers in Alan Jones, Bernard Hedges, Jim Pressdee to get the runs and Ossie Wheatley, Don

Shepherd and Jeff Jones, the fast left-armer, to do the bowling. As usual, they were an excellent fielding side.

BOYCOTT'S ARRIVAL

DM: Geoffrey Boycott had made his debut the previous season; now he was playing regularly and scoring heavily. Brian Bolus, in his first season with Nottinghamshire, topped 2,000 runs and they climbed six places up the table. Stuart Leary, of Kent, had a good season; he was a good South African-born all-round sportsman, playing soccer for Charlton Athletic and Queen's Park Rangers. Clive Inman was a left-hand batsman from Ceylon who hit the ball very hard and Graham Atkinson was an expatriate Yorkie who gave years of service to Somerset as an opening batsman. We see something of the emergence of

Somerset in the bowling figures, too. Ken Palmer was a consistent all-rounder who could open the bowling and the batting, too. He must have batted in every position from No. 1 to 11 during his career. Now a first-class and Test umpire.

FST: Eight of the top ten bowlers that year were medium-fast or quicker and as you can discount Parfitt's 18 wickets with questionable off-spin that leaves Alan Oakman as the most successful slow bowler around. *Wisden* had already blamed the lbw rule and the 75-yard boundaries (introduced *seven years earlier*) for the decline of slow left-arm and leg-spin bowling. Limited overs cricket was to get further blame for this decline and yet we have seen that the slow men were outstandingly useful in the first Gillette Final. Tony Nicholson came on the scene for Yorkshire—the best of my many opening partners and the best bowler never to play for England.

Sir Jack Hobbs and Sir Pelham ('Plum') Warner died in 1963.

Ossie Wheatley, a great worker for Glamorgan in many ways

1964

Winter Tour to India (1963–64):

Madras	Match drawn
Bombay	Match drawn
Calcutta	Match drawn
Delhi	Match drawn
Kanpur	Match drawn

Summer Series with Australia:

Trent Bridge	Match drawn
Lord's	Match drawn
Headingley	Australia won by seven wickets
Old Trafford	Match drawn
Oval	Match drawn

County Champions Worcestershire   **Gillette Cup** Sussex

TEST AVERAGES ENGLAND V INDIA 1963–64

	M	I	NO	HS	Runs	Av	100	50	Ct/St
M. C. Cowdrey	3	4	1	151	309	103.00	2	–	4
P. H. Parfitt	3	3	0	121	192	64.00	1	1	1
M. J. K. Smith	5	8	2	75*	306	51.00	–	2	4
J. B. Bolus	5	8	0	88	391	48.87	–	4	1
J. M. Parks	5	7	2	51*	211	42.20	–	1	7/2
J. B. Mortimore	3	4	1	73*	113	37.66	–	1	3
F. J. Titmus	5	6	2	84*	143	35.75	–	1	4
B. R. Knight	5	6	0	127	186	31.00	1	–	1
J. G. Binks	2	4	0	55	91	22.75	–	1	8/–
J. S. E. Price	4	3	1	32	33	16.50	–	–	2
D. Wilson	5	6	1	42	70	14.00	–	–	1
J. D. F. Larter	3	3	1	2*	2	1.00	–	–	2

Also batted: K. F. Barrington (1 match) 80; J. H. Edrich (2 matches) 41, 35, 1ct; I. J. Jones (1 match) 5; P. J. Sharpe (1 match) 27, 31*; M. J. Stewart (2 matches) 15.

	Overs	M	Runs	Wkts	Av	5w	10w	BB
J. S. E. Price	124.1	18	383	14	27.35	1	–	5–73
F. J. Titmus	398.5	156	747	27	27.66	2	–	6–73
D. Wilson	212	84	398	9	44.22	–	–	2–17
J. D. F. Larter	71.3	11	231	5	46.20	–	–	2–27
J. B. Mortimore	194	79	344	6	57.33	–	–	3–74
P. H. Parfitt	115	40	288	5	57.60	–	–	2–71
B. R. Knight	106.2	19	357	6	59.50	–	–	2–28

Also bowled: K. F. Barrington 6–0–29–0; J. B. Bolus 3–0–16–0; M. C. Cowdrey 5–0–34–0; J. H. Edrich 4–1–17–0; I. J. Jones 24–1–79–0; J. M. Parks 6–0–43–1; M. J. K. Smith 13–0–52–0.

TEST AVERAGES ENGLAND V AUSTRALIA 1964

	M	I	NO	HS	Runs	Av	100	50	Ct/St
K. F. Barrington	5	8	1	256	531	75.85	1	2	3
G. Boycott	4	6	0	113	291	48.50	1	1	–
E. R. Dexter	5	8	0	174	384	48.00	1	2	4
M. C. Cowdrey	3	5	1	93*	188	47.00	–	1	2
J. H. Edrich	3	4	0	120	161	40.25	1	–	1
P. J. Sharpe	2	3	1	35*	71	35.50	–	–	–
J. M. Parks	5	7	0	68	207	29.57	–	2	5/1
F. J. Titmus	5	8	0	56	138	17.25	–	1	1
P. H. Parfitt	4	5	0	32	73	14.60	–	–	7
F. S. Trueman	4	6	1	14	42	8.40	–	–	3
J. A. Flavell	2	3	0	7	17	5.66	–	–	–
N. Gifford	2	3	1	5	7	3.50	–	–	1

Also batted: D. A. Allen (1 match) 21, 3; R. W. Barber (1 match) 24, 29; T. W. Cartwright (2 matches) 4, 0; L. J. Coldwell (2 matches) 0*, 0*, 6*; J. B. Mortimore (1 match) 12; J. S. E. Price (2 matches) 1, 0*, 2ct; F. E. Rumsey (1 match) 3*; K. Taylor (1 match) 9, 15.

	Overs	M	Runs	Wkts	Av	5w	10w	BB
F. S. Trueman	133.3	25	399	17	23.47	1	–	5–48
N. Gifford	83	35	140	5	28.00	–	–	2–14
F. J. Titmus	202	92	301	10	30.10	–	–	4–69
T. W. Cartwright	139	55	228	5	45.60	–	–	3–110

Also bowled: D. A. Allen 16–8–22–1; R. W. Barber 6–1–23–0; K. F. Barrington 1–0–4–0; G. Boycott 1–0–3–0; L. J. Coldwell 64–14–158–4; E. R. Dexter 49–7–118–3; J. A. Flavell 49.2–8–136–2; J. B. Mortimore 49–13–122–0; J. S. E. Price 66–6–250–4; F. E. Rumsey 35.5–4–99–2; K. Taylor 2–0–6–0.

CHAMPIONSHIP TABLE 1964

					First Inns Lead in Match			
	P	Won	Lost	D	NR	Lost	D	Pts
Points Awarded	–	10	–	–	–	2	2	–
WORCESTERSHIRE (14)	28	18	3	6	1	0	5	191±
Warwickshire (4)	28	14	5	9	0	0	5	150
Northamptonshire (7)	28	12	4	11	1	0	5	130
Surrey (11)	28	11	3	13	1	0	9	129±
Yorkshire (1)	28	11	3	14	0	0	8	126
Middlesex (6)	28	9	6	12	1	2	9	112
Kent (13)	28	9	6	12	1	3	6	108
Somerset (3)	28	8	8	8	4	4	4	96
Sussex (4)	28	8	9	10	1	1	3	88
Essex (12)	28	7	11	8	2	5	3	86
Glamorgan (2)	28	7	7	12	2	1	6	84
Derbyshire (17)	28	5	9	12	2	4	5	68
Hampshire (10)	28	5	8	14	1	1	5	68*@
Lancashire (15)	28	4	10	13	1	4	8	64
Nottinghamshire (9)	28	4	13	11	0	3	4	54
Leicestershire (16)	28	3	18	5	2	7	0	44
Gloucestershire (8)	28	3	15	10	0	2	4	43*

± includes one point for tie on first innings in match drawn
* includes one point for tie on first innings in match lost
@ includes five points for fourth innings of drawn match when the final scores were level
1963 positions are shown in brackets

FIRST-CLASS AVERAGES 1964

	I	NO	HS	Runs	Av	100
K. F. Barrington (Surrey)	35	5	256	1872	62.40	4
B. L. D'Oliveira (Worcestershire)	8	2	119	370	61.66	2
M. C. Cowdrey (Kent)	37	5	117	1763	55.09	4
T. W. Graveney (Worcestershire)	51	7	164	2385	54.20	5
G. Boycott (Yorkshire)	44	4	177	2110	52.75	6
M. J. Stewart (Surrey)	44	5	227*	1980	50.76	6
±R. C. Wilson (Kent)	49	5	156	2038	46.31	4
W. E. Russell (Middlesex)	56	5	193	2342	45.92	5
M. D. Willett (Surrey)	51	12	126	1789	45.87	4
J. M. Brearley (Camb U/Middlesex)	54	5	169	2178	44.44	5

	Overs	M	Runs	Wkts	Av	BB
J. A. Standen (Worcestershire)	422.2	131	832	64	13.00	7–34
L. J. Coldwell (Worcestershire)	736.1	211	1518	98	15.48	7–25
A. G. Nicholson (Yorkshire)	581.4	159	1193	76	15.69	7–32
T. W. Cartwright (Warwickshire)	1146.2	502	2141	134	15.97	7–28
N. I. Thomson (Sussex)	925.5	293	1891	116	16.30	10–49
±J. C. Balderstone (Yorkshire)	81.1	37	187	11	17.00	3–28
F. J. Titmus (Middlesex)	1135.3	441	2106	123	17.12	9–57
R. Illingworth (Yorkshire)	1012.2	374	2131	122	17.46	7–49
±C. Forbes (Nottinghamshire)	442.3	143	950	53	17.92	7–80
J. A. Flavell (Worcestershire)	786.3	170	1934	107	18.07	9–56

Geoffrey Boycott, England's highest scorer of Test runs (8, 114)

Freddie Trueman: The heat and humidity of Madras was not the best place to play the first Test of the '63–64 tour of India when the English players had just left England in the very heart of mid-winter. Within days of the tour starting, several players were down with stomach upsets; by the time the Second Test took place in Bombay the party was reduced to ten fit men. Four of my Yorkshire colleagues (Phil Sharpe, Jimmy Binks, Don Wilson and Brian Bolus) were on the tour and I can tell you it was miserable.

Don Mosey: Mike Smith was England's latest captain and whatever plans he had for his Test side went out of the window in Bombay because Edrich, Sharpe, John Mortimore (the Gloucestershire off-spinner), Barrington and Mickey Stewart all had upsets of one form or another and the ten available men were the ones who played. That's how Jimmy Binks, the Yorkshire wicket-keeper, made his Test debut alongside Jeff Jones from Glamorgan, and John Price the big Middlesex fast bowler. Reinforcements were summoned from England and Parfitt and Cowdrey arrived in time for the Third Test to replace Barrington and Stewart, who took no further part in the tour. All five Tests were drawn and I imagine most of the men who undertook the tour would prefer to forget it. At least it gave England's batsmen a first glimpse of Chandrasekhar who was to torment them with his right-arm leg breaks and assorted funny stuff in the future.

FST: The two batsmen who arrived late, Parfitt and Cowdrey, were the men who came out best in the averages but once again it was an off-spinner who took most wickets—Fred Titmus getting 27. Not so much success for the left-armer, Don Wilson, but at least he got his maiden first-class hundred on the tour in a game in Hyderabad. Later he became chief coach at Lord's.

BOYCOTT'S TEST CAREER BEGINS

DM: Geoffrey Boycott played the first of his 108 Tests at Trent Bridge to start the 1964 series against Bobby Simpson's Australians. His first opening partner was Fred Titmus! This happened because Edrich was unfit so it delayed the start of England's most consistent and reliable opening partnership since Hutton and Washbrook

FST: It was a pretty poor summer, as I recall. There was rain all through the First Test and no play at all on the first two days at Lord's so not surprisingly both were drawn. And there was a remarkable number of injuries during the series. Apart from having to open the batting at Trent Bridge, Titmus had to open the bowling at Headingley as another emergency measure. That was the only match to provide a result and the Aussies won.

DM: For the Fourth Test at Old Trafford the Selectors decided on a new opening pair of John Price, who had

done well in India, and Fred Rumsey, the left-arm quickie from Somerset. You would be glad to sit that one out, Fred. . . .

FST: You are quite correct, Don. Only 19 wickets fell while 1271 runs were scored and that wasn't the sort of pitch that I really enjoy. Rumsey and Tom Cartwright, the third seamer, on their joint debut, together with Price, bowled a total of 157 overs. When England batted Tom Veivers, the Queensland off-spinner, got through 95 overs, and Graham McKenzie, the No. 1 strike bowler, had to bowl 70. At least he had figures of seven for 153 to show for his efforts. That was fine bowling on a horrible killer of a pitch.

DM: Bobby Simpson's 311 for Australia was remarkable in that he had never scored a century in 51 previous Test innings so he certainly made up for lost time. He was out there for nearly 12¾ hours and when you think what an obdurate batsman his partner, Bill Lawry, was, it must have been utterly heart-breaking for the England attack. Simpson and Lawry put on 201 before the first wicket fell—and that was Lawry, run out. And so to an historic Test at The Oval where Cowdrey got his 5,000th Test run. Barrington his 4,000th and Boycott his first century—but the rest of it is your story, Fred.

FST: I had 297 wickets when I started that game on 13 August. We were bowled out for 182 with Neil Hawke taking six for 47 and the Aussies then started the slow grind to put themselves in an unassailable position. They were one up in the series and they weren't going to lose the

Tom Cartwright, a fine-all-rounder and coach

last match. It was getting close to lunch on the Saturday and I could see Ted Dexter was wondering what to do next. It seemed as though he was going to ask Parfitt to bowl his comic off-spinners and I just couldn't have that. I virtually snatched the ball out of his hand, bowled off the short run and got one to cut back and bowl Ian Redpath—298 wickets. In came 'Garth' McKenzie and Cowdrey caught him at slip first ball—299 and now I was on a hat-trick as well. But the luncheon interval was now taken. I sat through it with a cup of tea thinking about a record 300 test wickets and the possibility of my fifth hat-trick. They were very happy thoughts. Upstairs, the next batsman—my good friend Neil Hawke (we had become good friends during the 1962–63 tour of Australia when he made his debut in Sydney)—was thinking, too. He was a modest man and he reasoned: 'No one's ever going to remember me for what I have done in Test cricket but the man who becomes Fred's 300th victim will be remembered for all time.' But he wasn't going to give anything away, of course. He was an Australian.

My first ball to him after lunch went past the off-stump and he didn't have to play a shot. The waiting hadn't done my concentration much good. He got 14 runs before I found the edge, Cowdrey took the catch—and that was No. 300. Hawkeye grinned at me, 'Well done, mate. I should be all right for champagne now, eh?'

DM: To put Fred's achievement in perspective, let us record that it had been done in 65 Tests. Not only had no one ever done it before but at the rate players came and went in the England side (and others, too) it seemed highly improbable that anyone would ever do it again. We did not know that in less than 20 years Tests would be played all round the world almost on a treadmill basis with sometimes two separate series in one winter. We did not know that players would be selected automatically in one Test after another for years on end because the competition for England places had virtually disappeared. Fred's 65 Tests had been spread over 13 seasons; his striking rate was four-and-a-half wickets per Test and his average of 21.57 was achieved despite the fact that he was essentially an attacking bowler with much of his bowling being carried out with fiercely attacking fields.

WORCESTERSHIRE'S CHAMPIONSHIP

FST: Worcestershire's first championship title came that year by a clear margin of 41 points in the new scoring system. They had been threatening for a couple of years and with three bowlers in the top ten it was not surprising

Norman Gifford, a new career at Edgbaston after 22 years with Worcestershire

The outstanding close catchers in action—Philip Sharpe (Yorkshire) and Mickey Stewart (Surrey)

to see them pull it off at last. Coldwell and Flavell were Test bowlers, Jim Standen was a medium pacer for whom 1964 was a big year. He not only topped the averages and won a championship medal but he kept goal for West Ham United in the FA Cup Final at Wembley. A championship and a Cup-winners medal in the same year—a unique double. Tony Nicholson crept up to third in the order with his out-swingers and off-cutters and Tom Cartwright had taken over from Derek Shackleton as the outstanding exponent of accurate medium pace bowling, doing a little bit in the air and a little bit off the seam. Carlton Forbes, a genial Jamaican who bowled left arm medium pace was a useful all-rounder for Nottinghamshire and, taking out the nominal figures of Chris Balderstone (at that time a Yorkshire Colt—he later went to Leicestershire), the two outstanding off-spinners in the country, Titmus and Illingworth, are the only slow bowlers in the list.

ENTER D'OLIVEIRA

DM: Tom Graveney's 2,385 runs played a major part in Worcestershire's success; Basil D'Oliveira's average of 61.66 played no part at all because he was still qualifying for the county after coming over from South Africa to play Central Lancashire League cricket. His runs were scored in 1964 in non-championship matches but he was soon to become an outstanding all-rounder for England. Boycott, now capped by Yorkshire and England, hit six centuries, a figure equalled only by Mickey Stewart in a generally wet summer.

GILLETTE CUP

FST: Sussex won their second Gillette beating Warwickshire by eight wickets, and everyone started to think a little more about this sort of cricket. Ted Dexter, ever a great theorist, seemed to have organised a funnel-shaped field stretching outwards from the batsman and ordered his bowlers to pitch the ball up so that the stroke to play was the drive—into the funnel. Clearly there was more to this cricket than simply bowling well and batting well!

Winter Tour to South Africa (1964–65):

Durban	England won by an innings & 104 runs
Johannesburg	Match drawn
Cape Town	Match drawn
Johannesburg	Match drawn
Port Elizabeth	Match drawn

Summer Series with New Zealand:

Edgbaston	England won by nine wickets
Lord's	England won by seven wickets
Headingley	England won by an innings & 187 runs

South Africa:

Lord's	Match drawn
Trent Bridge	South Africa won by 94 runs
Oval	Match drawn

County Champions   Worcestershire

Gillette Cup   Yorkshire

TEST AVERAGES ENGLAND V SOUTH AFRICA 1964–65

	M	I	NO	HS	Runs	Av	100	50	Ct/St
K. F. Barrington	5	7	2	148*	508	101.60	2	2	3
R. W. Barber	4	4	0	97	290	72.50	–	4	6
E. R. Dexter	5	7	1	172	344	57.33	1	1	4
G. Boycott	5	8	2	117	298	49.66	1	2	2
P. H. Parfitt	5	6	1	122*	240	48.00	1	1	3
J. M. Parks	5	6	1	108*	238	47.60	1	1	8/–
M. J. K. Smith	5	6	0	121	257	42.83	1	–	10
D. A. Allen	4	3	1	38*	62	31.00	–	–	1
N. I. Thomson	5	4	1	39	69	23.00	–	–	3
F. J. Titmus	5	5	0	13	32	6.40	–	–	2

Also batted: T. W. Cartwright (1 match) 9, 8*, 2ct; K. E. Palmer (1 match) 10; J. S. E. Price (4 matches) 0, 0*, 0, 2ct; J. T. Murray (1 match) 4, 8*.

	Overs	M	Runs	Wkts	Av	5w	10w	BB
D. A. Allen	255.5	87	458	17	26.94	1	–	5–41
G. Boycott	61	16	157	5	31.40	–	–	3–47
F. J. Titmus	309.1	88	694	18	38.55	1	–	5–66
J. S. E. Price	138	35	417	8	52.12	–	–	2–66
N. I. Thomson	248	68	568	9	63.11	–	–	2–55

Also bowled: R. W. Barber 37–4–103–3; K. F. Barrington 7.1–1–33–3; T. W. Cartwright 79–24–196–2; E. R. Dexter 37–3–153–2; K. E. Palmer 63–7–189–1; P. H. Parfitt 33–6–114–1; M. J. K. Smith 11–1–43–0.

TEST AVERAGES ENGLAND V NEW ZEALAND 1965

	M	I	NO	HS	Runs	Av	100	50	Ct/St
E. R. Dexter	2	4	2	80*	199	99.50	–	3	1
M. C. Cowdrey	3	4	1	119	211	73.66	1	1	2
G. Boycott	2	4	1	76	157	52.33	–	1	–
R. W. Barber	3	5	0	51	142	28.40	–	1	2
M. J. K. Smith	3	3	1	44	46	23.00	–	–	3
F. J. Titmus	3	3	0	13	27	9.00	–	–	4

Also batted: K. F. Barrington (2 matches) 137, 163, 3ct; T. W. Cartwright (1 match) 4; J. H. Edrich (1 match) 310*; P. H. Parfitt (2 matches) 11, 32, 1ct; J. M. Parks (3 matches) 34, 2, 10ct/1st; F. E. Rumsey (3 matches) 21*, 3; J. A. Snow (1 match) 2*, 1ct; F. S. Trueman (2 matches) 3, 3, 1ct. R. Illingworth and J. D. F. Larter played in one match but did not bat.

	Overs	M	Runs	Wkts	Av	5w	10w	BB
F. J. Titmus	171	85	234	15	15.60	1	–	5–19
J. D. F. Larter	50.1	16	120	6	20.00	–	–	4–66
F. E. Rumsey	104	32	229	9	25.44	–	–	4–25
R. W. Barber	100	36	236	9	26.22	–	–	4–132
F. S. Trueman	96.3	23	237	6	39.50	–	–	3–79

Also bowled: K. F. Barrington 5–0–25–0; T. W. Cartwright 19–9–26–2; E. R. Dexter 13–3–45–1; R. Illingworth 35–14–70–4; P. H. Parfitt 6–2–25–1; J. A. Snow 35–6–80–4.

TEST AVERAGES ENGLAND V SOUTH AFRICA 1965

	M	I	NO	HS	Runs	Av	100	50	Ct/St
M. C. Cowdrey	3	6	1	105	327	65.40	1	2	5
P. H. Parfitt	2	4	0	86	174	43.50	–	1	2
K. F. Barrington	3	6	0	91	202	33.66	–	2	5
J. M. Parks	3	5	1	44*	131	32.75	–	–	4/1
F. J. Titmus	3	5	2	59	94	31.33	–	1	4
R. W. Barber	3	6	0	56	172	28.66	–	1	2
M. J. K. Smith	3	6	1	32	112	22.40	–	–	2
G. Boycott	2	4	0	31	75	18.75	–	–	–
J. D. F. Larter	2	3	1	10	12	6.00	–	–	1
D. J. Brown	2	3	0	5	6	2.00	–	–	1

Also batted: L. T. W. Cartwright (1 match) 1*, 0; J. H. Edrich (1 match) 0, 7*, 1ct; K. Higgs (1 match) 2; W. E. Russell (1 match) 0, 70; F. E. Rumsey (1 match) 3, 0*; J. A. Snow (1 match) 3, 0; J. B. Statham (1 match) 0.

	Overs	M	Runs	Wkts	Av	5w	10w	BB
T. W. Cartwright	31.3	9	94	6	15.66	1	–	6–94
K. Higgs	65.1	13	143	8	17.87	–	–	4–47
J. B. Statham	53.2	12	145	7	20.71	1	–	5–40
F. E. Rumsey	51	17	133	6	22.16	–	–	3–49
D. J. Brown	90	27	200	8	25.00	–	–	3–30
J. D. F. Larter	89	25	207	7	29.57	1	–	5–68
F. J. Titmus	149.4	51	316	8	39.50	–	–	2–46

Also bowled: R. W. Barber 60.3–12–193–3; G. Boycott 26–10–70–0; J. A. Snow 55–12–146–4.

CHAMPIONSHIP TABLE 1965

						First Inns Lead in Match		
	P	Won	Lost	D	NR	Lost	D	Pts
Points Awarded	–	10	–	–	–	2	2	–
WORCESTERSHIRE (1)	28	13	4	10	1	1	6	144
Northamptonshire (3)	28	13	4	9	2	0	5	140
Glamorgan (11)	28	12	6	8	2	2	4	132
Yorkshire (5)	28	9	4	14	1	1	11	114
Kent (7)	28	8	5	14	1	0	8	96
Middlesex (6)	28	8	7	12	1	0	7	94
Somerset (8)	28	8	11	8	1	2	4	92
Surrey (4)	28	7	4	15	2	1	8	92±
Derbyshire (12)	28	7	9	11	1	2	6	86
Gloucestershire (17)	28	7	8	11	2	1	5	82
Warwickshire (2)	28	5	5	18	0	1	9	70
Hampshire (12)	28	5	4	17	2	0	8	66
Lancashire (14)	28	5	13	9	1	0	5	60
Leicestershire (16)	28	5	11	11	1	2	2	58
Essex (10)	28	4	7	16	1	0	7	54
Sussex (9)	28	4	10	14	0	2	4	52
Nottinghamshire (15)	28	3	11	13	1	3	6	48

± includes six points for first innings lead in match restricted by rain to last third of time allotted
1964 positions are shown in brackets

FIRST-CLASS AVERAGES 1965

	I	NO	HS	Runs	Av	100
M. C. Cowdrey (Kent)	43	10	196*	2093	63.42	5
±J. H. Edrich (Surrey)	44	7	310*	2319	62.67	8
±P. H. Parfitt (Middlesex)	44	9	128	1774	50.68	3
T. W. Graveney (Worcestershire)	45	9	126	1768	49.11	4
M. D. Willett (Surrey)	9	3	83*	271	45.16	–
B. L. D'Oliveira (Worcestershire)	45	6	163	1691	43.35	6
E. R. Dexter (Sussex)	19	3	98	676	42.25	–
B. L. Reed (Hampshire)	9	1	79	334	41.75	–
W. E. Russell (Middlesex)	54	5	156	1930	39.38	4
W. J. Stewart (Warwickshire)	39	8	102	1187	38.29	1

*denotes not out
±denotes left-hand batsman

	Overs	M	Runs	Wkts	Av	BB
H. J. Rhodes (Derbyshire)	646.5	187	1314	119	11.04	7–38
A. B. Jackson (Derbyshire)	807.5	262	1491	120	12.42	7–32(2)
J. B. Statham (Lancashire)	771	205	1716	137	12.52	8–69
T. W. Cartwright (Warwickshire)	735.1	305	1505	108	13.93	8–59
F. S. Trueman (Yorkshire)	754.4	180	1811	127	14.25	8–36
J. A. Flavell (Worcestershire)	910	217	2100	142	14.78	8–74
J. D. F. Larter (Northamptonshire)	589.2	169	1333	87	15.32	8–28
D. J. Shepherd (Glamorgan)	1062.2	460	1765	112	15.75	9–48
±I. J. Jones (Glamorgan)	654.3	203	1336	84	15.90	8–11
D. Shackleton (Hampshire)	1246	529	2316	144	16.08	7–32

±denotes left-arm bowler

THE AGE OF THE POLLOCKS

Freddie Trueman: Graeme Pollock was to become one of the finest international batsmen of all time (and, incidentally, to start the trend towards heavier bats) so it was a disappointment not to go to South Africa in the winter of 1964–65. Bradman's bats weighed 2lb 4oz, I believe, while Len Hutton used one weighing 2lb 2oz, Everton Weekes 2lb 3oz. Pollock, a big, broad-shouldered man, introduced bats several ounces heavier, which in turn developed into the monsters of more than 3lb which are popular today. Is it any wonder no one plays the late cut any more? My Yorkshire partner, Tony Nicholson, was picked for the tour then had to withdraw because he was unfit and he never got another chance to play for his country. Ian Thomson, of Sussex, had had a good summer in 1964 which won him a place and he made his debut in Durban in the only Test of the tour which brought a result.

Don Mosey: A win for England by an innings and 104 was really the work of the two off-spinners, Titmus and Allen,

but Ken Barrington's 148 not out meant that he had now scored a hundred in all seven Test-playing countries—the first man to do so. In the Second Test (Johannesburg) Dexter scored what was to be his ninth and last international hundred and he had made at least one against all the other six Test-playing countries. Mike Smith led his second successive winter tour abroad and enhanced his reputation as a splendid tour captain. In his home town of Port Elizabeth Graeme Pollock made his third Test hundred before he had reached the age of 21 and his elder, fast-bowling brother Peter took 12 wickets in the series. In the Final Test, with three men injured, England called up Ken Palmer, who was coaching in Johannesburg, to open the bowling with Thomson, and thus the Somerset man won his only Test cap.

DOUBLE TOUR

FST: The summer of 1965, which began with the most miserable weather, saw a double tour with New Zealand

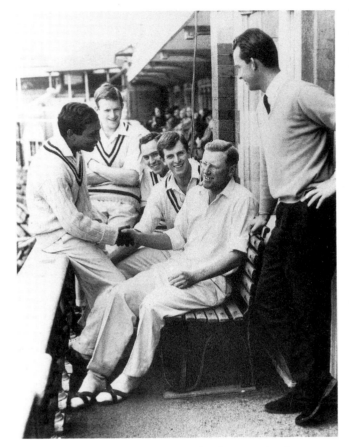

Congratulations to M. J. K. Smith on his England captaincy appointment from Warwickshire colleagues Ibadulla, Amiss, Jameson, D. J. Brown and Bob Barber

and South Africa playing three Tests each. Barrington's 137 at Edgbaston took him 437 minutes and he was dropped by the Selectors for the next Test as a disciplinary measure against his slow batting. England won by nine wickets. The final Test of my career was the Second, at Lord's. The 306th and 307th wickets were both clean bowled—Bruce Taylor and Richard Collinge—and I was glad to be able to go out in style at Headquarters.

DM: And in the same game we saw for the first time John Snow, of Sussex, who was to become England's new main strike bowler. England won all three Tests against New Zealand but South Africa took their rubber with a win at Trent Bridge with the other two games drawn.

FIELDING AS AN ART FORM

FST: Colin Bland, the South African cover point, showed us new standards of fielding at international level in the second half of the summer. His lightning pick-up and brilliantly accurate throwing were talked about everywhere. A big crowd at Lord's will certainly remem-

ber how he ran out Barrington and Parks by the speed and accuracy of his throwing.

DM: Then, at Trent Bridge, the Pollock brothers demolished England, with Graeme, going in at 16 for two, stroking 125 glorious runs out of 160 while he was at the wicket. It was a privilege to see that innings. Brother Peter took five wickets in each innings (for 53 and 35 respectively) and as their father was a newspaper editor in Port Elizabeth he would enjoy reading his own headlines. South Africa won by 94 runs despite an innings of 86 by Parfitt. At The Oval rain prevented what might well have been an England win to square the series. Statham was recalled by England after an absence of 20 Tests and this proved to be his last one. He retired from the international scene to skipper Lancashire with 252 wickets in 70 Tests. England were never to play South Africa again and the glories of Graeme Pollock's batting were lost to a whole generation of cricket-watchers.

John Snow, England's outstanding fast bowler in the late 1960s and early 1970s

WORCESTERSHIRE'S TITLE AGAIN

FST: Worcestershire won their second title in succession and this time it was Jack Flavell's turn to be their leading bowler, and while Tommy Cartwright was certainly going to take over the 'Shack' role in the future, the old warhorse showed he was by no means finished by taking 144 wickets. Derbyshire had by now found another Jackson—Brian, no relation to Les—who that year had the best of his six seasons with the county. With his partner, Harold Rhodes, topping the list, in *his* best season, you might have expected to see Derbyshire doing better than ninth place but they just couldn't score runs quickly enough. With Larter doing well, Northamptonshire climbed up to second place and were only a whisker away from winning what would have been their first honour in the game and Glamorgan's improvement was a reflection of the bowling of Jeff Jones and Don Shepherd.

DM: Cowdrey, now in his 16th season, made it his best in terms of runs scored and Basil D'Oliveira, now qualified for Worcestershire, hit six hundreds, more than anyone except John Edrich. I am glad to see the name of Jim Stewart in the list. Six years earlier I had paid a random visit to Stanley Park, Blackpool, to watch Lancashire play Warwickshire and Stewart had treated a holiday crowd to ten sixes. Dexter at this time was having some injury problems and increasingly developing business interests so that his appetite for full-time cricket was beginning to wane. Indeed, he made that his last full season and it was a great loss; he had been an outstanding entertainer in the purest cricket sense. Barry Reed, the Hampshire opener, had learned a sound technique at Winchester and his best years were still to come.

GILLETTE CUP

FST: I can't claim that we had now mastered the special art of limited-overs cricket. We still believed the game was about bowling the other side out rather than containing them but it worked for us in 1965 when we dismissed the opposition in all four games. The competition had been reduced to 60 overs a side and has remained at that up to the present time.

DM: Boycott's innings of 146 remained his outstanding achievement in terms of stroke-making in his 25-year career and seven of the Surrey wickets fell to spin bowling.

ICC

DM: In 1965 the Imperial Cricket Conference, which had existed since 1909 (founder-members England, Australia and South Africa), was renamed the *International* Cricket Conference and empowered to elect, as full or associate members, countries outside the Commonwealth. The first associate members were the USA, Ceylon and Fiji.

David Larter, Northants' giant fast bowler

1966

Winter Tour to Australia (1965–66):

Brisbane	Match drawn
Melbourne	Match drawn
Sydney	England won by an innings & 93 runs
Adelaide	Australia won by an innings & 9 runs
Melbourne	Match drawn

New Zealand:

Christchurch	Match drawn
Dunedin	Match drawn
Auckland	Match drawn

Summer Series with West Indies:

Old Trafford	West Indies won by an innings & 40 runs
Lord's	Match drawn
Trent Bridge	West Indies won by 139 runs
Headingley	West Indies won by an innings & 55 runs
Oval	England won by an innings & 34 runs

County Champions Yorkshire

Gillette Cup Warwickshire

TEST AVERAGES ENGLAND V AUSTRALIA 1965–66

	M	I	NO	HS	Runs	Av	100	50	Ct/St
K. F. Barrington	5	8	1	115	464	66.28	2	3	3
F. J. Titmus	5	6	2	60	258	64.50	–	3	5
M. C. Cowdrey	4	6	1	104	267	53.40	1	1	5
J. M. Parks	5	6	0	89	290	48.33	–	3	12/3
J. H. Edrich	5	8	0	109	375	46.87	2	1	4
G. Boycott	5	9	2	84	300	42.85	–	3	1
R. W. Barber	5	9	1	185	328	41.00	1	–	4
D. A. Allen	4	5	2	50*	62	20.66	–	1	1
M. J. K. Smith	5	7	1	41	107	17.83	–	–	4
I. J. Jones	4	5	2	16	29	9.66	–	–	–
D. J. Brown	4	5	0	12	17	3.40	–	–	–

Also batted: K. Higgs (1 match) 4; B. R. Knight (2 matches) 1, 13; W. E. Russell (1 match) 0*.

	Overs	M	Runs	Wkts	Av	5w	10w	BB
B. R. Knight	83.7	10	250	8	31.25	–	–	4–84
I. J. Jones	129	15	533	15	35.53	1	–	6–118
D. J. Brown	108	14	409	11	37.18	1	–	5–63
D. A. Allen	137	33	403	9	44.77	–	–	4–47
F. J. Titmus	210.3	52	517	9	57.44	–	–	4–40

Also bowled: R. W. Barber 55.1–2–261–3; K. F. Barrington 7.4–0–47–2; G. Boycott 23–4–89–2; K. Higgs 30–6–102–2; M. J. K. Smith 2–0–8–0.

TEST AVERAGES ENGLAND V NEW ZEALAND 1965–66

	M	I	NO	HS	Runs	Av	100	50	Ct/St
J. M. Parks	2	4	2	45*	117	58.50	–	–	11/–
D. A. Allen	3	3	1	88	104	52.00	–	1	–
M. C. Cowdrey	3	5	1	89*	196	49.00	–	2	2
M. J. K. Smith	3	5	0	87	209	41.80	–	2	8
P. H. Parfitt	3	5	1	54	137	34.25	–	1	2
B. R. Knight	2	3	1	25	50	25.00	–	–	3
W. E. Russell	3	5	0	56	123	24.60	–	1	3
J. H. Edrich	3	3	0	36	40	13.33	–	–	–
K. Higgs	3	3	2	8*	8	8.00	–	–	2
G. Boycott	2	3	0	5	13	4.33	–	–	2

Also batted: D. J. Brown (2 matches) 44, 0, 1ct; I. J. Jones (3 matches) 0, 0, 1ct; J. T. Murray (1 match) 50, 4ct.

	Overs	M	Runs	Wkts	Av	5w	10w	BB
K. Higgs	128	50	157	17	9.23	–	–	4–9
I. J. Jones	122.4	40	242	14	17.28	–	–	4–71
D. J. Brown	60.1	14	126	6	21.00	–	–	3–80
D. A. Allen	190.4	72	359	13	27.61	1	–	5–123

Also bowled: G. Boycott 12–6–30–0; J. H. Edrich 1–0–6–0; B. R. Knight 69–32–105–3; P. H. Parfitt 28–9–58–3; J. M. Parks 3–1–8–0.

TEST AVERAGES ENGLAND V WEST INDIES 1966

	M	I	NO	HS	Runs	Av	100	50	Ct/St
T. W. Graveney	4	7	1	165	459	76.50	1	1	5
C. Milburn	4	8	2	126*	316	52.66	1	1	2
B. L. D'Oliveira	4	6	0	88	256	42.66	–	3	2
R. W. Barber	2	3	0	55	97	32.33	–	1	2
M. C. Cowdrey	4	8	0	96	252	31.50	–	2	3
G. Boycott	4	7	0	71	186	26.57	–	2	–
J. M. Parks	4	8	0	91	181	22.62	–	1	9/–
J. A. Snow	3	5	2	59*	62	20.66	–	1	–
K. Higgs	5	8	0	63	147	18.37	–	1	1
W. E. Russell	2	4	0	26	61	15.25	–	–	1
K. F. Barrington	2	4	0	30	59	14.75	–	–	–
F. J. Titmus	3	5	0	22	61	12.20	–	–	3
D. L. Underwood	2	4	2	12*	22	11.00	–	–	2
R. Illingworth	2	3	0	4	7	2.33	–	–	2

Also batted: D. A. Allen (1 match) 37, 1; D. L. Amiss (1 match) 17; D. J. Brown (1 match) 14, 10; D. B. Close (1 match) 4, 1ct; J. H. Edrich (1 match) 35, 1ct; I. J. Jones (2 matches) 0*, 0*, 0*; B. R. Knight (1 match) 6, 1ct; J. T. Murray (1 match) 112, 3ct; M. J. K. Smith (1 match) 5, 6, 2ct.

	Overs	M	Runs	Wkts	Av	5w	10w	BB
K. Higgs	236.4	49	611	24	25.45	1	–	6–91
R. W. Barber	51.1	7	182	6	30.33	–	–	3–49
J. A. Snow	138.5	29	451	12	37.58	–	–	4–82
F. J. Titmus	81	20	190	5	38.00	1	–	5–83
B. L. D'Oliveira	160	48	329	8	41.12	–	–	2–51

Also bowled: D. A. Allen 31.1–8–104–2; D. J. Brown 28–4–84–0; D. B. Close 12–3–28–1; R. Illingworth 63–24–165–4; I. J. Jones 74–11–259–1; B. R. Knight 51–3–169–4; D. L. Underwood 69–25–172–1.

CHAMPIONSHIP TABLE 1966

	P	Won	Lost	D	NR	First Inns Lead	Pts
Points Awarded	–	10	–	–	–	2	–
YORKSHIRE (4)	28	15	5	8	0	17	184
Worcestershire (1)	28	13	5	9	1	18	166
Somerset (7)	28	13	7	7	1	13	156
Kent (5)	28	11	8	8	1	17	144
Northamptonshire (2)	28	10	9	9	0	15	130
Warwickshire (11)	28	8	8	10	2	16	113±
Surrey (8)	28	8	3	16	1	15	110
Leicestershire (14)	28	8	7	12	1	14	108
Derbyshire (9)	28	8	12	7	1	8	96
Sussex (16)	28	6	11	11	0	16	92
Hampshire (12)	28	5	4	18	1	16	87*
Lancashire (13)	28	6	11	8	3	13	86
Middlesex (6)	28	6	5	14	3	13	86
Glamorgan (3)	28	6	8	13	1	10	85*
Gloucestershire (10)	28	6	12	9	1	7	75±
Essex (15)	28	4	10	11	3	10	60
Nottinghamshire (17)	28	3	11	12	2	8	46

± includes one point for tie on first innings
* includes five points for fourth innings in drawn matches when final scores were level
1965 positions are shown in brackets

FIRST-CLASS AVERAGES 1966

	I	NO	HS	Runs	Av	100
T. W. Graveney (Worcestershire)	40	6	166	1777	52.26	4
C. Milburn (Northamptonshire)	44	6	203	1861	48.97	6
W. J. Stewart (Warwickshire)	14	3	166	505	45.90	1
M. J. K. Smith (Warwickshire)	50	9	140	1824	44.48	4
±J. H. Edrich (Surrey)	49	3	137	1978	43.00	3
A. R. Lewis (Glamorgan)	61	8	223	2198	41.47	5
±P. H. Parfitt (Middlesex)	57	8	114*	2018	41.18	2
R. M. Prideaux (Northamptonshire)	55	7	153*	1947	40.56	6
G. Boycott (Yorkshire)	50	3	164	1854	39.44	6
B. L. D'Oliveira (Worcestershire)	45	5	126	1536	38.40	2

	Overs	M	Runs	Wkts	Av	BB
±D. L. Underwood (Kent)	1104.5	475	2167	157	13.80	9–37
J. A. Flavell (Worcestershire)	822.3	199	1891	135	14.00	7–36
J. B. Statham (Lancashire)	624.4	135	1479	102	14.50	7–24
A. G. Nicholson (Yorkshire)	879.3	297	1752	113	15.50	6–32
O. S. Wheatley (Glamorgan)	865.3	269	1642	103	15.94	6–27
±N. Gifford (Worcestershire)	806.5	366	1458	91	16.02	8–54
D. J. Shepherd (Glamorgan)	1025.1	427	1844	111	16.61	7–7
D. R. Smith (Gloucestershire)	358.1	73	947	57	16.61	6–34
R. Illingworth (Yorkshire)	830.1	316	1680	100	16.80	6–30
Mushtaq Mohammad (Northants)	403	113	976	57	17.12	5–48

LAWRY'S MARATHONS

Freddie Trueman: England's opening attack in Australia in the winter of 1965–66 was now David Brown and Jeff Jones (in four Tests) and Brown and Ken Higgs in the other and the way Bill Lawry batted in that series, they were welcome to the job. He was a hard man to move at the best of times; in this series it was damn near impossible to shift him. He batted for more than 40 hours against the tourists and that included a duck in Sydney. He was a *very* hard man to dismiss. England won the Third Test in Sydney but Australia won the next at the Adelaide Oval so with three Tests drawn, the Aussies retained the Ashes. England were now pairing Bob Barber, the Warwickshire (and former Lancashire) left-hander, with Boycott to open the innings and they had some useful partnerships, notably 234 in 242 minutes in the Third Test, where Barber reached 185. It was his only century in 28 tests.
Don Mosey: Barber had a chequered career. After an outstanding school record at Ruthin, he got Blues at Cambridge in 1956 and '57 and then became captain of Lancashire where he had a pretty rough ride. With a committee which insisted on the captain staying in a different hotel from his team, Barber found it difficult to get the players behind him and Lancashire affairs were torn by controversy in the early sixties. He moved to Warwickshire in 1963 and soon confessed, 'I never realised that playing cricket could be fun.' His batting blossomed and he bowled leg-spin to good effect. Fred Titmus was second in the batting averages on tour and this was no freak resulting from a series of not outs. He batted with great consistency throughout the five Tests and showed why he was able to do the double on eight occasions. It was a good tour for the batsmen but the bowlers found it hard work, as the averages show.

DRAWN SERIES IN NEW ZEALAND

FST: All three Tests in New Zealand were drawn, which was rather unusual, but the series included a few landmarks, especially for Colin Cowdrey. He held his 100th test catch in Christchurch and scored his 6,000th Test run in Auckland. The quick bowlers did better than they had fared in Australia and Ken Higgs took 17 wickets at 9.23.

Edrich was struck down with appendicitis during the Third Test and had to have an operation. Although he had started the game, he was unable to bat in either innings.

THREE ENGLAND CAPTAINS

DM: Gary Sobers led the 1966 West Indians in England and tossed up with three different England captains during the series. At Old Trafford, Mike Smith skippered his country for the 25th and last time as England lost by an innings and 40 runs. Cowdrey took over for the next three matches and then gave way to Brian Close at The Oval, to start a run of seven Tests without defeat before he lost the captaincy for reasons unconnected with Test cricket. Colin Milburn made his debut at Old Trafford and was run out without scoring in his first innings. A dazzling 94 in the second innings, however, earned him a place at Lord's where he scored a maiden Test hundred which helped save the game. Sobers' cousin, David Holford, who had made his first appearance, like Milburn, at Old Trafford, also scored a maiden century at Lord's where Jim Parks completed a wicket-keeping double of 1,000 runs and 100 victims in Tests and Basil D'Oliveira played his first Test.

FST: Close's first Test as captain coincided with Dennis Amiss's as a batsman and he went on to play in 50 internationals. But the most remarkable thing about that Oval Test was seeing England, after being 166 for seven, finish on 527 all out with John Murray, at No. 9, hitting 112; Ken Higgs, No. 10, 63; and John Snow, last man in, 59 not out. Close's special brand of captaincy had a lot to do with Sobers' dismissal, first ball, in the second innings and that was the vital factor in England's win by an innings and 34 runs. But Sobers had clearly established himself as the finest all-rounder in the world with 722 runs at an average of 103.14, 20 wickets and ten catches. Graveney was England's outstanding batsman, but it was an impressive series for Ollie Milburn who averaged 52.66.

GILLETTE CUP

DM: It was Warwickshire's turn to win the Gillette Cup with the dynamic batting of men like Mike Smith, Amiss, Stewart, John Jameson (his Test career still ahead of him) and 'Billy' Ibadulla compensating for a fairly modest bowling line-up. They beat the reigning county champions, Worcestershire, by five wickets.

COUNTY CHAMPIONSHIP

FST: Now Yorkshire were back at the top of the table with a clear lead over Worcestershire and we see Somerset, after a couple of lean years, up near the top again. Kent had moved up one place, largely because of the emergence of Derek Underwood, who was still only 21. He had impressed us a great deal when we first saw him in Hull in 1963 and he was clearly a bowler with a big future. He bowled his left-arm spinners at something nearer medium pace than the traditional slow, flighted deliveries. Underwood had made his Test debut at Trent Bridge on 30 June (Third Test), and was destined to be a leading spin bowler for the next 20 years or so. By the time he was 25, he had already taken 1,000 first-class wickets.

DM: Remarkable to see Glamorgan slipping from third place to 14th in spite of Tony Lewis's emergence as a leading batsman. His 223 that year was made against Kent at Gravesend and he topped 2,000 runs. Not many players were doing that any more. Roger Prideaux, who had joined Northamptonshire from Kent in 1962, fell just 53 runs short of 2,000. (He is usually the joker in the pack when someone asks: 'How many first-class cricketers can you think of with an "x" in the name?')

REMARKABLE FAMILY

FST: We see the spinners coming back into their own in that year's averages with Mushtaq Mohammad entering the list for the first time. What a cricketing family tree he

An unproductive shot by Roger Prideaux (Northants and England). Parfitt is the fieldsman

had! Three brothers who played first-class cricket, and three nephews as well. He was a good leg-spinner as well as a gifted middle-order batsman and got 1,000 runs in a season 12 times as well as four double centuries. He played Test cricket for Pakistan before he was 16 but his brothers were all prodigies too—a remarkable family. It was a good season for my partner Tony Nicholson, in fact the best of his career, and with Ossie Wheatley and Don Shepherd both topping the 100 wicket mark it makes that slump of Glamorgan's look stranger than ever. David Smith, the Gloucestershire seamer, was a good, honest county bowler who could be very useful if there was anything in the pitch. We remember him in Yorkshire—with Tony Brown he once bowled us out for 35 at Bristol only a few days before we won the championship! Brian Statham was in his second year as captain of Lancashire and he was awarded the CBE in 1966 for his services to cricket. Ray Illingworth, now 34, had matured into a very complete and thoughtful player who was the ideal lieutenant to Close. In fact he was the first man Brian asked for when he was made captain of England that year.

Tony Nicholson, 'the best opening bowler never to play for England'

Mushtaq Mohammad in aggressive mood for Northants

1967

Summer Series with India:

Headingley	England won by six wickets
Lord's	England won by an innings & 124 runs
Edgbaston	England won by 132 runs

Pakistan:

Lord's	Match drawn
Trent Bridge	England won by ten wickets
Oval	England won by eight wickets

County Champions Yorkshire

Gillette Cup Kent

TEST AVERAGES ENGLAND V INDIA 1967

	M	I	NO	HS	Runs	Av	100	50	Ct/St
G. Boycott	2	3	1	246*	277	138.50	1	–	2
B. L. D'Oliveira	2	3	1	109	166	83.00	1	–	4
K. F. Barrington	3	5	0	97	324	64.80	–	3	2
T. W. Graveney	3	5	0	151	251	50.20	1	1	2
D. B. Close	3	4	1	47	102	34.00	–	–	2
D. L. Amiss	2	3	0	45	79	26.33	–	–	4
J. T. Murray	3	4	0	77	92	23.00	–	1	9/1
D. J. Brown	2	3	1	29*	37	18.50	–	–	–
J. A. Snow	3	3	1	10	27	13.50	–	–	2
R. N. S. Hobbs	3	3	1	15*	24	12.00	–	–	4
J. H. Edrich	2	3	0	22	35	11.66	–	–	1
R. Illingworth	3	4	1	12*	28	9.33	–	–	2

Also batted: C. Milburn (1 match) 40, 15, 2ct. K. Higgs played in one match but did not bat.

	Overs	M	Runs	Wkts	Av	5w	10w	BB
R. Illingworth	154.3	68	266	20	13.30	1	–	6–29
D. J. Brown	36	12	89	6	14.83	–	–	3–17
D. B. Close	60.4	20	144	8	18.00	–	–	4–68
J. A. Snow	112.4	29	264	10	26.40	–	–	3–49
R. N. S. Hobbs	112.1	34	259	9	28.77	–	–	3–25

Allso bowled: K. F. Barrington 9–1–38–0; B. L. D'Oliveira 35–15–89–3; K. Higgs 38–11–90–1.

TEST AVERAGES ENGLAND V PAKISTAN 1967

	M	I	NO	HS	Runs	Av	100	50	Ct/St
K. F. Barrington	3	5	2	148	426	142.00	3	–	3
T. W. Graveney	3	4	0	81	216	54.00	–	2	1
B. L. D'Oliveira	3	4	1	81*	150	50.00	–	2	3
D. B. Close	3	5	0	41	95	19.00	–	–	6
M. C. Cowdrey	2	4	1	16	41	13.66	–	–	1
K. Higgs	3	4	1	14	22	7.33	–	–	–

Also batted: D. L. Amiss (1 match) 26, 3*; G. G. Arnold (2 matches) 14, 59, 1ct; G. Boycott (1 match) 15, 1*; R. N. S. Hobbs (1 match) 1*, 1*, 1ct; R. Illingworth (1 match) 4, 9; A. P. E. Knott (2 matches) 0, 28, 12ct/1st; C. Milburn (1 match) 3, 32, 1ct; J. T. Murray (1 match) 0, 0, 1ct; W. E. Russell (1 match) 43, 12; J. A. Snow (1 match) 0, 7; F. J. Titmus (2 matches) 13, 65, 1ct; D. L. Underwood (2 matches) 2*, 1ct.

	Overs	M	Runs	Wkts	Av	5w	10w	BB
K. Higgs	119	45	249	17	14.64	1	–	5–58
D. L. Underwood	66	27	129	8	16.12	1	–	5–52
G. G. Arnold	68	22	147	8	18.37	1	–	5–58
F. J. Titmus	72.1	28	133	6	22.16	–	–	2–21

Also bowled: K. F. Barrington 32–5–81–3; D. B. Close 27–10–65–2; B. L. D'Oliveira 50–22–85–1; R. N. S. Hobbs 51–25–74–1; R. Illingworth 46–25–58–3; J. A. Snow 49.1–13–126–3.

CHAMPIONSHIP TABLE 1967

	P	Won	Lost	D	Tied	NR	First Inns Lead	Pts
Points Awarded	–	8	–	2	4	–	4	–
YORKSHIRE (1)	28	12	5	9	0	2	18	186
Kent (4)	28	11	3	12	0	2	16	176
Leicestershire (8)	28	10	3	12	0	3	18	176
Surrey (7)	28	8	4	12	0	4	15	148
Worcestershire (2)	28	6	6	16	0	0	13	132
Derbyshire (9)	28	5	5	17	0	1	14	130
Middlesex (12)	28	5	4	14	1	4	14	128
Somerset (3)	28	5	7	14	0	2	13	120
Northamptonshire (5)	28	7	8	11	0	2	10	118
Warwickshire (6)	28	5	4	15	0	4	11	118±*
Lancashire (12)	28	4	3	17	0	4	12	116*
Hampshire (11)	28	5	6	13	1	3	10	114±*
Sussex (10)	28	5	9	12	0	2	10	104
Glamorgan (14)	28	4	7	15	0	2	9	100*
Essex (16)	28	3	9	14	0	2	9	88
Nottinghamshire (17)	28	0	4	22	0	2	11	88
Gloucestershire (15)	28	3	11	9	0	5	11	86

± includes four points instead of two for fourth innings in drawn matches when final scores were level
* includes two points for tie on first innings
1966 positions are shown in brackets

FIRST-CLASS AVERAGES 1967

	I	NO	HS	Runs	Av	100
K. F. Barrington (Surrey)	40	10	158*	2059	68.63	6
D. L. Amiss (Warwickshire)	43	9	176*	1850	54.41	5
G. Boycott (Yorkshire)	40	4	246*	1910	53.05	4
±J. H. Edrich (Surrey)	47	5	226*	2077	49.45	5
R. M. Prideaux (Northamptonshire)	41	6	125	1637	46.77	3
C. A. Milton (Gloucestershire)	49	4	145	2089	46.42	7
B. L. D'Oliveira (Worcestershire)	44	8	174*	1618	44.94	6
W. E. Russell (Middlesex)	47	5	167	1885	44.88	4
T. W. Graveney (Worcestershire)	42	4	151	1668	43.89	4
M. J. Stewart (Surrey)	31	3	112	1184	42.28	2

*denotes not out
±denotes left-hand batsman

	Overs	M	Runs	Wkts	Av	BB
±D. L. Underwood (Kent)	979.1	459	1686	136	12.39	7–33
G. A. Cope (Yorkshire)	277.4	129	553	40	13.82	5–23
J. N. Graham (Kent)	906.2	353	1446	104	13.90	7–27
T. W. Cartwright (Warwickshire)	1194	488	2282	147	15.52	8–50
B. R. Knight (Leicestershire)	146.4	35	357	23	15.52	4–23
H. J. Rhodes (Derbyshire)	820.1	263	1585	102	15.53	6–28
A. S. M. Oakman (Sussex)	159.4	61	271	17	15.94	5–14
R. Illingworth (Yorkshire)	881.3	365	1613	101	15.97	7–6
±D. R. Cook (Warwickshire)	160.5	45	330	20	16.50	4–66
J. B. Statham (Lancashire)	635.2	153	1530	92	16.63	6–58

±denotes left-arm bowler

CLOSE'S CAPTAINCY

Don Mosey: This year was one of triumph and disaster for Brian Close and it brought a Selectorial rebuke to Geoffrey Boycott. Close's mixture of ruthlessness and imagination as captain overwhelmed India in all three Tests of the summer, and Pakistan managed to avoid a whitewash only because of a characteristic piece of batting obduracy by Hanif Mohammad allied to the loss of 3½ hours' play because of rain. Yet Close was dropped from the captaincy of the winter tour to the West Indies after leading England in seven Tests, only one of which was not won—the draw with Pakistan at Lord's. Towards the end of the season, Warwickshire needed 142 to win in 102 minutes to beat Yorkshire at Edgbaston. On the following morning (Saturday, 19 August) the national newspapers proclaimed loudly that Yorkshire had avoided defeat because Close had slowed down the game, and four days later he was severely censured by a specially-appointed MCC sub-committee for using delaying tactics. The day after that he led England to victory in the Final Test to win the series and during the game, at The Oval, he was told that he would not be leading England on the winter tour.

Freddie Trueman: Slowing down the over rate to prevent a side scoring quickly was not new and it was very soon after that to become commonplace, and all attempts by the Test and County Cricket Board to prevent delaying tactics by Test captains were to prove fruitless, at least up to and including 1987. We saw the West Indies regularly bowling only 12 and 13 overs an hour throughout the day and once, in India, Sunil Gavaskar slowed the rate down to nine an hour with two slow bowlers operating! During that final afternoon at Edgbaston we played through light rain for much of the time so the ball had to be wiped frequently. There was an actual stoppage for rain and we still bowled 16 overs in the first hour. I bowled an over which took six minutes because I bowled two no balls and took a wicket so that wasn't out of the ordinary.

DM: Close to this day insists that he did nothing to slow play deliberately but he was certainly tried in the public press before he faced the MCC sub-committee where he refused to accept that he had anything to apologise for. If he had publicly said he had done wrong the probability is that he would have retained the captaincy but that was not Close's way. He felt he was right and stood by his captaincy. Colin Cowdrey was appointed to lead England in the West Indies.

INDIA OVERWHELMED

FST: The First Test against India was won at Headingley despite the fact that India, following on, scored 510 in their second innings. Robin Hobbs played his first Test and restored the art of leg-spin bowling to England's attack, though he had only modest success as a wicket-taker—ten for 333 in four Tests that summer.

DM: Boycott's 246 not out at Headingley took him 573 minutes and 555 balls and, following on Barrington's punishment in 1965 for slow batting, Boycott was dropped for the Second Test at Lord's. Barrington opened in his place and hit 97 in his only innings of the game. In the same match Murray took six catches in the first innings which equalled the then record held by Wally Grout (Australia) and Denis Lindsay (South Africa). In the First Test against Pakistan, also at Lord's, Hanif made Boycott's innings against India seem positively frenzied. His 187 not out occupied 542 minutes and 556 balls, and it was also Wasim Bari's first appearance as Pakistan's wicket-keeper in a career which was to cover 73 Tests and five tours to England.

FST: Alan Knott came on the scene for the first time in the Second Test at Trent Bridge, along with Geoff Arnold, the Surrey seamer. Ken Barrington hit centuries there and at The Oval, the latter making him the first man to score a hundred on all six Test grounds in this country. And Ken Higgs had a successful series against Pakistan with 17 wickets.

GOOD YEAR FOR KENT

DM: Kent had an outstanding year, beating Somerset by 32 runs in the Gillette Cup final and finishing second to Yorkshire in the county championship. Cowdrey, in his 11th season as captain, saw the continuing development of Underwood as outstandingly the best left-arm spinner of his generation and he topped the first-class bowling averages but we now saw some quick bowling support from Norman Graham, a six ft seven and a half young man from Hexham, Northumberland. He topped 100 wickets and was awarded his county cap in 1967.

FST: Norman's great asset was that he could get a lot of bounce. When there was a bit of moisture in the wicket he could be quite devastating. He went back to play for his native Northumberland when he retired from Kent in 1977. An interesting name creeps into the list at No. 9—David Cook, who played one game for Warwickshire in 1962, then disappeared until 1967. He was a left-arm seamer and a fine rugby player with Coventry and Warwickshire. There are three off-spinners in the list with Geoff Cope appearing for the first time. Geoff was being groomed as Ray Illingworth's understudy but his action caused a bit of comment and twice in the 1970s he was to be suspended for a suspect action. We always felt he was harshly treated because there were one or two actions in the game at the time which were more doubtful, but no one complained about *West Indian* bowlers!

DM: Ken Barrington had a marvellous record through the 1960s and we see him topping the 2,000 mark for the third time in his career. He was sometimes criticised for slow scoring but paradoxically, at one stage of his career, he developed a penchant for reaching 100 with a hit for six. Arthur Milton scored more centuries than anyone else but Gloucestershire finished bottom of the table—they were short of penetrative bowling. Somerset slipped a little, as did Northamptonshire, Warwickshire and Worcestershire, but generally speaking the success of counties was achieved in direct relation to the success of the bowlers.

'How's that? I know he was plumb'—Ken Higgs

'I don't mind how or where I catch 'em'—Alan Knott

1968

Winter Tour to West Indies (1967-68):

Port-of-Spain	Match drawn
Kingston	Match drawn
Bridgetown	Match drawn
Port-of-Spain	England won by seven wickets
Georgetown	Match drawn

Summer Series with Australia:

Old Trafford	Australia won by 159 runs
Lord's	Match drawn
Edgbaston	Match drawn
Headingley	Match drawn
Oval	England won by 226 runs

County Champions Yorkshire   **Gillette Cup** Warwickshire

TEST AVERAGES ENGLAND V WEST INDIES 1967–68

	M	I	NO	HS	Runs	Av	100	50	Ct/St
A. P. E. Knott	2	3	2	73*	149	149.00	–	2	4/–
M. C. Cowdrey	5	8	0	148	534	66.75	2	4	3
G. Boycott	5	8	1	116	463	66.14	1	4	1
J. H. Edrich	5	8	0	146	340	42.50	1	1	4
K. F. Barrington	5	7	0	143	288	41.14	1	1	2
T. W. Graveney	5	8	0	118	261	32.62	1	1	9
G. A. R. Lock	2	3	0	89	94	31.33	–	1	2
B. L. D'Oliveira	5	8	2	51	137	22.83	–	1	3
F. J. Titmus	2	3	0	19	38	12.66	–	–	1
J. M. Parks	3	4	0	42	48	12.00	–	–	9/–
J. A. Snow	4	5	0	37	48	9.60	–	–	1
D. J. Brown	4	5	1	22*	37	9.25	–	–	–
P. I. Pocock	2	3	0	13	19	6.33	–	–	1
I. J. Jones	5	6	4	2	4	2.00	–	–	3

Also batted: R. N. S. Hobbs (1 match) 2, 1ct.

	Overs	M	Runs	Wkts	Av	5w	10w	BB
J. A. Snow	165	28	504	27	18.66	3	1	7–49
D. J. Brown	162	32	458	14	32.71	–	–	3–27
I. J. Jones	198.2	31	656	14	46.85	–	–	3–63
K. F. Barrington	79	14	257	5	51.40	–	–	1–41
P. I. Pocock	96	23	277	5	55.40	–	–	2–66

Also bowled: M. C. Cowdrey 1–0–1–0; B. L. D'Oliveira 118–34–293–3; R. N. S. Hobbs 28–3–78–2; G. A. R. Lock 69–11–212–4; F. J. Titmus 68–24–165–4.

TEST AVERAGES ENGLAND V AUSTRALIA 1968

	M	I	NO	HS	Runs	Av	100	50	Ct/St
B. L. D'Oliveira	2	4	1	158	263	87.66	1	1	1
J. H. Edrich	5	9	0	164	554	61.55	1	4	2
K. F. Barrington	3	4	1	75	170	56.66	–	1	3
T. W. Graveney	5	9	1	96	337	42.12	–	2	4
C. Milburn	2	3	0	83	109	36.33	–	1	2
M. C. Cowdrey	4	6	0	104	215	35.83	1	–	5
G. Boycott	3	5	0	49	162	32.40	–	–	1
E. R. Dexter	2	4	0	38	97	24.25	–	–	2
B. R. Knight	2	3	1	27*	34	17.00	–	–	1
A. P. E. Knott	5	8	1	33	116	16.57	–	–	11/4
J. A. Snow	5	7	2	19	56	11.20	–	–	3
R. Illingworth	3	4	0	27	51	12.75	–	–	1
D. J. Brown	4	4	0	14	17	4.25	–	–	3

Also batted: D. L. Amiss (1 match) 0, 0; R. W. Barber (1 match) 20, 46; K. W. R. Fletcher (1 match) 0, 23*; K. Higgs (1 match) 2, 0, 1ct; P. I. Pocock (1 match) 6, 10, 2ct; R. M. Prideaux (1 match) 64, 2; D. L. Underwood (4 matches) 14*, 45*, 9*, 1*, 2ct.

	Overs	M	Runs	Wkts	Av	5w	10w	BB
D. L. Underwood	209.5	103	302	20	15.10	1	–	7–50
R. Illingworth	183.2	82	291	13	22.38	1	–	6–87
P. I. Pocock	58	15	156	6	26.00	1	–	6–79
J. A. Snow	203	44	508	17	29.88	–	–	4–97
D. J. Brown	144	34	401	12	33.41	1	–	5–42

Also bowled: R. W. Barber 21–1–87–3; K. F. Barrington 8–1–26–1; E. R. Dexter 8–0–28–0; B. L. D'Oliveira 39–20–49–3; K. Higgs 58.3–19–121–2; B. R. Knight 40.4–16–85–4.

CHAMPIONSHIP TABLE 1968

						Bonus Pts		
Win = 10 points	P	Won	Lost	D	NR	Bat	Bowl	Pts
YORKSHIRE (1)	28	11	4	13	0	46	114	270
Kent (2)	28	12	5	11	0	41	95	256
Glamorgan (14)	28	11	6	9	2	42	85	237
Nottinghamshire (15)	28	7	3	17	1	53	99	222
Hampshire (12)	28	8	5	15	0	43	92	215
Lancashire (11)	28	8	6	14	0	24	105	209
Worcestershire (5)	28	8	7	13	0	26	97	203
Derbyshire (6)	28	6	5	16	1	47	92	199
Leicestershire (2)	28	6	10	12	0	52	85	197
Middlesex (7)	28	8	6	14	0	21	91	192
Warwickshire (10)	28	7	8	12	1	38	82	190
Somerset (8)	28	5	11	11	1	36	86	172
Northamptonshire (9)	28	5	6	17	0	34	86	170
Essex (15)	28	5	6	16	1	31	88	169
Surrey (4)	28	4	7	17	0	25	92	157
Gloucestershire (17)	28	2	8	17	1	40	93	153
Sussex (13)	28	2	12	14	0	43	77	140

1967 positions are shown in brackets

FIRST-CLASS AVERAGES 1968

	I	NO	HS	Runs	Av	100
G. Boycott (Yorkshire)	30	7	180*	1487	64.65	7
B. A. Richards (Hampshire)	55	5	206	2395	47.90	5
R. B. Kanhai (Warwickshire)	42	3	253	1819	46.64	6
±J. H. Edrich (Surrey)	50	5	164	2009	44.64	5
±G. St A. Sobers (Nottinghamshire)	44	7	105*	1590	42.97	2
M. C. Cowdrey (Kent)	28	2	129	1093	42.03	5
R. M. Prideaux (Northants)	53	5	108*	1993	41.52	2
K. W. R. Fletcher (Essex)	54	8	228*	1890	41.08	4
F. S. Goldstein (Oxford Univ)	25	1	155	980	40.83	1
D. M. Green (Gloucestershire)	54	1	233	2137	40.32	4

	Overs	M	Runs	Wkts	Av	BB
O. S. Wheatley (Glamorgan)	549	222	1062	82	12.95	9–60
A. Ward (Derbyshire)	147.5	41	399	30	13.30	6–56
±D. Wilson (Yorkshire)	815.5	335	1521	109	13.95	7–36
R. Illingworth (Yorkshire)	957.2	360	1882	131	14.36	7–73
±D. L. Underwood (Kent)	957.4	435	1821	123	14.80	7–17
K. Higgs (Lancashire)	778.2	223	1637	108	15.15	7–41
±J. C. J. Dye (Kent)	254.2	65	535	35	15.28	5–26
T. W. Cartwright (Warwickshire)	608.4	258	1145	71	16.12	7–36
B. L. D'Oliveira (Worcestershire)	467.3	145	990	61	16.22	6–29
A. G. Nicholson (Yorkshire)	677	225	1430	87	16.43	8–22

±denotes left-arm bowler

TCCB ESTABLISHED

Freddie Trueman: This was the most momentous year in modern times in the administration of the game. On 20 May the MCC announced the setting up of a Council as the governing body of the game with representation from the National Cricket Association, the Test and County Cricket Board and the MCC itself. Three months earlier the Advisory County Cricket Committee of MCC (replaced in May by the TCCB) had decided on a bonus points system designed to bring about more positive cricket from the start of a game. In the county championship ten points were now awarded for a win and five for a tie, one point was awarded in the first 85 overs of each innings for every 25 runs scored above 150 and for each two wickets taken by the bowling side. Points for a draw were abolished.

Don Mosey: And as a direct result of events at Edgbaston in August 1967, a minimum of 20 overs had to be bowled in the last hour of every match, whatever the official finishing time. In this new climate of county cricket, Yorkshire still won the championship (although it was destined to be for the last time for the next 20 years) but Kent actually brought off 12 outright wins to Yorkshire's 11. This was achieved largely because of Yorkshire's

bowling which brought them more bonus points than any other county's, while Nottinghamshire scored the highest number of batting bonus points. Significantly, they had been joined as captain by Gary Sobers. Yorkshire, at the end of that summer, bade a sad farewell to Freddie Trueman; Lancashire to Brian Statham. It was the end of an era in more ways than one.

FST: It still gave me my proudest moment in the whole of my career. That came on 2 July when, in Close's absence, I led Yorkshire to victory over Bill Lawry's Australians at Bramall Lane, Sheffield, by an innings and 69 runs. No Yorkshire side had beaten the Aussies since 1902 and I wanted that win more than I had ever wanted anything in my cricketing life. I retired a happy man at the end of the season.

DM: A win in Trinidad (Fourth Test) gave England the winter rubber against West Indies, but the tour was marred by an accident to Fred Titmus who was involved in an accident while swimming which cost him four toes. Happily, the Middlesex off-spinner recovered sufficiently to continue his county career and also played Test cricket on the tour to Australia in 1974–75. His accident in Barbados gave Pat Pocock, of Surrey, his first taste of Test cricket. Sobers' somewhat quixotic declaration at Port of Spain gave England the only win of the series by either side. He set a target of 215 runs in 165 minutes which scarcely gave him time to bowl out England who won with three minutes remaining. Boycott's 80 not out was one of his outstanding Test innings.

FST: Alan Knott took over from Jim Parks in the last two Tests and after that was established as England's regular wicket-keeper. His batting was always to prove a bonus which tipped the scales in his favour against any challengers; in his three innings in those two West Indian Tests he scored 69 not out, 7 and 73 not out. John Snow had a good series and his 27 wickets beat my 21 in 1959–60. And Pat Pocock, in his second Test, spent 82 minutes before scoring his first run.

DM: England had their first glimpse of Clive Lloyd on that tour. He had made his debut for West Indies during their tour of India in 1966–67, and now scored two hundreds in the series as well as making his mark as one of the outstanding fieldsmen of his day.

COWDREY'S 100 TESTS

FST: Not for the first time, it was a bit difficult to know what was in the Selectors' minds (Doug Insole, Peter May, Alec Bedser and Don Kenyon) when the summer series against Australia began. 'Percy' Pocock took six wickets for 79 in the Aussies' second innings at Old Trafford and Basil D'Oliveira scored 87 not out, by far England's best score in their vain attempt to avoid defeat, but both were dropped for the next match at Lord's. That was drawn, but nearly half the playing time was washed out, and so was the Third Test at Edgbaston: but this was a notable match for Colin Cowdrey. He became the first man to appear in 100 Tests and got his 21st century as well as passing 7,000 runs. At Headingley (Fourth Test) both sides were skippered by men doing the job for the first and only time in their careers. Cowdrey and Lawry were both injured and Graveney and Barry Jarman, the Australian wicket-keeper, led the sides. Keith Fletcher and Roger Prideaux made their England debuts.

DM: At The Oval, England squared the series but that still left Australia with the Ashes. Basil D'Oliveira was recalled by England and hit 158 in a game which finished on a note of high drama. A torrential rainstorm flooded the ground at lunchtime on the last day, but volunteers from the crowd helped the groundstaff to mop up and bright sunshine then provided Underwood with the sort of pitch which gave him his nickname, 'Deadly'. With five minutes' play remaining, John Inverarity—who had batted right through the innings for 56—offered no stroke and was out lbw. Underwood had taken seven wickets for 50. It was very much a spinners' series with Underwood, Illingworth and Pocock leading the English averages. England used 20 players in the five matches. Underwood was never dismissed in any of his four innings and started a career as the Test side's No. 1 nightwatchman.

OVERSEAS PLAYERS

FST: Counties were now allowed immediate registration, without residential qualification, of one overseas player every three years and Barry Anderson Richards, one of the most exciting batsmen the game has ever seen, played the first of his ten years with Hampshire in 1968, scoring 2,395 runs, with five centuries, and punishing bowling of all types. His career with Hampshire compensated to some extent for his absence from the Test scene (because of the ban on South Africa after the D'Oliveira Affair at the end of 1968). Richards was to become a sort of roving mercenary, playing in the English and Australian and/or South African summers alternately. His career in first-class cricket saw him score 28,358 runs and average 54.74 with a top score of a marvellous 356 for South Australia v Western Australia. His Tests numbered just four—with two centuries and an average of 72.57.

DM: With Rohan Kanhai in his first season with Warwickshire, the trickle of overseas players resulting from the new regulations was becoming a steady flow—Richards, Kanhai and Sobers appearing in the top ten in their first seasons here (Goldstein, though Rhodesian-

Barry Richards, one of the most dazzling batsmen of all time, and Farokh Engineer outstanding wicketkeeper-batsman for India and Lancashire

born, figured only briefly for Northamptonshire).

FST: Ossie Wheatley had another outstanding season, and his nine wickets for 60 against Sussex at Ebbw Vale was the best performance of his career; Don Wilson had his best season for Yorkshire and the new name in the bowling list is that of John Dye, the left-arm fast-medium bowler who followed a long run with Kent with five years at Northamptonshire.

THE D'OLIVEIRA AFFAIR

DM: As we have seen, Basil D'Oliveira was dropped after the first Test of the summer against Australia and he had a modest season, especially with the bat, for Worcestershire. Consequently, when Prideaux dropped out of the side for the Final Test because of illness, D'Oliveira was something of a surprise choice. His 158 now provided something of an embarrassment for the Selectors as they sat down at the end of that Test to pick the tour party for South Africa. Newspapers had already started extensive speculation about the reaction of the South African Government if D'Oliveira, a Cape Coloured, was chosen to tour there during the coming winter. He was, in the event, omitted from the party as initially chosen and Doug Insole explained the reason for this as being that D'Oliveira's claims for inclusion as a batsman could not be seen as better than those of the seven batters actually selected. This explanation was seen in some quarters here as being politically expedient since the indications from South Africa were that the government would not welcome D'Oliveira as a member of a touring party. Correspondence to national newspapers on the subject began to come from very distinguished circles indeed. Then the *News of the World* announced that D'Oliveira would report the series for them, and this was seen in South Africa as a politically provocative move. On 16 September Tom Cartwright reported that he was unfit to tour and the Selectors named D'Oliveira as his replacement. In view of the fact that Doug Insole had earlier indicated the non-selection of D'Oliveira was on his merits as a batsman, his inclusion now as an all-rounder fuelled South African suspicions that the whole affair was now a political matter aimed at trying to interfere with internal South African laws as they affected coloured races in that country. In Bloemfontein, the heartland of Afrikaanerdom, the Prime Minister, Mr Vorster, made a speech in which he made it crystal clear that South Africa would not receive a team which had been forced on her by people with certain political aims. On 24 September the MCC cancelled the tour and there have been no Tests between the two countries since that time. South African-born players have, however, continued to play for English counties and, indeed, for England Test sides.

Basil D'Oliveira pensively considers the furore created by his selection to tour South Africa

1969

Winter Tour to Pakistan (1968–69):

Lahore	Match drawn
Dacca	Match drawn
Karachi	Match drawn (abandoned – riots)

Summer Series with West Indies:

Old Trafford	England won by ten wickets
Lord's	Match drawn
Headingley	England won by 30 runs

New Zealand:

Lord's	England won by 230 runs
Trent Bridge	Match drawn
Oval	England won by eight wickets

County Champions Glamorgan

Gillette Cup Yorkshire

John Player League Lancashire

TEST AVERAGES ENGLAND V PAKISTAN 1968–69

	M	I	NO	HS	Runs	Av	100	50	Ct/St
A. P. E. Knott	3	4	1	96*	180	60.00	–	2	6/–
B. L. D'Oliveira	3	4	1	114*	161	53.66	1	–	4
T. W. Graveney	3	4	0	105	176	44.00	1	–	–
D. J. Brown	3	4	2	44*	80	40.00	–	–	1
K. W. R. Fletcher	3	4	0	83	157	39.25	–	1	2
M. C. Cowdrey	3	4	0	100	133	33.25	1	–	–
J. H. Edrich	3	5	1	54	130	32.50	–	1	–
R. M. Prideaux	2	4	1	18*	36	12.00	–	–	–
D. L. Underwood	3	3	0	22	28	9.33	–	–	–

Also batted: R. M. H. Cottam (2 matches) 4*, 4, 2ct; C. Milburn (1 match) 139; P. I. Pocock (1 match) 12, 1, 3ct; J. A. Snow (2 matches) 9, 9, 1ct. R. N. S. Hobbs played in one match but did not bat.

	Overs	M	Runs	Wkts	Av	5w	10w	BB
D. J. Brown	58	13	159	8	19.87	–	–	3–43
R. M. H. Cottam	92.3	31	180	9	20.00	–	–	4–50
D. L. Underwood	106	40	204	8	25.50	1	–	5–94

Also bowled: B. L. D'Oliveira 25–5–55–1; K. W. R. Fletcher 8–2–31–0; T. W. Graveney 6–0–11–0; P. I. Pocock 26–7–80–1; R. M. Prideaux 2–2–0–0; J. A. Snow 37–12–85–4.

TEST AVERAGES ENGLAND V NEW ZEALAND 1969

	M	I	NO	HS	Runs	Av	100	50	Ct/St
J. H. Edrich	3	5	0	155	376	75.20	2	1	1
P. J. Sharpe	3	5	1	111	270	67.50	1	–	5
B. R. Knight	2	3	1	49	96	48.00	–	–	2
B. L. D'Oliveira	3	4	0	45	95	23.75	–	–	1
R. Illingworth	3	4	0	53	90	22.50	–	1	3
G. Boycott	3	5	0	47	101	20.20	–	–	–
A. Ward	3	3	1	21	40	20.00	–	–	2
K. W. R. Fletcher	2	3	0	31	47	15.66	–	–	2
A. P. E. Knott	3	4	0	21	54	13.50	–	–	9/2
D. L. Underwood	3	4	0	16	24	6.00	–	–	–

Also batted: G. G. Arnold (1 match) 1, 2ct; D. J. Brown (1 match) 11*, 7, 1ct; M. H. Denness (1 match) 2, 55*, 3ct; J. A. Snow (2 matches) 4*, 21*.

	Overs	M	Runs	Wkts	Av	5w	10w	BB
D. L. Underwood	150	70	220	24	9.16	2	2	7–32
R. Illingworth	101.3	43	154	10	15.40	–	–	4–37
A. Ward	73.5	15	210	10	21.10	–	–	4–61

Also bowled: G. G. Arnold 18–5–30–0; D. J. Brown 17–8–23–0; B. L. D'Oliveira 53–21–77–2; K. W. R. Fletcher 3–1–14–0; B. R. Knight 35.5–8–83–2; J. A. Snow 61–14–154–3.

TEST AVERAGES ENGLAND V WEST INDIES 1969

	M	I	NO	HS	Runs	Av	100	50	Ct/St
G. Boycott	3	6	1	125	270	54.00	2	–	–
R. Illingworth	3	5	1	113	163	40.75	1	–	4
J. H. Edrich	3	6	1	79	169	33.80	–	2	3
J. H. Hampshire	2	4	0	107	135	33.75	1	–	4
B. L. D'Oliveira	3	5	0	57	162	32.40	–	1	1
A. P. E. Knott	3	5	0	53	139	27.80	–	1	10/1
J. A. Snow	3	4	3	15*	25	25.00	–	–	1
P. J. Sharpe	3	5	0	86	120	24.00	–	1	8
B. R. Knight	3	5	1	31	66	16.50	–	–	–
D. J. Brown	3	4	0	34	62	15.50	–	–	–
D. L. Underwood	2	3	1	16	31	15.50	–	–	3

Also batted: T. W. Graveney (1 match) 75, 1ct; P. H. Parfitt (1 match) 4, 39.

	Overs	M	Runs	Wkts	Av	5w	10w	BB
D. L. Underwood	53	29	101	6	16.83	–	–	4–55
D. J. Brown	110.3	25	288	14	20.57	–	–	4–39
B. R. Knight	120.1	29	279	11	25.36	–	–	4–63
J. A. Snow	139.3	26	406	15	27.06	1	–	5–114
R. Illingworth	93	32	218	5	43.60	–	–	3–66

Also bowled: B. L. D'Oliveira 75–25–169–4; P. H. Parfitt 1–0–8–0.

CHAMPIONSHIP TABLE 1969

Win = 10 points	P	Won	Lost	D	Bonus Pts Bat	Bowl	Pts
GLAMORGAN (3)	24	11	0	13	67	73	250
Gloucestershire (16)	24	10	6	8	26	93	219
Surrey (15)	24	7	1	16	64	76	210
Warwickshire (11)	24	7	3	14	41	89	205±
Hampshire (5)	24	6	7	11	56	87	203
Essex (14)	24	6	6	12	44	85	189
Sussex (17)	24	5	8	11	46	89	185
Nottinghamshire (4)	24	6	2	16	49	75	184
Northamptonshire (13)	24	5	7	12	47	66	163
Kent (2)	24	4	6	14	35	76	151
Middlesex (10)	24	3	7	14	40	76	146
Worcestershire (7)	24	5	7	12*	30	62	142
Yorkshire (1)	24	3	6	15	30	77	142±
Leicestershire (9)	24	4	7	13	26	64	130
Lancashire (6)	24	2	1	21	39	67	126
Derbyshire (8)	24	3	5	16*	22	67	119
Somerset (12)	24	1	9	14	17	69	96

* includes one match abandoned without a ball bowled
± includes five points for fourth innings in drawn matches when final scores were level
1968 positions are shown in brackets

FIRST-CLASS AVERAGES 1969

	I	NO	HS	Runs	Av	100
±J. H. Edrich (Surrey)	39	7	181	2238	69.93	8
E. J. O. Hemsley (Worcestershire)	16	5	138*	676	61.45	1
Mushtaq Mohammad (Northants)	40	9	156*	1831	59.06	6
B. A. Richards (Hampshire)	31	6	155	1440	57.60	5
±C. H. Lloyd (Lancashire/WI)	36	6	201*	1458	48.60	2
B. W. Luckhurst (Kent)	44	4	169	1914	47.85	4
±Younis Ahmed (Surrey)	46	9	127*	1760	47.56	5
M. J. Stewart (Surrey)	37	7	105	1317	43.90	2
C. Milburn (Northants)	8	0	158	341	42.62	1
±G. St A. Sobers (Notts/WI)	26	2	104	1023	42.62	2

*denotes not out
±denotes left-hand batsman

	Overs	M	Runs	Wkts	Av	BB
A. Ward (Derbyshire)	482.5	135	1023	69	14.82	5–32
M. J. Procter (Gloucestershire)	639.3	160	1623	108	15.02	7–65
±D. L. Underwood (Kent)	808.3	355	1561	101	15.45	7–32
T. W. Cartwright (Warwickshire)	880.5	373	1748	108	16.18	7–34
±D. Wilson (Yorkshire)	964.1	384	1772	102	17.37	7–19
±D. N. F. Slade (Worcestershire)	393.1	156	734	42	17.47	5–31
H. J. Rhodes (Derbyshire)	507.3	142	1167	64	18.23	6–17
J. N. Graham (Kent)	726	218	1460	79	18.48	8–20
C. M. Old (Yorkshire)	433	98	1061	57	18.61	7–20
R. Illingworth (Leicestershire)	599.1	206	1186	62	19.12	7–27

JOHN PLAYER LEAGUE

Freddie Trueman: Events, and the game itself, were now changing very rapidly indeed. This year saw the start of the 40 overs a side, Sunday afternoon frolic sponsored by the John Player tobacco firm. This was limited-overs cricket but played on a league basis, rather than knock-out, and the first winners were Lancashire who, under the leadership of Jackie Bond from 1968 to 1972, had a tremendous run of success in one-day cricket. Television gave the competition a great boost but it has never become popular with players, especially bowlers. It is no fun bowling to a field where there are no slips or other close-catchers.

Don Mosey: The original prize money was £1,000 to the winners, £500 for second place and £250 for third place and each winning side got £50 per victory. John Player remained the Sunday League sponsors until 1986 and in 1987 it was taken over by the Refuge Assurance Company.

GRIM TOUR

FST: With a pleasant trip to South Africa cancelled England sent a team to Pakistan under Colin Cowdrey, and it cannot have been very pleasant for anyone. All three matches were drawn but two of them were interrupted by riots and fighting; in fact the third match, in Karachi, was abandoned after three of the five days when a mob broke down the gates and invaded the National Stadium. It was a bit unlucky for Alan Knott, who was 96 not out at the time, and he didn't get the chance to complete his first Test hundred.

DM: The only match which was played peacefully was the second, in Dacca, which at that time was the capital of East Pakistan before it became the independent state of Bangladesh. There were no police or Army in sight and the crowd was controlled by student leaders. D'Oliveira got a marvellous 114 not out on a terrible pitch. Bob Cottam, of Hampshire, made his debut in Lahore (First Test) and the third, riot-ruined, match saw the first appearance for Pakistan of Sarfraz Nawaz who was to be a major force in their cricket (and Northamptonshire's) during the next decade before turning to a political career. His first bowling analysis was 34–6–78–0 as Tom Graveney and Colin Milburn hit centuries. In the case of both players, it was their last for England.

FST: After returning home, Milburn was involved in a terrible car accident near Northampton and, amongst

The most successful of all West Indian captains—the superb Clive Lloyd

Colin Milburn—hard-hitting career cut short by a terrible road accident

other injuries, lost his left eye. He made a gallant attempt to overcome his handicap and to carry on playing but finally had to give it up. Happily, he is still involved in cricket in various ways and joins us from time to time in the *Test Match Special* commentary box.

DOUBLE TOUR

DM: West Indies and New Zealand were the opposition in the double tour of 1969 and Ray Illingworth took over the captaincy from the injured Colin Cowdrey. He started with a ten-wickets win over West Indies at Old Trafford where Vanburn Holder (later to play for Worcestershire) and John Shepherd (Kent and Gloucestershire) made their debuts. At Lord's the Second Test was drawn but it was a notable match for John Hampshire, of Yorkshire, who became the first man to score a century in his Test debut at Lord's. Ray Illingworth got his first Test century in the same game, his second as captain. He had, incidentally, moved from Yorkshire and joined Leicestershire as captain in 1969 so it was as a Leicestershire player that he captained England in 31 Tests.

FST: Never mind that. He was still a Yorkshireman. England won at Headingley and so retained the Wisden Trophy which they had won in the Windies in the winter of 1967–68. The interesting thing to me about that series is the way the wickets were shared out—only Snow (at Lord's) had a five wickets in an innings return.

GLENN TURNER

DM: England won the first Test of the New Zealand series easily enough but the crowd at Lord's had their first glimpse of Glenn Turner who was to become the greatest New Zealand-born batsman, even though most of his runs were scored with Worcestershire. He had made his debut the previous winter, at home to West Indies, but now, on his first appearance at Lord's, aged 22, he carried his bat through the entire second innings for 43 not out. He was very much a strokeless wonder in his younger days but he became one of the best batsmen in the world. He made 34,346 first-class runs including 103 centuries and after retiring became, first, a TV commentator and then a successful manager of the New Zealand Test side.

FST: Alan Ward (Derbyshire) started his Test career at Lord's (v New Zealand) but it was Underwood's game—11 for 70 in the match including seven for 32 in the second innings. The Second Test (Trent Bridge) was drawn but Philip Sharpe made his only Test century there and John Edrich reached 25,000 first-class runs during his innings of 155. In the Final Test at The Oval, Mike Denness came on the scene but again it was Underwood's match—12 for 101. In the series he had taken 24 wickets at 9.16.

GLAMORGAN CHAMPIONS

DM: Glamorgan won their second championship title in a season which saw a reduction to 24 in the number of three-day matches and a huge turn-round in the fortunes of many counties. Overseas players were beginning to dominate as batsmen but not yet as bowlers, with one notable exception: Mike Procter, the South African-born Gloucestershire all-rounder—one of the finest the game has ever seen. In spite of an unusual action he bowled very fast; he could switch to off-spinners and as a batsman he hit with ferocious power. His achievements were to include a hat-trick (of lbw decisions) in the same game in which he scored a hundred. His 108 wickets in 1969 undoubtedly played a major part in Gloucestershire's leap from next to the bottom of the table the previous season to next to the top. Surrey and Sussex also made remarkable advances but Yorkshire and Lancashire slumped dis-

Another of the all-time great all-rounders—Mike Procter (Gloucestershire)

astrously. Significantly, it was Yorkshire's first season without Trueman, and Lancashire's first without Statham.

FST: At the same time, my successor, Chris Old, did well and Don Wilson took more than 100 wickets. The thing to remember is that Ray Illingworth and Ken Taylor had gone as well; Ray topped the Leicestershire batting and bowling averages in his first season at Grace Road. Tommy Cartwright was well into his stride now but at 34, Warwickshire must have decided he was past his best because they let him go to Somerset at the end of the season. A fine bowler, Tom Cartwright—a fine cricketer.

DM: In the batting averages we see the name of Ted Hemsley, one of those valuable bread-and-butter cricketers who came originally from the splendid Minor County production line in Staffordshire to play for 20 seasons for Worcestershire. He was a good footballer with Shrewsbury Town, Sheffield United and Doncaster Rovers. Clive Lloyd divided his season between the West Indian tourists and Lancashire who had signed him the previous year, after initially trying to persuade Sobers to Old Trafford. Lloyd was to become one of the favourite players there up to 1986. The top ten in the averages include two West Indians, two Pakistanis and one South African but John Edrich, with eight centuries, had one of the six 2,000-run seasons of his 20 years with Surrey and topped the list. And it's marvellous to see Colin Milburn's name there—his season limited to four matches by that accident—but averaging 42.62. Jimmy Binks retired as Yorkshire's wicket-keeper. He had not missed a championship match since his debut in 1955 (412 consecutive games). Ken Suttle, the Sussex left-hand batsman, went one better—he also retired in 1969 after 423 consecutive championship appearances.

Ken Suttle—423 consecutive county matches for Sussex

No official Tests were played in England in 1970 and there was no 1969 winter tour.

Rest of the World beat England in four of the five unofficial matches played during the summer. England won the remaining game.

County Champions Kent

Gillette Cup Lancashire

John Player League Lancashire

CHAMPIONSHIP TABLE 1970

Win = 10 points	P	Won	Lost	D	Bonus Pts Bat	Bowl	Pts
KENT (10)	24	9	5	10	70	77	237
Glamorgan (1)	24	9	6	9	48	82	220
Lancashire (15)	24	6	2	16	78	78	216
Yorkshire (13)	24	8	5	11	49	86	215
Surrey (3)	24	6	4	14	60	83	203
Worcestershire (12)	24	7	1	16	46	84	200
Derbyshire (16)	24	7	7	10	51	78	199
Warwickshire (4)	24	7	6	11	53	71	199±
Sussex (7)	24	5	7	12	62	87	199
Hampshire (5)	24	4	6	14	69	88	197
Nottinghamshire (8)	24	4	8	12	71	73	184
Essex (6)	24	4	6	14	64	76	180
Somerset (17)	24	5	10	9	40	86	176
Northamptonshire (9)	24	4	6	14	60	74	174
Leicestershire (14)	24	5	6	13	46	77	173
Middlesex (11)	24	5	5	14	47	69	166
Gloucestershire (2)	24	3	8	13	56	80	166

± includes five points for fourth innings in drawn match when final scores were level

1969 positions are shown in brackets

FIRST-CLASS AVERAGES 1970

	I	NO	HS	Runs	Av	100
±G. St A. Sobers (Nottinghamshire)	32	9	183	1742	75.73	7
T. W. Graveney (Worcestershire)	34	13	114	1316	62.66	2
G. M. Turner (Worcestershire)	46	7	154*	2379	61.00	10
R. B. Kanhai (Warwickshire)	37	4	187*	1894	57.39	7
G. Boycott (Yorkshire)	42	5	260*	2051	55.43	4
B. A. Richards (Hampshire)	33	2	153	1667	53.77	3
±D. W. White (Hampshire)	12	9	57	150	50.00	–
J. B. Bolus (Nottinghamshire)	53	9	147*	2143	48.70	2
B. W. Luckhurst (Kent)	38	4	203*	1633	48.02	4
R. T. Virgin (Somerset)	47	0	178	2223	47.29	7

	Overs	M	Runs	Wkts	Av	BB
Majid Khan (Camb U/ Glamorgan)	93	28	207	11	18.81	3–17
D. J. Shepherd (Glamorgan)	1123.3	420	2031	106	19.16	7–48
B. Wood (Lancashire)	287	80	601	31	19.38	5–54
E. J. Barlow (Rest of World)	152	33	396	20	19.80	7–64
±N. Gifford (Worcestershire)	965.5	331	2092	105	19.92	6–43
G. D. McKenzie (Leicestershire)	736.4	186	1860	91	20.43	7–67
V. A. Holder (Worcestershire)	707.3	141	1773	84	21.10	6–21
J. Sullivan (Lancashire)	183.2	51	470	22	21.36	4–44
P. Lever (Lancashire)	690.2	175	1774	83	21.37	7–83
R. N. S. Hobbs (Essex)	736	176	2183	102	21.40	7–59

REST OF THE WORLD

Freddie Trueman: Because of the D'Oliveira affair, South Africa's visit to England in the summer of 1970 was cancelled. Instead a series of five matches was staged between an England XI led by Ray Illingworth and a team designated Rest of the World, under the captaincy of Gary Sobers, for the Guinness Trophy. The matches are not recognised as official Tests although they were played at Lord's, The Oval, Headingley, Trent Bridge and Edgbaston with all the trappings and ceremonial of Tests.

Don Mosey: Although England's tour *to* South Africa had been cancelled, there was no thought in most cricketing minds that South Africa's 1970 visit to England would be called off. The circumstances were obviously entirely different. However, when the tour details were announced in September 1969, the Labour Minister of Sport, Denis Howell, offered the view that the South Africans should 'stay away'. Peter Hain, a 19-year-old student who at that time described himself as a Young Liberal, then started a 'Stop the Tour' campaign which gained a great deal of publicity but made no impact upon the Cricket Council, TCCB, MCC nor, it seemed, the vast majority of the cricket public. In November and December, confirmation was given from Lord's that the tour would go on, despite considerable disruption to certain aspects of the Springbok rugby tour currently taking place. Still the Cricket Council refused to yield and in January, 1970, they were given the backing of the Cricketers' Association, 81 per cent of whose membership had expressed themselves in favour of the tour. On the night of 19–20 January, 12 county cricket grounds suffered damage from vandals (or political protesters, depending on the viewpoint). On 16 April the Prime Minister (Harold Wilson) said in a TV appearance that 'MCC had made a big mistake by inviting the South Africans to tour.' This was followed by the opening of 'The 1970 Cricket Fund' by those in favour of the tour to raise £200,000 for the protection of grounds where the tourists were due to play. Clive Lloyd and Farokh Engineer, then playing for Lancashire, received threats of violence to their families if they played against the tourists. The TCCB decided to insure the lives of players competing against the tourists for £15,000. On 14 May, the House of Commons debated the issue to give MPs of all parties an opportunity to air (and hear) different points of view but no vote was taken. On 16 May the Cricket Council—refusing to bow to what it saw as outside and political pressure—confirmed again that the tour would take place but in an attempt to placate its critics added that no future meetings with South Africa would take place until teams were selected, and cricket played, on a multi-racial basis. Preparations were made to play matches in the series behind barbed wire and on artificial pitches if the natural ones were sabotaged. On 21 May, the Home Secretary (James Callaghan) formally requested the Cricket Council to cancel the tour and, faced with such an official approach, there was seen to be no alternative. The tour was cancelled on 22 May.

FST: I cannot think of many people within the game who saw this as anything but a crying shame. It opened the door to political interference with cricket which has gone on increasingly since that time. I didn't look forward to watching cricket played behind barbed wire any more than anyone else could have done. At the same time, if a stand had been made in 1970 it might have helped the game avoid a whole series of problems in the future.

Returning to purely cricketing matters, 1970 saw a change in the lbw Law which made it possible for a batsman to be out if he offered no stroke to a ball pitching outside the off stump when, in the opinion of the umpire, the ball would have carried on to hit the stumps but for the intervention of a pad. The batsman was still given protection by the Law if the ball struck his pad while he was playing a stroke. Sonny Ramadhin would have been happy if the change had been introduced 13 years earlier!

DM: Ironically, some of the outstanding cricket in the series was played by South Africans. The full list of overseas players who represented Rest of the World is: Eddie Barlow, South Africa (five matches); Farokh Engineer, India (2); Lance Gibbs, West Indies (4); Intikhab Alam, Pakistan (5); Rohan Kanhai, West Indies (5); Clive Lloyd, West Indies (5); Graham McKenzie, Australia (3); Deryck Murray, West Indies (3); Mushtaq Mohammad, Pakistan (2); Peter Pollock, South Africa (1); Graeme Pollock, South Africa (5); Mike Procter, South Africa (5); Barry Richards, South Africa (5), Gary Sobers, West Indies (5). The England players who were awarded caps for the series were: Dennis Amiss (one match), Geoff Boycott (2), David Brown (2), Colin

Peter Lever (Lancashire and England)

Cowdrey (4), Mike Denness (1), Basil D'Oliveira (4), John Edrich (2), Keith Fletcher (4), Tony Greig (3), Ray Illingworth (5), Alan Jones (1), Alan Knott (5), Peter Lever (1), Brian Luckhurst (5), Chris Old (2), Philip Sharpe (1), Ken Shuttleworth (1), John Snow (5), Derek Underwood (3), Alan Ward (1), Don Wilson (2). One or two interesting names there, Fred?

FST: The most interesting one to me is Alan Jones, the Glamorgan left-hand opener. He played county cricket from 1957 to 1983—610 matches—and never got an official Test even though he scored over 36,000 runs. The new Lancashire opening bowlers are there, Peter Lever and Ken Shuttleworth (Ken Higgs had retired a year after Statham only to re-appear at Leicestershire in 1972). And there's Tony Greig coming into the international picture for the first time. He had started with Sussex in 1967 (hitting a century in his first match) and he was soon to become the country's leading all-rounder.

DM: The 'Tests' might not have been official but the performances certainly rate as first-class, and we find Eddie Barlow getting into the averages that season with his 20 wickets at 19.80. I remember his hat-trick at Headingley—he actually took four wickets in five balls which wasn't bad for an opening batsman!

FST: Oh, Eddie was a fine all-rounder, bowling a brisk medium pace, and he could deliver a mean leg-break, too. He got two centuries for the Rest of the World and others were scored by Sobers (two), Kanhai, Lloyd (two) and Graeme Pollock. Boycott, D'Oliveira and Luckhurst got tons for England.

KENT'S CHAMPIONSHIP

DM: Kent's championship was not surprising with Luckhurst developing as an opening batsman and Cowdrey still scoring heavily. They had Underwood and Graham with splendid strike-rates as bowlers, Asif Iqbal, the Pakistani all-rounder, and Knott behind the stumps.

FST: Lancashire came back well, from 15th place to third because Lever and Shuttleworth had developed into a very useful opening pair of bowlers, and Glamorgan only slipped one place because Don Shepherd was still bowling so well in his 21st season. In all, Don took 2,200 first-class wickets and like his team-mate Alan Jones, he never got a Test—I find that a strange parallel. A lot of counties have moaned about not getting men in the England ranks because they were unfashionable but no county can say it with more truth than Glamorgan. We now begin to see overseas bowlers making their mark—Graham McKenzie

and Vanburn Holder for a start—and there are four overseas batsmen in the top ten. Kanhai had the best of his ten seasons with Warwickshire, and there's a nice little freak average for 'Butch' White who managed nine not outs in his ten innings. He was always rather proud of that season. (Butch was christened David William but I've never heard either name used.)

DM: I'm glad to see the name of Roy Virgin getting into the list. He was a sound opening bat for Somerset for 15 years, then had five years with Northamptonshire. He was still with Somerset when he had his best season in 1970. And how about Robin Hobbs, a leg-spinner, topping 100 wickets, Fred?

FST: A bit of a character, Hobbsie—one of the wittiest men in the game, and I suppose you've got to have a good sense of humour if you bowl that stuff. But he could bat a bit, as well. He once hit 100 in 44 minutes off an Australian touring side.

ONE-DAY COMPETITIONS

DM: Lancashire beat Sussex by six wickets to win the Gillette Cup for the first time and they also topped the John Player League for the second year in succession.

Bob Woolmer and Derek ('Deadly') Underwood, well pleased with a day's work at Lord's for Kent

1971

Winter Tour to Australia (1970–71):

Brisbane	Match drawn
Perth	Match drawn
Melbourne	Match abandoned without a ball bowled
Sydney	England won by 299 runs
Melbourne	Match drawn
Adelaide	Match drawn
Sydney	England won by 62 runs

One-Day International:

Melbourne	Australia won by five wickets

New Zealand:

Christchurch	England won by eight wickets
Auckland	Match drawn

Summer Series with Pakistan:

Edgbaston	Match drawn
Lord's	Match drawn
Headingley	England won by 25 runs

India:

Lord's	Match drawn
Old Trafford	Match drawn
Oval	India won by four wickets

County Champions Surrey

Gillette Cup Lancashire

John Player League Worcestershire

TEST AVERAGES ENGLAND V AUSTRALIA 1970–71

	M	I	NO	HS	Runs	Av	100	50	Ct/St
G. Boycott	5	10	3	142*	657	93.85	2	5	4
J. H. Edrich	6	11	2	130	648	72.00	2	4	5
B. W. Luckhurst	5	9	1	131	455	56.87	2	2	5
R. Illingworth	6	10	1	53	333	37.00	–	1	4
B. L. D'Oliveira	6	10	0	117	369	36.90	1	2	4
A. P. E. Knott	6	9	2	73	222	31.71	–	1	21/3
K. W. R. Fletcher	5	9	0	80	225	25.00	–	1	3
J. A. Snow	6	7	1	38	141	23.50	–	–	2
J. H. Hampshire	2	4	0	55	92	23.00	–	1	2
M. C. Cowdrey	3	4	0	40	82	20.50	–	–	3
R. G. D. Willis	4	5	3	15*	37	18.50	–	–	3
P. Lever	5	6	0	36	83	13.83	–	–	5
D. L. Underwood	5	6	3	8*	16	5.33	–	–	4

Also batted: K. Shuttleworth (2 matches) 7, 2, 1ct.

	Overs	M	Runs	Wkts	Av	5w	10w	BB
J. A. Snow	225.5	47	708	31	22.83	2	–	7–40
R. G. D. Willis	88	16	329	12	27.41	–	–	3–58
D. L. Underwood	194.6	50	520	16	32.50	–	–	4–66
P. Lever	143.5	25	439	13	33.76	–	–	4–49
K. Shuttleworth	75.5	13	242	7	34.57	1	–	5–47
R. Illingworth	132	43	349	10	34.90	–	–	3–39
B. L. D'Oliveira	114	29	290	6	48.33	–	–	2–15

Also bowled: G. Boycott 1–0–7–0; M. C. Cowdrey 6–0–36–0; K. W. R. Fletcher 20–1–101–1.

TEST AVERAGES ENGLAND V NEW ZEALAND 1970–71

	M	I	NO	HS	Runs	Av	100	50	Ct/St
B. L. D'Oliveira	2	3	0	100	163	54.33	1	1	–
J. H. Hampshire	2	4	1	51*	100	33.33	–	1	1
B. W. Luckhurst	2	4	1	29*	68	22.66	–	–	2
P. Lever	2	3	0	64	68	22.66	–	1	–
R. Illingworth	2	3	0	36	58	19.33	–	–	2
J. H. Edrich	2	4	0	24	39	9.75	–	–	2
K. Shuttleworth	2	3	0	11	16	5.33	–	–	–

Also batted: M. C. Cowdrey (1 match) 54, 45; K. W. R. Fletcher (1 match) 4, 2, 3ct; A. P. E. Knott (1 match) 101, 96; R. W. Taylor (1 match) 4, 2ct/1st; D. L. Underwood (2 matches) 0*, 1*, 8*, 3ct; R. G. D. Willis (1 match) 7, 3; D. Wilson (1 match) 5.

	Overs	M	Runs	Wkts	Av	5w	10w	BB
D. L. Underwood	84.1	28	205	17	12.05	3	1	6–12
K. Shuttleworth	41	5	102	5	20.40	–	–	3–14

Also bowled: B. L. D'Oliveira 3–1–2–0; R. Illingworth 41–12–102–0; P. Lever 41–10–80–1; B. W. Luckhurst 2–0–6–0; R. G. D. Willis 20–3–69–2; D. Wilson 25–8–68–2.

TEST AVERAGES ENGLAND V PAKISTAN 1971

	M	I	NO	HS	Runs	Av	100	50	Ct/St
G. Boycott	2	3	1	121*	246	123.00	2	–	–
B. W. Luckhurst	3	6	2	108*	242	60.50	1	1	2
B. L. D'Oliveira	3	4	0	74	241	60.25	–	3	2
A. P. E. Knott	3	4	1	116	137	45.66	1	–	10/1
R. A. Hutton	2	3	1	58*	90	45.00	–	1	4
D. L. Amiss	3	5	1	56	124	31.00	–	1	1
P. Lever	3	3	0	47	74	24.66	–	–	2
J. H. Edrich	3	5	0	37	87	17.40	–	–	4
R. Illingworth	3	4	0	45	67	16.75	–	–	–

Also batted: M. C. Cowdrey (1 match) 16, 34, 1ct; N. Gifford (2 matches) 3*, 2*, 1ct; R. N. S. Hobbs (1 match) 6, 0, 2ct; K. Shuttleworth (1 match) 21; D. L. Underwood (1 match) 9*, 1ct; A. Ward (1 match) 0. J. S. E. Price played in one match but did not bat.

	Overs	M	Runs	Wkts	Av	5w	10w	BB
B. L. D'Oliveira	99	47	162	8	20.25	–	–	3–46
N. Gifford	99.4	46	133	6	22.16	–	–	3–69
R. A. Hutton	63	13	126	5	25.20	–	–	3–72
R. Illingworth	87	36	162	6	27.00	–	–	3–58
P. Lever	88.3	20	239	7	34.14	–	–	3–10

Also bowled: R. N. S. Hobbs 24–5–70–0; J. S. E. Price 11.4–5–29–3; K. Shuttleworth 23–2–83–0; D. L. Underwood 41–13–102–0; A. Ward 29–3–115–0.

TEST AVERAGES ENGLAND V INDIA 1971

	M	I	NO	HS	Runs	Av	100	50	Ct/St
A. P. E. Knott	3	5	0	90	223	44.60	–	2	10/1
B. W. Luckhurst	3	6	0	101	244	40.66	1	1	1
J. A. Jameson	2	4	0	82	141	35.25	–	1	–
R. Illingworth	3	5	0	107	175	35.00	1	–	4
R. A. Hutton	3	5	1	81	129	32.25	–	1	5
J. H. Edrich	3	6	0	62	180	30.00	–	2	2
J. A. Snow	2	4	0	73	85	21.25	–	1	1
B. L. D'Oliveira	3	6	1	30	88	17.60	–	–	1
N. Gifford	2	3	1	17	32	16.00	–	–	1
K. W. R. Fletcher	2	4	1	28*	30	10.00	–	–	1
J. S. E. Price	3	5	2	5	9	3.00	–	–	1

Also batted: D. L. Amiss (1 match) 9, 0, 2ct; G. Boycott (1 match) 3, 33, 1ct; P. Lever (1 match) 88*; D. L. Underwood (1 match) 22, 11, 1ct.

	Overs	M	Runs	Wkts	Av	5w	10w	BB
N. Gifford	64.3	18	127	8	15.87	–	–	4–43
P. Lever	33	7	84	5	16.80	1	–	5–70
J. S. E. Price	81	21	207	8	25.87	–	–	2–30
J. A. Snow	74	21	169	6	28.16	–	–	2–64
R. Illingworth	118.3	43	202	7	28.85	1	–	5–70

Also bowled: B. L. D'Oliveira 58–28–83–3; R. A. Hutton 60–14–131–4; B. W. Luckhurst 2–0–9–1; D. L. Underwood 63–20–121–4.

CHAMPIONSHIP TABLE 1971

					Bonus Pts		
Win = 10 points	P	Won	Lost	D	Bat	Bowl	Pts
SURREY (5)	24	11	3	10	63	82	255
Warwickshire (8)	24	9	9	6	73	92	255
Lancashire (3)	24	9	4	11	76	75	241
Kent (1)	24	7	6	11	82	82	234
Leicestershire (15)	24	6	2	16	76	74	215±
Middlesex (16)	24	7	6	11	61	81	212
Somerset (13)	24	7	4	13	50	89	209
Gloucestershire (17)	24	7	3	14*	50	81	201
Hampshire (10)	24	4	6	14	70	82	192
Essex (12)	24	6	5	13	43	84	187
Sussex (9)	24	5	9	10	55	77	182
Nottinghamshire (14)	24	3	7	14	58	83	171
Yorkshire (4)	24	4	8	12	47	75	162
Northamptonshire (14)	24	4	8	12	36	83	159
Worcestershire (6)	24	3	7	14	46	76	152
Glamorgan (2)	24	3	5	16*	55	63	148
Derbyshire (7)	24	1	4	19	51	81	142

± includes five points for fourth innings in drawn match when final scores were level
* includes one match abandoned without a ball bowled
1970 positions are shown in brackets

FIRST-CLASS AVERAGES 1971

	I	NO	HS	Runs	Av	100
G. Boycott (Yorkshire)	30	5	233	2503	100.12	13
K. W. R. Fletcher (Essex)	41	12	164*	1490	51.37	3
M. J. Harris (Nottinghamshire)	45	1	177	2238	50.86	9
B. W. Luckhurst (Kent)	41	3	155*	1861	48.97	6
R. B. Kanhai (Warwickshire)	41	9	135*	1529	47.78	3
B. A. Richards (Hampshire)	45	4	141*	1938	47.26	2
±J. H. Edrich (Surrey)	44	1	195*	2031	47.23	6
±G. St A. Sobers (Nottinghamshire)	38	6	151*	1485	46.40	3
Asif Iqbal (Kent)	34	6	120	1294	46.21	2
M. J. K. Smith (Warwickshire)	48	9	127	1951	50.02	6

*denotes not out
±denotes left-hand batsman

	Overs	M	Runs	Wkts	Av	BB
G. G. Arnold (Surrey)	632	171	1421	83	17.12	6–31
±P. J. Sainsbury (Hampshire)	845.5	332	1874	107	17.51	8–76
T. W. Cartwright (Somerset)	976.4	407	1852	104	17.80	7–72
±D. Wilson (Yorkshire)	527.2	210	1095	60	18.25	6–35
N. G. Featherstone (Middlesex)	128.3	33	329	18	18.27	3–32
L. R. Gibbs (Warwickshire)	1024.1	295	2475	131	18.89	7–23
M. J. Procter (Gloucestershire)	535	149	1232	65	18.95	5–45
±D. L. Underwood (Kent)	945.5	368	1986	102	19.47	7–28
±J. C. Balderstone (Leicestershire)	162.5	59	354	18	19.66	6–84
R. Illingworth (Leicestershire)	633	230	1269	64	19.82	7–18

±denotes left-arm bowler

ONE-DAY INTERNATIONAL

Don Mosey: The first ever one-day International took place at the Melbourne Cricket Ground on 5 January 1971 and it occurred because of an accident of the weather. Ray Illingworth's tour party were already scheduled for a long and arduous series of six Tests in Australia. When the Third—due to start on New Year's Eve—was completely washed out by the first three days of continuous rain, officials of the MCC and the Australian Board of Control agreed to play an extra match at the end of the scheduled six so that a total of six would, in fact, have been played. But as compensation to the Melbourne cricketing public, who had lost their holiday attraction, a one-day fixture of 40 overs a side duration was staged on what would have been the last day of the Test. England were all out for 190 to the fourth ball of their scheduled 40 eight-ball overs, and John Edrich (82) became the scorer of the first 50 in this type of cricket. Australia (191 for five) then won by five wickets. In view of what we have already seen in the early days of the Gillette Cup in England it is worth recording that six English and three Australian wickets (nine of the 14 to fall to bowlers) were claimed by spinners. A crowd of 46,000 watched the match and suddenly limited-over Internationals were seen as an attraction which could be valuable to the finances of the game. By the 1980s, one-day Internationals were far outnumbering the Tests in Australia.

Freddie Trueman: The tour started in October and it didn't end, in New Zealand, until mid-March and Illingworth had to put up with a great deal before he brought home the Ashes. In the First Test (Brisbane) Keith Stackpole was run out by a couple of feet when he was 18 and was given not out. He went on to get 207 and it took a lot of solid batting by England to draw the match. The Second Test was the first to be played on Australia's newest Test ground, the WACA at Perth. Peter Lever got his first cap for England, and Australia gave *his* first to Greg Chappell who scored 108 batting at No. 7. Luckhurst, who had made his Test debut in Brisbane, got 100 in Perth and the match was drawn. The Third, as we have seen, was abandoned without a ball being bowled, but even so, Illy had problems. When the extra Test had been agreed it was announced that the Australian players would get an extra fee for this game but the tour management said nothing about more money for the England men. Some of them were on the verge of refusing to agree to play the extra game before a 'phone call to Lord's resulted in an extra fee (£50) being agreed. England won in Sydney (Fourth Test) where Bob Willis got a wicket in his first Test; drew in Melbourne (Fifth); and the Sixth (Adelaide) saw the first appearance of one of the greatest fast

bowlers—Dennis Lillee, who took five for 84. The Sixth Test was drawn as well and so Australia had to win the Seventh, in Sydney, to save the Ashes.

DM: They looked to have a good chance of doing so when Ian Chappell, taking over the captaincy from Bill Lawry, put England in to bat and bowled them out for 184. The second day was marred by crowd interruptions and bottle-throwing after Snow had struck Jenner on the head with a delivery, and Illingworth took the team off the field because he felt it was impossible for the game to continue. In the end, England won by 62 runs after being 80 behind on the first innings. Illingworth was very critical of some of the umpiring in a series in which not one lbw decision went England's way. Boycott, until he broke a forearm before the Seventh Test, scored 657 runs in the series and averaged 93.85; Snow, at the peak of his career on that tour, took 31 wickets and Knott claimed 21 catches and three stumpings. But Illy has always said that tour was outstandingly a team effort.

NEW ZEALAND

FST: Bob Taylor, who for so much of his career was understudy to Knott, got his first chance of Test cricket in Christchurch, and Underwood (in the course of taking six for 12) chalked up his 1,000th first-class victim. Charlie Elliott, the senior English umpire, who was in New Zealand at the time, stood in the First Test. In the Second, Knott made 101 in the first innings and 96 in the second. Four more runs and he would have been the first wicket-keeper to make two separate hundreds in a Test.

ZAHEER'S 200

DM: Summer brought another double-header with visits from Pakistan and India and at Edgbaston, Zaheer Abbas scored the first double century by a Pakistani against England and was promptly signed up to join Gloucestershire the following season. Rain saved England from what looked like being an overwhelming defeat. The Second Test (Lord's) saw Richard Hutton (Yorkshire) play in his first Test, and John Price took two wickets in two balls only to find the last man was unfit to bat (Pervez Sajjad). Boycott scored a third successive century at Headingley and Illingworth completed his personal double of 1,000 Test runs and 100 wickets. In the First Test against India, Snow made his highest score (73) but was dropped for the next match as a disciplinary measure when it was decided he *deliberately* collided with Sunil Gavaskar as the little Indian opener was taking a quick single. Gavaskar, destined to become one of the greatest opening batsmen of all time and by far the highest scorer in Tests, had played for India for the first time in the West Indies the previous

The first Pakistan player to hit a hundred hundreds—Zaheer Abbas

ership and the shrewd recruiting of their manager, Mike Turner. Chris Balderstone, for instance, had been a Yorkshire Colt for eight years without ever looking likely to become established in the side either with his batting or his slow left-arm bowling. Now at Leicestershire, in five years' time he was to play for England. Surrey were helped to their title by the bowling of Willis, but released him at the end of the 1971 season to join Warwickshire.

FST: I thought I remembered bowling at Mike Smith in the late sixties in what was supposed to be his final championship game but now we see him popping up again with nearly 2,000 runs. Kanhai, Richards, Sobers and Asif Iqbal are all overseas players taking four of the top ten positions but only Mike Procter and Lance Gibbs of the serious bowlers were imports.

DM: Boycott, appointed Yorkshire's captain after the dramatically sudden dismissal of Brian Close during the winter, had a personally brilliant season with 13 centuries and an average of 100, but Yorkshire nevertheless crashed winter and had scored 65, 67 not out, 116, 64 not out, 1, 117 not out, 124 and 220.

FST: The Final Test, at The Oval, saw India win in England for the first time and ended England's run of 26 Tests without defeat. It was Illingworth's first reverse as captain. It was largely achieved by the bowling of Chandrasekhar who took six for 38 to dismiss England for 101 in the second innings. The Indian series was a pretty thin one for batsmen and no one averaged 50 but Knott, without the help of a single not out, scored 223 runs at 44.60, and the summer as a whole brought him another 22 wicket-keeping victims.

DOMESTIC COMPETITIONS

DM: For the second year running Lancashire took the Gillette Cup (after one match against Gloucestershire which finished at 8.54 pm) but Worcestershire won the John Player League and Surrey were county champions. Glamorgan slumped from runners-up to next to the bottom of the table and we now see Leicestershire, accustomed for so long to the lower reaches of the championship, begin to respond to Illingworth's lead-

Peter Sainsbury, a great all-round servant to Hants

from fourth to 13th position. Close had now moved to Somerset and the results of that will be seen shortly. Geoff Arnold's bowling along with that of Willis and Pocock, was a factor in Surrey's success and the name of Peter Sainsbury conjures up memories of a great all-round servant to Hampshire through 23 seasons and 593 matches. Tom Cartwright is now taking his 100 wickets a season for Somerset, and Lance Gibbs is enjoying his best season with Warwickshire. But my lasting memory of that season is seeing David Hughes, of Lancashire, hitting 23 off an over from John Mortimore in that Gillette Cup win over Gloucestershire when the finish was televised live into the BBC News (then timed at 8.50 pm).

Lance Gibbs, second bowler in the world to take 300 Test wickets

1972

Summer Series with Australia:

Old Trafford	England won by 89 runs
Lord's	Australia won by eight wickets
Trent Bridge	Match drawn
Headingley	England won by nine wickets
Oval	Australia won by five wickets

Prudential One-Day Internationals:

Old Trafford	England won by six wickets
Lord's	Australia won by five wickets
Edgbaston	England won by two wickets

County Champions Warwickshire **John Player League** Kent

Gillette Cup Lancashire **Benson & Hedges Cup** Leicestershire

TEST AVERAGES ENGLAND V AUSTRALIA 1972

	M	I	NO	HS	Runs	Av	100	50	Ct/St
A. W. Greig	5	9	1	62	288	36.00	–	3	8
R. Illingworth	5	8	2	57	194	32.33	–	1	6
B. L. D'Oliveira	5	9	1	50*	233	29.12	–	1	3
A. P. E. Knott	5	8	0	92	229	28.62	–	2	17/–
B. W. Luckhurst	4	8	1	96	168	24.00	–	1	3
P. H. Parfitt	3	6	1	51	117	23.40	–	1	5
M. J. K. Smith	3	6	0	34	140	23.33	–	–	4
J. H. Edrich	5	10	0	49	218	21.80	–	–	1
G. Boycott	2	4	0	47	72	18.00	–	–	–
J. A. Snow	5	8	0	48	111	13.87	–	–	2
N. Gifford	3	5	1	16*	50	12.50	–	–	2
G. G. Arnold	3	5	2	22	28	9.33	–	–	–
D. L. Underwood	2	3	2	5	8	8.00	–	–	–

	Overs	M	Runs	Wkts	Av	5w	10w	BB
D. L. Underwood	125	49	266	16	16.62	1	1	6–45
G. G. Arnold	110.5	25	279	13	21.46	–	–	4–62
J. A. Snow	205.5	46	555	24	23.12	2	1	5–57
R. Illingworth	88	28	197	7	28.14	–	–	2–32
B. L. D'Oliveira	83	23	176	5	35.20	–	–	1–13
A. W. Greig	162.3	44	398	10	39.80	–	–	4–53

Also bowled: N. Gifford 34–6–116–1; P. Lever 45–11–137–1; B. W. Luckhurst 0.5–0–5–0; P. H. Parfitt 2–0–10–0; J. S. E. Price 33.1–5–115–3.

Also batted: K. W. R. Fletcher (1 match) 5; J. H. Hampshire (1 match) 42, 20, 1ct; P. Lever (1 match) 9; J. S. E. Price (1 match) 4*, 19; B. Wood (1 match) 26, 90.

CHAMPIONSHIP TABLE 1972

Win = 10 points	P	Won	Lost	D	Bonus Pts Bat	Bowl	Pts
WARWICKSHIRE (2)	20	9	0	11	68	69	227
Kent (4)	20	7	4	9	69	52	191
Gloucestershire (8)	20	7	4	9	38	77	185
Northamptonshire (14)	20	7	3	10	34	77	181
Essex (10)	20	6	4	10	50	63	173
Leicestershire (5)	20	6	2	12	43	68	171
Worcestershire (15)	20	4	4	12	59	68	167
Middlesex (6)	20	5	5	10	48	61	159
Hampshire (9)	20	4	6	10	50	64	154
Yorkshire (13)	20	4	5	11	39	73	152
Somerset (7)	20	4	2	14	34	71	145
Surrey (1)	20	3	5	12	49	61	140
Glamorgan (16)	20	1	7	12	55	61	126
Nottinghamshire (12)	20	1	6	13	38	73	121
Lancashire (3)	20	2	3	15*	42	56	118
Sussex (11)	20	2	8	10	46	49	115
Derbyshire (17)	20	1	5	14*	27	60	97

* includes one match abandoned without a ball bowled
1971 positions are shown in brackets

FIRST-CLASS AVERAGES 1972

	I	NO	HS	Runs	Av	100
G. Boycott (Yorkshire)	22	5	204*	1230	72.35	6
R. B. Kanhai (Warwickshire)	30	5	199	1607	64.28	8
Majid Khan (Camb Univ/ Glamorgan)	38	4	204	2074	61.00	8
Mushtaq Mohammad (Northants)	40	7	137*	1949	59.06	6
K. W. R. Fletcher (Essex)	36	6	181*	1763	58.76	5
D. L. Amiss (Warwickshire)	29	7	192	1219	55.40	5
B. W. Luckhurst (Kent)	37	6	184*	1706	55.03	3
D. S. Steele (Northamptonshire)	39	8	131	1618	52.19	5
G. M. Turner (Worcestershire)	38	4	170	1764	51.88	7
±D. B. Close (Somerset)	33	6	135	1396	51.70	3

	Overs	M	Runs	Wkts	Av	BB
A. Ward (Derbyshire)	164.5	35	506	31	16.32	4–45
M. J. Procter (Gloucestershire)	426.1	107	960	58	16.55	6–56
C. M. Old (Yorkshire)	378.5	101	931	54	17.24	6–69
C. T. Spencer (Leicestershire)	164	46	333	19	17.52	3–14
G. A. Cope (Yorkshire)	221.5	97	407	23	17.69	6–40
±J. C. J. Dye (Northamptonshire)	530.1	132	1427	79	18.06	6–41
R. M. H. Cottam (Northamptonshire)	364.3	109	918	50	18.36	8–14
T. W. Cartwright (Somerset)	863	373	1827	98	18.64	8–94
±N. Gifford (Worcestershire)	580	157	1395	74	18.85	7–27
A. G. Nicholson (Yorkshire)	547.3	152	1203	62	19.40	7–49

ONE-DAY INTERNATIONALS

Freddie Trueman: After 46,000 people had turned out in Melbourne to watch a hastily-arranged knockabout match, three one-day Internationals were arranged the following year in England to take place after the Test series over the Bank Holiday weekend. Illingworth withdrew from the squad because of injury and Brian Close was appointed to lead England in the three games. In the first, at Old Trafford, Dennis Amiss became the first man to score a hundred in this type of game; he opened the batting with Boycott. Australia totalled 222 for eight in 55 overs and England scored 226 for four. For the record, the men to play in this original match were: Boycott, Amiss, Fletcher, Close, Hampshire, D'Oliveira, Greig, Knott, Woolmer, Snow and Arnold. Australia were represented by Stackpole, Watson, Ian Chappell, Greg Chappell, Edwards, Sheahan, Walters, Marsh, Mallett, Lillee and Massie.

At Lord's England scored 236 for nine in 55 overs, and Australia (240 for five) won by five wickets. At Edgbaston, Barry Wood came into the England side for John Hampshire and after limiting Australia to 179 for nine (Arnold four for 27) England replied with 180 for eight in 51.3 overs. Three original members of the England squad of 15 who did not play in any match were Chris Old, Graham Roope and Derek Underwood. The Prudential Assurance Company put up a trophy for the series together with £30,000 in sponsorship money. Of this, £4,000 was prize money for the teams.

BENSON & HEDGES CUP

Don Mosey: The third limited-overs competition, sponsored by Benson & Hedges, was played for the first time in 1972, and in a rather dreary event at Lord's Leicestershire beat Yorkshire in the final. The new competition involved

Ray Illingworth with his Benson & Hedges Cup-winning side of 1972

55 overs a side, thus proving a variation on the theme of both the other limited-overs contests. It was Leicestershire's first success in the county's 78-year history and heralded the start of a golden age for them. Yorkshire, captained by Philip Sharpe in the absence of the injured Boycott, were bowled out for 136 and lost by five wickets. **FST**: The summer series against Ian Chappell's Australians started with a win at Old Trafford where Tony Greig made his first Test appearance and was top scorer in both innings (57 and 62). At Lord's (Second Test) it was an Australian debutant who startled everyone. Bob Massie, a Western Australian with the ability to swing the ball at medium-fast pace, found heavily humid conditions very much to his liking and took a record 16 wickets in the match, eight in each innings, for 137 runs. It was a record for any bowler in his first Test and yet Massie played in only five more after that—and took only another 15 wickets altogether! All the same, his performance was crucial in winning the Second Test and squaring the series. It was a draw at Trent Bridge and then in the Fourth, at Headingley, there was a row about the pitch (that was to become a regular thing), which was short of grass after a fungus-growth had developed on the square, and Underwood took ten wickets in the match (six for 45 in the second innings). The Ashes were safe for another series but Australia squared the rubber by winning at The Oval where Barry Wood made his Test debut. It was a damp summer, not a good one for batsmen, but one where you would have expected Laker, Lock, Wardle or Appleyard if they had still been playing to have taken a bundle of wickets. Instead, we see the few fast bowlers about struggling to top 50 wickets, only two spinners in the top ten in the country and the medium and medium-fast seamer beginning to dominate.

Two Pakistan captains who played in English county championship cricket: Asif Iqbal (Kent) and Majid Khan (Glamorgan)

FEWER CHAMPIONSHIP GAMES

DM: There were two causes of this, both connected with the three limited-overs competitions now in existence. The first was the increasing use of the medium-pacer in the one-day matches; the other was the reduced number of first-class games now being played. The figure had been reduced to 24 by the arrival of the John Player League; it was now down to 20 because of the zonal games which started the Benson & Hedges competition. The county championship was becoming a less realistic indication of the best side in the country. On the other hand, the honours of the game were now beginning to go round some counties where success was otherwise unknown. **FST**: John Dye enjoyed his first season at Northamptonshire by taking 79 first-class wickets, but once again we see Tom Cartwright bowling superbly at Somerset and just missing his 100 wickets. Close had played his first season with Somerset under Brian Langford's captaincy but now took over the leadership himself and hit five centuries, three in the championship and one of them against Yorkshire! This took him into the top ten of the first-class averages where we now see just three overseas players—Kanhai, Majid Khan (who hit his highest score for Glamorgan that season) and Mushtaq, who was becoming a consistently heavy scorer for Northamptonshire. **DM**: Norman Gifford is the only really successful slow bowler in the averages because Geoff Cope was now beginning to have problems with his action. He was suspended during 1972 for the first time and went to great lengths to correct what were seen officially as faults in his delivery. Gifford, now in his second season as captain of Worcestershire, had lost his left-arm partner, Doug Slade, at the end of 1971. For 11 years Worcester had enjoyed the luxury of *two* bowlers of a type which ten years later was to become almost extinct. Boycott once again headed the batting averages and in Warwickshire's championship year (only the third in their history) Northamptonshire made an advance of ten places in the table.

NOTABLE RETIREMENTS

FST: Brian ('Tonker') Taylor, the Essex wicket-keeper and captain, completed 301 consecutive appearances for his county, a sequence broken the following year when he was appointed a Test Selector and retired from the county game. It was the end of the line, too, for Jackie Bond, who had been a player since 1955 and captain since 1968. He took over at a low point in Lancashire history and led the side to three successive Gillette Cup final victories and the first two John Player championships. In his final Gillette he held the catch to dismiss Asif Iqbal who had looked like swinging the game in Kent's favour.

Winter Tour to India (1972–73):

Delhi	England won by six wickets
Calcutta	India won by 28 runs
Madras	India won by four wickets
Kanpur	Match drawn
Bombay	Match drawn

Pakistan:

Lahore	Match drawn
Hyderabad	Match drawn
Karachi	Match drawn

Summer Series with New Zealand:

Trent Bridge	England won by 38 runs
Lord's	Match drawn
Headingley	England won by an innings & 1 run

West Indies:

Oval	West Indies won by 158 runs
Edgbaston	Match drawn
Lord's	West Indies won by an innings & 226 runs

Prudential One-Day Internationals:

Swansea	England beat New Zealand by seven wickets
Old Trafford	Match abandoned – rain
Headingley	England beat West Indies by one wicket
Oval	West Indies won by eight wickets

County Champions Hampshire   **John Player League** Kent

Gillette Cup Gloucestershire   **Benson & Hedges Cup** Kent

TEST AVERAGES ENGLAND V INDIA 1972–73

	M	I	NO	HS	Runs	Av	100	50	Ct/St
A. W. Greig	5	8	2	148	382	63.66	1	2	9
K. W. R. Fletcher	5	8	1	113	312	44.57	1	2	6
J. Birkenshaw	2	3	0	64	112	37.33	–	1	–
A. R. Lewis	5	9	2	125	234	33.42	1	1	–
M. H. Denness	5	8	0	76	257	32.12	–	1	3
C. M. Old	4	6	2	33*	95	23.75	–	–	5
G. R. J. Roope	2	3	1	26*	47	23.50	–	–	3
A. P. E. Knott	5	8	0	56	168	21.00	–	1	11/1
G. G. Arnold	4	5	0	45	101	20.20	–	–	–
B. Wood	3	6	0	45	101	16.83	–	–	3
D. L. Amiss	3	6	0	46	90	15.00	–	–	1
R. M. H. Cottam	2	3	0	13	19	6.33	–	–	–
D. L. Underwood	4	5	1	9	19	4.75	–	–	3
P. I. Pocock	4	6	1	5	10	2.00	–	–	1

Also batted: N. Gifford (2 matches) 19, 3*, 1ct.

	Overs	M	Runs	Wkts	Av	5w	10w	BB
G. G. Arnold	137.3	42	300	17	17.64	1	–	6–45
A. W. Greig	143.5	52	247	11	22.45	1	–	5–24
C. M. Old	135.2	31	371	15	24.73	–	–	4–43
P. I. Pocock	177	49	410	14	29.28	–	–	4–28
R. M. H. Cottam	58	12	147	5	29.40	–	–	3–45
D. L. Underwood	214.4	82	457	15	30.46	–	–	4–56
J. Birkenshaw	80	14	227	5	45.40	–	–	2–66

Also bowled: N. Gifford 49.5–19–103–3; G. R. J. Roope 5–1–14–0; B. Wood 2–0–13–0.

TEST AVERAGES ENGLAND V PAKISTAN 1972–73

	M	I	NO	HS	Runs	Av	100	50	Ct/St
D. L. Amiss	3	6	1	158	406	81.20	2	1	2
A. W. Greig	3	5	0	72	261	52.20	–	2	3
A. P. E. Knott	3	5	1	71	199	49.75	–	2	4/–
K. W. R. Fletcher	3	6	1	78	221	44.20	–	3	2
A. R. Lewis	3	5	0	88	219	43.80	–	2	–
M. H. Denness	3	5	0	68	173	34.60	–	2	4
G. R. J. Roope	2	4	0	27	60	15.00	–	–	5
P. I. Pocock	3	3	0	33	41	13.66	–	–	3
G. G. Arnold	3	5	2	19*	32	10.66	–	–	–

Also batted: J. Birkenshaw (1 match) 21, 1ct; N. Gifford (2 matches) 24, 4*, 2ct; C. M. Old (1 match) 0, 17*; D. L. Underwood (2 matches) 6*, 20*; B. Wood (1 match) 3, 5.

	Overs	M	Runs	Wkts	Av	5w	10w	BB
J. Birkenshaw	49.3	10	146	6	24.33	1	–	5–57
N. Gifford	127	36	265	10	26.50	1	–	5–55
A. W. Greig	78.2	10	255	6	42.50	–	–	4–86
P. I. Pocock	129	25	377	8	47.12	1	–	5–169

Also bowled: G. G. Arnold 105–17–306–3; K. W. R. Fletcher 3–0–22–0; C. M. Old 27–2–98–0; D. L. Underwood 96–35–215–3.

TEST AVERAGES ENGLAND V NEW ZEALAND 1973

	M	I	NO	HS	Runs	Av	100	50	Ct/St
G. Boycott	3	5	0	115	320	64.00	1	3	1
D. L. Amiss	3	5	1	138*	250	62.50	1	1	–
K. W. R. Fletcher	3	5	0	178	309	61.80	1	1	2
A. W. Greig	3	5	0	139	216	43.20	1	1	1
N. Gifford	2	3	2	25*	35	35.00	–	–	–
G. G. Arnold	3	5	3	26	68	34.00	–	–	–
G. R. J. Roope	3	5	0	56	155	31.00	–	2	7
R. Illingworth	3	5	0	65	101	20.20	–	1	1
C. M. Old	2	3	0	34	48	16.00	–	–	–
A. P. E. Knott	3	5	0	49	72	14.40	–	–	12/–
J. A. Snow	3	5	0	8	23	4.60	–	–	–

Also batted: A. R. Lewis (1 match) 2, 2; D. L. Underwood (1 match) 20*.

	Overs	M	Runs	Wkts	Av	5w	10w	BB
C. M. Old	75.5	12	225	11	20.45	1	–	5–113
G. G. Arnold	161	48	351	16	21.93	2	–	5–27
A. W. Greig	74.5	15	185	8	23.12	–	–	4–33
J. A. Snow	135.1	27	320	13	24.61	–	–	3–21

Also bowled: N. Gifford 56–13–142–0; R. Illingworth 68–20–139–0; G. R. J. Roope 15–3–32–0; D. L. Underwood 18–6–41–0.

TEST AVERAGES ENGLAND V WEST INDIES 1973

	M	I	NO	HS	Runs	Av	100	50	Ct/St
K. W. R. Fletcher	3	6	2	86*	266	66.50	–	3	–
G. Boycott	3	5	1	97	202	50.50	–	2	2
D. L. Amiss	3	6	1	86*	231	46.20	–	2	2
F. C. Hayes	3	6	1	106*	159	31.80	1	–	2
A. W. Greig	3	5	0	44	122	24.40	–	–	5
R. Illingworth	3	5	0	40	107	21.40	–	–	–
B. W. Luckhurst	2	4	0	42	67	16.75	–	–	1
A. P. E. Knott	3	5	1	21	35	8.75	–	–	7/–
G. G. Arnold	3	5	0	24	38	7.60	–	–	2
D. L. Underwood	3	5	0	14	35	7.00	–	–	2

Also batted: C. M. Old (1 match) 0; G. R. J. Roope (1 match) 9, 31, 2ct; J. A. Snow (1 match) 0, 1; R. G. D. Willis (1 match) 5*, 0, 2ct.

	Overs	M	Runs	Wkts	Av	5w	10w	BB
G. G. Arnold	149.1	37	390	15	26.00	1	–	5–113
D. L. Underwood	133	38	330	8	41.25	–	–	3–40
R. Illingworth	128.4	39	311	6	51.83	–	–	3–50
A. W. Greig	105.1	12	402	7	57.42	–	–	3–180

Also bowled: B. W. Luckhurst 4–2–12–0; C. M. Old 44–3–151–4; G. R. J. Roope 6–1–26–0; J. A. Snow 49–12–133–3; R. G. D. Willis 35–3–118–4.

CHAMPIONSHIP TABLE 1973

Win = 10 points Tie = 5 points	P	Won	Lost	D	Tied	Bonus Pts Bat	Bonus Pts Bowl	Pts
HAMPSHIRE (9)	20	10	0	10	0	84	81	265
Surrey (12)	20	9	3	8	0	71	73	234
Northamptonshire (4)	20	8	4	8	0	53	75	208
Kent (2)	20	4	3	13	0	98	59	197
Gloucestershire (3)	20	6	4	10*	0	63	70	193
Worcestershire (7)	20	6	4	10	0	56	75	191
Warwickshire (1)	20	5	5	10	0	74	62	186
Essex (5)	20	6	5	9	0	46	72	178
Leicestershire (6)	20	4	3	13*	0	66	60	166
Somerset (11)	20	7	2	11	0	29	60	159
Glamorgan (13)	20	4	8	8	0	44	68	152
Lancashire (15)	20	4	6	10	0	44	67	151
Middlesex (8)	20	4	5	10	1	49	54	148
Yorkshire (10)	20	3	5	11	1	28	69	132
Sussex (16)	20	2	10	8	0	42	67	129
Derbyshire (17)	20	2	10	8	0	15	67	102
Nottinghamshire (14)	20	1	8	11	0	28	63	101

* includes one match abandoned without a ball bowled
1972 positions are shown in brackets

FIRST-CLASS AVERAGES 1973

	I	NO	HS	Runs	Av	100
G. M. Turner (Worcestershire/NZ)	44	8	153*	2416	67.11	9
G. Boycott (Yorkshire)	30	6	141*	1527	63.62	5
R. B. Kanhai (Warwickshire/WI)	22	4	230*	1129	62.72	4
M. J. Procter (Gloucestershire)	29	5	152	1475	61.45	6
D. L. Amiss (Warwickshire)	39	9	146*	1634	54.46	3
±Younis Ahmed (Surrey)	38	7	155*	1620	52.25	4
B. A. Richards (Hampshire)	30	2	240	1452	51.85	5
B. D. Julien (Kent/WI)	17	2	127	772	51.46	3
±G. St A. Sobers (Notts/WI)	29	5	150*	1215	50.62	3
K. W. R. Fletcher (Essex)	31	6	178	1259	50.36	2

*denotes not out
±denotes left-hand batsman

	Overs	M	Runs	Wkts	Av	BB
T. W. Cartwright (Somerset)	810.4	349	1410	89	15.84	7–37
±P. J. Sainsbury (Hampshire)	549.1	253	945	53	17.83	6–29
J. S. E. Price (Middlesex)	185.1	43	466	26	17.92	6–27
±B. S. Bedi (Northamptonshire)	864.2	309	1884	105	17.94	6–60
G. Edwards (Nottinghamshire)	86.4	27	224	12	18.66	5–44
P. G. Lee (Lancashire)	740.3	181	1901	101	18.82	8–53
A. G. Nicholson (Yorkshire)	553.5	165	1232	65	18.95	6–44
B. M. Brain (Worcestershire)	577.3	117	1621	84	19.29	6–32
P. Lever (Lancashire)	409.5	117	1011	52	19.44	5–35
R. G. D. Willis (Warwickshire)	470.1	133	1164	58	20.06	5–42

±denotes left-arm bowler

NEW CAPTAIN

Don Mosey: The 12 months which followed the end of the 1972 season were the most hectic in the history of England cricket with 14 Tests and four one-day Internationals being played. Illingworth opted out of the long winter tour to India and Pakistan and Tony Lewis took over as captain in his first Test match, played in New Delhi, joining a band of notables by failing to score in his first innings. In the second, however, he made 70 not out, which played a major part in England's victory by six wickets. He followed this up with 125 in Kanpur (Fourth Test) but England lost the series by two Tests to one with two drawn. Chris Old made his Test debut in Calcutta in the Third Test.

Freddie Trueman: Not the best pitch in the world for a fast bowler to start. England had trouble with Chandrasekhar on that tour, I seem to remember—35 wickets in the series—and with Prasanna and Bedi in action as well, India didn't really need opening bowlers except to take the shine off the ball. They used a couple of little medium pacers, Solkar and Abid Ali, but sometimes they had only a couple of overs and that was it. Greig had a good tour of India, topping the batting and coming second in the bowling and I was glad to see Chris Old take 15 wickets in his four Tests. Jackie Birkenshaw (Leicestershire) and Graham Roope (Surrey) got their first caps in the Fourth Test (Kanpur). Then the party moved on to Pakistan for three more Tests—it must have been a long four months!

DM: Dennis Amiss enjoyed himself in the second half. After a very thin time in India he scored 112 in Lahore, 158 in Hyderabad (the first Test ever played there) and 99 in Karachi when, as usual, there were riots on and off during the Third Test. In that game both Majid Khan and Mushtaq Mohammad were out on 99 as well. Not surprisingly, Amiss topped the Test batting averages but I think the bowlers would rather forget their experiences in Pakistan. Certainly they'll want to forget the innings of Intikhab Alam (who played for Surrey from 1969 to 1981 and was an excellent manager of the 1982 tour to England). He hit four sixes and 15 fours in his 138 and not many innings like that have been seen in Pakistan.

SUMMER AT HOME

FST: It was another double-header at home, with New Zealand looking a stronger side than we had seen before even though they lost two and drew one. Congdon and Pollard got centuries during the same innings at Trent Bridge, and at Lord's the same two players plus Mark Burgess topped the hundred mark. England used the regular opening pair of Boycott and Amiss throughout the double series of six Tests that summer.

ONE-DAY INTERNATIONALS

FST: New Zealand had given themselves a taste of the limited-overs stuff by playing a match against Pakistan in Christchurch in February of that year and they won by 22 runs but they were well beaten by England in the first representative game to be played at Swansea. Snow and Arnold rolled them over for 158 and Amiss hit his second one-day International century in England's win by seven wickets. Frank Hayes (Lancashire), who was to start his Test career eight days later, made his first appearance for an England XI. At Old Trafford, rain washed out the tail-end of the England innings and the rest of the game.

WEST INDIES SERIES

DM: The rubber against West Indies showed to what an extent their players had become established in county cricket in this country and were thus very much at home in English conditions. In the First Test at The Oval (where Frank Hayes marked his debut with a second innings 106

Tony Lewis and his 1972–73 touring party set off for India and Pakistan

not out) only Inshan Ali, the slow left-armer, was not on the strength of an English county. In the Second at Lord's, West Indies were represented by Fredericks (Glamorgan, 1971–73), Headley (Worcestershire, 1958–74), Kanhai (Warwickshire, 1968–77), Lloyd (Lancashire, 1968–86), Kallicharran (Warwickshire, 1971–), Sobers (Nottinghamshire, 1968–74), Murray (Nottinghamshire, 1966–68, Warwickshire, 1972–75), Julien (Kent, 1970–77), Boyce (Essex, 1966–77), Holder (Worcestershire, 1968–80) and Gibbs (Warwickshire, 1967–72). It was a series played with a certain amount of acrimony which reached a high point in the Second Test at Edgbaston when Boycott (who retired and returned twice during an innings after suffering bruised ribs and a damaged arm) was given not out by Arthur Fagg on an appeal for a catch by the wicket-keeper. Kanhai, captain of West Indies, expressed his displeasure at the decision so forcibly that Fagg refused to continue on the third morning. The Final Test, played at Lord's, cost Illingworth his England captaincy after 31 of his 61 Tests, so great was the West Indies margin of victory—an innings and 226 runs. (Scores: West Indies 652 for eight declared; England 233 and 193). On the Saturday afternoon the first bomb scare occurred on an England ground and a hoax 'phone call resulted in a delay of an hour and a half.

DENNESS AS CAPTAIN

FST: Mike Denness took over as captain for the two one-day Internationals and won his first game at Heading-

Tony Greig—England captain but Packer's man as well

ley, but the second was lost. Gary Sobers, who had been dogged by injury during the Test series (but had still scored a magnificent 150 not out at Lord's) only ever played in one limited-overs International. He got a duck at Headingley. Bob Taylor played in his first game of this type and brought off two catches and a stumping; he was run out in both matches. At The Oval, Fredericks became the second man to score a one-day International hundred.

UNBEATEN HAMPSHIRE

DM: Hampshire won their second county championship title by going through the first-class season unbeaten. They were now skippered by Richard Gilliat, a handsome left-hand batsman with the pedigree of Charterhouse and Oxford. Roy Marshall had retired the previous season but there was a ready-made replacement in Gordon Greenidge, who was capped in 1972 and with Barry Richards formed the most formidable opening pair in the country. Also in 1973, Hampshire had been joined by Andy Roberts from Antigua who was to become the outstanding fast bowler of his day. His debut was against the West Indian touring team and he became qualified for championship cricket the following season. Roughly the same teams occupied the lower half of the table as in previous season and the chief advance was made by Surrey, climbing from 12th position to runners-up.

FST: With so many West Indians called up from the county championship for the Test series it is not surprising to find only the Indian slow left-armer, Bishen Singh Bedi, in the top ten of the bowling averages. He had joined Northamptonshire the previous season and in an era when we see fewer and fewer bowlers claiming 100 in a season, he's there with 105. The other centurion bowler is Peter ('Leapy') Lee, of the high-bounding action, who had moved from Northamptonshire after four years there to spend the next ten at Old Trafford. He could be a very useful performer if there was any grass on the pitch or any damp about, and the start to the 1973 season was very damp indeed in the North.

DM: Right in the middle of the top ten, Fred, we find the name of Gordon Edwards who played in nine games for Nottinghamshire as an off-spinner, and so far as I can discover never played first-class cricket again.

FST: Tom Cartwright is still bowling 'em out for Somerset and Peter Sainsbury's all-round ability obviously had a lot to do with Hampshire's championship title. John Price was beginning to experience one or two injury problems and was now getting towards the end of his career with Middlesex.

OVERSEAS BATSMEN

DM: There might not have been too many overseas bowlers available that season, Fred, but look at the batsmen—seven out of the top ten. Turner only scored 116 in his five Test innings for New Zealand so what a season he had for Worcestershire! He got 1,018 runs before the end of May and no one had done that since Bill Edrich in 1938.

LIMITED-OVERS COMPETITIONS

FST: Lancashire's domination of the Gillette Cup had come to an end and Gloucestershire became the sixth county to get their name on the trophy. They beat Sussex (appearing at Lord's for the fifth time in this competition) by 40 runs and their skipper, Tony Brown, was Man of the Match with 77 not out and one for 33. Earlier in the season, Durham had become the first Minor County to beat a first-class outfit when they won by five wickets at Harrogate. Yorkshire were getting into a bit of a sorry state. It was an exceptionally good season for Kent who were fourth in the championship and won both the Benson & Hedges and the John Player. They beat Worcestershire

Glenn Turner (Worcestershire and New Zealand) congratulated by Northants players after completing 1,000 runs in May 1973

by a comfortable 39 runs and won the John Player for the second successive year. Yorkshire, on the receiving end of a Bob Willis hat-trick at Edgbaston, were runners-up.

Gillette Cup victory celebrations for Gloucestershire—Mike Procter, Tony Brown, David Shepherd

1974

Winter Tour to West Indies (1973–74):

Port-of-Spain	West Indies won by seven wickets
Kingston	Match drawn
Bridgetown	Match drawn
Georgetown	Match drawn
Port-of-Spain	England won by 26 runs

Summer Series with India:

Old Trafford	England won by 113 runs
Lord's	England won by an innings & 285 runs
Edgbaston	England won by an innings & 78 runs

Pakistan:

Headingley	Match drawn
Lord's	Match drawn
Oval	Match drawn

One-Day Internationals:

Headingley	England beat India by four wickets
Oval	England won by six wickets
Trent Bridge	Pakistan beat England by seven wickets
Edgbaston	Pakistan won by eight wickets

County Champions	Worcestershire
Gillette Cup	Kent
John Player League	Leicestershire
Benson & Hedges Cup	Surrey

TEST AVERAGES ENGLAND V WEST INDIES 1973–74

	M	I	NO	HS	Runs	Av	100	50	Ct/St
D. L. Amiss	5	9	1	262*	663	82.87	3	–	–
A. W. Greig	5	9	0	148	430	47.77	2	–	7
G. Boycott	5	9	0	112	421	46.77	1	3	2
A. P. E. Knott	5	9	1	87	365	45.62	–	3	4/–
K. W. R. Fletcher	4	7	1	129*	262	43.66	1	–	6
M. H. Denness	5	9	0	67	231	25.66	–	1	5
R. G. D. Willis	3	5	4	10*	25	25.00	–	–	3
J. A. Jameson	2	4	0	38	73	18.25	–	–	–
D. L. Underwood	4	7	3	24	67	16.75	–	–	2
F. C. Hayes	4	7	0	24	60	8.57	–	–	2
G. G. Arnold	3	5	1	13	34	8.50	–	–	1
P. I. Pocock	4	7	0	23	52	7.42	–	–	3
C. M. Old	4	7	0	19	50	7.14	–	–	–
J. Birkenshaw	2	3	0	8	15	5.00	–	–	2

	Overs	M	Runs	Wkts	Av	5w	10w	BB
A. W. Greig	207.1	46	543	24	22.62	3	1	8–86
R. G. D. Willis	73	15	255	5	51.00	–	–	3–97
P. I. Pocock	200	50	550	9	61.11	1	–	5–110
C. M. Old	87.4	15	313	5	62.60	–	–	3–89
D. L. Underwood	137.5	45	314	5	62.80	–	–	2–48

Also bowled: G. G. Arnold 49.3–11–148–2; J. Birkenshaw 40–9–96–2; K. W. R. Fletcher 0.5–0–5–0; J. A. Jameson 7–2–17–1.

TEST AVERAGES ENGLAND V INDIA 1974

	M	I	NO	HS	Runs	Av	100	50	Ct/St
K. W. R. Fletcher	3	3	2	123*	189	189.00	1	1	1
J. H. Edrich	3	3	1	100*	203	101.50	1	1	1
M. H. Denness	3	4	1	118	289	96.33	2	–	2
D. L. Amiss	3	4	0	188	370	92.50	1	2	–
D. L. Underwood	3	3	0	9	25	8.33	–	–	2

Also batted: G. G. Arnold (2 matches) 5, 1ct; G. Boycott (1 match) 10, 6, 1ct; A. W. Greig (3 matches) 53, 106, 2ct; M. Hendrick (3 matches) 1*, 4ct; A. P. E. Knott (3 matches) 0, 26, 15ct/1st; D. Lloyd (2 matches) 46, 214*, 1ct; C. M. Old (3 matches) 12, 3, 1ct; R. G. D. Willis (1 match) 24, 1ct.

	Overs	M	Runs	Wkts	Av	5w	10w	BB
C. M. Old	89	19	249	18	13.83	1	–	5–21
M. Hendrick	85	14	215	14	15.35	–	–	4–28
R. G. D. Willis	36	8	97	5	19.40	–	–	4–64
G. G. Arnold	65.5	13	204	10	20.40	–	–	4–19
A. W. Greig	70.1	16	176	6	29.33	–	–	3–35

Also bowled: D. Lloyd 2–0–4–0; D. L. Underwood 67–25–146–4.

TEST AVERAGES ENGLAND V PAKISTAN 1974

	M	I	NO	HS	Runs	Av	100	50	Ct/St
K. W. R. Fletcher	3	4	1	122	208	69.33	1	1	2
D. L. Amiss	3	5	1	183	220	55.00	1	–	1
C. M. Old	3	4	1	65	116	38.66	–	1	2
J. H. Edrich	3	4	0	70	144	36.00	–	1	–
A. P. E. Knott	3	4	0	83	132	33.00	–	1	7/–
D. L. Underwood	3	3	1	43	64	32.00	–	–	–
D. Lloyd	3	5	1	48	96	24.00	–	–	4
M. H. Denness	3	4	0	44	91	22.75	–	–	4
A. W. Greig	3	4	0	37	90	22.50	–	–	11
G. G. Arnold	3	3	0	10	13	4.33	–	–	1

Also batted: M. Hendrick (2 matches) 1*, 6, 2ct; R. G. D. Willis (1 match) 1*.

	Overs	M	Runs	Wkts	Av	5w	10w	BB
D. L. Underwood	113.5	48	218	17	12.82	2	1	8–51
A. W. Greig	79.5	23	222	8	27.75	–	–	3–23
G. G. Arnold	121	28	300	10	30.00	–	–	3–36
M. Hendrick	68	16	195	6	32.50	–	–	3–39
C. M. Old	88.3	8	324	7	46.28	–	–	3.54

Also bowled: D. Lloyd 2–0–13–0; R. G. D. Willis 35–4–129–2.

CHAMPIONSHIP TABLE 1974

Win = 10 points Tie = 5 points	P	Won	Lost	D	Tied	Bonus Pts Bat	Bowl	Pts
WORCESTERSHIRE (6)	20	11	3	6	0	45	72	227
Hampshire (1)	20	10	3	7*	0	55	70	225
Northamptonshire (3)	20	9	2	9	0	46	67	203
Leicestershire (9)	20	7	7	6	0	47	69	186
Somerset (10)	20	6	4	10	0	49	72	181
Middlesex (13)	20	7	5	8	0	45	56	171
Surrey (2)	20	6	4	10	0	42	69	171
Lancashire (9)	20	5	0	15	0	47	66	163
Warwickshire (7)	20	5	5	10	0	44	65	159
Kent (4)	20	5	8	7	0	33	63	146
Yorkshire (14)	20	4	7	9*	0	37	69	146
Essex (8)	20	4	3	12	1	44	52	141
Sussex (15)	20	4	9	6	1	29	63	137
Gloucestershire (5)	20	4	9	7*	0	29	55	124
Nottinghamshire (17)	20	1	9	10	0	42	66	118
Glamorgan (11)	20	2	7	11*	0	28	56	104
Derbyshire (16)	20	1	6	13	0	23	62	95

*includes one match abandoned without a ball bowled
1973 positions are shown in brackets

FIRST-CLASS AVERAGES 1974

	I	NO	HS	Runs	Av	100
±C. H. Lloyd (Lancashire)	31	8	178*	1458	63.39	4
B. A. Richards (Hampshire)	27	4	225*	1406	61.13	4
G. M. Turner (Worcestershire)	31	9	202*	1332	60.54	3
G. Boycott (Yorkshire)	36	6	160*	1783	59.43	6
R. T. Virgin (Northamptonshire)	39	5	144*	1936	56.94	7
D. L. Amiss (Warwickshire)	31	3	195	1510	53.92	5
±J. H. Edrich (Surrey)	23	2	152*	1126	53.61	3
J. H. Hampshire (Yorkshire)	23	6	158	901	53.00	2
R. B. Kanhai (Warwickshire)	22	4	213*	936	52.00	3
J. A. Jameson (Warwickshire)	42	2	240*	1932	48.30	6

	Overs	M	Runs	Wkts	Av	BB
A. M. E. Roberts (Hampshire)	727.4	198	1621	119	13.62	8–47
G. G. Arnold (Surrey)	487	139	1069	75	14.25	6–32
V. A. Holder (Worcestershire)	659	146	1493	94	15.88	7–40
M. J. Procter (Gloucestershire)	311.3	80	776	47	16.51	5–29
B. L. D'Oliveira (Worcestershire)	345.3	105	697	40	17.42	5–49
M. N. S. Taylor (Hampshire)	541	147	1259	72	17.48	6–26
H. R. Moseley (Somerset)	661.5	198	1420	81	17.53	5–24
R. Illingworth (Leicestershire)	535.1	204	1014	57	17.78	7–18
±P. Carrick (Yorkshire)	405.4	167	840	47	17.87	6–43
S. Turner (Essex)	615.5	166	1317	73	18.04	6–87

WINTER IN WEST INDIES

Freddie Trueman: The series began with one of those incidents which might have spelled disaster for the tour as a whole. In the First Test (Trinidad), Tony Greig threw down Alvin Kallicharran's wicket as the batsman strayed out of his ground. It was the last ball of the day and although the umpire, Sang Hue, had no option but to give Kallicharran out it was generally felt in the England ranks that while Greig's gesture was within the letter of the law it wasn't quite within the spirit. Greig was ever a competitor and never more so when up against the Windies. It's perhaps as well the crowd were drifting home when the decision was given and that some of those remaining hadn't noticed what had taken place. When the teams got inside the pavilion there was a long conference between captains, umpires and West Indian officials and England management and the upshot of it all was that the appeal was withdrawn and 'Kally' batted on the following morning. As he was 142 at the time and was finally out for 158, honour had been served and a crisis avoided. It's not a good thing to start a West Indies tour with an incident, especially one involving umpires.

Don Mosey: The Second (Jamaica), Third (Barbados) and Fourth (Guyana) Tests were drawn but Amiss, having

a marvellous tour, followed his 174 in Trinidad with 262 not out in Jamaica and 118 in Guyana. Sobers became the first batsman in the world to top 8,000 runs in Tests during the Second, and Roberts played his first Test in Barbados and became the first Antiguan to represent West Indies. Sobers ended his Test career in the Final Test, his 93rd, by becoming the first West Indian bowler to take 100 wickets against England. This was in Trinidad (Tests were not yet played in Antigua so Trinidad, with the largest ground capacity, got two matches) second time round and England won to square the series. It is generally regarded as the Boycott/Greig Test as Boycott scored 99 and 112 while Greig took eight for 86 and five for 70, the best match analysis by an England bowler against the Windies.

INDIAN SERIES

FST: Mike Hendrick played his first match for England in the First Test at Old Trafford and took a wicket (Solkar) with his third ball. This was the first match to be played under the new regulation allowing for an extra hour's play on any of the first four days if more than an hour was lost to the weather. It was necessary to use the extra hour at OT, needless to say. A couple of beautiful

Mike Hendrick (Derbyshire, Notts and England)

England, 240 in Pakistan's 600 for seven declared at The Oval. Once again it is possible to see overseas players benefiting from playing in the English county championship because in that Test their side included Sadiq Mohammad (Gloucestershire, 1972–82), Majid Khan (Glamorgan, 1968–76), Mushtaq Mohammad (Northamptonshire, 1964–77), Sarfraz Nawaz (Northamptonshire, 1969–82), Asif Iqbal (Kent, 1968–82), Imran Khan (Worcestershire, 1971–76, later Sussex), Intikhab Alam (Surrey, 1969–81). David Lloyd got a not out 116 at Trent Bridge in the first one-day International but was on the losing side as the first five Pakistani batsmen—all with experience of England conditions and limited-overs competitions—knocked up 246 for three. The second Prudential Trophy match was scheduled for Edgbaston on 2 September but the weather made play impossible and a game of 35 overs was arranged for the following day. England reached 81 for nine and the only men to reach double figures were Bob Taylor (26 not out) batting at No. 8 and Derek Underwood (17) at No. 10. Zaheer was 57 not out in Pakistan's eight-wickets win.

COUNTY CHAMPIONSHIP

DM: As we have seen, it was a pretty wet summer once again and Worcestershire won the championship by just two points from Hampshire for whom Andy Roberts, qualified for the first time, took 119 wickets, while at the other end Mike Taylor (who had joined Hampshire from Nottinghamshire the previous season) reaped the benefit of having an outstanding partner with 72 wickets, and Bob

A champagne soaking for Norman Gifford to celebrate Worcestershire's County Championship success. Joining in the festivities are (left to right) Glenn Turner, John Inchmore, Ron Headley, Jim Yardley, Brian Brain, Vanburn Holder and Alan Ormrod

pitches then followed at Lord's and Edgbaston, which produced some remarkable batting averages for one or two of the England players. . . .

DM: . . . with one notable exception—Geoffrey Boycott—for whom this was a troubled period in his cricketing life. He was at loggerheads with a large section of the Yorkshire Committee; he was in the throes of his Benefit year; and for some reason which seemed inexplicable he had failed with the bat in three encounters with the touring Indians—for MCC, for Yorkshire and for England. He asked the chairman of the Selectors, Alec Bedser, to rest him after the First Test and he did not, in fact, return to Test cricket until 1977. David Lloyd of Lancashire took his place for the remainder of the summer and scored 214 not out in his second match (Edgbaston).

FST: England won all three Tests easily and both one-day Internationals as well, but it was a different story in the second half of the summer with three drawn Tests and two defeats in the one-days. Zaheer Abbas, who had been signed by Gloucestershire after his previous successful tour in 1971, hit his second double-century in a Test in

Andy Roberts—the West Indian fast bowling menace really begins with his arrival at Hampshire

Herman, the other fast bowler, took 73. Richards, after another record-breaking season at home in South Africa (1,285 runs at 80.31), topped 1,000 runs for Hampshire for the seventh successive season. If they had not had one game abandoned without a ball bowled, Hampshire might well have won their second successive championship. Worcestershire owed a great deal to their overseas-born players, Turner, Headley and D'Oliveira all topping 1,000 runs and Holder falling six short of his 100 wickets.

FST: Roy Virgin won his Northamptonshire cap in 1974 after moving from Somerset the previous year and he topped their averages as well as hitting seven centuries. John Jameson's 240 not out against Gloucestershire was part of a record second-wicket partnership with Rohan

Kanhai of 465. The top three batsmen in the first-class averages were all overseas players and so were four of the top five bowlers.

GILLETTE WASH-OUT

DM: For the first time since the competition began, rain prevented any play in the Gillette Final on the appointed day (9 September) so the match was played the following Monday. The rain-affected pitch proved difficult and the only man in the entire match to score more than 20 runs was Clive Lloyd who was run out after slipping on the greasy surface. With him went Lancashire's last hope and they were all out for 118. Not without a few scares, Kent won by four wickets: their highest scorer, John Shepherd, made 19! After making only 170, Surrey won another disappointing Benson & Hedges Final by 27 runs. Somehow the B & H has rarely reached the heights of excitement which occurred in the Gillette/NatWest except on a very few occasions. Leicestershire, bowled out for 143 in the penultimate over of the Benson & Hedges final, gained some compensation by winning the John Player League by two points from Somerset. As this was a direct Illingworth/Close captaincy confrontation it had an added piquancy. Leicestershire had now got a nice blend which was beginning to look good but their best year was yet to come.

A new world record for the second wicket by the Warwickshire pair John Jameson and Rohan Kanhai

1975

Winter Tour to Australia (1974–75):

Brisbane	Australia won by 166 runs
Perth	Australia won by nine wickets
Melbourne	Match drawn
Sydney	Australia won by 171 runs
Adelaide	Australia won by 163 runs
Melbourne	England won by an innings & 4 runs

New Zealand:

Auckland	England won by an innings & 83 runs
Christchurch	Match drawn

One-Day Internationals:

Melbourne	England beat Australia by three wickets
Dunedin Wellington	Matches v New Zealand abandoned

Summer Series with Australia:

Edgbaston	Australia won by an innings & 85 runs
Lord's	Match drawn
Headingley	Match drawn
Oval	Match drawn

Prudential World Cup:

Lord's	England beat India by 202 runs
Headingley	Australia beat Pakistan by 73 runs
Edgbaston	New Zealand beat East Africa by 181 runs
Old Trafford	West Indies beat Sri Lanka by 9 wickets
Lord's	Australia beat Sri Lanka by 52 runs
Headingley	India beat East Africa by 10 wickets
Trent Bridge	England beat New Zealand by 80 runs
Edgbaston	West Indies beat Pakistan by 1 wicket
Oval	West Indies beat Australia by 7 wickets
Edgbaston	England beat East Africa by 196 runs
Old Trafford	New Zealand beat India by 4 wickets
Trent Bridge	Pakistan beat Sri Lanka by 192 runs

SEMI FINALS:

Headingley	Australia beat England by 4 wickets
Oval	West Indies beat New Zealand by 5 wickets

FINAL:

Lord's	West Indies beat Australia by 17 runs

County Champions	Leicestershire
Gillette Cup	Lancashire
John Player League	Hampshire
Benson & Hedges Cup	Leicestershire

TEST AVERAGES ENGLAND V AUSTRALIA 1974–75

	M	I	NO	HS	Runs	Av	100	50	Ct/St
J. H. Edrich	4	7	1	70	260	43.33	–	2	2
A. W. Greig	6	11	0	110	446	40.54	1	3	12
A. P. E. Knott	6	11	1	106*	364	36.40	1	3	22/1
K. W. R. Fletcher	5	9	0	146	324	36.00	1	1	3
M. H. Denness	5	9	0	188	318	35.33	1	1	6
D. Lloyd	4	8	0	49	196	24.50	–	–	6
D. L. Amiss	5	9	0	90	175	19.44	–	1	3
M. C. Cowdrey	5	9	0	41	165	18.33	–	–	3
F. J. Titmus	4	8	0	61	138	17.25	–	1	–
C. M. Old	2	3	0	43	50	16.66	–	–	–
R. G. D. Willis	5	10	5	15	76	15.20	–	–	1
B. W. Luckhurst	2	4	0	27	54	13.50	–	–	–
D. L. Underwood	5	9	0	30	111	12.33	–	–	–
P. Lever	2	3	1	14	24	12.00	–	–	2
M. Hendrick	2	4	2	8*	12	6.00	–	–	–
G. G. Arnold	4	7	1	14	22	3.66	–	–	–

	Overs	M	Runs	Wkts	Av	5w	10w	BB
P. Lever	61	8	214	9	23.77	1	–	6–38
R. G. D. Willis	140.4	15	522	17	30.70	1	–	5–61
D. L. Underwood	185	42	595	17	35.00	1	1	7–113
C. M. Old	51.6	4	210	6	35.00	–	–	3–50
G. G. Arnold	141.1	23	528	14	37.71	1	–	5–86
A. W. Greig	167.5	19	681	17	40.05	–	–	4–56
F. J. Titmus	122.3	30	360	7	51.42	–	–	2–43

Also bowled: M. Hendrick 34.6–6–119–2.

TEST AVERAGES ENGLAND V AUSTRALIA 1975

	M	I	NO	HS	Runs	Av	100	50	Ct/St
D. S. Steele	3	6	0	92	365	60.83	–	4	4
R. A. Woolmer	2	4	0	149	218	54.50	1	–	1
J. H. Edrich	4	8	0	175	428	53.50	1	2	1
A. P. E. Knott	4	8	1	69	261	37.28	–	2	4/–
A. W. Greig	4	8	0	96	284	35.50	–	2	4
B. Wood	3	6	0	52	146	24.33	–	1	–
K. W. R. Fletcher	2	4	0	51	79	19.75	–	1	2
C. M. Old	3	6	1	25*	60	12.00	–	–	4
J. A. Snow	4	7	0	34	84	12.00	–	–	–
P. H. Edmonds	2	4	1	13*	32	10.66	–	–	–
G. A. Gooch	2	4	0	31	37	9.25	–	–	2
D. L. Amiss	2	4	0	10	19	4.75	–	–	1
D. L. Underwood	4	7	3	10	16	4.00	–	–	1

Also batted: G. G. Arnold (1 match) 0*, 6*, 1ct; M. H. Denness (1 match) 3, 8, 1ct; J. H. Hampshire (1 match) 14, 0, 1ct; P. Lever (1 match) 4, 1ct; G. R. J. Roope (1 match) 0, 77, 1ct.

	Overs	M	Runs	Wkts	Av	5w	10w	BB
J. A. Snow	135.5	29	355	11	32.27	–	–	4–66
P. H. Edmonds	81.1	20	224	6	37.33	1	–	5–28
A. W. Greig	97	23	322	8	40.25	–	–	3–107
C. M. Old	91	22	283	7	40.42	–	–	3–74
D. L. Underwood	131	51	266	6	44.33	–	–	1–5

Also bowled: G. G. Arnold 33–3–91–3; P. Lever 35–5–138–2; D. S. Steele 11.4–5–21–2; B. Wood 6–2–16–0; R. A. Woolmer 34–9–72–2.

CHAMPIONSHIP TABLE 1975

Win = 10 points	P	Won	Lost	D	Bonus Pts Bat	Bonus Pts Bowl	Pts
LEICESTERSHIRE (4)	20	12	1	7	61	59	240
Yorkshire (11)	20	10	1	9	56	68	224
Hampshire (2)	20	10	6	4	51	72	223
Lancashire (8)	20	9	3	8	57	72	219
Kent (10)	20	8	4	8	59	70	209
Surrey (7)	20	8	3	9	55	67	202
Essex (12)	20	7	6	7	61	67	198
Northamptonshire (3)	20	7	9	4	40	72	182
Glamorgan (16)	20	7	8	5	45	66	181
Worcestershire (1)	20	5	6	9	55	63	168
Middlesex (6)	20	6	7	7	45	59	164
Somerset (5)	20	4	8	8	51	65	156
Nottinghamshire (15)	20	3	9	8	59	67	156
Warwickshire (9)	20	4	10	6	48	65	153
Derbyshire (17)	20	5	7	8	33	69	152
Gloucestershire (14)	20	4	10	6	43	62	145
Sussex (13)	20	2	13	5	37	62	119

1974 positions are shown in brackets

FIRST-CLASS AVERAGES 1975

	I	NO	HS	Runs	Av	100
R. B. Kanhai (Warwickshire)	22	9	178*	1073	82.53	3
G. Boycott (Yorkshire)	34	8	201*	1915	73.65	6
±C. H. Lloyd (Lancashire)	27	4	167*	1423	61.86	6
B. A. Richards (Hampshire)	32	5	135*	1621	60.03	3
G. M. Turner (Worcestershire)	29	5	214*	1362	56.75	3
B. F. Davison (Leicestershire)	34	6	189	1498	53.50	3
J. M. Brearley (Middlesex)	39	8	150	1656	53.41	4
D. S. Steele (Northamptonshire)	39	3	126*	1756	48.77	3
Asif Iqbal (Kent)	30	4	140	1262	48.53	4
P. A. Todd (Nottinghamshire)	9	1	178	385	48.12	1

*denotes not out
±denotes left-hand batsman

	Overs	M	Runs	Wkts	Av	BB
A. M. E. Roberts (Hampshire)	418.3	141	901	57	15.80	6–69
M. Hendrick (Derbyshire)	493.1	148	1077	68	15.83	6–36
±B. D. Julien (Kent)	270	76	707	40	17.67	7–66
P. Lever (Lancashire)	419.1	116	1098	61	18.00	5–16
±D. L. Underwood (Kent)	576.1	233	1210	67	18.05	7–44
K. D. Boyce (Essex)	471	92	1309	72	18.18	6–25
P. G. Lee (Lancashire)	799.5	199	2067	112	18.45	7–8
B. Wood (Lancashire)	127	47	244	13	18.76	4–43
T. E. Jesty (Hampshire)	383.5	108	960	50	19.20	6–40
K. Shuttleworth (Lancashire)	304.5	86	717	37	19.37	6–28

±denotes left-arm bowler

WORLD CUP

Freddie Trueman: The first-ever World Cup took place in June, 1975, with some marvellous one-day cricket crammed into a fortnight (in fact five actual playing days) and a magnificent final which finished just before a quarter to nine at night with the West Indies, led by Clive Lloyd, beating Ian Chappell's Australians who were also that season's tourists for four Tests. At first, it didn't look too good. The Indians, who were to win the Cup (sponsored by Prudential) in 1983, had not yet come to terms with the requirements of one-day cricket and after England had scored 334 for four at Lord's in the opening match a crowd of 20,000 saw India bat anti-climactically through their whole 60 overs to finish at 132 for three. Gavaskar carried his bat for 36 and many people must have wondered if the competition could possibly be a success. Sri Lanka and East Africa, the two invited sides, were plainly nowhere near the standard of the six senior countries and it was not until West Indies met Pakistan at Edgbaston on 11 June that the public saw a really great match. Pakistan scored 266 for seven with fifties from their captain Majid Khan, Mushtaq Mohammad and Wasim Raja, and then Sarfraz Nawaz (four for 44) reduced the West Indies to 203 for

World Cup drama at Headingley—but it's a near miss for a run-out and Australia win

nine in the 46th over. Deryck Murray and Andy Roberts, however, scored 64 for the last wicket to steer the Windies home with two balls to spare. England reached the semi-final only to be destroyed at Headingley by the left-arm swing bowling of Gary Gilmour whose figures were 12–6–14–6. He then went on to make the top Australian score of 28 not out: England 93, Australia 94–6. In the other semi-final, West Indies comfortably beat New Zealand by five wickets and the final was dominated by an innings of 102 off 82 balls by Clive Lloyd (his first limited-overs international century) but Gilmour again bowled splendidly (five for 48). The Australians lost five batsmen to run-outs but a last-wicket partnership between Lillee and Thomson, then the most formidable pair of opening bowlers in the world, took them to within 17 runs before Thomson became the fifth run-out. A crowd of 26,000 paid £66,950 to watch the final. The World Cup was a success in a summer which provided a lot of fine weather.

MISERABLE WINTER

Don Mosey: It followed a miserable winter tour to Australia and New Zealand. England lost four of the six Tests in Australia, drew one and won the sixth and last in Melbourne. Lillee and Thomson were at the height of their powers and in the First Test (Brisbane), Amiss fractured a thumb and Edrich a hand and Cowdrey was flown out to shore up the batting. Denness, England's captain since Illingworth had been deposed, dropped himself for the Fourth Test (Sydney) and John Edrich had his first and only game as captain of England. He was hit in the ribs by the first ball he received from Lillee and went to hospital, returning to bat with *two* fractures. Until the Sixth Test, England simply had no answer to Lillee and Thomson on the tour. Thomson injured a shoulder on rest day in the Fifth Test and was unable to bowl in England's second innings or in the Final Test, yet he took 33 wickets in the series and Lillee 21. In Adelaide (Fifth Test) Knott claimed his 200th Test victim and got a not out hundred as well and in Melbourne (Sixth), Denness made 188, the highest score by an England captain in Australia. Cowdrey played his last Test with a record of 114 matches and 7.624 runs (22 centuries). Notwithstanding these individual highlights, England returned from Australia more or less shell-shocked by the pace attack to play the World Cup and then face Australia (with Lillee and Thomson) again. They started with an innings defeat at Edgbaston which was the end of Denness as captain (Greig took over) and provided a short-lived introduction to Test cricket for Graham Gooch. Not only did he join the club of those not troubling the scorers in his first Test innings; he bagged a

Mike Denness, captain in Australia, pictured just before he announced he had dropped himself for the Fourth Test

pair and his second dismissal was quite the most devastating delivery (from Thomson) I have personally witnessed from the commentary box.

STEELE'S DEBUT

FST: In his quest for ever greater speed, Thomson was no-balled 22 times on the first day at Lord's; he was at all times a menace to England's batsmen with the back-up of Lillee and Max Walker—and of course Gilmour who took six wickets in the first innings at Headingley. On the

David Steele, an inspired choice by the Selectors to bat against Lillee and Thomson

Monday afternoon at Lord's, Test cricket had its first streaker. Michael Angelow, a ship's cook, gave the crowd an exhibition of nude hurdling over both sets of stumps before being taken into custody. It provided BBC Archives with a classic piece of John Arlott commentary. The Selectors by this time were desperate to find someone capable of standing up to Lillee and Thomson and hit on an inspired choice in David Steele, of Northamptonshire. He wasn't the sort of batsman you thought about in terms of taking an attack to pieces but he had a good defence and a good temperament. In his first six Test innings he scored 50, 45, 75, 92, 39 and 66. The Third Test was never finished because on the Monday night the pitch was sabotaged by people campaigning for the release from prison of a man they claimed had been wrongfully convicted—parts of the wicket were dug up and oil was poured on it as well. It was impossible for the game to continue so it goes in the book as a draw. At the time both sides fancied their chances with Australia needing 225 to win and seven wickets in hand. Phil Edmonds made his debut in the match with five for 28 and Underwood claimed his 200th wicket. It was another draw at The Oval

where Bob Woolmer, of Kent, got 149 in his third Test match.

LEICESTERSHIRE'S YEAR

DM: It had been an eventful summer at international level; on the county scene, it was very much Leicestershire's year as all the building undertaken by Mike Turner and Ray Illingworth came to fruition. Leicestershire won the championship with two wins more than their closest rivals, Yorkshire, and they took the Benson & Hedges Cup as well, bowling out Middlesex for 146 and winning by five wickets with Illingworth hitting the winning run. The championship was finally won in a remarkable match against Derbyshire at Chesterfield which will certainly be remembered by all-rounder Chris Balderstone. He was also a good footballer, starting with Huddersfield Town, then moving to Carlisle United and he was with Doncaster Rovers at this time. On the Monday night of that week-end game he was one of the not-out batsmen. With the permission (and not a little anxiety) of his captain, he took off his pads, jumped into a car driven by the Doncaster Rovers manager, Stan Anderson, and played a League match for Rovers before returning to continue his innings the following morning. He scored a century in the game and played a major part in bowling out Derbyshire in their second innings! Leicestershire were largely a side of more-than-useful bits-and-pieces players; almost every one who batted could do a bit of bowling as well and above all they worked well together. Leicestershire's first championship had been a long time arriving but it was the happiest moment of Illingworth's cricketing life. And learning his trade in the Leicestershire ranks during that season was an 18-year-old batsman called David Gower.

LANCASHIRE'S FOURTH GILLETTE

FST: David Lloyd had taken over the captaincy of Lancashire after the retirement of Jackie Bond and although Middlesex looked a much stronger batting side on paper (Mike Smith, Brearley, Radley, Featherstone, Barlow and the West Indian Larry Gomes) they could only score 180 for eight in the Gillette Cup final. Then they dropped Clive Lloyd when he had scored only eight and he went on to make 73 not out and Lancashire won by seven wickets. It was their fifth final and fourth win in six years and they were very much the one-day kings in the first half of the seventies.

FIRST-CLASS AVERAGES

DM: Geoff Boycott was the only Englishman in the top five but Mike Brearley was one of seven players who averaged more than 50. Andy Roberts again topped the first-class bowling, where Lancashire had no fewer than four names in the list with Peter Lee taking more than 100 wickets once again. That took them up from eighth to fourth place in the championship but there were set-backs for Worcestershire, Middlesex and Somerset. They, however, were about to make their mark as never before—Vivian Richards and Ian Botham were now playing alongside each other.

Peter ('Leapy') Lee, dangerous when any moisture in the pitch

1976

Summer Series with West Indies:

Trent Bridge	Match drawn
Lord's	Match drawn
Old Trafford	West Indies won by 425 runs
Headingley	West Indies won by 55 runs
Oval	West Indies won by 231 runs

Prudential One-Day Internationals:

Scarborough	West Indies won by six wickets
Lord's	West Indies won by 36 runs
Edgbaston	West Indies won by 50 runs

County Champions	Middlesex
Gillette Cup	Northamptonshire
John Player League	Kent
Benson & Hedges Cup	Kent

CHAMPIONSHIP TABLE 1976

Win = 10 points	P	Won	Lost	D	Bonus Pts Bat	Bowl	Pts
MIDDLESEX (11)	20	11	5	4	57	67	234
Northamptonshire (8)	20	9	3	8	54	74	218
Gloucestershire (16)	20	9	5	6*	54	66	210
Leicestershire (1)	20	9	3	8	51	68	209
Warwickshire (14)	20	6	7	7	65	70	195
Essex (7)	20	7	4	9	57	62	189
Somerset (12)	20	7	8	5	47	63	180
Yorkshire (2)	20	6	6	8	49	67	176
Surrey (6)	20	6	4	10	54	61	175
Sussex (17)	20	5	8	7	49	71	170
Worcestershire (10)	20	6	3	11*	50	59	169
Hampshire (3)	20	4	10	6	52	67	159
Nottinghamshire (13)	20	4	7	9	58	60	158
Kent (5)	20	5	7	8	48	57	155
Derbyshire (15)	20	4	7	9	39	70	149
Lancashire (4)	20	3	7	10	43	75	148
Glamorgan (9)	20	3	10	7	37	60	127

*includes one match abandoned without a ball bowled
1975 positions are shown in brackets

TEST AVERAGES ENGLAND V WEST INDIES 1976

	M	I	NO	HS	Runs	Av	100	50	Ct/St
J. H. Edrich	2	4	1	76*	145	48.33	–	1	1
D. B. Close	3	6	1	60	166	33.20	–	1	4
D. S. Steele	5	10	0	106	308	30.80	1	1	3
A. W. Greig	5	9	1	116	243	30.37	1	1	6
A. P. E. Knott	5	9	0	116	270	30.00	1	2	5/1
P. Willey	2	4	0	45	115	28.75	–	–	–
R. A. Woolmer	5	9	0	82	245	27.22	–	1	2
C. M. Old	2	3	0	33	65	21.66	–	–	2
J. A. Snow	3	5	2	20*	54	18.00	–	–	2
J. M. Brearley	2	4	0	40	70	17.50	–	–	1
J. C. Balderstone	2	4	0	35	39	9.75	–	–	1
F. C. Hayes	2	4	0	18	25	6.25	–	–	3
M. W. W. Selvey	2	4	2	4*	10	5.00	–	–	1
D. L. Underwood	5	9	0	31	40	4.44	–	–	3
P. I. Pocock	2	4	1	7	13	4.33	–	–	–
M. Hendrick	2	3	1	5	5	2.50	–	–	3
R. G. D. Willis	2	4	2	5*	5	2.50	–	–	1

Also batted: D. L. Amiss (1 match) 203, 16; G. Miller (1 match) 36, 24; A. Ward (1 match) 0, 0, 1ct; B. Wood (1 match) 6, 30.

	Overs	M	Runs	Wkts	Av	5w	10w	BB
R. G. D. Willis	57.3	11	234	9	26.00	1	–	5–42
J. A. Snow	106.4	16	423	15	28.20	–	–	4–53
D. L. Underwood	224	59	631	17	37.11	1	–	5–39
C. M. Old	68.3	11	248	6	41.33	–	–	3–80
M. W. W. Selvey	67	8	263	6	43.83	–	–	4–41
A. W. Greig	98	15	336	5	67.20	–	–	2–42

Also bowled: J. C. Balderstone 16–0–80–1; M. Hendrick 69–14–192–4; G. Miller 27–4–106–1; P. I. Pocock 61–15–173–4; D. S. Steele 3–0–18–0; A. Ward 24–2–128–4; P. Willey 4–0–15–0; R. A. Woolmer 40–2–194–1.

FIRST-CLASS AVERAGES 1976

	I	NO	HS	Runs	Av	100
Zaheer Abbas (Gloucestershire)	39	5	230*	2554	75.11	11
G. Boycott (Yorkshire)	24	5	207*	1288	67.78	5
D. L. Amiss (Warwickshire)	38	6	203	2110	65.93	8
Javed Miandad (Sussex)	10	1	162	523	58.11	2
B. F. Davison (Leicestershire)	41	9	132	1818	56.81	6
K. W. R. Fletcher (Essex)	36	7	128*	1588	54.75	4
H. Pilling (Lancashire)	35	5	149*	1569	52.30	3
Mushtaq Mohammad (Northants)	36	4	204*	1620	50.62	4
G. M. Turner (Worcestershire)	37	2	169	1752	50.05	4
±G. D. Barlow (Middlesex)	37	7	160*	1478	49.26	3

	Overs	M	Runs	Wkts	Av	BB
N. G. Featherstone (Middlesex)	232	64	569	36	15.80	5–58
R. M. H. Cottam (Northamptonshire)	213.5	54	584	36	16.22	7–39
Asif Iqbal (Kent)	69.4	12	214	13	16.46	3–20
±P. J. Sainsbury (Hampshire)	572.3	228	1236	66	18.72	8–114
E. J. Barlow (Derbyshire)	308.5	60	897	46	19.50	5–63
P. B. Clift (Leicestershire)	572.5	128	1493	74	20.17	8–17
W. Larkins (Northamptonshire)	67.2	9	245	12	20.41	3–34
R. D. Jackman (Surrey)	563.4	120	1760	85	20.70	8–79
M. W. W. Selvey (Middlesex)	644.3	130	1913	90	21.25	7–20
K. Higgs (Leicestershire)	473.4	114	1175	55	21.36	4–36

GOLDEN SUMMER

Don Mosey: This was a golden summer, if not for English cricket then for the most superb sunshine and absence of rain in living memory. By the beginning of August an official state of drought had been declared and Mr Denis Howell, the Minister for Sport, had been given a special, additional portfolio to deal with the chronic shortage of water in the country's reservoirs. (Even so—and it would scarcely have been an English summer without something of the kind happening—one county championship game between Gloucestershire and Worcestershire was abandoned without a ball being bowled.) But the abiding memories of the summer of 1976 are of day after day of dry, sunny weather and, unfortunately for England, conditions in which the visiting West Indians felt very much at home. They came here in prime form after a winter series in Australia followed by four Tests at home to India. In Australia they had introduced Michael Holding to international cricket and arrived in England under Clive Lloyd's leadership able to perm four fast bowlers from a battery of five in the party—Roberts, Holding, Holder, Wayne Daniel, Bernard Julien. They had a slow left-armer (Jumadeen), an off-spinner (Padmore) and a brilliant array of stroke-playing batsmen including Richards, already an established Test player, who hit a dazzling 232 at Trent Bridge in the First Test of the summer.

Freddie Trueman: Mike Brearley played his first Test and joined The Club—no score in his first innings—but Steele carried on where he had left off against the Australians in 1975 and got 106 at Nottingham. Close had been recalled to Test cricket at the age of 45, presumably on the same basis as Steele—he wouldn't flinch against fast bowling. After two drawn Tests (Trent Bridge and Lord's), England brought in Mike Selvey, of Middlesex, at Old Trafford where he took three wickets for six runs in his first 3.2 overs. It was a terrible pitch for a Test and the ball went right through the top before the game was a day old. In these circumstances, Gordon Greenidge's 134 out of 211 was a marvellous innings. England were bowled out for 71 of which Steele made 20 and extras totalled 19 (Holding five for 17). In the second innings extras (25) represented the main item in the scorecard. Close and Edrich, who opened (combined ages adding up to 84) were battered black and blue when England went in for the second time late on Saturday, but England had no form of retaliation with an opening attack of Selvey and Hendrick, neither of them much more than medium-fast. West Indies won by a massive 425 runs. It was the end of Close's Test career in which his 22 matches spanned 27 years. It was the end of the line for Edrich as well, yet the two veterans topped the batting averages at the end of the series. At Headingley, England brought in Chris Balderstone and Peter Willey for the first time and in an effort to find some pace in attack they called up Snow, Willis and Ward. West Indies' response was an opening partnership of 192 and a total of 450. Snow took his 200th Test wicket; Greig and Knott each scored 116 and Knott's innings included a seven which caused confusion on the scoreboard—a single, followed by two overthrows and then four overthrows! West Indies' win meant they retained the Wisden Trophy and they made it three in a row at The Oval.

DM: The groundsman had done his best for England by preparing a slow, flat wicket on which Richards made a brilliant 291 in West Indies' total of 687 for eight declared. Geoff Miller, Derbyshire's off-spinning all-rounder, played his first Test and Knott passed Evans' record of 219 dismissals but the game was unforgettable for Michael Holding's bowling. On a pitch which gave him no help of

Michael Holding—brilliant bowling at The Oval

Cause for rejoicing? Richards out for 291 at The Oval

any kind he took eight first-innings wickets for 92 and six for 57 in the second by sheer pace which blasted through the sleepiness of the pitch. Greig, the England captain, had made a half-joking remark about 'making the West Indies grovel' which was picked up by the Press and fiercely resented by the West Indians. They had given him their answer.

ONE-DAY INTERNATIONAL
FST: Scarborough's first game of this kind saw the introduction of Ian Botham to International cricket along with Graham Barlow (Middlesex), and John Lever (Essex). Barlow got 80 not out, Botham one run and one wicket for 26 from three overs, Lever 0–38, and West Indies won by six wickets. At Lord's, Derek Randall (Nottinghamshire) started his international career with 88 in a game which started on Saturday and had to be finished on Sunday because of the weather. West Indies won again, as they did at Edgbaston where no play was possible on Bank Holiday Monday and the match was reduced to 32 overs when a start was finally made just before two o'clock

on Tuesday, 31 August. The golden summer was over. This really was the dawn of the modern era of West Indies cricket in which their ability to find genuinely fast bowlers almost at will has given them a dominance in world cricket. Jumadeen bowled 28 overs in the only Test in which he appeared (Lord's) and Padmore had three overs in *his* only Test (Old Trafford). Clive Lloyd was not slow to recognise the physical and psychological advantage four genuinely quick bowlers gave him and this was to form the basis of West Indies policy for the next decade and beyond.

MIDDLESEX CHAMPIONS
DM: Middlesex, led by Brearley, were now beginning to look a formidable side with Barlow winning his cap that year and a young man called Mike Gatting, back from touring West Indies with England Young Cricketers, looking very promising material in the middle order. Edmonds was established at a time when slow left-armers

Middlesex are county champions (Mike Selvey, Mike Brearley, Graham Barlow)

were beginning to disappear from the ranks of other counties and the best was yet to come from the off-spinner, John Emburey. Selvey's 90 wickets had earned him a couple of England caps and Wayne Daniel, the West Indian, had been signed to play the following season. With Zaheer's runs and Procter's wickets (and runs), Gloucestershire made a dramatic leap up the table from next to bottom to third from the top but Lancashire plunged in the opposite direction, as did Kent and Hampshire. For Kent, however, there was compensation in other competitions while Hampshire could scarcely have expected to fare so well with Roberts and Greenidge absent for most of the season. Javed Miandad, the young Pakistan batsman, had now qualified for Sussex (after scoring 227 in a second eleven game the previous year) and in a limited number of appearances he looked a considerable prospect. Harry Pilling, at five ft three the smallest man in English cricket, had been contemplating retirement when, at the age of 33, he got a new lease of life and had his best seasonal average as well as hitting a career-best 149 against Glamorgan at Liverpool. Eddie Barlow, the talented South African who had done well in the Rest of the World series six years earlier, had joined Derbyshire for three years and took over the captaincy from Bob Taylor in mid-season to prove a great motivator. His medium-fast bowling took

him into the 1976 first-class averages but batting was his main forte, as his 217 against Surrey at Ilkeston showed. Wayne Larkins, at this time 22 years old, figured as a medium-pace bowler in the averages but it was his batting which won him his Northamptonshire cap in 1976, notably 167 against Warwickshire at Edgbaston. Paddy Clift, the Rhodesian all-rounder, won his cap for Leicestershire in a season which saw him do the hat-trick against Yorkshire at Grace Road.

LIMITED-OVERS COMPETITIONS

FST: Kent won two competitions in the same season and their future prospects looked bright when Chris Cowdrey, elder son of Colin, was made captain of the England Young Cricketers in the West Indies with Paul Downton (also the son of a former Kent player) as his vice-captain. Kent beat Worcestershire by 43 runs to take the Benson & Hedges Cup and topped the John Player table for the third time—the first county to do that—but Northamptonshire won the Gillette, their first title of any kind, beating Lancashire (their sixth appearance in seven finals) by four wickets.

1977

Winter Tour to India (1976–77):

Delhi	England won by an innings & 25 runs
Calcutta	England won by ten wickets
Madras	England won by 200 runs
Bangalore	India won by 140 runs
Bombay	Match drawn

Australia:

Melbourne	Australia won by 45 runs (Centenary Test)

Summer Series with Australia:

Lord's	Match drawn
Old Trafford	England won by nine wickets
Trent Bridge	England won by seven wickets
Headingley	England won by an innings & 85 runs
Oval	Match drawn

One-Day Internationals:

Old Trafford	England beat Australia by two wickets
Edgbaston	England won by 101 runs
Oval	Australia won by two wickets

County Champions (joint)   Middlesex/Kent

Gillette Cup   Middlesex

John Player League   Leicestershire

Benson & Hedges Cup   Gloucestershire

TEST AVERAGES ENGLAND V INDIA 1976–77

	M	I	NO	HS	Runs	Av	100	50	Ct/St
D. L. Amiss	5	9	1	179	417	52.12	1	2	1
A. W. Greig	5	8	0	103	342	42.75	1	2	5
A. P. E. Knott	5	8	1	81*	268	38.28	–	2	13/2
J. M. Brearley	5	8	0	91	215	26.87	–	2	9
R. W. Tolchard	4	7	2	67	129	25.80	–	1	5
K. W. R. Fletcher	3	5	1	58*	91	22.75	–	1	4
J. K. Lever	5	8	1	53	122	17.42	–	1	5
C. M. Old	4	6	0	52	95	15.83	–	1	4
R. A. Woolmer	2	3	0	22	42	14.00	–	–	3
D. W. Randall	4	7	0	37	86	12.28	–	–	3
D. L. Underwood	5	7	1	23	71	11.83	–	–	5
G. D. Barlow	2	3	1	7*	11	5.50	–	–	–
R. G. D. Willis	5	7	2	7	19	3.80	–	–	3

Also batted: M. W. W. Selvey (1 match) 5*.

	Overs	M	Runs	Wkts	Av	5w	10w	BB
J. K. Lever	149.4	29	380	26	14.61	2	1	7–46
R. G. D. Willis	135	25	335	20	16.75	2	–	6–53
D. L. Underwood	252.5	95	509	29	17.55	1	–	5–84
C. M. Old	88.5	20	201	10	20.10	–	–	3–38
A. W. Greig	131	28	336	10	33.60	–	–	3–64

Also bowled: M. W. W. Selvey 15–1–80–0; R. A. Woolmer 1–0–2–0.

TEST AVERAGES ENGLAND V AUSTRALIA 1977

	M	I	NO	HS	Runs	Av	100	50	Ct/St
G. Boycott	3	5	2	191	442	147.33	2	1	–
R. A. Woolmer	5	8	1	137	394	56.28	2	1	2
A. P. E. Knott	5	7	0	135	255	36.42	1	1	12/–
D. W. Randall	5	8	2	79	207	34.50	–	2	4
A. W. Greig	5	7	0	91	226	32.28	–	2	9
J. M. Brearley	5	9	0	81	247	27.44	–	1	7
R. G. D. Willis	5	6	4	24*	49	24.50	–	–	2
D. L. Underwood	5	6	2	20	66	16.50	–	–	3
C. M. Old	2	3	0	37	46	15.33	–	–	2
D. L. Amiss	2	4	1	28*	43	14.33	–	–	2
M. Hendrick	3	3	0	15	20	6.66	–	–	5
J. K. Lever	3	4	0	10	24	6.00	–	–	2

Also batted: G. D. Barlow (1 match) 1, 5; I. T. Botham (2 matches) 25, 0, 1ct; G. Miller (2 matches) 6, 13; G. R. J. Roope (2 matches) 34, 38.

	Overs	M	Runs	Wkts	Av	5w	10w	BB
R. G. D. Willis	166.4	36	534	27	19.77	3	–	7–78
I. T. Botham	73	16	202	10	20.20	2	–	5–21
M. Hendrick	128.4	33	290	14	20.71	–	–	4–41
D. L. Underwood	169.1	61	362	13	27.84	1	–	6–66
A. W. Greig	77	25	196	7	28.00	–	–	2–64
J. K. Lever	75	22	197	5	39.40	–	–	3–60
C. M. Old	77	14	199	5	39.80	–	–	2–46

Also bowled: G. Miller 24–7–47–3; R. A. Woolmer 16–5–31–1.

CHAMPIONSHIP TABLE 1977

Win = 12 points	P	Won	Lost	D	Bonus Pts Bat	Bowl	Pts
MIDDLESEX (1)	22	9	5	8	43	76	227
KENT (14)	22	9	2	11★	54	65	227
Gloucestershire (3)	22	9	5	8±	44	70	222
Somerset (7)	22	6	4	12★	58	64	194
Leicestershire (4)	22	6	4	12	44	73	189
Essex (6)	22	7	5	10★	38	65	187
Derbyshire (15)	22	7	3	12★	38	64	186
Sussex (10)	22	6	5	11	52	60	184
Northamptonshire (2)	22	6	6	10±	43	68	183
Warwickshire (5)	22	4	8	10	61	72	181
Hampshire (12)	22	6	5	11	53	54	179
Yorkshire (8)	22	6	5	11★	36	63	171
Worcestershire (11)	22	5	10	7	29	55	144
Glamorgan (17)	22	3	7	12★	36	60	132
Surrey (9)	22	3	6	13★	42	54	132
Lancashire (16)	22	2	4	16★	36	57	117
Nottinghamshire (13)	22	1	11	10	34	52	98

± includes two matches abandoned without a ball bowled
★ includes one match abandoned without a ball bowled
1976 positions are shown in brackets

FIRST-CLASS AVERAGES 1977

	I	NO	HS	Runs	Av	100
R. P. Baker (Surrey)	12	9	77★	215	71.66	–
G. Boycott (Yorkshire)	30	5	191	1701	68.04	7
I. V. A. Richards (Somerset)	35	2	241★	2161	65.48	7
C. G. Greenidge (Hampshire)	32	3	208	1771	61.06	6
G. R. J. Roope (Surrey)	31	5	115	1431	55.03	5
Zaheer Abbas (Gloucestershire)	36	6	205★	1584	52.80	5
K. S. McEwan (Essex)	37	4	218	1702	51.57	8
D. L. Amiss (Warwickshire)	34	5	162★	1513	52.17	6
B. Wood (Lancashire)	34	6	155★	1439	51.39	3
F. C. Hayes (Lancashire)	26	3	157★	1152	50.08	3

★denotes not out

	Overs	M	Runs	Wkts	Av	BB
R. A. Woolmer (Kent)	134.1	50	289	19	15.21	3–7
M. Hendrick (Derbyshire)	562.3	189	1068	67	15.94	6–19
W. W. Daniel (Middlesex)	516.1	142	1233	75	16.44	6–33
Sarfraz Nawaz (Northamptonshire)	486.4	130	1246	73	17.06	7–37
R. W. Hills (Kent)	215.3	60	566	33	17.15	5–44
G. Miller (Derbyshire)	655.4	224	1551	87	17.82	7–54
M. J. Procter (Gloucestershire)	777.3	226	1967	109	18.04	7–35
J. E. Emburey (Middlesex)	686.1	205	1488	81	18.37	7–36
±D. L. Underwood (Kent)	436.2	164	896	46	19.47	7–43
M. W. W. Selvey (Middlesex)	629.1	158	1540	78	19.74	5–19

±denotes left-arm bowler

INDIAN WINTER

Freddie Trueman: The winter tour in India was remarkable in that four of the five Tests produced positive results and as England won the first three, all kinds of history was made: in New Delhi (First Test) they won by an innings for the first time in India; in Calcutta (Second) it was the first time they had won successive Tests in India and their first victory in that city; in Madras (Third) they won a rubber in India for the first time since 1933–34. Barlow won his first cap in Delhi and started with a duck. Lever was the other debutant in that match and fared rather differently—he took ten wickets in the match. He swung the ball so much at various stages of the tour that it led to allegations that he was using illegal methods to shine it. Randall played his first Test in Calcutta along with Roger Tolchard, the Leicestershire wicket-keeper who played as a batsman. Greig, the captain, reached 3,000 runs and 100 Test wickets during the Second Test, the first man to do so for England. India won the Fourth Test in Bangalore and the Fifth (Bombay) was drawn. Underwood's 29 wickets equalled my record 29 in a series against India in 1952. It was a long tour because after the five Tests in India the party went on to play in Sri Lanka (still not a first-class cricketing country) and then to Australia for the Centenary Test in Melbourne.

CENTENARY TEST

FST: The game which is officially recognised as the first Test ever played took place at the MCG on 15, 16, 17 and 19 March 1977 and Australia won by 45 runs. By a miracle of organisation the Victoria Cricket Association (with sponsorship) gathered together as many former Test players who had competed in Australia–England matches as they could find and persuade to make the trip to be part of the celebrations. It was one of the greatest experiences of my life to be there and by a miracle of a different kind the game ended in a win for Australia by exactly the same margin as 100 years previously—45 runs. Derek Randall made the top score in the game, 174 in England's second innings and Underwood's first wicket was his 250th in Tests. The teams in this historic match were Australia: IC Davis, RM McCosker, GJ Cosier, GS Chappell (captain), DW Hookes, KD Walters, RW Marsh (wk), GJ Gilmour, KJ O'Keefe, DK Lillee, MHN Walker. England: RA Woolmer, JM Brearley, DL Underwood (going in as night-watchman), DW Randall, DL Amiss, KWR Fletcher, AW Greig (captain), APE Knott (wk), CM Old, JK Lever, RGD Willis. Australia scored 138 and 419 for nine (declared), England 95 and 417.

KERRY PACKER

Don Mosey: Before the summer series began the whole of the cricketing world was rocked by the news that Kerry Packer, the Australian newspaper and television magnate, had bought up many of the best players in the game to take part in a series of one-day matches to be staged in the 1977–78 Australian summer. As this was without any authority or approval from any established cricket body the matches would obviously be unofficial. Tony Greig, it soon emerged, had played an important role in recruiting the English players Amiss, Woolmer, Knott and Underwood and was to play a leading part in the competition himself. He was immediately relieved of the England captaincy but remained a member of the side, now led by Brearley in the three one-day Internationals of 1977 and all five Tests. For the first time, the limited-overs game took place before the Test series. England won at Old Trafford and Edgbaston and there was an extraordinary ending to the third match at The Oval. Rain stopped play and made a finish seem unlikely but as the following day (7 June) was to be a national holiday to celebrate the Royal Jubilee the teams agreed to play on with pools of water lying around the ground. Australia won with ten balls to spare at a quarter past eight in the evening.

JUBILEE TEST

FST: The First Test, unusually, was played at Lord's and named the Jubilee Test to mark 25 years of the Queen's reign. It brought receipts which at that time were a record (£220,384) and Chris Old took his 100th Test wicket in the match, which was drawn. Bob Woolmer scored 79 and 120 at Lord's and 137 in the Second Test at Old Trafford where Underwood took five wickets in an innings for the last time in a Test in England.

DM: The Third Test, at Trent Bridge, saw the return to Test cricket of Geoff Boycott for the first time since 1974. He had missed 30 Tests and after expressing his wish to return, earlier that season, the Selectors decided to 'let him wait' for a couple of matches. In the same game that Boycott returned (with a century), Ian Botham played his first Test, taking five wickets for 74 in Australia's first innings. He was played primarily as a bowler and batted at No. 8, scoring 25 in his only innings. At Headingley (Fourth Test) Boycott scored 191 in making what was his hundredth first-class century and so became the first man to achieve this in a Test match. Knott made his 250th dismissal in his 88th Test and Willis took his 100th wicket. England had regained the Ashes. Rain washed out almost two days of playing time at The Oval where the Final Test was the last to be played before Packer's World Series in Australia divided the cricketing world. Boycott scored his

Derek Randall turns a cartwheel of delight as Australia are beaten at Trent Bridge

5,000th Test run and averaged 147.33 on his return to the international scene.

JOINT CHAMPIONS

FST: Kent, capitalising on their success in limited-overs cricket in 1976, climbed 13 places up the championship table to share the title with Middlesex, for whom Wayne Daniel had made an immediate impact with 75 first-class wickets. Selvey took 78 and the now-emerging Emburey 81 while Gatting topped 1,000 runs and was capped. For Kent, the 19-year-old Chris Cowdrey had made his maiden century against Glamorgan and Chris Tavaré, after three Blues at Oxford, would be available full time for Kent in the following year. Gloucestershire, for whom the two Pakistanis, Zaheer Abbas and Sadiq Mohammad, again scored heavily with excellent support from Andy Stovold, were once again in third place with Procter topping 100 wickets again.

DM: Once again we see one of those mathematical flukes which leaves at the top of the country's batting averages one Raymond Paul Baker, a medium pace bowler for Surrey. In a career of 54 matches spread over six seasons he scored only 563 runs, but nine not-outs in 1977 saw him top of the list—ahead of Boycott, Richards, Greenidge and the rest—and no one can ever take it away from him.

FST: The same sort of thing happened with the bowling—Bob Woolmer's 19 wickets at 15.21 taking him to the top—but the real bowlers are not far away and only three out of the top ten are overseas players. Lancashire were still down next to the bottom of the table because their bowling by now was a bit thin. Lever and Shuttleworth had retired, Lee's 71 wickets cost 23.56 apiece and Colin Croft, the West Indian fast bowler from Guyana, their new overseas signing, had only one five-wicket performance in the season.

DM: But at least Lancashire have two men in the top ten batsmen, Barry Wood and Frank Hayes, who that season took 34 in an over off Malcolm Nash at Swansea—same bowler, same ground as Sobers' 36 off one over in 1968.

LIMITED-OVERS COMPETITIONS

FST: Middlesex added their first limited-overs success to their joint championship when they won the Gillette Cup with a comfortable five-wickets margin over Glamorgan. Mike Llewellyn hit one six almost to the top of the pavilion—it hit the commentary box—but the batting was never solid enough. Five of the nine Glamorgan wickets fell to spinners. Interesting to see Tom Cartwright in the side. Somerset let him go after the 1976 season and he became player, coach, then cricket manager for Glamorgan. Clive Radley got 85 not out for Middlesex, who had reached the final in unusual circumstances. The semi-final with Somerset was first of all washed out on all three days allocated for the fixture. An alternative date was decided upon, a week later, but after two days still no play had been possible. It was then agreed to play a match of 15 overs a side which Middlesex won by six wickets. This was a terrible disappointment to Brian Close, who was about to retire and badly wanted to see Somerset win their first trophy and to bow out personally at Lord's.

DM: Gloucestershire had a notable win in the Benson & Hedges in view of Kent's recent successes, beating them by 64 runs, and Leicestershire just edged out Essex for the John Player League title. Both teams finished level on points but Leicestershire's 13th win (against Essex's 12) was only achieved on the last day when they beat a Glamorgan side depressed by their Gillette defeat the previous day.

Frank Hayes (Lancs and England), 34 off one over

1978

Winter Tour to Pakistan (1977–78):

Lahore	Match drawn
Hyderabad	Match drawn
Karachi	Match drawn

One-Day Internationals:

Sahiwal	England won by three wickets
Sialkot	England won by six wickets
Lahore	Pakistan won by 36 runs

New Zealand:

Wellington	New Zealand won by 72 runs
Christchurch	England won by 174 runs
Auckland	Match drawn

Cornhill Insurance Tests:

Edgbaston	England beat Pakistan by an innings & 57 runs
Lord's	England beat Pakistan by an innings & 120 runs
Headingley	Match drawn
Oval	England beat New Zealand by seven wickets
Trent Bridge	England beat New Zealand by an innings & 119 runs
Lord's	England beat New Zealand by seven wickets

Prudential One-Day Internationals:

Old Trafford	England beat Pakistan by 132 runs
Oval	England won by 94 runs
Scarborough	England beat New Zealand by 19 runs
Old Trafford	England won by 126 runs

County Champions — Kent

Gillette Cup — Sussex

John Player League — Hampshire

Benson & Hedges Cup — Kent

TEST AVERAGES ENGLAND V PAKISTAN 1977–78

	M	I	NO	HS	Runs	Av	100	50	Ct/St
G. Boycott	3	5	1	100*	329	82.25	1	3	–
G. Miller	3	4	1	98*	117	39.00	–	1	2
J. M. Brearley	2	3	0	74	114	38.00	–	1	3
G. R. J. Roope	3	4	1	56	109	36.33	–	1	3
R. W. Taylor	3	4	1	36	86	28.66	–	–	5/1
D. W. Randall	3	4	0	55	104	26.00	–	1	–
J. K. Lever	3	4	2	33*	37	18.50	–	–	1
B. C. Rose	3	4	0	27	56	14.00	–	–	1
R. G. D. Willis	3	3	1	14	27	13.50	–	–	1
G. A. Cope	3	3	0	22	40	13.33	–	–	1

Also batted: P. H. Edmonds (2 matches) 4, 6, 5ct; M. W. Gatting (1 match) 5, 6, 2ct; C. M. Old (1 match) 2.

	Overs	M	Runs	Wkts	Av	5w	10w	BB
P. H. Edmonds	87	15	236	10	23.60	1	–	7–66
R. G. D. Willis	59	8	190	7	27.14	–	–	2–26
G. A. Cope	108	29	277	8	34.62	–	–	3–102

Also bowled: G. Boycott 3–0–4–0; J. K. Lever 67.6–14–195–4; G. Miller 72–14–262–4; C. M. Old 25–7–81–1; D. W. Randall 1–0–2–0; G. R. J. Roope 1–0–2–0.

TEST AVERAGES ENGLAND V NEW ZEALAND 1977–78

	M	I	NO	HS	Runs	Av	100	50	Ct/St
I. T. Botham	3	5	1	103	212	53.00	1	1	5
G. R. J. Roope	3	5	1	68	164	41.00	–	2	8
G. Boycott	3	5	0	77	166	33.20	–	2	2
G. Miller	3	4	0	89	132	33.00	–	1	3
P. H. Edmonds	3	4	0	50	73	18.25	–	1	9
R. W. Taylor	3	4	0	45	69	17.25	–	–	9/–
R. G. D. Willis	3	4	3	6*	15	15.00	–	–	–
B. C. Rose	2	4	1	21	44	14.66	–	–	1
D. W. Randall	3	5	0	30	56	11.20	–	–	2
C. M. Old	2	4	0	10	28	7.00	–	–	–

Also batted: M. W. Gatting (1 match) 0, 1ct; M. Hendrick (1 match) 0, 0; J. K. Lever (1 match) 1; C. T. Radley (2 matches) 15, 158.

	Overs	M	Runs	Wkts	Av	5w	10w	BB
R. G. D. Willis	103.6	27	255	14	18.21	1	–	7–66
I. T. Botham	101	17	311	17	18.29	1	–	5–73
C. M. Old	60	21	150	8	18.75	1	–	6–54
P. H. Edmonds	99	31	201	9	22.33	–	–	4–38
J. K. Lever	51	9	155	5	31.00	–	–	3–96

Also bowled: M. W. Gatting 1–0–1–0; M. Hendrick 27–4–62–2; G. Miller 31–11–99–3; D. W. Randall 1–0–1–0; G. R. J. Roope 1–0–2–0.

TEST AVERAGES ENGLAND V NEW ZEALAND 1978

	M	I	NO	HS	Runs	Av	100	50	Ct/St
G. A. Gooch	3	5	2	91*	190	63.33	–	2	1
D. I. Gower	3	5	0	111	285	57.00	1	1	–
G. Boycott	2	3	0	131	159	53.00	1	–	–
C. T. Radley	3	5	0	77	187	37.40	–	2	2
J. M. Brearley	3	5	1	50	104	26.00	–	1	5
I. T. Botham	3	3	0	22	51	17.00	–	–	2
P. H. Edmonds	3	3	0	28	39	13.00	–	–	4
R. W. Taylor	3	3	0	22	31	10.33	–	–	12/1

Also batted: J. E. Emburey (1 match) 2, 2ct; M. Hendrick (2 matches) 7, 12, 3ct; G. Miller (2 matches) 0, 4, 1ct; C. M. Old (1 match) 16; G. R. J. Roope (1 match) 14, 10*; R. G. D. Willis (3 matches) 3*, 1*, 7*.

	Overs	M	Runs	Wkts	Av	5w	10w	BB
I. T. Botham	142.1	42	337	24	14.04	3	1	6–34
P. H. Edmonds	112	48	145	10	14.50	–	–	4–20
R. G. D. Willis	99.2	33	229	12	19.08	1	–	5–42

Also bowled: J. E. Emburey 29.1–14–40–2; G. A. Gooch 10–0–29–0; M. Hendrick 63–30–87–3; G. Miller 71–33–90–4; C. M. Old 25–9–56–1.

TEST AVERAGES ENGLAND V PAKISTAN 1978

	M	I	NO	HS	Runs	Av	100	50	Ct/St
I. T. Botham	3	3	0	108	212	70.66	2	–	4
D. I. Gower	3	3	0	58	153	51.00	–	2	–
C. T. Radley	3	3	0	106	121	40.33	1	–	2
G. R. J. Roope	3	3	0	69	112	37.33	–	1	6
G. Miller	3	3	1	48	66	33.00	–	–	1
J. M. Brearley	3	3	0	38	40	13.33	–	–	6

Also batted: P. H. Edmonds (3 matches) 4*, 36*, 1*, 1ct; G. A. Gooch (2 matches) 54, 20, 2ct; C. M. Old (3 matches) 5, 0, 1ct; R. W. Taylor (3 matches) 10, 2, 8ct; R. G. D. Willis (3 matches) 18, 1ct; B. Wood (1 match) 14.

	Overs	M	Runs	Wkts	Av	5w	10w	BB
P. H. Edmonds	61	24	95	8	11.87	–	–	4–6
C. M. Old	114.2	47	191	13	14.69	1	–	7–50
I. T. Botham	75.5	19	209	13	16.07	1	–	8–34
R. G. D. Willis	88.4	16	233	13	17.92	1	–	5–47

Also bowled: G. Miller 30–10–50–2; B. Wood 3–2–2–0.

SCHWEPPES CHAMPIONSHIP TABLE 1978

					Bonus Pts		
Win = 12 points	P	Won	Lost	D	Bat	Bowl	Pts
KENT (1)	22	13	3	6	56	80	292
Essex (6)	22	12	1	9	55	74	273
Middlesex (1)	22	11	5	6*	48	75	255
Yorkshire (12)	22	10	3	9	58	55	233
Somerset (4)	22	9	4	9	44	76	228
Leicestershire (5)	22	4	5	13	57	68	173
Nottinghamshire (17)	22	3	7	12	63	67	166
Hampshire (11)	22	4	6	12*	53	60	161
Sussex (8)	22	4	7	11	39	64	151$
Gloucestershire (3)	22	4	8	10*	42	55	145
Warwickshire (10)	22	4	5	13	39	56	143
Lancashire (16)	22	4	8	10*	28	59	135$
Glamorgan (14)	22	3	8	11	43	54	133
Derbyshire (7)	22	3	7	12	33	63	132
Worcestershire (13)	22	2	5	15	56	51	131
Surrey (14)	22	3	7	12	36	58	130
Northamptonshire (9)	22	2	6	14±	41	56	121

± includes two matches abandoned without a ball bowled
* includes one match abandoned without a ball bowled
$ six points deducted for breach of regulations (Lancashire had not registered C. E. H. Croft and C. H. Lloyd with the TCCB)
1977 positions are shown in brackets

FIRST-CLASS AVERAGES 1978

	I	NO	HS	Runs	Av	100
C. E. B. Rice (Nottinghamshire)	37	9	213*	1871	66.82	5
G. M. Turner (Worcestershire)	38	7	202*	1711	55.19	6
C. G. Greenidge (Hampshire)	34	1	211	1771	53.66	5
D. L. Amiss (Warwickshire)	41	3	162	2030	53.42	7
J. H. Hampshire (Yorkshire)	36	6	132	1596	53.20	3
G. Boycott (Yorkshire)	25	1	131	1233	51.37	6
B. F. Davison (Leicestershire)	35	3	180*	1644	51.37	4
M. J. Procter (Gloucestershire)	36	3	203	1655	50.15	3
K. S. McEwan (Essex)	37	3	186	1682	49.47	5
Asif Iqbal (Kent)	25	6	171	934	49.15	3

	Overs	M	Runs	Wkts	Av	BB
±A. J. Mack (Glamorgan)	77.3	26	195	16	12.18	4–28
±D. L. Underwood (Kent)	815.1	359	1594	110	14.49	9–32
R. A. Woolmer (Kent)	135.4	46	292	20	14.60	6–27
W. W. Daniel (Middlesex)	453.3	113	1114	76	14.65	5–42
M. Hendrick (Derbyshire)	473.5	167	895	59	15.16	5–32
±J. K. Lever (Essex)	681.1	160	1610	106	15.18	7–32
±P. H. Edmonds (Middlesex)	503	174	912	60	15.20	7–34
M. W. Gatting (Middlesex)	168.3	36	411	26	15.80	5–59
J. Garner (Somerset)	170.1	61	351	22	15.95	5–50
R. J. Hadlee (Notts/New Zealand)	497.1	120	1269	78	16.26	7–77

SLOW BATTING

Don Mosey: The First Test of the winter double tour was certainly the most excruciating I have ever seen (when cricket was actually taking place), but there were also two riots, the second more serious than the first, during which a tear-gas shell landed between my feet and made subsequent broadcasting slightly difficult. The game itself was historic in a number of negative ways: Mudassar Nazar spent 557 minutes reaching the slowest hundred in all first-class cricket; Geoff Cope, in his first Test, did the hat-trick and then had it taken away from him when Brearley, the captain, pointed out he had not made the catch although Iqbal Qasim had already been given out by the umpire; Geoff Miller refused at least a dozen singles to shield Bob Willis from the strike in a last-wicket partnership of 25. Any two of those singles would have given Miller his maiden first-class hundred—in fact he had to wait another six-and-a-half years to record it. With the Second Test (Hyderabad) hopelessly beyond salvation and Boycott on 99, England took the optional last half-hour and Lever came out to be non-striker while Boycott completed his hundred, which won him 100 bottles of champagne on his return to England. The Third Test, in Karachi, had its usual complement of riots; saw Mike Gatting make his debut and Boycott lead England for the first time as Brearley had sustained a fractured forearm in a one-day 'friendly'! All three Tests were drawn and England moved on to New Zealand.

FIRST DEFEAT IN NZ

Freddie Trueman: John Wright, who had just completed his first season in English cricket (with Derbyshire), batted right through the first day of the First Test (Wellington) for 55 to frustrate England completely. Boycott then responded by batting 442 minutes for 77, but England were still 13 behind on the first innings. When NZ could make only 123 in the second innings, victory for England looked a formality, but Richard Hadlee returned six for 26 (ten for 100 in the match) to dismiss them for 64. England had lost to New Zealand for the first time. In Christchurch (Second Test) Botham scored a first Test hundred and took five for 73 in New Zealand's first innings. Clive Radley made his England debut after being flown from Australia to Pakistan as Brearley's replacement, then flying back with the party to the Andipodes before having his first game. The Third Test (Auckland) was drawn with Geoff Howarth (Surrey) getting a century in each innings for New Zealand and Radley 158 for England.

ONE-DAY INTERNATIONALS

DM: Three one-day Internationals were played in Pakistan; none in New Zealand. England won in Sahiwal (where Paul Downton had his first International match but did not bat) and Sialkot, skippered by Boycott who pencilled in his name at No. 7 and did not have to bat. In Lahore, Pakistan won on a day when I was colder than I have ever been at a cricket match anywhere in the world.

PACKER ERA

FST: The same two countries provided the summer opposition in England and Pakistan in particular were handicapped by the loss of such players as Zaheer Abbas, Asif Iqbal and Javed Miandad to Packer's World Series. The first of two Prudential Internationals against Pakistan went over into the second day because of bad light on the first, a game in which Boycott captained England at home for the first and only time. Pakistan were skippered on tour by their wicket-keeper, Wasim Bari. England won both one-day matches easily.

SPONSORED TESTS

DM: In consequence of the money shown by the Packer World Series to be available for injection into the game, sponsorship (in addition to the one-day tournaments) now came prominently into English cricket. Cornhill Insurance signed a five year contract with the TCCB which meant an injection of £1 million over that period. The tour fee for the winter trip to Pakistan and New Zealand went up from £3,000 to £5,000; players' match fees for Tests jumped from £200 to £1,000 and umpires got a rise from £175 to £750 a match. Schweppes became the first sponsors of the county championship, putting in £175,000 initially. With around £130,000 coming in from both the Benson & Hedges and John Player and £100,000 from Gillette, first-class cricket was now better off than at any time in the game's history. Costs, of course, were increasing every year, too.

FST: The year 1978 saw the introduction of the protective helmet worn by batsmen, later extended to close fieldsmen as well. One of the earliest batsmen to wear the helmet was Dennis Amiss, who (coincidentally or not) was the only batsman to score 2,000 runs that season. Amiss, in fact, went into the helmet business as a commercial venture and I remember seeing his car at Bradford Park Avenue with dozens of the fibre-glass helmets, made in Birmingham and retailing at £29 each, packed into the back. Other brands of defensive head-gear quickly followed onto the market and cricket had entered another new era.

Philippe Edmonds in the posture his wife Frances likes most to see him

TEST SERIES

DM: David Gower played in his first Test match at Edgbaston with a score of 58 in his only innings, but it was really Chris Old's match. He took seven for 50 including four wickets in five balls, the middle one a no-ball. Radley and Botham got hundreds in their first Test against Pakistan and Botham followed his with another in the Second Test (Lord's), on each occasion batting at No. 7. In Pakistan's second innings at Lord's he returned 20.5–8–34–8, the first instance of a player getting a hundred plus eight wickets in an innings of the same Test. Rain ruined the Third Test (Headingley) where Old had another remarkable bowling performance—41 overs and four balls for 41 runs and four wickets. Better weather in the second half of the summer saw England beat New Zealand in both one-day Internationals at Scarborough and Old Trafford. Gooch, after his traumatic Test debut at Edgbaston in 1975, and three one-day appearances against the West Indies in 1976 as a middle-order

batsman, now returned to the international scene as an opener and made a handsome 94 at Scarborough and at Old Trafford Lance Cairns, the New Zealand swing bowler, conceded a record 84 runs from 11 overs, then hit 60 of the last 67 New Zealand runs, including four sixes.

FST: Gower got a maiden Test hundred at The Oval (First Test) and was run out on 111 (who said it was just superstition?). Emburey joined his Middlesex spin twin Edmonds in his first Test match at Lord's (Third Test) where Botham had a five-wicket return for the eighth time in his first 11 Tests. England won all three Tests easily.

NEW OVERSEAS FACES

DM: Two significant new faces now appeared amongst the overseas players for English counties. Richard Hadlee had joined Nottinghamshire, and though his 1978 appearances were limited to seven matches, because of the New Zealand tour he topped the county's bowling averages with 37 wickets at 15.00 and was second in the batting (48.25) with 101 not out against Derbyshire. Hadlee was 27 years old in July 1978. He had already played 23 Tests over a six-year period and few suspected that in the second

Hadlee, one of the world's outstanding all-rounders, starts his ten-year career with Notts

half of his playing life he was to become one of the outstanding bowlers in the history of the game and a considerable all-rounder. When we assess how English county cricket has helped to develop overseas players, Hadlee's name must be high on the list. The other new face was that of Joel Garner, an unforgettable figure at six ft eight. The Barbadian fast bowler played in mid-week matches for Somerset in 1977 and 1978 while he was professional for Littleborough, in the Central Lancashire League at week-ends and in limited appearances had topped the averages in each season.

FST: And we now see overseas players taking over the batting well and truly—only Amiss, Hampshire and Boycott of the top ten are English-born. Clive Rice, the brilliant South African all-rounder, topped the list despite having a few personal problems at this time. He had been appointed captain of Nottinghamshire for 1978 but because he had signed for Packer's World Series the appointment was cancelled; he was, however, reinstated the following year. The season provided the one purple patch in Andy Mack's first-class career which extended over ten matches with Surrey and 21 with Glamorgan. A left-arm medium-pacer, he joined Glamorgan in 1978 and his 16 wickets put him into the record books. Only two spinners figure in the top ten—Underwood and Edmonds.

Joel Garner, 6ft 8ins of menace

KENT CHAMPIONS AGAIN

DM: Kent won the championship in their own right this season and the Benson & Hedges Cup as well. They were untroubled by Test calls while their 1977 rivals, Middlesex, lost Brearley, Radley, Edmonds and, at the end, Emburey as well. Knott, after his World Series winter, did not play for Kent in 1978 and Downton (still only 21 but with an official tour behind him) claimed 57 wicket-keeping victims. Tavaré won his cap with 1,432 runs and a big blond 19-year-old fast bowler named Graham Dilley took five for 32 against Middlesex at Lord's. Essex were improving steadily in Keith Fletcher's fifth year of captaincy with Gooch and McEwan scoring well and Lever's 102 wickets were backed up by 92 from Ray East, the best comedian on the circuit but a fine slow left-armer, nonetheless, and 71 from Norbert Phillip, their fast bowler from Dominica. Nottinghamshire made a spectacular jump from the bottom of the table to seventh although they actually won only three matches.

ONE-DAY GAMES

FST: Sussex were surprise winners of the Gillette Cup after some good fortune in the earlier rounds—a ten overs slog against Yorkshire, for instance, and a narrow escape from defeat by Staffordshire who lost by only two runs—but in the end they had a comfortable margin of five wickets over Somerset, the firm favourites. Kent won the Benson & Hedges because Derbyshire (147) never got anything like enough runs and Hampshire took their second John Player championship on a superior run rate over Somerset and Leicestershire after all three counties had finished on 48 points.

Another Gillette Cup win for Sussex, skippered by Arnold Long

Winter Tour to Australia (1978–79):

Brisbane	England won by seven wickets
Perth	England won by 166 runs
Melbourne	Australia won by 103 runs
Sydney	England won by 93 runs
Adelaide	England won by 205 runs
Sydney	England won by nine wickets

One-Day Internationals for the Benson & Hedges Cup:

Melbourne	Abandoned without a ball bowled
Sydney	Abandoned
Melbourne	England won by seven wickets
Melbourne	Australia won by four wickets
Melbourne	Australia won by six wickets

Cornhill Tests v India:

Edgbaston	England won by an innings & 83 runs
Lord's	Match drawn
Headingley	Match drawn
Oval	Match drawn

Second Prudential World Cup:

Lord's	England beat Australia by six wickets
Trent Bridge	New Zealand beat Sri Lanka by nine wickets
Headingley	Pakistan beat Canada by eight wickets
Edgbaston	West Indies beat India by nine wickets
Oval	West Indies v Sri Lanka – abandoned without a ball being bowled
Headingley	New Zealand beat India by eight wickets
Trent Bridge	Pakistan beat Australia by 89 runs
Old Trafford	England beat Canada by eight wickets
Edgbaston	Australia beat Canada by seven wickets
Headingley	England beat Pakistan by 14 runs
Trent Bridge	West Indies beat New Zealand by 32 runs
Old Trafford	Sri Lanka beat India by 47 runs

SEMI-FINALS

Old Trafford	England beat New Zealand by 9 runs
Oval	West Indies beat Pakistan by 43 runs

FINAL

Lord's	West Indies beat England by 92 runs

County Champions	Essex
Gillette Cup	Somerset
John Player League	Somerset
Benson & Hedges Cup	Essex

TEST AVERAGES ENGLAND V AUSTRALIA 1978–79

	M	I	NO	HS	Runs	Av	100	50	Ct/St
D. I. Gower	6	11	1	102	420	42.00	1	1	4
D. W. Randall	6	12	2	150	385	38.50	1	2	4
I. T. Botham	6	10	0	74	291	29.10	–	2	11
R. W. Taylor	6	10	2	97	208	26.00	–	1	18/2
G. Miller	6	10	0	64	234	23.40	–	1	1
G. A. Gooch	6	11	0	74	246	22.36	–	1	9
G. Boycott	6	12	0	77	263	21.91	–	1	2
J. M. Brearley	6	12	1	53	184	16.72	–	1	5
J. E. Emburey	4	7	1	42	67	11.16	–	–	6
R. G. D. Willis	6	10	2	24	88	11.00	–	–	3
M. Hendrick	5	9	4	10	34	6.80	–	–	3

Also batted: P. H. Edmonds (1 match) 1, 1ct; J. K. Lever (1 match) 14, 10; C. M. Old (1 match) 29*.

	Overs	M	Runs	Wkts	Av	5w	10w	BB
G. Miller	177.1	54	346	23	15.04	1	–	5–44
J. K. Lever	15.1	2	48	5	9.60	–	–	4–28
M. Hendrick	145	30	299	19	15.73	–	–	3–19
J. E. Emburey	144.4	49	306	16	19.12	–	–	4–46
R. G. D. Willis	140.3	23	461	20	23.05	1	–	5–44
I. T. Botham	158.4	25	567	23	24.65	–	–	–

Also bowled: G. Boycott 1–0–6–0; P. H. Edmonds 13–2–27–0; G. A. Gooch 6–1–15–0; C. M. Old 26.7–2–84–4.

TEST AVERAGES ENGLAND V INDIA 1979

	M	I	NO	HS	Runs	Av	100	50	Ct/St
G. Miller	3	3	1	63*	152	76.00	–	2	1
G. Boycott	4	5	0	155	378	75.60	2	–	1
D. I. Gower	4	5	1	200*	289	72.25	1	1	1
I. T. Botham	4	5	0	137	244	48.80	1	–	8
G. A. Gooch	4	5	0	83	207	41.40	–	2	6
D. W. Randall	3	3	0	57	83	27.66	–	1	4
P. H. Edmonds	4	4	1	27*	81	27.00	–	–	1
J. M. Brearley	4	5	0	34	96	19.20	–	–	5

Also batted: D. L. Bairstow (1 match) 9, 59; A. R. Butcher (1 match) 14, 20; M. Hendrick (4 matches) 0, 0, 1ct; J. K. Lever (1 match) 6*; R. W. Taylor (3 matches) 64, 1, 5ct; P. Willey (1 match) 52, 31; R. G. D. Willis (3 matches) 4*, 10*.

	Overs	M	Runs	Wkts	Av	5w	10w	BB
M. Hendrick	129.2	51	218	12	18.16	–	–	4–45
I. T. Botham	179	49	472	20	23.60	2	–	5–35
R. G. D. Willis	102	23	298	10	29.80	–	–	3–53
P. H. Edmonds	161	56	323	6	53.83	–	–	2–60

Also bowled: G. Boycott 7–3–8–0; A. R. Butcher 2–0–9–0; G. A. Gooch 25–9–49–1; J. K. Lever 33.5–10–98–2; G. Miller 69–23–134–2; P. Willey 47.5–16–106–2.

SCHWEPPES CHAMPIONSHIP TABLE 1979

Win = 12 points	P	Won	Lost	D	Bonus Pts Bat	Bowl	Pts
ESSEX (2)	22	13	4	5*	56	69	281
Worcestershire (15)	22	7	4	11*	58	62	204
Surrey (16)	22	6	3	13*	50	70	192
Sussex (9)	22	6	4	12@	47	65	184
Kent (1)	22	6	3	13	49	60	181
Leicestershire (6)	22	4	5	13*	60	68	176
Yorkshire (4)	22	5	3	14*	52	63	175
Somerset (5)	22	5	1	16*	56	53	171
Nottinghamshire (7)	22	6	4	12±	43	54	169
Gloucestershire (10)	22	5	4	13@	53	54	167
Northamptonshire (17)	22	3	6	13*	59	58	153
Hampshire (8)	22	3	9	10*	39	66	141
⎱Lancashire (12)	22	4	4	14	37	55	140
⎰Middlesex (3)	22	3	3	16@	44	60	140
Warwickshire (11)	22	3	7	12*	46	51	133
Derbyshire (14)	22	1	6	15*	46	60	118
Glamorgan (13)	22	0	10	12*	35	58	93

± includes three matches abandoned without a ball bowled
@ includes two matches abandoned without a ball bowled
* includes one match abandoned without a ball bowled
1978 positions are shown in brackets

FIRST-CLASS AVERAGES 1979

	I	NO	HS	Runs	Av	100
G. Boycott (Yorkshire)	20	5	175*	1538	102.53	6
±Younis Ahmed (Worcestershire)	30	8	221*	1539	69.95	4
G. M. Turner (Worcestershire)	31	2	150*	1669	57.55	8
±Sadiq Mohammad (Gloucestershire)	30	2	171	1595	56.96	8
±K. C. Wessels (Sussex)	36	2	187	1800	52.94	6
±A. I. Kallicharran (Warwickshire)	26	5	170*	1098	52.28	4
C. G. Greenidge (Hampshire)	30	2	145	1404	50.14	3
A. J. Lamb (Northamptonshire)	34	8	178	1747	67.19	4
D. L. Amiss (Warwickshire)	37	3	232*	1672	49.17	6
±C. H. Lloyd (Lancashire)	22	4	104*	880	48.88	3

*denotes not out
±denotes left-hand batsman

	Overs	M	Runs	Wkts	Av	BB
M. F. Malone (Lancashire)	102.3	32	230	19	12.10	7–88
C. M. Wells (Sussex)	73.1	30	137	10	13.70	4–23
J. Garner (Somerset)	393.1	127	761	55	13.83	6–80
±D. L. Underwood (Kent)	799.2	335	1575	106	14.85	8–28
±D. Lloyd (Lancashire)	59.3	19	164	11	14.90	6–60
Imran Khan (Sussex)	415.4	106	1091	73	14.94	6–37
H. R. Moseley (Somerset)	196.4	50	495	31	15.96	6–52
R. J. Hadlee (Nottinghamshire)	317	103	753	47	16.02	7–23
R. D. Jackman (Surrey)	628.1	173	1595	93	17.15	8–64
±J. K. Lever (Essex)	700	166	1834	106	17.30	8–49

±denotes left-arm bowler

SECOND WORLD CUP

Don Mosey: This was another desperate year for weather as a quick glance at the county championship table will show, some counties having as many as three matches abandoned without a ball being bowled. All the rain, however, could not prevent another World Cup (again sponsored by the Prudential Assurance Company) being completed with its share of surprises and heroics. There was also, between 22 May and 16 June a mini-World Cup with 14 teams competing for the ICC Trophy. (Gibraltar withdrew at the last moment from an original 15 and Wales were granted a non-competitive place in the tournament.) Bermuda, Denmark, Sri Lanka and Canada reached the semi-finals and the latter two—who progressed to the final where Sri Lanka won by 61 runs—then took part in the World Cup proper.

Freddie Trueman: Australia had been hit by the World Series calls harder than any other country involved and the team sent to play in the World Cup, led by Kim Hughes, was hardly representative—no Chappells, no Marsh, no Thomson or Lillee. England had, in fact, given Australia a five Tests to one beating in Australia during the winter and

the great decline of Australian cricket was very much under way. They didn't get a semi-final place in the World Cup. One of the great matches was at Headingley where England beat Pakistan by 14 runs in a low-scoring match—165 for nine, 151 all out in 56 overs, and it was the tail-enders of both sides who were the batting heroes. Willis and Taylor put on 43 for England's ninth wicket and Pakistan's last four wickets added 110 runs. The semi-final at Old Trafford between England and New Zealand produced a margin of just nine runs and at The Oval, West Indies had 43 runs to spare over Pakistan but it was a fine game which produced 543 runs. An all-ticket crowd of 25,000 saw the final at Lord's but some strange selection policy saw England compelled to cobble together 12 overs from a combination of Gooch, Boycott and Wayne Larkins. West Indies totalled 286 with a superb 138 not out from Viv Richards and 86 off 67 balls by Collis King. Brearley and Boycott started with a partnership of 129 for England's first wicket but as this occupied 38 of the 60 overs it put all the later batsmen under pressure and they could manage only 194.

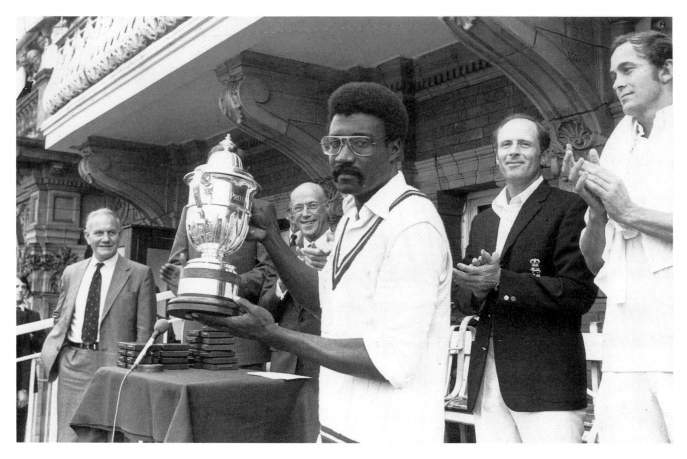

A second World Cup for West Indies—Clive Lloyd, watched by Alec Bedser, Charles Palmer, Geoff Boycott and Phil Edmonds

WINTER TOUR

DM: The extent to which Australia had been devastated by Packer's World Series had already been seen during the winter tour when England won every Test except the Third, in Melbourne, where Allan Border made his debut. It was a good tour for Geoff Miller, who topped the wicket-takers and the averages and scored a respectable 234 runs in the lower reaches of the order. In the Fourth Test (Sydney) I remember Randall's laboured innings of 150 in 571 minutes but essentially it has to be seen in context. It was a blazing hot day with a shade temperature at times above 100° so it must have been blistering out in the middle and it was an innings which undoubtedly put England in a position to win. The same game saw Boycott out first ball for the only time in any of his 193 Test innings. Rodney Hogg, who developed a great but friendly rivalry with Ian Botham, took 41 wickets in the six-Test series. In an inaugural Benson & Hedges Cup competition of one-day Internationals, Australia beat England by two victories to one.

SUMMER SERIES

DM: At Edgbaston, Gower made 200 not out, his maiden double century in first-class cricket against the summer visitors, India, who played four Tests after the World Cup competition. In the same game Boycott completed 6,000 Test runs as well as a century on each of England's six Test grounds.

FST: At Lord's, Botham took five wickets in an innings for the tenth time and Gavaskar was his 100th victim in two years, nine days of international games. It was another poor summer as far as the weather was concerned and the Second, Third, and Fourth Tests were all drawn but at Headingley we saw a remarkable century by Botham— 137 out of 270 with five sixes and 16 fours. At The Oval, David Bairstow and Alan Butcher played their first Tests and Botham got his 1,000th run to complete the Test double in 21 Tests—the shortest time ever. India made a great effort to get 438 runs to win and fell just nine short in a marvellous last day.

John Edrich and Robin Jackman demonstrate the 'John Edrich Bowling Machine' at The Oval

ESSEX'S GREAT YEAR

DM: After 103 years of labouring without reward, Essex achieved their first success on 21 July by winning the Benson & Hedges Cup but the foundations had already been laid for a greater success—the county championship. Essex went to the top early, due in no small measure to the bowling of Lever who took 53 championship wickets in the month of June. By the end of July, Essex had developed a commanding lead at the top of the table, ultimately winning by a margin of 77 championship points from Worcestershire. In fact with four games still to play, Essex could not be overtaken. They lost Gooch for the four Tests and Lever for one of them but McEwan, Fletcher, Hardie and Denness (who had moved from Kent three years earlier) all topped 1,000 runs. It was a popular win and one which had been threatening for some time under Fletcher's shrewd and experienced captaincy. Boycott averaged more than 100 for the second time but once again Yorkshire finished out of the prize-money, in seventh place. Boycott had been deposed as captain (John

Keith Fletcher and Graham Gooch enjoy the first Essex win in a major competition, the Benson & Hedges Cup

Ken McEwan (Essex), another great South African batsman

Hampshire taking over) and Ray Illingworth had returned from Leicestershire to become the cricket manager but the establishment of a Reform Group (in fact a Boycott support group) started a revolution in Yorkshire affairs which was to bedevil the county's cricket for the next seven years. Younis Ahmed, having moved from Surrey to Worcestershire in 1979, continued to score heavily and his 1,539 runs, together with 1,669 from the consistent Turner, played a major part in Worcestershire's climb of 13 places up the championship table. Five left-handers appear in the top ten of the batting averages, all of them overseas players. If you add Greenidge, Lamb and Turner, the only Englishmen in the group are Boycott and Amiss, aged 38 and 36 respectively. Where were the young Englishmen?

FST: At the top of the bowling we have Mike Malone, who had played in his only Test during Australia's 1977 tour, then joined the World Series. He played two seasons for Lancashire, 1979 and 1980, but really had only one outstanding performance in that time. Underwood, in his 17th season, had another 100 wicket haul and, as we have seen, so had John Lever. Kepler Wessels, the South African-born soldier of fortune who was to play Test cricket for Australia, had his best batting season for Sussex, for whom Colin Wells quickly made his mark to be followed into the side by his brother, Alan, two years later.

ONE-DAY COMPETITIONS

DM: Garner was now available full-time for Somerset who were developing well under Brian Rose's captaincy but they caught a cold in the Benson & Hedges by trying to be too clever by half. On 24 May, Somerset went to Worcester for their final Benson & Hedges zonal game, knowing that they were certain to qualify for the knock-out stages providing their striking-rate of wickets taken per balls bowled was not bettered by the two rivals, Worcestershire and Glamorgan. Batting first, Rose declared after one delivery—a no-ball, incidentally—and Somerset's striking rate of 33.32 could then not be beaten. They headed Group A and thus were through to the quarter finals. There was uproar throughout the game of cricket: the spectators had their money refunded and *Wisden* referred to the incident as 'sacrificing all known cricketing principles by deliberately losing the game'. A week later, the TCCB disqualified Somerset from the later stages. Essex beat Surrey by 35 runs in the final after totalling 290 for six (Gooch 120, the first century in a B & H Final). Somerset gained consolation handsomely by beating Northamptonshire by 45 runs in the final of the Gillette (Richards 117, Garner six for 29) to score their first success in 104 years of existence and the following day made it a double by finishing at the top of the John Player League, two points ahead of Kent.

1980

Tests v Australia (1979–80):

Perth	Australia won by 138 runs
Sydney	Australia won by six wickets
Melbourne	Australia won by eight wickets

India:

Bombay (Jubilee Test)	England won by ten wickets

One-Day Internationals (Benson & Hedges World Series):

v West Indies (1979–80): (in Australia)

Sydney (D/N)	England won by 2 runs
Brisbane	West Indies won by nine wickets
Melbourne	Abandoned without a ball bowled
Adelaide	West Indies won by 107 runs

v Australia:

Melbourne	England won by three wickets
Sydney (D/N)	England won by 72 runs
Sydney (D/N)	England won by four wickets
Sydney (D/N)	England won by two wickets

Best-of-three Final

Melbourne	West Indies won by 2 runs
Sydney	West Indies won by eight wickets

v West Indies (Summer Series):

Trent Bridge	West Indies won by two wickets
Lord's	Match drawn
Old Trafford	Match drawn
Oval	Match drawn
Headingley	Match drawn

v Australia:

Lord's (Centenary Test)	Match drawn

Prudential One-Day Internationals:

West Indies:

Headingley	West Indies won by 24 runs
Lord's	England won by three wickets

Australia:

Oval	England won by 23 runs
Edgbaston	England won by 47 runs

County Champions	Middlesex
Gillette Cup	Middlesex
John Player League	Warwickshire
Benson & Hedges Cup	Northamptonshire

TEST AVERAGES ENGLAND V AUSTRALIA 1979–80

	M	I	NO	HS	Runs	Av	100	50	Ct/St
G. A. Gooch	2	4	0	99	172	43.00	–	2	1
G. R. Dilley	2	4	2	38*	80	40.00	–	–	1
I. T. Botham	3	6	1	119*	187	37.40	1	–	3
G. Boycott	3	6	1	99*	176	35.20	–	1	2
J. M. Brearley	3	6	1	64	171	34.20	–	2	3
D. I. Gower	3	6	1	98*	152	30.40	–	1	3
R. W. Taylor	3	6	0	32	102	17.00	–	–	10/1
D. L. Underwood	3	6	0	43	71	11.83	–	–	4
D. W. Randall	2	4	0	25	26	6.50	–	–	1
P. Willey	3	6	0	12	35	5.83	–	–	2
R. G. D. Willis	3	6	0	11	21	3.50	–	–	–

Also batted: W. Larkins (1 match) 25, 3, 1ct; J. K. Lever (1 match) 22, 12, 1ct; G. Miller (1 match) 25, 8, 1ct.

	Overs	M	Runs	Wkts	Av	5w	10w	BB
I. T. Botham	173.1	62	371	19	19.52	2	1	6–78
D. L. Underwood	160.2	48	405	13	31.15	–	–	3–71

Also bowled: G. R. Dilley 53–5–143–3; G. A. Gooch 19–6–36–2; J. K. Lever 60.4–18–129–4; G. Miller 21–2–66–0; P. Willey 19–2–56–0; R. G. D. Willis 98–26–224–3.

TEST AVERAGES ENGLAND V WEST INDIES 1980

	M	I	NO	HS	Runs	Av	100	50	Ct/St
B. C. Rose	3	6	1	70	243	48.60	–	2	2
G. Boycott	5	10	1	86	368	40.88	–	3	–
G. A. Gooch	5	10	0	123	394	39.40	1	2	5
P. Willey	5	9	2	100*	262	37.42	1	1	1
R. A. Woolmer	2	4	1	46	109	36.33	–	–	–
M. W. Gatting	4	7	0	56	172	24.57	–	1	1
J. E. Emburey	3	5	2	28*	70	23.33	–	–	2
R. G. D. Willis	4	6	3	24*	61	20.33	–	–	–
I. T. Botham	5	9	0	57	169	18.77	–	1	2
C. J. Tavaré	2	4	0	42	65	16.25	–	–	2
W. Larkins	3	6	0	33	90	15.00	–	–	2
A. P. E. Knott	4	7	0	9	36	5.14	–	–	11/–
G. R. Dilley	3	4	0	2	2	0.50	–	–	1

Also batted: D. L. Bairstow (1 match) 40, 9*, 2ct; D. I. Gower (1 match) 20, 1, 1ct; M. Hendrick (2 matches) 7*, 2*, 10*, 1ct; J. K. Lever (1 match) 15, 4, 1ct; C. M. Old (1 match) 6; D. L. Underwood (1 match) 3.

	Overs	M	Runs	Wkts	Av	5w	10w	BB
J. E. Emburey	39.3	13	83	6	13.83	–	–	3–20
G. R. Dilley	74	19	183	11	16.63	–	–	4–57
R. G. D. Willis	110.1	27	407	14	29.07	1	–	5–65
I. T. Botham	131	41	385	13	29.61	–	–	3–50

Also bowled: G. Boycott 7–2–11–0; G. A. Gooch 25–7–59–3; M. Hendrick 44–11–141–2; J. K. Lever 28–4–101–1; C. M. Old 28.5–9–64–2; D. L. Underwood 29.2–7–108–1; P. Willey 43–16–111–2.

SCHWEPPES CHAMPIONSHIP TABLE 1980

Win = 12 points	P	Won	Lost	D	Bonus Pts Bat	Bowl	Pts
MIDDLESEX (14)	22	10	2	10	58	80	258
Surrey (3)	22	10	4	8	51	74	245
Nottinghamshire (9)	22	6	5	11	42	64	178
Sussex (4)	22	4	3	15	60	60	168
Somerset (8)	22	3	5	14*	56	70	168±
Yorkshire (7)	22	4	3	15	51	64	163
Gloucestershire (10)	22	4	5	13*	39	74	161
Essex (1)	22	4	3	15	48	64	160
⎰Derbyshire (16)	22	4	3	15@	47	62	157
⎱Leicestershire (16)	22	4	2	16	45	58	157±
Worcestershire (2)	22	3	7	12*	54	61	151
Northamptonshire (11)	22	5	4	13	41	47	148
Glamorgan (17)	22	4	4	14*	43	57	148
Warwickshire (15)	22	3	4	15	55	54	145
Lancashire (13)	22	4	3	15@	26	58	132
Kent (5)	22	2	8	12	36	59	119
Hampshire (12)	22	1	10	11	34	56	102

± includes six points for fourth innings in drawn match when final scores level
@ includes two matches abandoned without a ball bowled
* includes one match abandoned without a ball bowled
1979 positions are shown in brackets

FIRST-CLASS AVERAGES 1980

	I	NO	HS	Runs	Av	100
A. J. Lamb (Northamptonshire)	39	12	152	1797	66.55	5
J. Whitehouse (Warwickshire)	19	8	197	725	65.90	1
±K. C. Wessels (Sussex)	29	5	254	1562	65.08	2
P. N. Kirsten (Derbyshire)	36	6	213*	1895	63.16	6
G. M. Turner (Worcestershire)	35	4	228*	1817	58.61	7
C. T. Radley (Middlesex)	34	8	136*	1491	57.34	5
Javed Miandad (Glamorgan)	32	5	181	1460	54.07	3
C. E. B. Rice (Nottinghamshire)	36	9	131*	1448	53.62	5
G. Boycott (Yorkshire)	28	4	154*	1264	52.66	3
J. H. Hampshire (Yorkshire)	27	8	124	987	51.94	2

	Overs	M	Runs	Wkts	Av	BB
R. J. Hadlee (Nottinghamshire)	222.1	82	410	29	14.13	5–32
V. A. P. Van der Bijl (Middlesex)	642.3	213	1252	85	14.72	6–47
R. D. Jackman (Surrey)	745.2	220	1864	121	15.40	8–58
±J. F. Steele (Leicestershire)	347.5	139	704	40	17.60	7–29
M. D. Marshall (Hampshire/WI)	477.3	128	1170	66	17.72	7–56
M. Hendrick (Derbyshire)	444.5	128	980	55	17.81	7–19
Imran Khan (Sussex)	402.5	109	967	54	17.90	6–80
M. J. Procter (Gloucestershire)	372.1	102	931	51	18.25	7–16
W. G. Merry (Middlesex)	96	21	300	15	20.00	4–24
J. E. Emburey (Middlesex)	735.2	243	1518	75	20.24	6–31

WORLD SERIES AFTERMATH

Don Mosey: Peace had now been declared between the Packer Organisation and the Australian Board of Control, but there were the strongest indications that cricket the world over would never be the same again. The World Series of one-day games had been very much a showbiz-style production, some played partly during the day and continuing at night under floodlights. Bouncers were delivered with such frequency that many games took on the appearance of Roman games with players being felled, batting with broken fingers and a variety of other injuries. Histrionics and naked aggression—some simulated but much of it all too real—became an essential part of the game and began to spill over into orthodox cricket when Packer's gladiators returned to it. In the winter of 1979–80, for instance (New Zealand v West Indies), we saw pictures of one of the saddest sights the game has ever seen—Michael Holding, the great West Indian fast bowler, kicking over the stumps in exaggerated dissent at an umpiring decision, and in the same series his colleague Colin Croft shoulder-charged a New Zealand umpire, Fred Goodall, to the ground in what was seen as a scarcely accidental collision. (Seven years later public pronouncements on another West Indies tour to New Zealand showed very clearly that the incident had not been forgotten.) Protective helmets are now a normal part of the English cricket scene and—sponsorship money having increased the pay-cheques of Test cricketers at home—*Wisden* wistfully reflected that money was now the main topic of discussion in most county dressing-rooms. Packer's 'circus' was disbanded after his television company, Channel 9 in Australia, had been granted exclusive rights for coverage of Test matches and other official games in that country but the influences of his regime, for good or ill, lingered on. His marketing company was now responsible for the promotion and staging of the game in Australia.

Freddie Trueman: One result of this was the large-scale development of one-day International cricket which now became a regular part of the Australian summer scene with orthodox Test cricket overshadowed. In the winter of 1979–80, England, West Indies and Australia played a triangular contest of 12 matches and a best-of-three final. West Indies beat England in the first two of the final three and thus won the first of these competitions which were to become a regular feature of the Australian season. The one-day contest was interspersed with orthodox Test matches—three each between Australia and England, three more between Australia and West Indies. As the Test series had been hastily arranged at the request of the Australian authorities, England naturally did not put the Ashes up for competition which caused resentment in Australia, especially when (strengthened by the return of their Packer men) they scored three straight wins. Graham Dilley made his first England appearance in the First Test (Perth) and Wayne Larkins in the Third (Melbourne). In Perth, Dennis Lillee played four balls from Botham using a bat made of aluminium, which (a) caused a large-scale row at the time, and (b) caused the words 'the bat shall be made of wood' to be included in the Laws of Cricket when they were re-written that year.

JUBILEE TEST

DM: On their way home, the England party played a match in Bombay to celebrate the 50th anniversary of the formation of the BCCI (Board of Control for Cricket in India). An eclipse of the sun took place during the course of the match, which England won by ten wickets, and Botham made more history. His 114 (out of a total of 296) and bowling returns of six for 58 and seven for 48 represented the first instance of a player scoring a century and taking ten wickets or more in a match. Bob Taylor held ten catches in the Test. Graham Stevenson (Yorkshire) made his first Test appearance in the match.

BOTHAM'S CAPTAINCY

FST: Mike Brearley gave up the England captaincy when the party returned to England for the home series against the West Indies and Ian Botham was appointed in his place, an appointment which did not have the unanimous approval of the Selectors. In the worst summer for weather since 1958, West Indies won the First Test (Trent Bridge) and the other four were drawn. Chris Tavaré (Kent) was England's only debutant during that series. Gooch scored his first Test century at Lord's (Second Test) and Willey scored *his* first in the Final Test at The Oval, where Botham collected his 150th Test wicket in the record time of three years.

CENTENARY TEST

DM: The rain failed to respect the celebration of 100 years of Test cricket in England, for which Australia made a special trip to play at Lord's on 28, 29 and 30 August, 1 and 2 September. On the third day (Saturday) while the sun shone brightly, the ground was still unfit for play and when the umpires, 'Dickie' Bird and David Constant, returned from their fifth inspection there was an angry scene as they passed through the Long Room and Constant was physically manhandled by a small group of

A great commentator bowed out in 1980—John Arlott

MCC members. During the game itself, in which Hughes and Wood scored centuries for Australia, Boycott hit 128 not out and completed 7,000 runs in Tests. And in mid-afternoon, when John Arlott completed his last 20-minute commentary period for Radio 3's *Test Match Special* and retired, the entire crowd—and players—stood to applaud our colleague and the end of an era of radio broadcasting.

ONE-DAY INTERNATIONALS

FST: West Indies won the first of the two one-day Internationals, played before the Test series, although Tavaré made an impressive first appearance with 82 not out from a total of 174. England won the second (Lord's) where the new captain steered them home with 42 not out after being mauled for 71 runs off nine overs. Before the Centenary Test England beat Australia at The Oval and at Edgbaston where Roland Butcher became the first West Indian-born player to represent England. Bill Athey (Yorkshire, later Gloucestershire) played in both one-day Internationals and made his first full international appearance in the Centenary Test.

OVERSEAS INFLUX

DM: Overseas players were now dominating almost every aspect of the English county championship and while Australia, like West Indies, were able to muster a battery of four—five if necessary—fast bowlers, the England Selectors' search for an answer was rendered largely futile because they might at any given moment of the season find no fewer than 20 imports opening county bowling—ten West Indians, four South Africans, two Pakistanis, two Australians, a Rhodesian and a New Zealander. Apart from Robin Jackman, of Surrey, who in his 35th year had his best season and was the country's leading wicket-taker, the first-class averages were largely dominated by overseas players, and I suppose the pedants could argue that even Jackman was born in Simla (India) and had spent the last ten winters playing in South Africa! Four of the top batsmen were South African-born, one was a New Zealander and one a Pakistani.

MIDDLESEX'S YEAR

FST: Middlesex won both the county championship and the Gillette Cup in the last year in which the 60-overs competition was played for that particular trophy. The biggest single influence in their success was, according to Mike Brearley, the bowling of Vintcent Van der Bijl; a genial giant of a man (six ft seven and a half, 17 stone) who bowled fast with generous bounce and tremendous accuracy. He was signed for one season from South Africa because Middlesex expected Wayne Daniel to be required by the West Indian tourists. He was not, in fact, called upon. Fred Titmus, at the age of 48, played in five matches when Emburey was away and thus had played in five decades.

ONE-DAY COMPETITIONS

DM: Middlesex had a seven-wicket margin over Surrey (who were also runners-up in the county championship) in the last Gillette Final with Brearley anchoring the innings (96 not out) and Roland Butcher finishing off the match with a brisk 50 not out. In the Benson & Hedges, rain prevented any play on Saturday 19 July, and the following Monday Northamptonshire beat Essex by six runs in an enthralling finish when Essex were unable to score 12 off the last over. In the year after they finished bottom of the John Player League table, Warwickshire won the title for the first time—two points ahead of Somerset and four in front of Middlesex, for whom it had, nevertheless, been a memorable season.

Left: Vintcent Van der Bijl almost topped the averages in his only full season

Winter Tour to West Indies (1980–81):

Port-of-Spain	West Indies won by an innings & 79 runs
Georgetown	Cancelled
Bridgetown	West Indies won by 298 runs
St John's	Match drawn
Kingston	Match drawn

One-Day Internationals:

St Vincent	West Indies won by 2 runs
Berbice	West Indies won by six wickets

Summer Series with Australia:

Trent Bridge	Australia won by four wickets
Lord's	Match drawn
Headingley	England won by 18 runs
Edgbaston	England won by 29 runs
Old Trafford	England won by 103 runs
Oval	Match drawn

Prudential One-Day Internationals v Australia

Lord's	England won by six wickets
Edgbaston	Australia won by 2 runs
Headingley	Australia won by 71 runs

County Champions	Nottinghamshire
Natwest Trophy	Derbyshire
John Player League	Essex
Benson & Hedges Cup	Somerset

TEST AVERAGES ENGLAND V AUSTRALIA 1981

	M	I	NO	HS	Runs	Av	100	50	Ct/St
A. P. E. Knott	2	4	1	70*	178	59.33	–	2	6/–
C. J. Tavaré	2	4	0	78	179	44.75	–	2	1
G. R. Dilley	3	6	2	56	150	37.50	–	1	1
I. T. Botham	6	12	1	149*	399	36.27	2	1	12
G. Boycott	6	12	0	137	392	32.66	1	1	2
M. W. Gatting	6	12	0	59	370	30.83	–	4	8
J. E. Emburey	4	7	2	57	134	26.80	–	1	1
D. I. Gower	5	10	0	89	250	25.00	–	1	3
P. Willey	4	8	0	82	179	22.37	–	1	–
C. M. Old	2	4	1	29	63	21.00	–	–	–
J. M. Brearley	4	8	0	51	141	17.62	–	1	4
G. A. Gooch	5	10	0	44	139	13.90	–	–	1
R. A. Woolmer	2	4	0	21	30	7.50	–	–	2
R. G. D. Willis	6	10	2	13	43	5.37	–	–	2
R. W. Taylor	3	6	0	9	23	3.83	–	–	13/–

Also batted: P. J. W. Allott (1 match) 52*, 14; P. R. Downton (1 match) 8, 3, 2ct; M. Hendrick (2 matches) 6*, 0*, 0*; W. Larkins (1 match) 34, 24; P. W. G. Parker (1 match) 0, 13.

	Overs	M	Runs	Wkts	Av	5w	10w	BB
G. R. Dilley	98	24	275	14	19.64	–	–	4–24
I. T. Botham	272.3	81	700	34	20.58	3	1	6–95
R. G. D. Willis	252.4	56	666	29	22.96	1	–	8–43
J. E. Emburey	193.5	58	399	12	33.25	–	–	4–43
C. M. Old	84	27	175	5	35.00	–	–	3–44
M. Hendrick	100.2	28	221	6	36.83	–	–	4–82

Also bowled: P. J. W. Allott 23–4–88–4; G. Boycott 3–2–2–0; M. W. Gatting 3–1–13–0; G. A. Gooch 10–4–28–0; P. Willey 16–3–35–1.

TEST AVERAGES ENGLAND V WEST INDIES 1980–81

	M	I	NO	HS	Runs	Av	100	50	Ct/St
G. A. Gooch	4	8	0	153	460	57.50	2	1	3
D. I. Gower	4	8	1	154*	376	53.71	1	1	2
P. Willey	4	8	3	102*	244	48.80	1	1	–
G. Boycott	4	8	1	104*	295	42.14	1	1	1
R. O. Butcher	3	5	0	32	71	14.20	–	–	3
P. R. Downton	3	5	1	26*	48	12.00	–	–	6/–
I. T. Botham	4	7	0	26	73	10.42	–	–	5
J. E. Emburey	4	6	1	17*	38	7.60	–	–	2
R. D. Jackman	2	3	0	7	14	4.66	–	–	–
G. R. Dilley	4	6	3	7*	11	3.66	–	–	–
C. W. J. Athey	2	4	0	3	7	1.75	–	–	1

Also batted: D. L. Bairstow (1 match) 0, 2, 5ct; M. W. Gatting (1 match) 2, 0, 1ct; G. Miller (1 match) 3, 8, 1ct; C. M. Old (1 match) 1, 0; B. C. Rose (1 match) 10, 5; G. B. Stevenson (1 match) 1.

	Overs	M	Runs	Wkts	Av	5w	10w	BB
I. T. Botham	145.2	31	492	15	32.80	–	–	4–77
R. D. Jackman	73.2	15	198	6	33.00	–	–	3–65
G. R. Dilley	129.4	25	450	10	45.00	–	–	4–116
J. E. Emburey	185	62	419	7	59.85	1	–	5–124

Also bowled: G. Boycott 3–2–5–0; G. A. Gooch 14–5–36–0; G. Miller 18–4–42–1; C. M. Old 16–4–49–1; G. B. Stevenson 33–5–111–3; P. Willey 47–12–111–1.

SCHWEPPES CHAMPIONSHIP TABLE 1981

					Bonus Pts		
Win = 12 points	P	Won	Lost	D	Bat	Bowl	Pts
NOTTINGHAMSHIRE (3)	22	11	4	7*	56	72	304
Sussex (4)	22	11	3	8@	58	68	302
Somerset (5)	22	10	2	10	54	65	279
Middlesex (1)	22	9	3	10*	49	64	257
Essex (8)	22	8	4	10*	62	64	254
Surrey (2)	22	7	5	10*	52	72	236
Hampshire (17)	22	6	7	9*	45	65	206
Leicestershire (9)	22	6	6	10*	45	58	199
Kent (16)	22	5	7	10	51	58	189
Yorkshire (6)	22	5	9	8	41	66	187
Worcestershire (11)	22	5	9	8	44	52	172$
Derbyshire (9)	22	4	7	11*	51	57	172
Gloucestershire (7)	22	3	4	15±	51	55	170
Glamorgan (13)	22	3	10	9*	50	69	167
Northamptonshire (12)	22	3	6	13*	51	67	166
Lancashire (15)	22	4	7	11	47	57	164$
Warwickshire (14)	22	2	11	9	56	47	135

± includes three matches abandoned without a ball bowled
@ includes two matches abandoned without a ball bowled
* includes one match abandoned without a ball bowled
$ includes twelve points for win in match reduced to one innings
1980 positions are shown in brackets

FIRST-CLASS AVERAGES 1981

	I	NO	HS	Runs	Av	100
Zaheer Abbas (Gloucestershire)	36	10	215*	2306	88.69	10
Javed Miandad (Glamorgan)	37	7	200*	2083	69.43	8
A. J. Lamb (Northamptonshire)	43	9	162	2049	60.26	5
I. V. A. Richards (Somerset)	33	3	196	1718	57.26	7
C. E. B. Rice (Nottinghamshire)	30	4	172	1462	56.23	6
P. N. Kirsten (Derbyshire)	35	6	228	1605	55.34	3
G. M. Turner (Worcestershire)	42	4	168	2101	55.28	9
M. W. Gatting (Middlesex)	33	6	186*	1492	55.25	4
±A. I. Kallicharran (Warwickshire)	23	6	135	923	54.29	3
C. J. Tavaré (Kent)	40	7	156	1770	53.63	4

*denotes not out
±denotes left-hand batsman

	Overs	M	Runs	Wkts	Av	BB
R. J. Hadlee (Nottinghamshire)	708.4	231	1564	105	14.89	7–25
S. T. Clarke (Surrey)	339.4	98	734	49	14.97	6–66
J. Garner (Somerset)	605.4	182	1349	88	15.32	7–25
M. A. Holding (Lancashire)	271.1	75	715	40	17.87	6–74
E. A. Moseley (Glamorgan)	355.4	88	942	52	18.11	6–23
A. Sidebottom (Yorkshire)	305.5	88	899	47	19.12	6–62
C. E. B. Rice (Nottinghamshire)	494.5	142	1248	65	19.20	6–44
I. A. Greig (Sussex)	477	100	1469	76	19.32	7–43
±P. J. Hacker (Nottinghamshire)	175.5	53	446	23	19.39	4–34
M. D. Marshall (Hampshire)	531.3	166	1321	68	19.42	6–57

±denotes left-arm bowler

A TRAGIC TOUR

Don Mosey: 'Tragic' is the only way to describe England's visit to the West Indies in January, February and March of 1981, firstly because of the death on tour of Ken Barrington, then assistant manager of the party and one of the best-loved men in the game. He suffered a heart attack during the match in Barbados. The second tragedy was that for the first time a government (in Guyana) interfered with the selection of a visiting tour party by declaring Robin Jackman *persona non grata* which caused the cancellation of the Second Test and the departure from that country of the England party. For a time the tour as a whole was in jeopardy.

Freddie Trueman: It wasn't such a good tour from a playing point of view, either, because England were completely outclassed until the later stages when one or two batsmen got a bit of confidence to face Roberts (replaced by Marshall in Jamaica), Holding, Croft and Garner: but then the bowling never looked capable of dismissing West Indies twice, either.

DM: It all started rather messily with demonstrations in Trinidad about the omission by the West Indies Selectors of Deryck Murray, at that time captain of Trinidad, and his supporters caused a bit of damage to the pitch which resulted in a delayed start. Bob Willis had had to go home before the Test series started with knee trouble and the remaining England bowlers took a hammering on the easiest-paced of the West Indian wickets. Paul Downton made his debut in this Test in which only Boycott seemed able to cope with the pace attack and Botham was savaged for a world (Test) record of 24 runs off one over by Andy Roberts. Then came Guyana and Jackman, flown in as Willis's replacement, found himself at the centre of a political controversy. The players flew to the Albion Sports Club, Berbice, to play a one-day International while the manager, Alan Smith, stayed behind in Georgetown to negotiate with the Guyanan government officials who had called in Jackman's passport. (Not surprisingly, in view of his winters in South Africa—and he was married to a South African wife—it bore generous indications of his visits to that country.) The party returned from Berbice to learn that the Guyanan part of the tour had now been cancelled and they would leave the following morning for Barbados. There they experienced a long delay before being told that the remainder of the matches could be played after conferences between the governments of Barbados, Antigua, Montserrat and Jamaica.

FST: Jackman made his Test debut in Barbados (it now became the Third Test although no Second had been played) and dismissed Greenidge with his fifth ball, and it was also the first appearance for England of Roland Butcher, who had been born, and lived for the first 13 years of his life, 14 miles from the ground in Bridgetown. Brian Rose, in the meantime, had flown home because of eye trouble which was to require him to play in spectacles during the rest of his career. England were beaten a second time in Barbados but managed to draw the remaining two Tests in St John's, Antigua (the first Test match to be played there), where Willey and Boycott got centuries, and in Kingston, Jamaica, where Gooch made 153 and Gower 154 not out. Vivian Richards was married three days before the Antigua Test and celebrated with 114 runs in his only innings. Botham's form undoubtedly suffered because of his problems as captain and he managed only 73 runs in his seven Test innings. He was leading wicket-taker with 15, however.

BREARLEY'S RECALL

DM: The summer series against Australia, which started with their first win at Trent Bridge since 1948, saw the debuts of Terry Alderman (who was to have such a good summer) and Trevor Chappell, youngest of three brothers to represent Australia. Rodney Marsh passed Knott's record of 244 wicket-keeping catches. Australia won by four wickets and there was an increasing chorus of calls for Botham to be relieved of the captaincy because his personal form was at a low ebb. When he bagged a pair in the Second Test (Lord's) and took three wickets for 81, the Selectors decided on a change and approached Brearley to ask whether he would be willing to return (he had stood down saying he did not wish to tour any more after the previous winter in Australia but he *was* willing to skipper the side in England). As he came off the field at Lord's, Botham forestalled the Selectors by resigning as captain—and the next two months became what will always be known as Botham's Summer.

FST: It began straightaway in the Third Test at Headingley when England, follow-on 227 behind, found themselves at 105 for five in the second innings when Botham went in at No. 7. He had already taken six for 95 in Australia's first innings and made the top score of 50 in England's. Now he hit 149 not out (aided by Dilley, 56,

Bob Willis on his way to 8–43 as England pull off an 'impossible' win at Headingley. Bob Taylor catches Geoff Lawson

and Old, 29) to see England to 356. Australia still needed only 130 to win but Willis produced the finest performance of *his* life and returned eight for 43 as Australia were tumbled out for 111. Only once had a side won after following on and that had been in 1894–95 (again, England beating Australia). In the course of the game, Marsh passed Knott's record of 263 dismissals (as opposed simply to catches, the record he had acquired at Lord's) and Bob Taylor passed John Murray's figure of 1,270 catches in first-class cricket. The First Test, incidentally, had involved Sunday play for the first time, with the match being played straight through without a rest day, and this was done also in the Fourth and Fifth Tests.

DM: At Edgbaston, Botham had a modest game with the bat and Australia looked set to win when they started the second Sunday of Test cricket that summer needing 142 to win with nine wickets in hand. Botham then took five wickets for one run in 28 deliveries and England won by 29 runs, but still the best was to come. At Old Trafford (Fifth Test), where Paul Allott made his Test debut with 52 not out, batting at No. 10, Botham hit 118 of the most spectacular runs I, personally, have seen in any Test. They came from 102 balls and the century was actually reached off only 86 deliveries with six sixes (including two off Lillee with the new ball). Alderman took 37 wickets in the series and with a record of another sort, Tavaré took 306 minutes to reach the slowest 50 in English first-class cricket, but there could be no doubt that it had been Botham's summer. He scored more runs and took more wickets than any other Englishman in the series and yet stubbornly denied at all times that his renaissance was due to his being relieved of the cares of captaincy. If ever a man proved himself wrong it was Ian Botham in the summer of '81. At The Oval (Sixth Test) he took his 200th wicket in another record time of four years and 34 days.

ONE-DAY INTERNATIONALS

FST: The series of three games, played for the Prudential Trophy as usual, took place before the Tests and the 2–1 margin for Australia undoubtedly gave them a boost which helped them to the First Test win. Jim Love, of Yorkshire, got his first International chance at Lord's, along with Geoff Humpage, the hard-hitting Warwickshire wicket-keeper, and England won easily by six wickets. At Edgbaston, however, England needed six to win off the last over but got only three while losing three wickets, and at Headingley Australia had a 71-run margin. It is interesting to note that Graeme Wood, the world's leading expert in running himself out, managed it in two of the one-day matches as well as one Test.

NOTTINGHAMSHIRE'S CHAMPIONSHIP

DM: Nottinghamshire's first county championship for 52 years owed much to their two overseas players: Rice scoring 1,462 runs and taking 65 wickets; Hadlee taking 105 wickets and adding 745 runs. Hadlee had had all kinds of injury problems during the 1980 season and it took a good deal of persuasion to coax him back from New Zealand. Once at Trent Bridge he discovered a new lease of life and he and his close friend, Clive Rice, played in every championship match of the season. There is a certain irony in seeing the name of Peter Hacker in the same bracket as Hadlee's (the top ten of the first-class averages). An ebullient character, and left-arm medium-fast bowler, he managed only 61 first-team games in a seven-year career at Trent Bridge but 1981 was clearly his best season. Sussex, after many years of toil, at last got close to a championship title and were crushingly disappointed to learn that they had been pipped on the penultimate day of the season. They were well led by John Barclay, the Etonian opening batsman and off-spinner (as well as excellent slip-catcher) and had a formidable opening attack of Imran Khan and the South African, Garth le Roux, both of whom were good batsmen. Paul Parker—as he had been for three years—was on the fringe of selection for England, finally achieving it at The Oval.

OVERSEAS MENACE

FST: But the overseas challenge was now becoming a menace in county cricket. Of the top ten batsmen, only Mike Gatting and Chris Tavaré were English-born and only two of the bowlers were not imports—Yorkshire's Arnie Sidebottom and Hacker, whose appearance in the list is largely nominal. Michael Holding, who was virtually playing 12 months a year round the world—from Australia to West Indies, from Tests to Lancashire League cricket—had seven games with Lancashire in 1981 and made his mark as you might expect. But seven out of those top ten are opening bowlers from overseas—can you wonder at the shortage of English-born talent in this department?

ONE-DAY COMPETITIONS

DM: The Gillette Cup was now the NatWest Trophy and the first holders were Derbyshire after a frenzied last-ball finish with Northamptonshire who scored 235 for nine. Off the last over, Derbyshire needed to score six runs to tie the scores and give them victory because they had only six wickets down. Miller and Tunnicliffe accumulated five runs off five deliveries, and Miller's race from the non-striker's end from the last ball got him home before the wicket was broken. The Benson & Hedges was a rather

Sylvester Clarke, one of the game's most feared bowlers

Derbyshire are the first winners of the NatWest Bank Trophy, captained by Barry Wood

different affair, Somerset scoring 197 for three to beat Surrey by seven wickets with ten and a half overs to spare. Vivian Richards hit a brilliant 132 not out after Somerset had lost their first two wickets for five runs. Essex, three times runners-up in the John Player League, at last won it and Somerset were runners-up for the fifth time.

1982

Winter Tour to India (1981–82):

Bombay	India won by 138 runs
Bangalore	Match drawn
Delhi	Match drawn
Calcutta	Match drawn
Madras	Match drawn
Kanpur	Match drawn

One-Day Internationals:

Ahmedabad	England won by five wickets
Jullundur	India won by six wickets
Cuttack	India won by five wickets

Sri Lanka (1981–82):

Colombo (Inaugural Test)	England won by seven wickets

One-Day Internationals:

Colombo	England won by 5 runs
Colombo	Sri Lanka won by 3 runs

Summer Series:

v India:

Lord's	England won by seven wickets
Old Trafford	Match drawn
Oval	Match drawn

v Pakistan:

Edgbaston	England won by 113 runs
Lord's	Pakistan won by ten wickets
Headingley	England won by three wickets

County Champions	Middlesex
Natwest Trophy	Surrey
John Player League	Sussex
Benson & Hedges Cup	Somerset

TEST AVERAGES ENGLAND V INDIA 1981–82

	M	I	NO	HS	Runs	Av	100	50	Ct/St
I. T. Botham	6	8	0	142	440	55.00	1	4	3
G. A. Gooch	6	10	1	127	487	54.11	1	4	4
D. I. Gower	6	9	1	85	375	46.87	–	4	2
G. Boycott	4	8	1	105	312	44.57	1	2	2
C. J. Tavaré	6	9	0	149	349	38.77	1	1	5
K. W. R. Fletcher	6	9	2	69	252	36.00	–	3	5
G. R. Dilley	4	5	0	52	70	14.00	–	1	1
M. W. Gatting	5	6	1	32	68	13.60	–	–	–
R. G. D. Willis	5	4	2	13	26	13.00	–	–	–
D. L. Underwood	6	7	4	13*	38	12.66	–	–	1
R. W. Taylor	6	7	1	33	57	9.50	–	–	15/1
J. E. Emburey	3	4	0	2	4	1.00	–	–	1

Also batted: P. J. W. Allott (1 match) 6; J. K. Lever (2 matches) 1, 2.

	Overs	M	Runs	Wkts	Av	5w	10w	BB
J. K. Lever	73	16	204	7	29.14	1	–	5–100
R. G. D. Willis	129.1	29	381	12	31.75	–	–	3–75
J. E. Emburey	99	31	222	6	37.00	–	–	2–35
I. T. Botham	240.3	52	660	17	38.82	1	–	5–61
D. L. Underwood	228	99	438	10	43.80	–	–	3–45
G. R. Dilley	105	17	350	7	50.00	–	–	4–47

Also bowled: P. J. W. Allott 31–4–135–0; K. W. R. Fletcher 6–2–20–1; M. W. Gatting 1–0–4–0; G. A. Gooch 33.1–6–77–2; D. I. Gower 2–0–2–1; C. J. Tavaré 2–0–11–0; R. W. Taylor 2–0–6–0.

TEST AVERAGES ENGLAND V PAKISTAN 1982

	M	I	NO	HS	Runs	Av	100	50	Ct/St
C. J. Tavaré	3	6	0	82	216	36.00	–	2	3
D. I. Gower	3	6	0	74	197	32.83	–	2	2
D. W. Randall	3	6	0	105	168	28.00	1	–	3
I. T. Botham	3	6	0	69	163	27.16	–	2	1
R. W. Taylor	3	6	2	54	108	27.00	–	1	12/–
M. W. Gatting	3	6	1	32*	111	22.20	–	–	3
E. E. Hemmings	2	4	0	10	41	10.25	–	–	2
R. D. Jackman	2	3	0	17	28	9.33	–	–	–
A. J. Lamb	3	6	0	33	48	8.00	–	–	1
I. A. Greig	2	4	0	14	26	6.50	–	–	–

Also batted: G. Fowler (1 match) 9, 86, 1ct; V. J. Marks (1 match) 7, 12*; G. Miller (1 match) 47, 5, 1ct; D. R. Pringle (1 match) 5, 14; R. G. D. Willis (2 matches) 0*, 28*, 1*, 3ct.

	Overs	M	Runs	Wkts	Av	5w	10w	BB
R. G. D. Willis	74	14	222	10	22.20	–	–	3–55
I. T. Botham	150.5	33	478	18	26.55	1	–	5–74
R. D. Jackman	105	30	247	8	30.87	–	–	4–110

Also bowled: M. W. Gatting 10–3–21–0; I. A. Greig 31.2–6–114–4; E. E. Hemmings 56.1–12–149–3; V. J. Marks 7–1–31–1; G. Miller 9.4–2–27–2; D. R. Pringle 26–9–62–0.

TEST AVERAGES ENGLAND V INDIA 1982

	M	I	NO	HS	Runs	Av	100	50	Ct/St
I. T. Botham	3	3	0	208	403	134.33	2	1	1
D. W. Randall	3	3	0	126	221	73.66	1	1	1
A. J. Lamb	3	5	1	107	207	51.75	1	–	–
C. J. Tavaré	3	5	1	75*	178	44.50	–	2	2
D. I. Gower	3	5	1	47	152	38.00	–	–	2
P. H. Edmonds	3	3	0	64	90	30.00	–	1	1
G. Cook	3	5	0	66	138	27.60	–	2	5
R. G. D. Willis	3	5	1	28	35	17.50	–	–	–
D. R. Pringle	3	3	0	23	39	13.00	–	–	–
R. W. Taylor	3	4	1	31	36	12.00	–	–	9/–

Also batted: P. J. W. Allott (2 matches) 41*, 3, 2ct; G. Miller (1 match) 98.

	Overs	M	Runs	Wkts	Av	5w	10w	BB
R. G. D. Willis	88	11	330	15	22.00	1	–	6–101
D. R. Pringle	82	22	219	7	31.28	–	–	2–16
I. T. Botham	93.3	16	320	9	35.55	1	–	5–46
P. H. Edmonds	102.2	35	261	6	43.50	–	–	3–89

Also bowled: P. J. W. Allott 49–9–147–2; G. Cook 1–0–4–0; G. Miller 16–4–51–1.

SCHWEPPES CHAMPIONSHIP TABLE 1982

Win = 16 points	P	Won	Lost	D	Bonus Pts Bat	Bowl	Pts
MIDDLESEX (4)	22	12	2	8	59	74	325
Leicestershire (8)	22	10	4	8	57	69	286
Hampshire (7)	22	8	6	8	48	74	250
Nottinghamshire (1)	22	7	7	8*	44	65	221
Surrey (6)	22	6	6	10	56	62	214
Somerset (3)	22	6	6	10	51	66	213
Essex (5)	22	5	5	12	57	75	212
Sussex (2)	22	6	7	9	43	68	207
Northamptonshire (15)	22	5	3	14	61	54	195
Yorkshire (10)	22	5	1	16*	48	51	179
Derbyshire (12)	22	4	3	15	45	64	173
Lancashire (16)	22	4	3	15	48	55	167
Kent (9)	22	3	4	15	55	63	166
Worcestershire (11)	22	3	5	14	43	54	141±
Gloucestershire (13)	22	2	9	11	46	55	133
Glamorgan (14)	22	1	8	13	43	60	119
Warwickshire (17)	22	0	8	14	58	53	111

* includes one match abandoned without a ball bowled
± includes twelve points for win in match reduced to one innings
1981 positions are shown in brackets

FIRST-CLASS AVERAGES 1982

	I	NO	HS	Runs	Av	100
G. M. Turner (Worcestershire)	16	3	311*	1171	90.07	5
Zaheer Abbas (Glos/Pakistan)	25	4	162*	1475	70.23	5
±A. I. Kallicharran (Warwickshire)	37	5	235	2120	66.25	8
P. N. Kirsten (Derbyshire)	37	7	164*	1941	64.70	8
G. Boycott (Yorkshire)	37	6	159	1913	61.70	6
M. W. Gatting (Middlesex)	34	6	192	1651	58.96	6
T. E. Jesty (Hampshire)	36	8	164*	1645	58.75	8
±J. G. Wright (Derbyshire)	39	6	190	1830	55.45	7
B. F. Davison (Leicestershire)	37	4	172	1800	54.54	7
±Younis Ahmed (Worcestershire)	29	6	122	1247	54.21	4

	Overs	M	Runs	Wkts	Av	BB
R. J. Hadlee (Nottinghamshire)	403.5	122	889	61	14.57	7–25
M. D. Marshall (Hampshire)	822	225	2108	134	15.73	8–71
M. W. Gatting (Middlesex)	135	40	343	21	16.33	5–34
Imran Khan (Sussex/Pakistan)	414.4	134	1079	64	16.85	7–52
W. W. Daniel (Middlesex)	468.5	107	1245	71	17.53	9–61
J. Garner (Somerset)	259.1	76	583	33	17.66	6–23
M. Hendrick (Nottinghamshire)	244.2	86	473	26	18.19	5–21
G. S. le Roux (Sussex)	467	116	1210	65	18.61	5–15
A. M. E. Roberts (Leicestershire)	427.2	114	1081	55	19.65	8–56
F. D. Stephenson (Gloucestershire)	197.2	40	632	32	19.75	5–64

TOUR OF INDIA AND SRI LANKA

Don Mosey: After England's defeat in the First Test in Bombay it was pretty obvious to everyone in the party that they would encounter the flattest of wickets throughout the remainder of the trip. And so it proved. In Bombay the groundsman had somehow wrought a miracle in providing a pitch which seamed; in Bangalore, New Delhi, Calcutta, Madras and Kanpur any bowler who could make the ball bounce shin-high (let alone deviate off the seam) might have expected to be 'called' for intimidation. And so five Tests creaked and groaned their inevitable way to drawn matches.

There were isolated moments of historic importance, of drama, of humour. On the first day in Delhi, when India bowled only 78 overs (43 of them by spinners), Geoffrey Boycott overtook Gary Sobers' world record of 8,032 runs and less than a fortnight later returned home to England, Boycott claiming that he was too ill to continue and the management asserting that his 'attitude was not right'. We saw the cynical slowing-down process reach its ultimate in Calcutta where Doshi and Shastri—slow left-armers both with short approaches to the wicket—could manage only nine overs an hour. In Madras, on the only pitch with any semblance of pace in it, we saw Paul Allott suffer the agony of two dropped catches early in his first spell and end with the heart-breaking figures 33–4–135–0 as Viswanath played an innings of rare brilliance (222) even by his standards.

At no stage of the tour (at least in Tests and one-day Internationals) did the England players do themselves justice, largely because in addition to encountering umpiring of modest standards they developed an almost paranoic belief that they were going to get bad decisions, come what may. Sri Lanka saw two limited-overs Internationals which ended frenetically in victory for England by five runs and a win for Sri Lanka by just three. These were followed by the gala occasion of Sri Lanka's first-ever official Test, which was duly won by England because of Underwood's spin in the first innings and Emburey's in the second, when it had been fairly confidently assumed that pace would be the tourists' most potent weapon.

SOUTH AFRICAN CONTROVERSY

Before the new season could begin back home, English cricket was divided by yet another controversy on the subject of playing in South Africa. The first whispers of a tour by English players had been heard the previous winter when England were on tour in the West Indies. They had been heard again while we were in India. Indeed, at one stage I became personally involved when Bob Woolmer, the Kent and former England batsman,

Two great all-rounders exchange a smile—Botham and Sobers

telephoned Broadcasting House in London, asking for a message to be passed to Ian Botham to call a telephone number in Cape Town. The message was relayed to me and I passed it on to Botham. Strenuous efforts to recruit Botham for the unofficial tour which took place in March 1982 failed, but a side went out to play which included Graham Gooch, Geoffrey Boycott, Alan Knott, John Emburey and Derek Underwood. The whole party then received a three-year ban from playing in Test cricket which was seen by many as grossly unfair.

The players' argument was that during the winter, when not required by England on official tours, they were free agents and, as professional cricketers, they had the right to seek employment where it was offered. The Test and County Cricket Board, on the other hand, had clearly warned that any member of an organised but unofficial team in going to play in South Africa would risk a ban.

Freddie Trueman: So it all seemed completely daft to some of us when the Selectors, chaired for the first time by Peter May, picked Allan Lamb to play international cricket for the first time the following June. Gooch and Emburey couldn't play because they had gone to play in South Africa three months earlier but Lamb, who was as South African as Table Mountain, could. And India, who had raised objections to Boycott and Geoff Cook touring with England during the winter because they had played a bit of cricket in South Africa, played against Lamb without a murmur of protest.

HIGHLIGHTS

DM: On Spring Bank Holiday Saturday, Glenn Turner hit 311 not out for Worcestershire against Warwickshire as the climax to a marvellous career. It gave him his one hundred hundreds in first-class cricket (only the 19th batsman in history to do that) and it was also the first triple century in the county championship for 33 years. Glenn might have started out as a strokeless wonder, but he developed his batting to become a great stroke-maker and as he had always been such a keen student of the game he was able later to become a fine TV commentator and then to take over the cricketing managership of New Zealand, when they won a series in Australia in 1985, and the Aussies didn't like that one little bit. England won the two one-day Internationals easily enough and we saw Alan Lamb justify his selection with 35 not out in the first one and 99 in the second. At Gloucester in June, Zaheer Abbas scored 162 not out and 107 against Lancashire to equal Wally Hammond's record of a century in both innings of a match on seven occasions and a week later Bob Willis began his reign as the England captain with a seven-wickets win in the First Test against India.

FST: For me the lasting memory of that Test is the sight of Derek Pringle, a bit of a controversial choice as an England all-rounder—certainly in my book—walking out to bat, all 6 ft 4½ ins of him, wearing a protective helmet to the bowling of Doshi and Shastri.

Kim Barnett, soon to become Derbyshire captain, got his maiden hundred against Lancashire and in the John Player League, too, where there isn't much time to hang around. That was at the beginning of July, and six days later Zimbabwe beat Bermuda in the final of the ICC Trophy (the mini-World Cup). In the meantime, Ian Botham had clocked up 208 off 255 deliveries in the Third Test.

PAKISTAN'S TOUR OF ENGLAND

The second half of the season brought Pakistan as tourists and after England had polished them off without any trouble in the one-day Internationals and the First Test they got a nasty shock at Lord's. Willis was unfit so Gower captained England for the first time and was probably as surprised as anyone to see Mudassar Nazar, opening batsman and bit of a change bowler, swing the ball all over

The future English captain and vice-captain—Mike Gatting and John Emburey

the shop and take six for 32 in England's second innings. If it had been little Abdul Qadir I could have understood it because no one ever sorted out his leg-spin, but Mudassar . . . ! He'd have been chuffed with figures like that bowling for Burnley in the Lancashire League where he's spent a lot of time.

THE BENSON & HEDGES FINAL

DM: The Benson & Hedges Final was a disappointing affair where Nottinghamshire couldn't find anything like their county championship form and never got enough runs and, for once, the NatWest final fizzled out as well with Warwickshire's miserable total of 158 not even causing Surrey to get into second gear. Like Somerset in the B & H, they won by nine wickets. The first-class averages painted a pretty unwholesome picture of the state of English cricket. Of the top ten batsmen, two were New Zealanders, two Pakistanis, one West Indian, one South African and one Rhodesian. The only Englishmen there were Geoffrey Boycott, Mike Gatting and Trevor Jesty. Of the top ten bowlers, if you take out Mike Gatting, who was really only an occasional bowler (but had taken the required ten wickets to qualify for the averages), you are left with five West Indians, one New Zealander, one Pakistani and one South African. Mike Hendrick was the only Englishman up there with them.

The most unfortunate incident of the season was when India refused to accept the experienced and expert umpire David Constant to 'stand' in the Tests. This was a quite obvious tit-for-tat measure because Keith Fletcher, in India the previous winter, had understandably objected to the umpiring of one Mohammed Ghouse. It resulted in a quite unjustified slur upon the professional reputation of Constant.

Winter Tour Tests in Australia (1982–83):

Perth	Match drawn
Brisbane	Australia won by seven wickets
Adelaide	Australia won by eight wickets
Melbourne	England won by 3 runs
Sydney	Match drawn

One-Day Internationals (Benson & Hedges World Series) (1982–83):

v Australia

Sydney (D/N)	Australia won by 31 runs
Brisbane	Australia won by seven wickets
Melbourne	Australia won by five wickets
Sydney (D/N)	England won by 98 runs
Adelaide	England won by 14 runs

v New Zealand:

Melbourne	New Zealand won by 2 runs
Brisbane	England won by 54 runs
Sydney (D/N)	England won by eight wickets
Adelaide	New Zealand won by four wickets
Perth	New Zealand won by seven wickets

England were eliminated from the best-of-three final and Australia beat New Zealand 2–0

One-Day Internationals in New Zealand:

Auckland	New Zealand won by six wickets
Wellington	New Zealand won by 103 runs
Christchurch	New Zealand won by 84 runs

Cornhill Tests in England v New Zealand:

Oval	England won by 189 runs
Headingley	New Zealand won by five wickets
Lord's	England won by 127 runs
Trent Bridge	England won by 165 runs

Third Prudential World Cup:

Oval	England beat New Zealand by 106 runs
Swansea	Pakistan beat Sri Lanka by 50 runs
Trent Bridge	Zimbabwe beat Australia by 13 runs
Old Trafford	India beat West Indies by 34 runs
Taunton	England beat Sri Lanka by 47 runs
Leicester	India beat Zimbabwe by five wickets
Edgbaston	New Zealand beat Pakistan by 52 runs
Headingley	West Indies beat Australia by 101 runs
Lord's	England beat Pakistan by eight wickets
Worcester	West Indies beat Zimbabwe by eight wickets
Trent Bridge	Australia beat India by 162 runs
Bristol	New Zealand beat Sri Lanka by five wickets
Edgbaston	New Zealand beat England by two wickets
The Oval	West Indies beat India by 66 runs
Headingley	Pakistan beat Sri Lanka by 11 runs
Southampton	Australia beat Zimbabwe by 32 runs
Old Trafford	England beat Pakistan by seven wickets
Lord's	West Indies beat Australia by seven wickets
Derby	Sri Lanka beat New Zealand by three wickets
Tunbridge Wells	India beat Zimbabwe by 31 runs
Headingley	England beat Sri Lanka by nine wickets
Edgbaston	West Indies beat Zimbabwe by ten wickets
Trent Bridge	Pakistan beat New Zealand by 11 runs
Chelmsford	India beat Australia by 118 runs

England topped Group A with Pakistan second, New Zealand third and Sri Lanka fourth; West Indies won Group B with India second, Australia third and Zimbabwe fourth.

SEMI-FINALS:

Oval	West Indies beat Pakistan by eight wickets
Old Trafford	India beat England by six wickets

FINALS:

India (183 in 54.4 overs) beat West Indies (140 in 52 overs) by 43 runs

County Champions	Essex	**John Player League**	Yorkshire
NatWest Trophy	Somerset	**Benson & Hedges Cup**	Middlesex

TEST AVERAGES ENGLAND V NEW ZEALAND 1983

	M	I	NO	HS	Runs	Av	100	50	Ct/St
A. J. Lamb	4	8	2	137*	392	65.33	2	1	10
D. I. Gower	4	8	1	112*	404	57.71	2	1	6
C. J. Tavaré	4	8	0	109	330	41.25	1	2	2
D. W. Randall	3	6	1	83	194	38.80	–	2	3
I. T. Botham	4	8	0	103	282	35.25	1	1	3
G. Fowler	2	4	0	105	134	33.50	1	–	–
M. W. Gatting	2	4	0	81	121	30.25	–	1	4
P. H. Edmonds	2	4	1	43*	63	21.00	–	–	1
C. L. Smith	2	4	0	43	78	19.50	–	–	2
R. G. D. Willis	4	7	2	25*	67	13.40	–	–	4
N. G. B. Cook	2	4	0	26	51	12.75	–	–	3
R. W. Taylor	4	7	1	21	63	10.50	–	–	11/–
N. G. Cowans	4	7	1	10	22	3.66	–	–	–

Also batted: G. R. Dilley (1 match) 0, 15, 1ct; N. A. Foster (1 match) 10, 3, 1ct; V. J. Marks (1 match) 4, 2.

	Overs	M	Runs	Wkts	Av	5w	10w	BB
R. G. D. Willis	123.3	38	273	20	13.65	1	–	5–35
N. G. B. Cook	135.2	56	275	17	16.17	2	–	5–35
I. T. Botham	112.5	27	340	10	34.00	–	–	4–50
N. G. Cowans	125	25	447	12	37.25	–	–	3–74

Also bowled: G. R. Dilley 25–6–52–0; P. H. Edmonds 87.1–30–221–4; N. A. Foster 28–5–75–1; M. W. Gatting 7–3–13–0; V. J. Marks 43–20–78–3; C. L. Smith 12–2–31–2.

TEST AVERAGES ENGLAND V AUSTRALIA 1982–83

	M	I	NO	HS	Runs	Av	100	50	Ct/St
D. W. Randall	4	8	0	115	365	45.62	1	2	3
D. I. Gower	5	10	0	114	441	44.10	1	3	4
A. J. Lamb	5	10	0	83	414	41.40	–	4	5
G. Fowler	3	6	0	83	207	34.50	–	2	1
E. E. Hemmings	3	6	1	95	157	31.40	–	1	2
I. T. Botham	5	10	0	58	270	27.00	–	1	9
D. R. Pringle	3	6	2	47	108	27.00	–	–	–
C. J. Tavaré	5	10	0	89	218	21.80	–	2	2
G. Miller	5	10	1	60	193	21.44	–	1	3
R. W. Taylor	5	10	3	37	135	19.28	–	–	13/–
N. G. Cowans	4	7	1	36	68	11.33	–	–	3
R. G. D. Willis	5	9	3	26	63	10.50	–	–	4
G. Cook	3	6	0	26	54	9.00	–	–	1

	Overs	M	Runs	Wkts	Av	5w	10w	BB
R. G. D. Willis	166.3	28	486	18	27.00	1	–	5–66
G. Miller	171	50	397	13	30.53	–	–	4–70
N. G. Cowans	107	14	396	11	36.00	1	–	6–77
I. T. Botham	213.5	35	729	18	40.50	–	–	4–75
E. E. Hemmings	188.3	59	409	9	45.44	–	–	3–68

Also bowled: G. Cook 6–3–23–0; A. J. Lamb 1–1–0–0; D. R. Pringle 73.5–12–214–4.

SCHWEPPES CHAMPIONSHIP TABLE 1983

Win = 16 points	P	Won	Lost	D	Bonus Pts Bat	Bowl	Pts
ESSEX (7)	24	11	5	8	69	79	324
Middlesex (1)	24	11	4	9*	60	72	308
Hampshire (3)	24	10	2	12	62	71	289$
Leicestershire (2)	24	9	3	12	52	81	277
Warwickshire (17)	24	10	3	11	52	64	276
Northamptonshire (9)	24	7	4	13	63	77	252
Kent (13)	24	7	4	13	68	70	250
Surrey (5)	24	7	4	13	65	70	247
Derbyshire (11)	24	7	5	12	46	65	219$
Somerset (6)	24	3	7	14	57	75	180
Sussex (8)	24	3	10	11*	50	72	170
⌐Gloucestershire (15)	24	3	8	14±	56	61	165
⌐Lancashire (12)	24	3	4	17	56	61	165
Nottinghamshire (4)	24	3	10	11	39	62	149
Glamorgan (16)	24	2	10	12	45	64	141
Worcestershire (14)	24	2	11	11	43	54	129
Yorkshire (10)	24	1	5	17	45	64	125

± includes two matches abandoned without a ball bowled
*includes one match abandoned without a ball bowled
$ includes twelve points for win in match reduced to one innings
1982 positions are shown in brackets

FIRST-CLASS AVERAGES 1983

	I	NO	HS	Runs	Av	100
I. V. A. Richards (Somerset)	20	4	216	1204	75.25	5
C. G. Greenidge (Hampshire)	27	5	154	1438	65.36	4
M. W. Gatting (Middlesex)	28	5	216	1494	64.95	6
J. A. Carse (Northamptonshire)	10	8	36*	129	64.50	–
K. S. McEwan (Essex)	39	5	189*	2176	64.00	8
Imran Khan (Sussex)	25	3	124*	1260	57.27	2
C. S. Cowdrey (Kent)	34	10	123	1364	56.83	5
A. J. Lamb (Northamptonshire)	29	7	137*	1232	56.00	5
G. Boycott (Yorkshire)	40	5	214*	1941	55.45	7
±A. I. Kallicharran (Warwickshire)	34	4	243*	1637	54.56	6

*denotes not out
±denotes left-hand batsman

	Overs	M	Runs	Wkts	Av	BB
Imran Khan (Sussex)	46.2	12	86	12	7.16	6–6
±J. K. Lever (Essex)	569	137	1726	106	16.28	7–55
M. D. Marshall (Hampshire)	532.5	143	1327	80	16.58	7–29
M. Hendrick (Nottinghamshire)	552.1	190	1122	66	17.00	6–17
R. A. Woolmer (Kent)	86	29	170	10	17.00	3–13
J. E. Emburey (Middlesex)	935	325	1842	103	17.88	6–13
P. B. Clift (Leicestershire)	619.4	167	1592	83	19.18	5–20
±D. L. Underwood (Kent)	936.3	358	2044	106	19.28	7–55
±K. D. James (Middlesex)	89	20	217	11	19.72	5–28
T. M. Lamb (Northamptonshire)	188.2	57	416	21	19.80	5–27

±denotes left-arm bowler

THIRD WORLD CUP

Freddie Trueman: The Third Prudential World Cup was on a larger scale than the two previous tournaments with 24 matches staged, some of them at a whole series of new international venues, as eliminators. These provided more than their share of heroics such as Zimbabwe's win over Australia, right at the beginning of the tournament. This historic event, roughly the equivalent of Durham's Gillette Cup win over Yorkshire, took place at Trent Bridge on 9 June and was no fluke. Put in by Kim Hughes, Zimbabwe totalled 239 for six in their 60 overs and then contained their illustrious opponents so successfully that they finished their overs on 226 for seven. Sri Lanka did well to score 286 against England at Taunton and went one better by beating New Zealand at Derby. Kapil Dev, the Indian captain, gave spectators at Tunbridge Wells *the* innings of the World Cup when he went to the wicket with a scoreboard reading 9 for four wickets against Zimbabwe and was not out 175 at the end of 60 overs. His innings included six sixes and 16 fours. India had already shaken

West Indies by beating them at Old Trafford in a match which went over into the second day, but their victory in the final still took everyone by surprise. When they beat England in the semi-final it was the signal for lots of plans to be changed in India and last-minute flights to be booked to England. Consequently all sorts of Indian supporters arrived unexpectedly for the final when all the tickets had been sold months earlier. It led to a certain resentment in Indian circles which was still being mentioned when the Fourth World Cup was played in India four years later!

The final was at no time spectacular but it was tense in the extreme from the first ball to the last. Against the bowling of Roberts, Garner, Marshall and Holding, the Indian batsmen showed they had come a long way since they batted through their overs to finish 202 in arrears at Lord's in 1975, and even further since they backed away from fast bowling in 1952. Even so, setting aside the undoubted class of their 23-year-old captain, it was difficult to see their threadbare attack having the ability to contain batsmen like Greenidge, Haynes, Richards,

Another crowd invasion—this time Indian supporters at Lord's as India beat West Indies in the third World Cup

Lloyd, Gomes and Bacchus. We reckoned without the experience in limited-overs cricket gained in the leagues of northern England by Madan Lal and Mohinder Amarnath and the way the Indians now surpassed themselves in the field: West Indies were all out 140. It was an epic victory by 43 runs for a well-organised team which fought every inch of the way. A day of national holiday was declared in India minutes after the last ball had been bowled at Lord's and the rejoicing amongst their supporters in this country went on for much longer than that. The highest individual score in the game was 33 (Richards) and Mike Brearley's Man-of-the-Match award went to Amarnath—26 runs and bowling figures of 7–0–12–3.

ASHES LOST

Don Mosey: The previous winter had seen the Ashes lost by a team led by Bob Willis, although Keith Fletcher had proved himself a capable and popular tour leader the previous winter in India. Norman Cowans, Middlesex's Jamaican-born fast bowler, won his first England cap in

the First Test (Perth) where an outbreak of football-type hooliganism marred the second day's play. England supporters were very much involved and Alderman, the Australian bowler, pursued one who had struck him and dislocated his shoulder so badly in bringing down the spectator that he missed the remainder of the season. It was, however, a notable game for Botham who scored his 3,000th Test run and took his 250th wicket. In Brisbane (Second Test), Kepler Wessels, Sussex's South African-born opening batsman, made his debut for Australia with a century and Rodney Marsh took his 300th catch. Australia won again in Adelaide to go 2–0 up but England pulled off a thrilling victory in Melbourne by just three runs and Botham, by taking the last wicket to complete that win, went to a double of 1,000 runs and 100 wickets against Australia. A drawn last Test in Sydney meant the return of the Ashes to Australia after five and a half years but Eddie Hemmings, the Nottinghamshire off-spinner, remembers the game for his night-watchman's innings of 95. England went on to New Zealand to play three one-day Internationals and were comprehensively beaten in all of them. Glenn Turner, having retired from English county cricket with Worcestershire after 1982, scored 88, 94 and 34 and New Zealand achieved their hat-trick of wins without the services of Richard Hadlee. It had been a miserable winter for the tourists.

NEW ZEALAND IN ENGLAND

FST: After the World Cup, England took on New Zealand again in a four-Test series and started with a win at The Oval in spite of Hadlee's return of six for 53 as they were dismissed in the first innings for 209. In the second innings, Fowler, Tavaré and Lamb all scored centuries. At Headingley (Second Test) New Zealand claimed their first Test win in England with Cairns taking seven for 74. Hadlee did not take a wicket in the match! On the eve of the Third Test (Lord's) Edmonds strained his back; Nick Cook, the Leicestershire slow left-arm bowler, was called up—and returned five for 35 in his first Test. Other debutants in the match were Neil Foster (Essex), and Chris Smith (Hampshire) who joined Allan Lamb as a pair of South African-born players in the England side. Smith not only joined the ranks of those who did not score in their first Test innings; he was out first ball. Hadlee took his 200th Test wicket at Trent Bridge where England completed a 3–1 win in the series. Cook, who retained his place in the Fourth Test, ended the series with 17 wickets at 16.17 which won him a place on the following winter's tour.

COUNTY CHAMPIONSHIP

DM: The number of county championship matches played by each side was increased by two to 24 in 1983 and Essex, once again a very solid outfit with star players but no mega-stars, won the Schweppes title for the second time although they won only the same number of games (11) as the runners-up, Middlesex. Essex scored nine more batting bonus points and seven more for bowling, with Lever again topping the 100-wicket mark. Yorkshire, in their fifth year of internal strife, reached total rock-bottom with a 17th placing unprecedented in 20th century cricket and paradoxically they won the John Player League—a form of cricket which all right-thinking Yorkshiremen utterly despise. Such were the eccentricities of the championship scoring system that although Yorkshire won only one first-class game they actually lost only five—the same number as the championship-winners, Essex. Nottinghamshire, with Hadlee involved in both Test series and World Cup, tumbled from fourth place to 14th and the most spectacular advance was made by Warwickshire—bottom to fifth, with ten wins. These were achieved by solid batting (five players topped 1,000 runs) and the bowling of the 43-year-old Norman Gifford, who had joined the county from Worcestershire, and Chris Old, recruited from Yorkshire. Chris Cowdrey had his best season for Kent so far, with five centuries plus a 122 not out in the NatWest and a 95 in the John Player.

SOMERSET'S NATWEST

FST: Somerset won their second 60-overs final, their first under the NatWest banner, and were now recognised as an outstanding limited-overs side. Their semi-final against Middlesex at Lord's was much more notable than their 24-run win over Kent in the final on the same ground. Middlesex, after making 222 for nine, had Somerset in deep trouble at 52 for five when Botham struck a majestic 96. The scores were level at the start of the last over and Somerset had by then lost eight wickets. Resisting the temptation to win with a six and reach his century, Botham played out a maiden over so that Somerset won by virtue of losing fewer wickets. The final did in fact provide a first because a delayed start reduced the match to 50 overs a side. The Benson & Hedges Cup produced a much more exciting final than usual with the 26-year-old Gatting, in his first season as Middlesex captain, keeping his head when almost everyone about him (notably in the Essex side) lost theirs. He was defending a total of only 196 for eight and saw Essex progress to 79 for one, 127 for two, 135 for three, 151 for four, and 156 for five. In fact they reached 185 without losing another wicket and so needed only 11 to win if they lost no more than two wickets, but it was the batting side who panicked and lost all five to give Middlesex the game with just five balls remaining. Earlier, Middlesex had become the first side to win a game on the toss of a coin—against Gloucestershire in the quarter-final at Bristol where not a ball was possible on all three days. Yorkshire, level on points with Somerset, won the John Player because of a greater number of away wins.

Botham smashes away another six

1984

Winter Tour to New Zealand (1983–84):

Wellington	Match drawn
Christchurch	New Zealand won by an innings & 132 runs
Auckland	Match drawn

One-Day Internationals v New Zealand (1983–84):

Christchurch	England won by 54 runs
Wellington	England won by six wickets
Auckland	New Zealand won by seven wickets

Winter Tour to Pakistan:

Karachi	Pakistan won by three wickets
Faisalabad	Match drawn
Lahore	Match drawn

One-Day Internationals v Pakistan:

Lahore	Pakistan won by six wickets
Karachi	England won by six wickets

Cornhill Tests in England:

West Indies:

Edgbaston	West Indies won by an innings & 180 runs
Lord's	West Indies won by nine wickets
Headingley	West Indies won by eight wickets
Old Trafford	West Indies won by an innings & 64 runs
Oval	West Indies won by 172 runs

Sri Lanka:

Lord's	Match drawn

Texaco One-Day Internationals v West Indies:

Old Trafford	West Indies won by 104 runs
Trent Bridge	England won by three wickets
Lord's	West Indies won by eight wickets

County Champions	Essex
NatWest Trophy	Middlesex
John Player League	Essex
Benson & Hedges Cup	Lancashire

TEST AVERAGES ENGLAND V NEW ZEALAND 1983–84

	M	I	NO	HS	Runs	Av	100	50	Ct/St
C. L. Smith	2	3	1	91	148	74.00	0	1	–
D. W. Randall	3	4	0	164	293	73.25	2	–	2
I. T. Botham	3	4	0	138	226	56.50	1	1	3
A. J. Lamb	3	4	0	49	82	20.50	–	–	1
M. W. Gatting	2	3	1	19*	38	19.00	–	–	2
C. J. Tavaré	2	4	1	36*	54	18.00	–	–	1
D. I. Gower	3	4	0	33	69	17.25	–	–	2
R. W. Taylor	3	4	0	23	54	13.50	–	–	9/–
N. G. Cowans	2	3	0	21	32	10.66	–	–	1
R. G. D. Willis	3	4	1	6	14	4.66	–	–	–
G. Fowler	2	3	0	10	14	4.66	–	–	–

Also batted: N. G. B. Cook (1 match) 7, 1ct; N. A. Foster (2 matches) 10, 18*, 1ct; V. J. Marks (1 match) 6; A. C. S. Pigott (1 match) 4, 8*.

	Overs	M	Runs	Wkts	Av	5w	10w	BB
R. G. D. Willis	115.1	28	306	12	25.50	–	–	4–51
N. G. Cowans	52	14	154	5	30.80	–	–	3–52
I. T. Botham	109.4	25	354	7	50.57	1	–	5–59

Also bowled: N. G. B. Cook 89.3–37–196–4; N. A. Foster 91–29–229–4; M. W. Gatting 10–4–28–1; V. J. Marks 40.2–9–115–3; A. C. S. Pigott 17–7–75–2; C. L. Smith 3–1–6–0.

TEST AVERAGES ENGLAND V PAKISTAN 1983–84

	M	I	NO	HS	Runs	Av	100	50	Ct/St
D. I. Gower	3	5	1	173*	449	112.25	2	2	3
G. Fowler	2	3	0	58	134	44.66	–	2	1
V. J. Marks	3	5	0	83	218	43.60	–	3	–
M. W. Gatting	3	5	0	75	158	31.60	–	2	6
C. L. Smith	3	5	0	66	132	26.40	–	1	3
D. W. Randall	3	5	0	65	103	20.60	–	1	–
A. J. Lamb	3	5	0	29	78	15.60	–	–	4
N. G. Cowans	2	4	3	3*	7	7.00	–	–	2
N. G. B. Cook	3	4	1	9	18	6.00	–	–	–
R. W. Taylor	3	5	0	19	29	5.80	–	–	3/–

Also batted: I. T. Botham (1 match) 22, 10, 4ct; G. R. Dilley (1 match) 2*; N. A. Foster (2 matches) 6, 0, 1ct; R. G. D. Willis (1 match) 6, 2, 1ct.

	Overs	M	Runs	Wkts	Av	5w	10w	BB
N. G. Cowans	57.3	11	175	7	25.00	1	–	5–42
G. R. Dilley	37	6	142	5	28.40	–	–	3–101
N. G. B. Cook	178.3	54	444	14	31.71	2	1	6–65
N. A. Foster	82	20	230	7	32.85	1	–	5–67

Also bowled: I. T. Botham 30–5–90–2; G. Fowler 1–0–3–0; M. W. Gatting 5–0–35–1; V. J. Marks 90–24–260–4; C. L. Smith 2–1–2–1; R. G. D. Willis 19–6–46–2.

TEST AVERAGES ENGLAND V WEST INDIES 1984

	M	I	NO	HS	Runs	Av	100	50	Ct/St
A. J. Lamb	5	10	1	110	386	42.88	3	–	3
I. T. Botham	5	10	0	81	347	34.70	–	3	5
G. Fowler	5	10	0	106	260	26.00	1	1	3
B. C. Broad	4	8	0	55	195	24.37	–	1	1
P. R. Downton	5	10	1	56	210	23.33	–	1	10/–
R. G. D. Willis	3	5	3	22	43	21.50	–	–	1
D. I. Gower	5	10	1	57*	171	19.00	–	1	3
D. R. Pringle	3	6	1	46*	81	16.20	–	–	3
P. J. W. Allott	3	6	0	26	67	11.16	–	–	2
N. G. B. Cook	3	6	0	13	25	4.16	–	–	1
G. Miller	2	4	0	22	42	10.50	–	–	2
V. P. Terry	2	3	0	8	16	5.33	–	–	2

Also batted: J. P. Agnew (1 match) 5, 2*; N. G. Cowans (1 match) 0, 14, 1ct; R. M. Ellison (1 match) 20*, 13; N. A. Foster (1 match) 6, 9*; M. W. Gatting (1 match) 1, 29, 2ct; T. A. Lloyd (1 match) 10*; P. I. Pocock (2 matches) 0, 0, 0, 0; D. W. Randall (1 match) 0, 1, 1ct; C. J. Tavaré (1 match) 16, 49, 2ct.

	Overs	M	Runs	Wkts	Av	5w	10w	BB
R. M. Ellison	44	10	94	5	18.80	–	–	3–60
P. J. W. Allott	104.5	26	282	14	20.14	1	–	6–61
I. T. Botham	163.2	30	667	19	35.10	2	–	8–103
D. R. Pringle	71.3	10	257	5	51.40	1	–	5–108
N. G. B. Cook	95	15	297	5	59.40	–	–	2–27
R. G. D. Willis	85	15	367	6	61.16	–	–	2–48

Also bowled: J. P. Agnew 26–4–97–2; N. G. Cowans 19–2–46–0; N. A. Foster 18–2–82–0; G. Miller 28–1–142–1; P. I. Pocock 53.3–17–145–4.

FIRST-CLASS AVERAGES 1984

	I	NO	HS	Runs	Av	100
M. W. Gatting (Middlesex)	43	10	258	2257	68.39	8
±P. W. Denning (Somerset)	8	3	90	338	67.60	–
G. A. Gooch (Essex)	45	7	227	2559	67.34	8
Javed Miandad (Glamorgan)	15	2	212*	832	64.00	2
G. Boycott (Yorkshire)	35	10	153*	1567	62.68	4
±J. G. Wright (Derbyshire)	21	1	177	1201	60.05	2
D. L. Amiss (Warwickshire)	50	10	122	2239	55.97	6
M. D. Crowe (Somerset)	41	6	190	1870	53.42	6
V. J. Marks (Somerset)	34	10	134	1262	52.58	3
±A. I. Kallicharran (Warwickshire)	50	6	200*	2301	52.29	9

	Overs	M	Runs	Wkts	Av	BB
R. J. Hadlee (Nottinghamshire)	772.2	248	1645	117	14.05	7–35
R. A. Harper (WI/D. B. Close XI)	314.1	109	676	37	18.27	6–57
P. J. W. Allott (Lancashire)	604.5	171	1496	79	18.93	7–72
±D. L. Underwood (Kent)	676.4	250	1511	77	19.62	8–87
T. M. Tremlett (Hampshire)	669.5	210	1444	71	20.33	5–48
A. Sidebottom (Yorkshire)	488.1	105	1292	63	20.50	6–41
G. S. Le Roux (Sussex)	604.2	154	1647	78	21.11	6–57
S. T. Clarke (Surrey)	651	165	1687	78	21.62	6–57
N. G. Cowans (Middlesex)	493.1	76	1593	73	21.82	6–64
±J. K. Lever (Essex)	874.5	195	2550	116	21.98	8–37

BRITANNIC ASSURANCE CHAMPIONSHIP TABLE 1984

Win = 16 points
Tie = 8 points

	P	Won	Lost	D	Tied	Bonus Pts Bat	Bonus Pts Bowl	Pts
ESSEX (1)	24	13	3	8	0	64	83	355
Nottinghamshire (14)	24	12	3	9	0	68	81	341
Middlesex (3)	24	8	7	9	0	63	78	269
Leicestershire (4)	24	8	2	14	0	60	78	266
Kent (7)	24	8	3	11	2	45	65	254
Sussex (11)	24	7	6	10	1	54	79	249±
Somerset (10)	24	6	7	11	0	60	78	234
Surrey (8)	24	6	6	12	0	62	72	230
Warwickshire (5)	24	6	7	11	0	71	60	227
Worcestershire (16)	24	5	5	14	0	66	74	220
Northamptonshire (6)	24	5	9	9	1	58	56	202
Derbyshire (9)	24	4	6	14	0	72	66	202
Glamorgan (15)	24	4	2	18	0	65	71	200
Yorkshire (17)	24	5	4	15	0	59	55	194
Hampshire (3)	24	3	13	8	0	58	62	168
Lancashire (12)	24	1	9	14	0	49	72	137
Gloucestershire (12)	24	1	10	13	0	56	61	133

± includes twelve points for win in match reduced to one innings
1983 positions are shown in brackets

PACIFIC NEW YEAR

Don Mosey: At 4.30 am on New Year's Eve, 1983, that winter's touring party broke new ground by arriving in Fiji, where no England cricketers had called since 1933—Jardine's bodyline tour, returning home, and they did not play any cricket. Bob Willis's group played two light-hearted limited-overs games during a five-day acclimatisation stop before continuing to New Zealand. In the drawn First Test (Wellington), Willis overtook the Trueman record of 307 wickets; Botham got another century plus five wickets in an innings; and Gatting took his first Test wicket (Martin Crowe, who had just completed a maiden Test hundred) while Randall, who spent something like an hour on 99, progressed in due course to 164. The Second Test (Christchurch) saw the debut in unusual circumstances of Tony Pigott, the Sussex fast bowler, who was spending the English winter playing in Wellington. With Foster and Dilley both injured, Pigott was called up to play in a match in which England were totally humiliated by being bowled out for 82 and 93 to lose for the second time in New Zealand—by an innings and 132 runs. Hadlee just missed a Botham-like performance by taking five for 28 (eight for 44 in the match) and scoring

England set off for Fiji, New Zealand and Pakistan

99. With the Third Test (Auckland) drawn, England had lost a series in (and to) New Zealand for the first time. Ian Smith, the New Zealand wicket-keeper, completed the unusual feat of claiming six victims in England's only innings including the dismissal of Fowler, first ball, immediately after completing his own (not out) maiden Test hundred. England then flew to Pakistan via Sydney (for an unscheduled stop because of engine trouble) and Bombay and lost a Test in Pakistan for the first time. Nick Cook, despite returns of six for 65 and five for 18, was on the losing side. Botham's run of 65 consecutive Tests ended in Karachi and before the Second Test (Faisalabad) he flew home for an operation on an injured knee. Willis, too, was out of action and Gower, taking over as captain, scored 152, completing 4,000 Test runs in the process. With the Final Test (Lahore) drawn, England had lost two series on the same winter tour. They won one and lost one of the two one-day Internationals. In New Zealand they had won two and lost one. Gower, who had totalled only 69 runs in four innings in New Zealand came good in Pakistan with 449 runs (avge 112.25). His captaincy, too, had been impressive in two Tests and he was given the job of leading England against the West Indies during the summer.

DISASTROUS DEBUT

Freddie Trueman: Andy Lloyd, the Warwickshire left-hand opener, played his first Test at the start of the 1984 summer series on his home ground and saw Fowler, then Randall, dismissed with only five runs scored, before he was struck on the helmet by a ball from Marshall. Despite the protection he did not return and did not play again in 1984. Eldine Baptiste, after three seasons with Kent, came into the West Indies pace attack and as a No. 9 batsman shared a stand of 150 with Michael Holding (No. 10) in 114 minutes. Chris Broad (who had moved from Gloucestershire to Nottinghamshire that season) came into the England side at Lord's (Second Test) for Lloyd and shared a first-wicket partnership of 101 with Fowler in a match which coincided with the centenary of Test cricket on the ground. Clive Lloyd topped 7,000 runs for West Indies, Botham reached 4,000 for England but the highlight of the game was a brilliant 214 not out (out of 344 for one) by Gordon Greenidge, with two sixes and 29 fours. Lamb, who was to have an outstanding season, scored a second-innings 110 to make possible an England declaration. Their subsequent defeat was the first after a second-innings declaration since Headingley, 1948. Paul

Quick reaction at silly point—David Gower catches Sandeep Patil

Terry, who had been scoring well for Hampshire, came into the side for the Third (Headingley) and Fourth (Old Trafford) Tests and in his third innings suffered a fractured forearm. He returned at the fall of the ninth wicket with his left arm in a sling but could not improve his score, one-handed, before he was bowled. Lamb scored successive centuries at Lord's, Headingley and Old Trafford. Jonathan Agnew (Leicestershire) and Richard Ellison (Kent) made their first appearances in the Final Test (The Oval) but West Indies completed a clean sweep of all five, the first side to do so in England. Pat Pocock, the Surrey off-spinner, returned to Test cricket at Old Trafford, 86 matches after his previous International which was on the same ground and against the West Indies. His laconic comment, when asked if things had changed much, was, 'They're not as fast as they used to be.' The current England batsmen did not agree with him! Willis played the last of his 90 Tests at Headingley and retired with 325 wickets and 55 not-out innings. Botham took his 300th Test wicket at The Oval.

Left: Andy Lloyd's brief Test career ends in his first innings—felled by Marshall at Edgbaston

ONE-DAY INTERNATIONALS

DM: England had the consolation of one success out of three in the one-day Internationals now sponsored by the oil company, Texaco, though it might have been a different story but for Vivian Richards. In the first match, at Old Trafford, he went in at 11 for two, saw the score go to 166 for nine and yet contrived a final total of 272 for nine with the greatest limited-overs innings (189 not out) in the history of the game. Those who saw both claim it surpassed Kapil Dev's 175 not out in the World Cup at Tunbridge Wells in more than arithmetical terms. He hit five sixes—one off Pringle went out of the ground—and 21 fours and faced only 170 deliveries. The last-wicket partnership with Holding realised 106 in 14 overs and Holding faced only 27 balls. Certainly I never expect to see an innings to equal Richards'.

FST: Significantly, England won at Trent Bridge where Richards scored only three, but his 84 not out at Lord's once again made the difference between the sides as far as batting was concerned. I agree—I don't ever expect to see another knock like Richards' at Old Trafford. The shot I remember was a six off Foster over long-off but that was always a speciality of Viv's . . . a truly marvellous innings.

HADLEE'S DOUBLE

DM: The Britannic Assurance Company were the new sponsors of the county championship and Essex (the winners) and Nottinghamshire gave them a magnificent start with a duel which went to the very last over of the season. With Hadlee available full time, Nottinghamshire based their challenge on his wonderful all-round perform-ance of 117 wickets at 14.05 and 1,179 runs, average 51.26. He hit two centuries, seven fifties, took ten wickets in a match once and five in an innings six times. It was the first time anyone had done the double in English cricket since Fred Titmus in 1967, when 28 championship matches were played. Tim Robinson topped 2,000 runs for Nottinghamshire and Rice scored 1,553. Against that, Essex could point to a magnificent 2,559 runs from Gooch, 1,755 from McEwan, three other players with more than 1,000 and another 116 wickets from Lever, now aged 35. Foster and Pringle were developing well but there was nothing like the employment for spinners in Essex that Nottinghamshire found for Hemmings. The last games of the season found Nottinghamshire in Taunton and Essex at Old Trafford. If both sides won, Nottinghamshire would take the title; if Essex won and Nottinghamshire didn't, it would be Essex's championship. They duly won in two days against Lancashire, playing very positive and indeed dynamic cricket to do so. Nottinghamshire responded in similar fashion when, on the third afternoon,

Botham set them a target of 297 in a minimum of 52 overs (which because of the use of spinners, ultimately became, in fact, 60 overs), a perfectly reasonable one in all the circumstances. Rice played a wonderful innings, helped by Hadlee and young Paul Johnson but when the captain was out, Nottinghamshire needed 39 from four overs which soon became 27 off two and another two wickets had gone. Mike Bore, a Yorkshire-born slow left-armer, faced Stephen Booth, a Yorkshire-born slow left-armer, for the final over with 14 still required. He hit the first two balls for four, turned the next for two, blocked the fourth and slammed the fifth high to long off where a substitute fieldsman, Richard Ollis, held the catch. A foot higher and Nottinghamshire would have won the game and the title. It was the most magnificent climax to Britannic's first championship.

ONE-DAY COMPETITIONS

FST: The most remarkable thing about the Benson & Hedges Cup Final—unless you count the fact that Lancashire were there at all in what was a terrible season for them—was that the Gold award, judged by Peter May, went to John Abrahams who was out for a duck and did not bowl! The reason given was Abrahams' leadership in a match where Warwickshire simply fell apart. From 102 for three, they were all out 139 in 50.4 overs and Lancashire won by six wickets. It was a different story in the NatWest which went to the very last ball. Tavaré, the Kent captain, was criticised for not using up Underwood's full complement of 12 overs after the veteran left-armer had bowled nine overs for only 12 runs, and Ellison's medium pace was used for the last over with Middlesex needing seven runs. They accumulated five singles off five and Ellison's last delivery was turned to leg for four. Essex became the first county to win both championship and the John Player League—the two extremes of the game—in the same season and Yorkshire slumped from first to 16th. Boycott's feud with the Yorkshire Committee had now reached revolutionary proportions. His supporters had won a majority on the Committee and Illingworth had been dismissed as manager.

SRI LANKA'S VISIT

DM: One of the great delights of the season was provided by the batting of Sri Lanka in their first Test appearance at Lord's (a one-off game played after the West Indies series). Cornhill sponsored the match as they did the West Indies series. Perhaps it was the preponderance of limited-overs cricket in this country which had reared a generation of spectators unaccustomed to orthodox batting but certainly a large number were unprepared for the grace and charm of the centuries by Wettimuny (190) and Mendis (111) after Gower had put Sri Lanka in to bat. They played correctly at all times and looked (to my eyes at least) like beautifully coached schoolboys who had gone on to develop their cricket at Fenner's or The Parks. England—a reaction, perhaps, after the traumas of the earlier summer—looked sloppy in the field and arrogantly unenthusiastic in their bowling, and a certain indiscipline which had crept into their cricket during the summer was now openly displayed. Sri Lankan batsmen registered three centuries (one not out), a 94 and an 84 in their two innings. Lamb (inevitably in that summer) scored England's only 100 in a drawn match. One felt the *Benson & Hedges Cricket Year* book summed it all up admirably with this comment on the match: 'England chose to dawdle and be flippant, Botham making low bows to the crowd when taking his first wicket. Sri Lanka played all the best cricket and were a delight to watch. One sighed for an England side with discipline and dignity.' Amen to that.

A Benson & Hedges Cup-winning captain and Gold Award winner—John Abrahams of Lancashire

1985

Winter Tour to India (1984–85):

Bombay	India won by eight wickets
Delhi	England won by eight wickets
Calcutta	Match drawn
Madras	England won by nine wickets
Kanpur	Match drawn

One-Day Internationals v India (1984–85):

Pune	England won by four wickets
Cuttack	England won on faster scoring rate
Bangalore	England won by three wickets
Nagpur	India won by three wickets
Chandigarh	England won by 7 runs

Benson & Hedges World Championship (in Australia):

Melbourne (D/N)	Australia won by seven wickets
Sydney (D/N)	India won by 86 runs
Melbourne (D/N)	Pakistan won by 67 runs

Cornhill Tests in England:

Headingley	England won by five wickets
Lord's	Australia won by four wickets
Trent Bridge	Match drawn
Old Trafford	Match drawn
Edgbaston	England won by an innings & 118 runs
Oval	England won by an innings & 94 runs

Texaco One-Day Internationals:

Australia:

Old Trafford	Australia won by three wickets
Edgbaston	Australia won by four wickets
Lord's	England won by eight wickets

Britannic County Champions	Middlesex
NatWest Trophy	Essex
John Player League	Essex
Benson & Hedges Cup	Leicestershire

TEST AVERAGES ENGLAND V INDIA 1984–85

	M	I	NO	HS	Runs	Av	100	50	Ct/St
M. W. Gatting	5	9	3	207	575	95.83	2	1	4
R. T. Robinson	5	9	2	160	444	63.42	1	2	–
P. R. Downton	5	6	3	74	183	61.00	–	2	14/2
G. Fowler	5	8	0	201	438	54.75	1	2	2
A. J. Lamb	5	7	1	67	241	40.16	–	3	9
P. H. Edmonds	5	6	0	49	175	29.16	–	–	–
D. I. Gower	5	7	1	78	167	27.83	–	1	6
C. S. Cowdrey	5	6	1	38	96	19.20	–	–	5
P. I. Pocock	5	5	2	22*	39	13.00	–	–	2
R. M. Ellison	3	4	0	10	12	3.00	–	–	–
N. G. Cowans	5	5	1	9	10	2.50	–	–	2

Also batted: N. A. Foster (2 matches) 5, 8.

	Overs	M	Runs	Wkts	Av	5w	10w	BB
N. A. Foster	87	18	286	14	20.42	2	1	6–104
P. H. Edmonds	276.1	104	584	14	41.71	–	–	4–60
N. G. Cowans	181.5	41	627	14	44.78	–	–	3–103
P. I. Pocock	237.5	53	655	13	50.38	–	–	4–93

Also bowled: C. S. Cowdrey 61–2–288–4; R. M. Ellison 105–24–289–4; G. Fowler 1–1–0–0; M. W. Gatting 13–1–36–0; D. I. Gower 3–0–13–0; A. J. Lamb 1–0–6–1; R. T. Robinson 1–1–0–0.

TEST AVERAGES ENGLAND V AUSTRALIA 1985

	M	I	NO	HS	Runs	Av	100	50	Ct/St
M. W. Gatting	6	9	3	160	527	87.83	2	3	–
D. I. Gower	6	9	0	215	732	81.33	3	1	6
R. T. Robinson	6	9	1	175	490	61.25	2	1	5
G. A. Gooch	6	9	0	196	487	54.11	1	2	4
A. J. Lamb	6	8	1	67	256	36.57	–	1	7
J. E. Emburey	6	6	2	33	130	32.50	–	–	3
I. T. Botham	6	8	0	85	250	31.25	–	2	8
P. R. Downton	6	7	1	54	114	19.00	–	1	19/1
P. H. Edmonds	5	5	0	21	47	9.40	–	–	8
P. J. W. Allott	4	5	1	12	27	6.75	–	–	–

Also batted: J. P. Agnew (1 match) 2*; N. G. Cowans (1 match) 22*; R. M. Ellison (2 matches) 3, 1ct; N. A. Foster (1 match) 3, 0; A. Sidebottom (1 match) 2; L. B. Taylor (2 matches) 1*, 1ct; P. Willey (1 match) 36, 3*.

	Overs	M	Runs	Wkts	Av	5w	10w	BB
R. M. Ellison	75.5	20	185	17	10.88	1	1	6–77
I. T. Botham	251.4	36	855	31	27.58	1	–	5–109
J. E. Emburey	248.4	75	544	19	28.63	1	–	5–82
P. H. Edmonds	225.5	59	549	15	36.60	–	–	4–40
P. J. W. Allott	113	22	297	5	59.40	–	–	2–74

Also bowled: J. P. Agnew 23–2–99–0; N. G. Cowans 33–6–128–2; N. A. Foster 23–1–83–1; M. W. Gatting 5–0–16–0; G. A. Gooch 41.2–10–102–2; A. J. Lamb 1–0–10–0; A. Sidebottom 18.4–3–65–1; L. B. Taylor 63.3–11–178–4.

BRITANNIC ASSURANCE CHAMPIONSHIP TABLE 1985

Win = 16 points	P	Won	Lost	D	Bonus Pts Bat	Bowl	Pts
MIDDLESEX (3)	24	8	4	12	61	85	274
Hampshire (15)	24	7	2	15	66	78	256
Gloucestershire (17)	24	7	3	14*	51	78	241
Essex (1)	24	7	2	15*	42	70	224
Worcestershire (10)	24	5	6	13	65	68	221±
Surrey (8)	24	5	5	14	62	76	218
Sussex (6)	24	6	1	17*	52	57	205
Nottinghamshire (2)	24	4	2	18	66	69	199
Kent (5)	24	4	5	15	51	71	186
Northamptonshire (11)	24	5	4	15	52	51	183
Yorkshire (14)	24	3	4	17*	58	59	165
Glamorgan (13)	24	4	4	16	41	50	163±
Derbyshire (12)	24	3	9	12	46	69	163
Lancashire (16)	24	3	7	14	44	67	159
Warwickshire (9)	24	2	8	14	47	74	153
Leicestershire (4)	24	2	3	19	48	65	145
Somerset (7)	24	1	7	16	70	45	131

* includes one match abandoned without a ball bowled
± includes eight points for fourth innings in drawn matches when final scores were level
1984 positions are shown in brackets

FIRST-CLASS AVERAGES 1985

	I	NO	HS	Runs	Av	100
I. V. A. Richards (Somerset)	24	0	322	1836	76.50	9
G. Boycott (Yorkshire)	34	12	184	1657	75.31	6
G. A. Gooch (Essex)	33	2	202	2208	71.22	7
I. T. Botham (Somerset)	27	5	152	1530	69.54	5
Imran Khan (Sussex)	21	8	117*	890	68.46	1
±Younis Ahmed (Glamorgan)	30	8	177	1421	64.59	5
Javed Miandad (Glamorgan)	29	6	200*	1441	62.65	4
R. T. Robinson (Nottinghamshire)	31	4	175	1619	59.96	6
C. L. Smith (Hampshire)	39	4	143*	2000	57.14	7
±J. G. Wright (Derbyshire)	16	2	177*	797	56.92	2

*denotes not out
±denotes left-hand batsman

	Overs	M	Runs	Wkts	Av	BB
R. M. Ellison (Kent)	432.1	113	1118	65	17.20	7–87
R. J. Hadlee (Nottinghamshire)	473.5	136	1026	59	17.38	8–41
M. D. Marshall (Hampshire)	688.1	193	1680	95	17.68	7–59
±G. E. Sainsbury (Gloucestershire)	178	59	481	27	17.81	7–38
C. A. Walsh (Gloucestershire)	560.3	124	1706	85	20.07	7–51
Imran Khan (Sussex)	422.1	114	1040	51	20.39	5–49
T. M. Tremlett (Hampshire)	665.5	181	1620	75	21.60	5–42
Kapil Dev (Worcestershire)	304.5	83	805	37	21.75	4–56
M. A. Holding (Derbyshire)	354.5	67	1124	50	22.48	6–65
P. J. W. Allott (Lancashire)	560.2	167	1328	58	22.89	6–71

±denotes left-arm bowler

LONGER TOURS

Freddie Trueman: Winter tours were now becoming ever longer and it was not surprising to find players who were certain of regular selection wanting to opt out of some of them. Tours took up a lot of time in my day but much of this was occupied by the journey by sea to our host country which, there and back, could take between six and eight weeks. The arrival of the jumbo-jet age meant that the furthest destination was now within 48 hours' travelling-time and in most cases no more than 36 hours'. Internal travel within the Indian sub-continent no longer meant a three-day train journey but a three-hour flight, with the result that more and more fixtures were now being crammed into the itinerary. Most of the extra games were one-day Internationals for this sort of game had really caught on in India since the 1983 World Cup. In Australia, the marketing men were ruling the roost and seemed quite capable of dreaming up an historical reason for a new competition every year. In 1985, for instance,

the 150th anniversary of the founding of the state of Victoria was the excuse for calling up England once again, when the tour party had been playing five Tests plus one-day Internationals in India for the previous four and a half months! With Benson & Hedges once again the sponsors, this new venture was given the title 'World Championship of Cricket' and it followed on another triangular 'World Series' involving Australia, West Indies and Sri Lanka. The 'World Championship' now brought together all the senior cricketing nations in a competition similar in construction to the World Cup. India beat New Zealand in one semi-final, Pakistan beat West Indies in the other and then India beat Pakistan by 8 wickets in the final. In the space of 18 months, India had become World Cup-holders and now World Champions. England, having played and lost three qualifying games, were quickly out of it all, but there were still a couple more one-day frolics to be played at Sharjah, in the Persian Gulf, before the jaded players could start thinking about the domestic

'Percy' Pocock—seven wickets in 11 balls v Sussex in 1972

season—the busiest of any country in the world—and a six-Test series during the summer against Australia. It had been a long, long winter, starting at the beginning of October and not ending, for most of the players, until mid-March.

SUCCESS IN INDIA

Don Mosey: Gower again led England on the tour of India, from which Botham opted out to spend more time with his family, and it could scarcely have got off to a worse start. First came the assassination of Mrs Gandhi, which raised doubts about whether the tour could take place at all. In fact the England party flew to Sri Lanka until the dust settled. Then, almost as soon as it *had* got under way, Martyn Moxon had to return to England because of the death of his father. (He returned later.) And then the First Test was lost at the Wankhede Stadium, Bombay, which is not one of England's happiest hunting grounds. In 1981 their destroyer had been the medium-pace seamer Madan Lal; now it was the young leg-spinner, Sivaramakrishnan, who had a match return of 12 for 181. In the Second (New Delhi), however, the bowling of

Edmonds and Pocock and the batting of Robinson (160), Downton (74) and Lamb (52) enabled England to square the series. This defeat resulted in a public disagreement between Gavaskar, the captain, and former captain Kapil Dev, who had led India to their World Cup success, and Kapil Dev was dropped for the Third Test which, being in Calcutta, was almost inevitably drawn. Kapil Dev was restored to the side for Madras (Fourth Test), in my view the quickest of the Indian wickets (though that is a relative term!), but with Fowler (201) and Gatting (207) leading England to 652 for seven declared, victory was achieved by nine wickets. With the Final Test drawn in Kanpur, England had won the series and restored a little pride on a tour which started badly and ended in good spirits under Gower's leadership and the management of Tony Brown, the Somerset secretary. As the team also won four of the five one-day Internationals it augured well for the summer series. Gatting, who had had to wait nearly seven years and 54 innings for his first Test century (which he accomplished in Bombay) had a magnificent tour averaging 95.83, and Robinson, Downton and Fowler all topped the 50 mark while two quick men and two spinners shared the wickets almost equally. Chris Cowdrey, who earned his first cap in Bombay, played in all five and if neither his bowling nor his fielding seemed quite up to Test standard, he proved a magnificent fielder at all times.

INNOVATIONS

FST: The 1985 season was the first in England in which no-balls and wides were debited against the bowlers' analyses and the First Test, played at Headingley, was the first in which a reserve umpire was appointed in case of injury or illness to one of the two standing. The first such reserve was Ray Julian, the former Leicestershire wicket-keeper, as back-up to Barrie Meyer and Ken Palmer. England won a match in which more than 1,200 runs were scored while 35 wickets fell and I did not notice anyone complaining about the pitch for a change. It was good to see England winning the series and regaining the Ashes but I am bound to say that the Aussies looked the poorest side I have ever seen from that country. We also saw a further deterioration in standards of behaviour on the field, especially by Botham and particularly at Trent Bridge, where his conduct caused an umpire, Alan Whitehead, to report him to his captain. Unfortunately, Gower seemed incapable of handling Botham and this was a major factor in his losing the captaincy to Mike Gatting in due course.

NEW FAST BOWLERS

DM: With Dilley having problems with his action and

Foster with his fitness, England tried a number of different opening-bowling permutations during the season, none of which proved entirely satisfactory. Arnie Sidebottom (Yorkshire) and Les Taylor (Leicestershire) were introduced without making any impact and Sidebottom broke down in his 19th over at Trent Bridge. Botham took by far the greatest number of wickets but was usually expensive and the best performance of the summer was Ellison's six for 77 (ten for 104 in the match) at Edgbaston. It was as well that Australia performed so modestly and to a great extent they were a two-man team, with Border batting splendidly throughout the season (in all games) and McDermott taking 30 wickets in the Tests (albeit at a fairly high cost—30.03). His eight for 141 at Old Trafford was the best bowling performance on either side. Gatting again batted splendidly for England and Gower did even better with a total of 732 runs but it was, in all truth, a poor Australian side. Before the Tests, the Aussies won the first two Texaco one-day Internationals, at Old Trafford and Edgbaston, and lost the third at Lord's, a remarkable game in which Wood for Australia and Gooch and Gower all scored centuries.

MIDDLESEX CHAMPIONS

FST: Once again it was a wet summer and even Middlesex, who fared better than most counties with the weather, lost the equivalent of nine playing days. Having

The England team which won the Ashes from Australia in the memorable summer of 1985. Standing: P. R. Downton, J. E. Emburey, R. M. Ellison, L. B. Taylor, P. H. Edmonds, R. T. Robinson, B. W. Thomas (physiotherapist). Seated: A. J. Lamb, M. W. Gatting, D. I. Gower (capt), I. T. Botham, G. A. Gooch

two class spinners undoubtedly helped them to the title and with Cowans, Daniel and Williams as their faster bowlers they had by far the best-balanced and the most penetrative attack in the country. On the other hand, they lost Gatting, Emburey and Downton for all six Tests, Edmonds for five and Cowans for one. Hampshire, with Greenidge and Marshall available for the whole season, Chris Smith scoring 1,720 runs and his younger brother Robin 1,351 in championship matches alone, made a spectacular advance under the new captaincy of Mark Nicholas from 15th place to runners-up. Essex compensated for their loss of the title by taking two of the one-day competitions but Somerset dropped from seventh to bottom of the table despite Richards topping the first-class averages. On 1 June, the crowd at Taunton were electrified by a dazzling innings of 322 by him. It was the highest innings for Somerset (beating Harold Gimblett's 310 in 1948) and the highest in England for 36 years (Jack Robertson, Middlesex v Worcestershire). Richards hit eight sixes, 42 fours and reached 300 off only 244 deliveries. During the year, Botham hit a record 80 sixes in 27 first-class innings. No county had more cause for reflection upon the role of the mega-star in a team game than Somerset as they contemplated that bottom of the table position. The side had scored more batting bonus points than any of the 16 counties above them!

ONE-DAY COMPETITIONS

DM: For the second successive year the NatWest Final went to the very last ball and it was the two counties involved in the previous year's breathless scramble for the county championship who were involved. As in that duel, Essex triumphed over Nottinghamshire at the very last moment. They totalled 280 for two, with Hardie making 110 and Gooch 91 (202 for the first wicket), and Nottinghamshire needed 18 to win from the last over. Randall gathered 16 from the first five balls and was beautifully caught at short mid-wicket off the last. Only seven wickets fell in the whole match, and two of them were run-outs. Essex won by one run. In the Benson & Hedges, Leicestershire had three overs to spare in beating Essex by five wickets and thus deprived Essex of the distinction of winning all three limited-overs competitions in the same season because they took the John Player League title by two points from Sussex. Up to 1979, Essex had never won an honour of any kind. In the next seven seasons they had now taken three county championships, three John Player Leagues, one Benson & Hedges Cup and one NatWest Trophy. Small wonder that Keith Fletcher was the most highly respected captain in the country.

Winter Tour to West Indies (1985–86):

Kingston	West Indies won by ten wickets
Port-of-Spain	West Indies won by seven wickets
Bridgetown	West Indies won by an innings & 30 runs
Port-of-Spain	West Indies won by ten wickets
St John's	West Indies won by 240 runs

One-Day Internationals v West Indies (1985–86):

Kingston	West Indies won by six wickets
Port-of-Spain	England won by five wickets
Bridgetown	West Indies won by 135 runs
Port-of-Spain	West Indies won by eight wickets

Cornhill Tests:

India:

Lord's	India won by five wickets
Headingley	India won by 279 runs
Edgbaston	Match drawn

New Zealand:

Lord's	Match drawn
Trent Bridge	New Zealand won by eight wickets
Oval	Match drawn

Texaco One-Day Internationals:

India:

Oval	India won by nine wickets
Old Trafford	England won by five wickets

New Zealand:

Headingley	New Zealand won by 47 runs
Old Trafford	England won by six wickets

Britannic County Champions	Essex
NatWest Trophy	Sussex
John Player League	Hampshire
Benson & Hedges Cup	Middlesex

TEST AVERAGES ENGLAND V WEST INDIES 1985–86

	M	I	NO	HS	Runs	Av	100	50	Ct/St
D. I. Gower	5	10	0	90	370	37.00	–	3	3
G. A. Gooch	5	10	0	53	276	27.60	–	4	6
A. J. Lamb	5	10	0	62	224	22.40	–	1	3
D. M. Smith	2	4	0	47	80	20.00	–	–	–
P. Willey	4	8	0	71	136	17.00	–	1	–
I. T. Botham	5	10	0	38	168	16.80	–	–	4
W. N. Slack	2	4	0	52	62	15.50	–	1	1
R. M. Ellison	3	6	0	36	82	13.66	–	–	–
J. G. Thomas	4	8	4	31*	45	11.25	–	–	–
J. E. Emburey	4	8	2	35*	64	10.66	–	–	–
P. R. Downton	5	10	1	26	91	10.11	–	–	6/2
R. T. Robinson	4	8	0	43	72	9.00	–	–	1
P. H. Edmonds	3	6	2	13	36	9.00	–	–	2
N. A. Foster	3	6	1	14	24	4.80	–	–	–

Also batted: M. W. Gatting (1 match) 15, 1, 2ct.

	Overs	M	Runs	Wkts	Av	5w	10w	BB
J. E. Emburey	153	34	448	14	32.00	1	–	5–78
N. A. Foster	83.5	8	285	7	40.71	–	–	3–76
R. M. Ellison	82.3	19	294	7	42.00	1	–	5–78
J. G. Thomas	86	13	364	8	45.50	–	–	4–70
I. T. Botham	134.5	16	535	11	48.63	1	–	5–71

Also bowled: P. H. Edmonds 92.3–16–260–3; G. A. Gooch 7–3–27–1; A. J. Lamb 0–0–1–0 (1 no-ball); P. Willey 4–0–15–1.

TEST AVERAGES ENGLAND V INDIA 1986

	M	I	NO	HS	Runs	Av	100	50	Ct/St
M. W. Gatting	3	6	2	183*	293	73.25	1	–	3
G. A. Gooch	3	6	0	114	175	29.16	1	–	5
D. I. Gower	2	4	0	49	101	25.25	–	–	2
D. R. Pringle	3	6	0	63	136	22.66	–	1	4
C. W. J. Athey	2	4	0	38	78	19.50	–	–	–
A. J. Lamb	2	4	0	39	65	16.25	–	–	2
J. E. Emburey	3	6	1	38	74	14.80	–	–	4
P. H. Edmonds	2	4	1	18	42	14.00	–	–	1
G. R. Dilley	2	4	1	10	18	6.00	–	–	1
B. N. French	2	4	0	8	22	5.50	–	–	9/–

Also batted: M. R. Benson (1 match) 21, 30; P. R. Downton (1 match) 5, 29, 1ct; R. M. Ellison (1 match) 12, 19; N. A. Foster (1 match) 17, 0; J. K. Lever (1 match) 0*, 0; N. V. Radford (1 match) 0, 1; R. T. Robinson (1 match) 35, 11; W. N. Slack (1 match) 0, 19, 2ct; C. L. Smith (1 match) 6, 28.

	Overs	M	Runs	Wkts	Av	5w	10w	BB
D. R. Pringle	126.3	31	302	13	23.23	–	–	4–73
P. H. Edmonds	85	27	178	7	25.42	–	–	4–31
J. K. Lever	53	9	166	6	35.25	–	–	4–64
G. R. Dilley	85.2	19	299	10	29.90	–	–	4–146

Also bowled: R. M. Ellison 35–11–80–1; J. E. Emburey 76.5–28–141–4; N. A. Foster 63–18–141–4; M. W. Gatting 2–0–10–0; G. A. Gooch 13–2–31–1; N. V. Radford 38–3–148–2.

TEST AVERAGES ENGLAND V NEW ZEALAND 1986

	M	I	NO	HS	Runs	Av	100	50	Ct/St
D. I. Gower	3	5	0	131	293	58.60	1	2	3
G. A. Gooch	3	5	0	183	268	53.60	1	–	6
J. E. Emburey	2	3	1	75	92	46.00	–	1	–
M. W. Gatting	3	5	0	121	170	34.00	1	–	2
B. N. French	3	3	2	21	33	33.00	–	–	3/–
M. D. Moxon	2	4	0	74	111	27.75	–	1	1
C. W. J. Athey	3	5	0	55	138	27.60	–	1	3
P. H. Edmonds	3	4	1	20	35	11.66	–	–	3

Also batted: I. T. Botham (1 match) 59*; G. R. Dilley (2 matches) 17; N. A. Foster (1 match) 8; A. J. Lamb (1 match) 0; D. R. Pringle (1 match) 21, 9; N. V. Radford (1 match) 12*; G. C. Small (2 matches) 2*, 12; J. G. Thomas (1 match) 28, 10; P. Willey (1 match) 44, 42.

	Overs	M	Runs	Wkts	Av	5w	10w	BB
G. R. Dilley	69.3	16	179	9	19.88	–	–	4–82
P. H. Edmonds	101	32	212	8	26.50	–	–	4–97

Also bowled: I. T. Botham 26–4–82–3; J. E. Emburey 79.5–33–141–4; N. A. Foster 28–7–69–1; G. A. Gooch 19–9–38–1; D. I. Gower 1–0–5–0; D. R. Pringle 22–1–74–0; N. V. Radford 25–4–71–1; G. C. Small 64–20–134–4; J. G. Thomas 43–5–140–2.

BRITANNIC ASSURANCE CHAMPIONSHIP TABLE 1986

					Bonus Pts		
Win = 16 points	P	Won	Lost	D	Bat	Bowl	Pts
ESSEX (4)	24	10	6	8	51	76	287
Gloucestershire (3)	24	9	3	12	50	65	259
Surrey (6)	24	8	6	10	54	66	248
Nottinghamshire (8)	24	7	2	15	55	80	247
Worcestershire (5)	24	7	5	12	58	72	242
Hampshire (2)	24	7	4	13*	54	69	235
Leicestershire (16)	24	5	7	12	55	67	202
Kent (9)	24	5	7	12	42	75	197
Northamptonshire (10)	24	5	3	16	53	60	193
Yorkshire (11)	24	4	5	15	62	59	193$
Derbyshire (13)	24	5	5	14	42	70	188±
⌠Middlesex (1)	24	4	9	11	47	65	176
⌡Warwickshire (15)	24	4	5	15	61	51	176
Sussex (7)	24	4	7	13*	46	56	166
Lancashire (14)	24	4	5	15*	41	51	156
Somerset (17)	24	3	7	14*	52	52	152
Glamorgan (12)	24	2	7	15	39	47	118

* includes one match abandoned without a ball bowled
± includes twelve points for win in match reduced to one innings
$ includes eight points for fourth innings in drawn matches when final scores were level
1985 positions are shown in brackets

FIRST-CLASS AVERAGES 1986

	I	NO	HS	Runs	Av	100
C. G. Greenidge (Hampshire)	34	4	222	2035	67.83	8
J. J. Whitaker (Leicestershire)	32	9	200*	1526	66.34	5
G. A. Hick (Worcestershire)	37	6	227*	2004	64.64	6
A. J. Lamb (Northamptonshire)	27	4	160*	1359	59.08	4
B. M. McMillan (Warwickshire)	21	4	136	999	58.76	3
R. J. Bailey (Northamptonshire)	43	9	224*	1915	56.32	4
±A. I. Kallicharran (Warwickshire)	23	5	163*	1005	55.83	5
M. W. Gatting (Middlesex)	23	3	183*	1091	54.55	4
G. Boycott (Yorkshire)	20	1	135*	992	52.21	2
±R. J. Hadlee (Notts/New Zealand)	21	5	129*	813	50.81	2

	Overs	M	Runs	Wkts	Av	BB
M. D. Marshall (Hampshire)	656.3	171	1508	100	15.08	6–51
R. J. Hadlee (Notts/New Zealand)	547.3	150	1215	76	15.98	6–31
±J. H. Childs (Essex)	640.1	212	1449	89	16.28	8–58
S. T. Clarke (Surrey)	341.3	95	806	48	16.79	5–31
C. A. Walsh (Gloucestershire)	789.5	193	2145	118	18.17	9–72
A. H. Gray (Surrey)	342.3	69	966	51	18.94	7–23
T. M. Alderman (Kent)	610	139	1882	98	19.20	8–46
M. A. Holding (Derbyshire)	388.1	110	1045	52	20.09	7–97
J. Simmons (Lancashire)	230.5	52	762	36	21.16	7–79
P. W. Jarvis (Yorkshire)	428.4	82	1332	60	22.20	7–55

HARD WINTER

Don Mosey: England's winter tour to the West Indies added up to one of the sorriest periods in the whole history of Test cricket. The results were bad enough in themselves—a clean sweep of five Test victories to the West Indies, all by massive margins, and a solitary win for the tourists out of four one-day Internationals—but an avalanche of publicity which engulfed the tour was very often not about the cricket at all. Botham's behaviour on and off the field during the previous summer, which brought him in front of the Test and County Cricket Board for his behaviour in the Test at Trent Bridge, resulted in an unprecedented Press presence in the West Indies. Not only were the cricket correspondents there in force but many newspapers also sent news reporters to watch off-duty activities, particularly those of Botham. In consequence, none of the tour party was ever able really to relax when off duty and certainly not able to let their hair down in time-honoured fashion for fear of who might be watching or listening and what the resultant publicity might be. This, allied to batting which once again proved too frail to stand up to the battery of fast bowlers (reinforced now by Patrick Patterson, who had limited experience with Lancashire but proved fearsomely fast and aggressive in his native Jamaica) and bowling which lacked the pace or penetration to disturb the West Indian batting, resulted in probably the most miserable tour any party has ever undertaken. In these circumstances, everything usually seems to go from bad to worse and in the first one-day International (Jamaica) Mike Gatting suffered a badly fractured nose which caused him to fly home for surgery. (Characteristically, Gatting returned to the fray after treatment in England and batted with great courage.) There was political interference once again (as in 1981), this time directed pointedly at Graham Gooch which caused him a great deal of concern. And some of the players—Botham and Gower, the captain, prominently amongst them—did not help by contributing ghosted columns to popular newspapers back home. Finally, a large number of British supporters took a winter holiday in the Caribbean to watch some cricket and not only saw England overwhelmingly vanquished but in some cases appearing not to take their humiliation to heart. In the course of the tour, Botham (in Trinidad) took his 350th Test wicket. Greg Thomas (Glamorgan) and David Smith (Surrey and Worcestershire) made their debuts in Jamaica, Wilf Slack (Middlesex) in the Second Test (Trinidad).

BOTHAM SUSPENDED

FST: It must have been an enormous relief to return home after all that and to contemplate what promised, on paper, to be a couple of relatively easy series against India and New Zealand. But by now it seemed to be impossible to keep the seedier side of cricket out of the headlines. In May Botham called off a threatened libel action against the *Mail on Sunday* (against which he had issued a writ in early 1984). The newspaper then published an article under Botham's name in which he admitted that he had been involved in drug-taking. The following day the Executive Committee of the TCCB instructed the Selectors to withdraw Botham from the squad of players picked to play the two one-day Internationals against India. On 29 May the Disciplinary Committee of the Board, having carried out an investigation, suspended Botham from first-class cricket until 31 July. On 12 July Botham's appeal against the decision was turned down. He missed the series against India and returned to play against New Zealand at The Oval where—predictably—he took a wicket with his first ball. This equalled Lillee's record of 355 Test wickets and with the last ball of his second over he had Jeff Crowe lbw to lead the world. In an innings of 59 not out before rain ruined the Test, Botham hit 24 off one over from Stirling, thus equalling the record set by Roberts off his

(Botham's) bowling in 1981. Nor was he idle for Somerset, once the suspension had ended. At Wellingborough School, in August, he hit a record 13 sixes, and 12 fours as well, in a John Player League innings of 175.

INDIA'S GREAT SERIES

DM: If England had expected an easy passage during the summer they were seriously disappointed. Just as Pakistan were to do a year later, India's batsmen showed superior technique in English conditions, winning the First and Second Tests (Lord's and Headingley) comfortably and they looked an odds-on bet to complete a hat-trick when bad light and rain caused a 48-minute stoppage on the final day at Edgbaston where Mark Benson (Kent) and Neal Radford (Worcestershire) won their first caps. Gatting replaced Gower as captain after the First Test. Vengsarkar was the outstanding batsman of the series and Chetan Sharma, whose 16 wickets beat everyone else on both sides, was a bowler who did not exactly set the world alight when bowling in the Northern League in Lancashire. At Headingley—where Roger Binny took five for 49 and Madan Lal three for 18 by simple, commonsense use of seaming conditions—England were bowled out for 102 and 128, and the critics blamed the wicket. The simple fact was that batsmen the world over (with the possible exception of Australia) were showing better technique than England players. India won one and lost one of the Texaco games but won the trophy on a superior scoring rate, as did New Zealand in the second half of the summer.

NEW ZEALAND WINNERS

FST: Hadlee played for New Zealand in the international matches but returned to Nottinghamshire when the tourists were involved in games against county sides and his 19 Test wickets took him to 334, now third in the world behind Lillee and Botham (in that order at that time). The First Test at Lord's saw a little bit of history made when England fielded *four* wicket-keepers in one innings. Bruce French, after winning his first cap against India at Headingley, was struck on the helmet by a bouncer from Hadlee in his first innings against New Zealand which left him groggy and dazed when England took the field. Gatting was given Coney's agreement to use Bob Taylor (now 45, retired from cricket and on duty as the Cornhill liaison officer) as a temporary substitute. While Taylor gathered together a collection of borrowed clothing and equipment, Athey went behind the stumps for the first two overs. Taylor then took over for the next 76 overs and was replaced by Bobby Parks (Hampshire) for almost the remainder of the innings. French finally resumed—for

Essex, the 1986 county champions. Back row (left to right): Paul Prichard, John Childs, Chris Gladwin, Alan Lilley, Ian Pont, Derek Pringle, Neil Foster, Donald Topley, Allan Border. Front row: David East, Brian Hardie, Stuart Turner, Graham Gooch (capt), Keith Fletcher (vice-capt), John Lever, David Acfield, Keith Pont

just one delivery on the Monday morning. As an indication of just how English batting technique had declined, both Athey (right hand) and Gower (left) were bowled round their legs by Evan Gray, the slow left-armer. New Zealand won the series by virtue of their victory at Trent Bridge where Hadlee took ten wickets in the match, Gladstone Small made his debut for England (Barbados-born), and Emburey was England's top scorer with 75 in the second innings.

OVERSEAS PLAYERS

DM: In another championship year for Essex, they proved to have made an inspired signing from Gloucestershire in John Childs, the slow left-arm bowler, to replace Ray East. He was the only Englishman in the first eight bowlers in the averages, alongside five West Indian quicks, one from New Zealand and one from Australia. The top ten batsmen included two born in the West Indies, two in South Africa, one in Rhodesia and the versatile Hadlee—tenth in the first-class batting, second in the bowling—in a season when his services were divided between New Zealand's requirements and those of Nottinghamshire. Of the four Englishmen, one was the 45-year-old Boycott, playing his last season in first-class cricket (he was not offered a contract by Yorkshire at the end of the season). The main rays of hope for the future were James Whitaker, Leicestershire's middle-order batsman from Uppingham School, and Robin Bailey, of Northamptonshire. By general consent, the two most gifted young batsmen in the world were Martin Crowe (a contracted Somerset player since 1984 but not qualified for England) and Graeme Hick, of Worcestershire, who (under the complex qualifying system) was ineligible to play for England for the next eight years. Gloucestershire,

Graeme Hick, still only 20 in 1986 but one of the most exciting batting talents in the world

with the substantial help of the Jamaican fast bowler Courtney Walsh's 118 wickets, kept their place in the top bracket but Middlesex, whose batting proved brittle in 1986, dropped from title-holders to joint 12th. Somerset, having relieved Botham of the captaincy and appointed Peter Roebuck before the season started improved their championship position by one place. On 23 August Somerset announced that the services of Richards and Garner would not be retained in 1987 and Botham immediately announced that he would leave the county in protest. There was an outcry amongst the county membership culminating in an extraordinary general meeting at Shepton Mallet at which a vote of no confidence in the Somerset Committee was defeated by a substantial majority (two and a half to one). During the winter Botham signed for Worcestershire in 1987 and also agreed to play during the Australian summer with Queensland. It had been a disturbed 12 months in English cricket.

ONE-DAY COMPETITIONS

FST: Sussex beat Lancashire in the Natwest Final with a measured and well-organised performance which saw them home by seven wickets and in a much more exciting affair Middlesex took the Benson & Hedges Cup with a two-run victory over Kent who batted in funereal light and (at the end) drizzling rain as well. Hampshire wrested the John Player League title from Essex in the last year of the tobacco company's sponsorship. They pulled out after the 18 years of the league's existence and the Refuge Assurance Company took over in 1987.

Winter Tour to Australia (1986–87):

Brisbane	England won by seven wickets
Perth	Match drawn
Adelaide	Match drawn
Melbourne	England won by an innings & 14 runs
Sydney	Australia won by 55 runs

Benson & Hedges Challenge (played in Perth):

v Australia	England won by 37 runs
v West Indies	England won by 19 runs
v Pakistan	England won by three wickets
v Pakistan (final)	England won by five wickets

Benson & Hedges World Series (1986–87):

v West Indies:

Brisbane	England won by six wickets
Adelaide	England won by 89 runs
Melbourne (D/N)	West Indies won by six wickets
Devonport	England won by 29 runs

v Australia:

Brisbane	Australia won by 11 runs
Sydney (D/N)	England won by three wickets
Adelaide	Australia won by 33 runs
Melbourne	Australia won by 109 runs

Best-of-three Final

Melbourne	England won by six wickets
Sydney	England won by 8 runs

Cornhill Tests:

Pakistan:

Old Trafford	Match drawn
Lord's	Match drawn
Headingley	Pakistan won by an innings & 18 runs
Edgbaston	Match drawn
Oval	Match drawn

Texaco One-Day Internationals:

Pakistan:

Oval	England won by seven wickets
Trent Bridge	Pakistan won by six wickets
Edgbaston	England won by one wicket

Fourth World Cup

Gurjanwala:	England beat West Indies by 2 wickets
Rawalpindi:	England lost to Pakistan by 18 runs
Peshawar:	England beat Sri Lanka by 138 runs
Karachi:	England lost to Pakistan by 7 wickets
Jaipur (India):	England beat West Indies by 34 runs
Pune (India):	England beat Sri Lanka by 8 wickets
SEMI-FINAL, Bombay:	England beat India by 35 runs
FINAL, Calcutta:	England lost to Australia by seven runs

Tour to Pakistan (1987):

Lahore	Pakistan won by an innings and 87 runs
Faisalabad	Match drawn
Karachi	Match drawn

One-day Internationals v Pakistan (1987):

Lahore	England won by two wickets
Karachi	England won by 23 runs
Peshawar	England won by 98 runs

TEST AVERAGES ENGLAND V AUSTRALIA 1986–87

	M	I	NO	HS	Runs	Av	100	50	Ct/St
B. C. Broad	5	9	2	162	487	69.57	3	–	5
D. I. Gower	5	8	1	136	404	57.71	1	2	1
M. W. Gatting	5	9	0	100	393	43.66	3	5	1
C. J. Richards	5	7	0	133	264	37.71	1	–	15/1
J. E. Emburey	5	7	2	69	179	35.80	–	1	3
C. W. J. Athey	5	9	0	96	303	33.66	–	3	3
I. T. Botham	4	6	0	138	189	31.50	1	–	10
P. A. J. DeFreitas	4	5	1	40	77	19.25	–	–	1
A. J. Lamb	5	9	1	43	144	18.00	–	–	6
G. C. Small	2	3	1	21*	35	17.50	–	–	1
P. H. Edmonds	5	5	1	19	44	11.00	–	–	2
G. R. Dilley	4	4	2	4*	6	3.00	–	–	1

Also batted: J. J. Whitaker (1 match) 11, 1ct.

	Overs	M	Runs	Wkts	Av	5w	10w	BB
G. C. Small	78.4	23	180	12	15.00	2	–	5–48
G. R. Dilley	176.1	38	511	16	31.93	1	–	5–68
I. T. Botham	106.2	24	296	9	32.88	1	–	5–41
P. H. Edmonds	261.4	78	538	15	35.86	–	–	3–45
J. E. Emburey	315.5	86	663	18	36.83	2	–	7–78
P. A. J. DeFreitas	141.4	24	446	9	49.55	–	–	3–62

Also bowled: M. W. Gatting 23–7–39–0; A. J. Lamb 1–1–0–0.

TEST AVERAGES ENGLAND V PAKISTAN 1987 (England)

	M	I	NO	HS	Runs	Av	100	50	Ct/St
M. W. Gatting	5	8	1	150*	445	63.57	2	1	2
R. T. Robinson	5	8	0	166	299	37.37	1	1	–
C. W. J. Athey	4	6	1	123	186	37.20	1	–	2
I. T. Botham	5	8	1	51*	232	33.14	–	1	3
J. E. Emburey	4	5	0	58	162	32.40	–	2	3
D. I. Gower	5	8	0	61	236	29.50	–	2	2
B. C. Broad	4	7	0	55	193	27.57	–	2	–
B. N. French	4	5	1	59	103	25.75	–	1	4
P. H. Edmonds	5	7	4	24*	66	22.00	–	–	3
N. A. Foster	5	6	0	29	93	15.50	–	–	1
G. R. Dilley	5	5	2	17	20	6.66	–	–	2

Also batted: D. J. Capel (1 match) 53, 28; P. A. J. DeFreitas (1 match) 11; N. H. Fairbrother (1 match) 0, 1ct; M. D. Moxon (1 match) 8, 15, 3ct; C. J. Richards (1 match) 6, 2, 2ct.

	Overs	M	Runs	Wkts	Av	5w	10w	BB
N. A. Foster	137.2	36	339	15	22.60	1	–	8–107
G. R. Dilley	133.3	26	388	14	27.71	2	–	6–154
I. T. Botham	134.3	30	433	7	61.85	–	–	3–217

Also bowled: D. J. Capel 18–1–64–0; P. A. J. DeFreitas 12–4–36–1; P. H. Edmonds 92.3–36–219–4; J. E. Emburey 107–21–222–0; M. W. Gatting 22–5–40–0; M. D. Moxon 6–2–27–0.

County Champions	Nottinghamshire
NatWest Trophy	Nottinghamshire
Refuge Assurance League	Worcestershire
Benson & Hedges Cup	Yorkshire

BRITANNIC ASSURANCE CHAMPIONSHIP TABLE 1987

Win = 16 points	P	Won	Lost	D	Bonus Pts Bat	Bowl	Pts
NOTTINGHAMSHIRE (4)	24	9	1	14*	68	80	292
Lancashire (15)	24	10	4	10	55	73	288
Leicestershire (7)	24	8	3	13	57	75	260
Surrey (3)	24	7	4	13	65	73	250
Hampshire (6)	24	7	3	14	59	73	244
Derbyshire (11)	24	6	5	12	51	70	225
Northamptonshire (9)	24	7	4	13	48	68	224±
Yorkshire (9)	24	7	3	14*	52	58	222
Worcestershire (10)	24	5	4	15	58	68	206
Gloucestershire (2)	24	5	8	10	62	50	200
Somerset (16)	24	2	3	19	61	70	163
Essex (1)	24	2	4	18	45	77	162$
Glamorgan (17)	24	3	9	12	40	70	158
Kent (8)	24	2	7	15	53	66	151
Warwickshire (12)	24	2	7	15	48	67	147
Middlesex (12)	24	2	8	14*	47	60	139
Sussex (14)	24	1	8	15*	47	56	119

* includes one match abandoned without a ball bowled
± includes twelve points for win in match reduced to one innings
$ includes eight points for fourth innings in drawn matches when final scores were level
1986 positions are shown in brackets

FIRST-CLASS AVERAGES 1987

	I	NO	HS	Runs	Av	100
M. D. Crowe (Somerset)	29	5	206*	1627	67.79	6
±K. D. James (Hampshire)	16	6	142*	620	62.00	2
M. W. Gatting (Middlesex/England)	29	2	196	1646	60.96	6
R. K. Illingworth (Worcestershire)	19	11	120*	448	56.00	1
±R. J. Hadlee (Nottinghamshire)	28	7	133*	1111	52.90	2
G. A. Hick (Worcestershire)	38	2	173	1879	52.19	8
P. M. Roebuck (Somerset)	29	5	165*	1199	49.95	5
C. G. Greenidge (Hampshire)	18	0	163	899	49.94	3
±D. R. Turner (Hampshire)	35	8	184*	1328	49.18	2
R. A. Smith (Hampshire)	25	7	209*	869	48.27	1

± denotes left-hand batsman

	Overs	M	Runs	Wkts	Av	BB
±R. J. Hadlee (Nottinghamshire)	591	189	1227	97	12.64	6–20
A. H. Gray (Surrey)	291.1	59	748	48	15.58	5–46
K. J. Barnett (Derbyshire)	88.2	27	225	13	17.30	4–31
S. T. Clarke (Surrey)	456.4	114	1160	67	17.31	8–62
N. G. Cowans (Middlesex)	341.3	78	958	51	18.78	5–43
T. M. Tremlett (Hampshire)	547	153	1407	72	19.54	6–53
O. H. Mortensen (Derbyshire)	432.5	111	1084	55	19.70	5–57
M. D. Marshall (Hampshire)	594.1	152	1508	76	19.84	5–49
P. J. W. Allott (Lancashire)	535.2	166	1222	59	20.71	7–42
N. V. Radford (Worcestershire)	741.5	125	2269	109	20.81	8–55

± denotes left-hand bowler

ANOTHER CHALLENGE

Don Mosey: The winter of 1986–87 brought another of those long tours with yet a new limited-overs contest dreamed up by the marketing whiz-kids: the four-team Benson & Hedges Challenge, played in Perth to coincide with the Americas Cup extravaganza being sailed off neighbouring Freemantle. After a summer of discontent and defeat, the tour as a whole has to be seen as a triumph for the England party because they cleaned up in everything—the Challenge, the World Series competition, the Test series and even another limited-overs jamboree in Sharjah on the way home where they defeated India. After sorting out both Australia and West Indies in the Perth Challenge, Gatting's forces then beat Pakistan in the play-off. In the World Series, they beat West Indies in three matches out of four and then disposed of Australia in the play-offs. And they won two Tests out of five, lost one and drew the other two. In terms of results it has to be seen as a huge success and yet, viewed in context, it was somewhat less encouraging. Australia looked an even more ramshackle side than the one which came to England in 1985; West Indies seemed jaded after a long winter journeying through Pakistan before arriving in Australia.

And yet there *were* encouraging signs for the future: Chris Broad had a superb tour, hitting three centuries in the Tests and doing well in the spate of one-day (or day and night) games; Gower and Gatting scored well; Richards provided some spectacular wicket-keeping at times and the 21-year-old Phillip DeFreitas showed tremendous promise in the early matches of his first tour. Dilley bowled a better line and length than at any previous stage of his career and got excellent support from Gladstone Small. The tour started well with a seven-wicket victory in Brisbane where Botham played his best innings of what was, for him, a modest sort of tour. The next two Tests (Perth and Adelaide) were drawn; England won by an innings in Melbourne and then surprisingly lost the Final Test in Sydney, where the Australian Selectors startled the nation by picking a 30-year-old off-spinning all-rounder called Peter Taylor who had played only six first-class matches. After disposing of Botham cheaply in the first innings and first ball in the second, Taylor was suddenly a national hero because Botham is the greatest bogeyman of all time to Australians. The World Series followed and although Australia scored three wins over England, the tourists' success in one game plus three against West Indies took them into the play-off and they then beat Australia twice in successive encounters. It had been a pleasant tour, a happy and successful one, with Mickey Stewart as England's first cricket manager and Peter Lush tour-managing a full England squad for the first time (he had been in charge of the 'B' party in Sri Lanka in 1985–86).

DEFEAT BY PAKISTAN

Freddie Trueman: It was a different story at home in the summer—another miserable one as far as weather was concerned—with Pakistan drawing four Tests and winning the other by an innings. This happened at Headingley and, not for the first time when England have been beaten there, there was an outcry against the pitch. Why? Pakistan showed us how to bowl on a seamer's wicket and then how to bat on it as well, just as India had done the previous year. In view of the results in Yorkshire matches there during the earlier part of the summer it wasn't the

wisest decision to bat first, but once again we saw a deplorable lack of technique by England batsmen when the ball was moving off the seam and, occasionally, in the air. England had given a first chance to the Northamptonshire all-rounder, David Capel, and were relying on his out-swing bowling to back up the opening attack of Dilley and Foster if Botham did not do his stuff as third seamer. These things rarely work out. Botham didn't bowl at all and Capel never looked remotely like taking a wicket, but he did come off with the bat—his 53 was more than twice as many runs as any other batsman scored in the first innings. Foster was the man who returned the outstanding bowling figures of eight for 107 by keeping the ball up to the bat and letting the pitch, and the atmosphere, do the rest. Because Pakistan batted so much better than Eng-

Chris Broad, the outstanding success of England's winter touring party to Australia, on his way to a maiden Test century

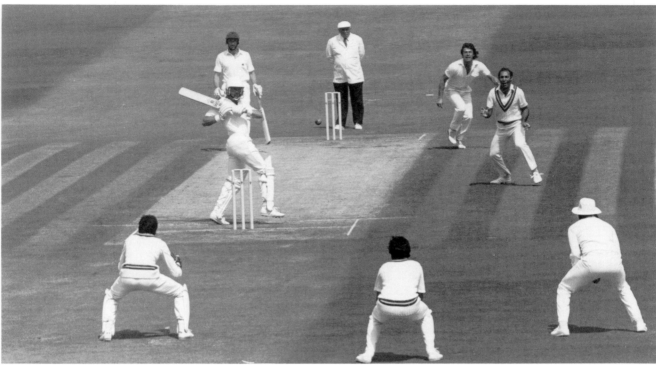

land, Foster conceded runs, but it was excellent seam bowling just the same. Salim Malik played a fine innings, then lost his momentum in the nineties (62 minutes there) only to fall to a catch at short extra-cover on 99. England's batting was not much better in the second innings than the first, but credit has to go to Imran Khan for a tremendous piece of bowling—seven for 40—and the game went less than half an hour into the fourth day. There was an exciting finish to the Fourth Test (Edgbaston) when it had looked almost from the first ball to be doomed to a draw. England should have won but rather lost their heads in the last hour and very nearly the game as well. Two of the one-day Internationals were won and one lost, and after a promising start to the Test series, England faded badly. Gatting's batting set the standard, but no one else approached it and some of the bowling looked very ordinary indeed. Foster and Dilley were very much the pick of the nine used during the Tests but Botham's seven wickets cost 61.85 apiece and at The Oval he had the horrifying figures of three for 217. Emburey did not take a single wicket in four Tests but averaged 32.4 with the bat; Edmonds' four wickets cost 219 runs. So England's two top spinners jointly managed four wickets for 441 runs. What had we come to?

COUNTY CHAMPIONSHIP

DM: Once again we had a breathtaking climax to the

Tim Robinson has edged the ball from Imran Khan and it's on its way into the hands of Salim Malik at slip. An excellent picture from the Third Test

Success for Yorkshire at last—a delighted Arnie Sidebottom, with Jim Love, make for the pavilion at Lord's after the Benson & Hedges Cup win over Northants

Tavaré c Rice b Hadlee—a picture from the Kent v Notts championship match involving the two all-rounders who played such an important part in Notts' title win

championship programme (in which wickets were left uncovered once play had started) and Nottinghamshire, who were saying farewell to Hadlee and Rice, had to wait until three days after they had completed their own programme to be certain of the title. Lancashire, in a season which saw them improve from 15th to second under the leadership for the first time of David Hughes, 40 years of age and in his 21st season, staged a brilliant finish to their programme, and victory by maximum points at Colchester would have given them the title. It proved just too much to ask, especially with the weather intervening, but they actually won one more game than Nottinghamshire, losing the title by four points because their haul of bonus-points—batting and bowling—was inferior. Once again Nottinghamshire were deeply indebted to Hadlee, who missed his second double by just three wickets. The runs were there—1,111 of them—and if Hemmings had not nipped in with five for 12 in Glamorgan's first innings of Nottinghamshire's final match, Hadlee might well have got the three wickets he needed. He signed off with six for 38 in the second innings, Rice with a not out 104. Less than a week earlier both had played a major part in an incredible win over Northamptonshire in the NatWest Trophy Final which spilled over into Monday, and Hadlee had hit a six and a four in the last over to win the game. He and Rice now ended their association with Nottinghamshire after ten and 13 seasons respectively on a tide of spectacular success and a huge wave of sentiment. Nottinghamshire just failed to pull off the John Player League as well, Worcestershire taking that title on the last day of the season. With Hadlee topping the first-class bowling averages and Martin Crowe heading the batsmen, New

Zealand's contribution to English cricket had been enormous. Three English-born players got into the top ten bowlers, one of them (Kim Barnett, the Derbyshire captain) on a nominal basis. Gatting led the English contingent in the batsmen apart from Kevan James, a left-handed all-rounder import from Middlesex who could not command a regular place in Hampshire's side. Graeme Hick hit eight centuries for Worcestershire and at all times looked a world-class player as did Crowe, with six hundreds for Somerset. Yorkshire, who enjoyed a renaissance (virtually under new management and certainly with a new captain, Phil Carrick) led the county championship for the first half of the season and won the Benson & Hedges Cup when Jim Love blocked the last ball with the scores level and Yorkshire having lost fewer wickets. Northamptonshire, as in the Natwest, were the losing side and while they looked a well-balanced and well-equipped outfit, they were crippled by injuries in the later stages of the season.

WORLD CUP

DM: For the two host countries the World Cup ended in something of an anti-climax when India were beaten by England and Pakistan by Australia in the semi-finals. Obviously the ideal final in Calcutta would have been between India and Pakistan but this did not prevent a full-house of more than 90,000 in the vast Eden Garden stadium supporting, quite simply, limited-overs cricket. They saw an exciting finish when, with England needing 34 from the last three overs with four wickets left, Emburey was run out and then DeFreitas hit 4–6–4–1 off McDermott's next four deliveries. But Australia kept their heads, no one more so than Allan Border, with immaculate field-setting, and Steve Waugh, whose medium-pace bowling was delivered with such pin-point accuracy that England were squeezed out.

FST: Looking at Waugh's cricket during the past 12 months it is impossible to avoid a comparison with Doug Walters in the 1960s and '70s. He was a good, middle-order batsman who seemed always the man who could come on and take a vital wicket just when one was needed. Perhaps Waugh was more than that. Certainly he batted well in the Australian summer of 1986–87 and took vital wickets, and in the World Cup he did even better. It has to be said that Australia bowled and fielded better in the final than England after getting off to a better start with the bat, but all in all the competition was a great success when a lot of people feared it might be something of a disaster. Most of all it was a great come-back by Australia, who had looked such a bedraggled lot for so long.

ENGLAND'S TOUR TO PAKISTAN

FST: There had obviously been a big reaction in Pakistan to the national side's failure to win the World Cup or even to reach the final. But it was still a surprise to find that the three one- day Internationals which preceded the Test series were watched by only very small crowds and—this was *not* surprising—they became smaller as Pakistan were beaten in all three. As the First Test approached, the reports in our newspapers seemed to be all about the preparation of a wicket in Lahore which would suit the Pakistan leg-spinner, Abdul Qadir. Now, at the risk of hearing a chorus of 'Tell me the old, old story,' I have got to say that 20 or 30 years ago this wouldn't have worried an England touring team unduly. Help for the home spinners would simply have meant help for the touring slow bowlers as well. It just doesn't work like that any more and, as predicted, England (within days, remember, of their third successive one-day International victory in a row) had been completely humiliated by the leg-spinner, exactly as predicted.

DM: It was only the second time England had ever lost a Test in Pakistan. The first, 3½ years pre- viously, was on a pitch in Karachi which helped spinners and Abdul Qadir did a good job there, too. But I think it is important to remember that on that occasion Sarfraz Nawaz (certainly *not* a spinner) took six wickets in the match for 69 and Abdul's match figures were eight for 133. Compare that return with Nick Cook's in the same match—11 for 83. The difference between the two sides was that Pakistan batted better (despite their panic in the second innings) and Abdul got better bowling support than Cook. But the First Test of 1987 was a very different affair. It seemed that the English side were convinced before they started that they were going to be cheated out of any chance of victory. Whatever the truth of that, the fact remained at the end of the Test that they had been beaten out of sight by a side which batted, fielded and bowled better than England did. And with the rare experience of Test cricket in Pakistan being televised 'live' in England, viewers were shocked to see Chris Broad refusing to leave the crease after being given out by one of two controversial umpires, Shakeel Khan. And from the 'quotes' published in our newspapers after the game it did seem that the captain, Mike Gatting, was more concerned with doubtful umpir- ing decisions than the inescapable fact that Pakistan had played better than England.

FST: But all that seemed rather subdued compared with the row which broke out during the Second Test when televiewers were treated to the sight of an England captain involved in a slanging match with another umpire,

Dissent: Broad refuses to go after being given out in the First Test until sympathetically advised by Gooch

Shakoor Rana, and shaking an accusing finger in front of the umpire's face. I have never seen anything like that in all my life and I hope I never see it again. It's a well-known fact amongst Test cricketers that life can be very difficult in Pakistan and there is no doubt that umpiring there is nothing like as good as it is in England but those scenes shocked an awful lot of people.

DM: The upshot of it all was that Shakoor Rana refused to take the field on the third day of the Second Test until he had received an apology in writing from Mike Gatting who, in turn, said he would not apologise unless Rana withdrew his claim that Gatting was a cheat (for allegedly moving a fieldsman while the bowler was running in). There was no play on the third day; the fourth was the rest day and play only resumed on the fifth day after Gatting, on orders from the TCCB in London, finally apologised in writing to umpire Rana. There was no reciprocal apology, and the England players issued a statement supporting their captain. The Pakistan Board refused to allow an extra day's play to compensate for the one which had been lost and the match was drawn. At the weekend (13 December) Raman Subba Row and A. C. Smith, chair- man and chief executive respectively of the TCCB, flew to Pakistan. The umpires appointed for the Third Test, Khizar Hayat and Mehboob Shah, were acceptable to the

Dispute: the confrontation between Gatting and Shakoor Rana during the Second Test

England party and no public complaints were voiced at any decisions during the match, played in Karachi, on the first three days. On the fourth, however, attention was drawn by both television reporters and newspaper correspondents to the unenthusiastic reaction to their dismissals by Broad, Gatting and Athey.

FST: It was noticeable, too, that reporters who had been pretty sympathetic towards the players a week earlier when that apology had been forced upon Gatting by the TCCB were now not too happy about the way those players behaved. Then came the announcement that the touring party were to receive a bonus of £1,000 a man because of the problems they had encountered in Pakistan. That rather took my breath away, remembering occasions when I had my tour bonus *cut* for what was regarded as improper behaviour 30 years earlier. Now players got a bonus for behaving twenty times worse than anything I could remember! Times had changed.

DM: One way and another, it had been a dreadful tour and everyone was very glad to fly home on 22 December. After Gatting's confrontation with Shakoor Rana in Faisalabad, I turned up my notes of the Third Test in Karachi in 1978— Gatting's first-ever Test. He was given out lbw to Abdul Qadir after scoring five and beside the dismissal I had written, 'Pitched about 18 inches outside leg stump.' The umpire was Shakoor Rana. Almost every player who has ever toured that country can point to a

similar experience, but for 30 years expressions of a natural sense of outrage had been confined to the dressing-room or the team's hotel. Now they were out in the open and the game would never be the same again. The Second and Third Tests were drawn but the results will not be what people remember about that tour.

TEST AVERAGES ENGLAND V PAKISTAN 1987 (Pakistan)

	M	I	NO	HS	Runs	Av	Ct/St
J. E. Emburey	3	6	3	74*	207	69.00	–
G. A. Gooch	3	6	0	93	225	37.50	3
B. C. Broad	3	6	0	116	204	34.00	1
M. W. Gatting	3	6	0	79	128	21.33	1
D. J. Capel	3	6	0	98	125	20.83	–
B. R. French	3	5	1	38*	80	20.00	8
C. W. J. Athey	3	6	0	27	92	15.33	–
N. A. Foster	2	4	0	39	40	10.00	–
P. A. J. DeFreitas	2	4	0	15	38	9.50	–
N. G. B. Cook	3	5	0	14	33	6.60	–
R. T. Robinson	2	4	1	7*	16	5.33	1

Also batted: G. R. Dilley (1 match) 0, 0; N. H. Fairbrother (1 match) 3, 1; E. E. Hemmings (1 match) 1.

	Overs	M	Runs	Wkts	Av	BB
N. A. Foster	44	10	104	6	17.33	4–42
N. G. B. Cook	93.3	35	195	7	27.85	3–87
P. A. J. DeFreitas	52.5	10	170	6	28.33	5–86
J. E. Emburey	124	48	251	7	35.85	3–49

Also bowled: B. C. Broad 1–0–4–0; D. J. Capel 13–1–59–1; G. R. Dilley 21–2–102–1; G. A. Gooch 2–1–4–0; E. E. Hemmings 25–8–51–1.

Titles

	Gillette Cup/ NatWest Trophy Winners	John Player League/Refuge Assurance League	Benson & Hedges Cup Winners
1963	Sussex	–	–
1964	Sussex	–	–
1965	Yorkshire	–	–
1966	Warwickshire	–	–
1967	Kent	–	–
1968	Warwickshire	–	–
1969	Yorkshire	Lancashire	–
1970	Lancashire	Lancashire	–
1971	Lancashire	Worcestershire	–
1972	Lancashire	Kent	Leicestershire
1973	Gloucestershire	Kent	Kent
1974	Kent	Leicestershire	Surrey
1975	Lancashire	Hampshire	Leicestershire
1976	Northamptonshire	Kent	Kent
1977	Middlesex	Leicestershire	Gloucestershire
1978	Sussex	Hampshire	Kent
1979	Somerset	Somerset	Essex
1980	Middlesex	Warwickshire	Northamptonshire
1981	Derbyshire	Essex	Somerset
1982	Surrey	Sussex	Somerset
1983	Somerset	Yorkshire	Middlesex
1984	Middlesex	Essex	Lancashire
1985	Essex	Essex	Leicestershire
1986	Sussex	Hampshire	Middlesex
1987	Nottinghamshire	Worcestershire	Yorkshire

County Champions 1946–1987

1946	Yorkshire	1967	Yorkshire
1947	Middlesex	1968	Yorkshire
1948	Glamorgan	1969	Glamorgan
1949	Middlesex/Yorkshire	1970	Kent
1950	Lancashire/Surrey	1971	Surrey
1951	Warwickshire	1972	Warwickshire
1952	Surrey	1973	Hampshire
1953	Surrey	1974	Worcestershire
1954	Surrey	1975	Leicestershire
1955	Surrey	1976	Middlesex
1956	Surrey	1977	Middlesex/Kent
1957	Surrey	1978	Kent
1958	Surrey	1979	Essex
1959	Yorkshire	1980	Middlesex
1960	Yorkshire	1981	Nottinghamshire
1961	Hampshire	1982	Middlesex
1962	Yorkshire	1983	Essex
1963	Yorkshire	1984	Essex
1964	Worcestershire	1985	Middlesex
1965	Worcestershire	1986	Essex
1966	Yorkshire	1987	Nottinghamshire

Gillette Cup Winners 1963–1980
Natwest Trophy Winners 1981–1987

1963	Sussex beat Worcestershire by 14 runs
1964	Sussex beat Warwickshire by eight wickets
1965	Yorkshire beat Surrey by 175 runs
1966	Warwickshire beat Worcestershire by five wickets
1967	Kent beat Somerset by 32 runs
1968	Warwickshire beat Sussex by four wickets
1969	Yorkshire beat Derbyshire by 69 runs
1970	Lancashire beat Sussex by six wickets
1971	Lancashire beat Kent by 24 runs
1972	Lancashire beat Warwickshire by four wickets
1973	Gloucestershire beat Sussex by 40 runs
1974	Kent beat Lancashire by four wickets
1975	Lancashire beat Middlesex by seven wickets
1976	Northamptonshire beat Lancashire by four wickets
1977	Middlesex beat Glamorgan by five wickets
1978	Sussex beat Somerset by five wickets
1979	Somerset beat Northamptonshire by 45 runs
1980	Middlesex beat Surrey by seven wickets
1981	Derbyshire beat Northamptonshire by losing fewer wickets with the scores level
1982	Surrey beat Warwickshire by nine wickets
1983	Somerset beat Kent by 24 runs
1984	Middlesex beat Kent by four wickets
1985	Essex beat Nottinghamshire by 1 run
1986	Sussex beat Lancashire by seven wickets
1987	Nottinghamshire beat Northamptonshire by 3 wickets

John Player League Winners 1969–1986
Refuge Assurance League Winner 1987

1969	Lancashire	1979	Somerset
1970	Lancashire	1980	Warwickshire
1971	Worcestershire	1981	Essex
1972	Kent	1982	Sussex
1973	Kent	1983	Yorkshire
1974	Leicestershire	1984	Essex
1975	Hampshire	1985	Essex
1976	Kent	1986	Hampshire
1977	Leicestershire	1987	Worcestershire
1978	Hampshire		

Benson & Hedges Cup Winners 1972–1987

1972	Leicestershire beat Yorkshire by five wickets
1973	Kent beat Worcestershire by 39 runs
1974	Surrey beat Leicestershire by 27 runs
1975	Leicestershire beat Middlesex by five wickets
1976	Kent beat Worcestershire by 43 runs
1977	Gloucestershire beat Kent by 64 runs
1978	Kent beat Derbyshire by six wickets
1979	Essex beat Surrey by 35 runs
1980	Northamptonshire beat Essex by 6 runs
1981	Somerset beat Surrey by seven wickets
1982	Somerset beat Nottinghamshire by nine wickets
1983	Middlesex beat Essex by 4 runs
1984	Lancashire beat Warwickshire by six wickets
1985	Leicestershire beat Essex by five wickets
1986	Middlesex beat Kent by 2 runs
1987	Yorkshire beat Northamptonshire with scores tied, Yorkshire having lost fewer wickets

Young Cricketers of the Year

Since 1950, the Cricket Writers' Club has made an award to the outstanding young cricketer of each year chosen by a ballot of the membership of the CWC. The complete list of Young Cricketers of the Year is:

1950 R. Tattersall (Lancashire)
1951 P. B. H. May (Surrey)
1952 F. S. Trueman (Yorkshire)
1953 M. C. Cowdrey (Kent)
1954 P. J. Loader (Surrey)
1955 K. R. Barrington (Surrey)
1956 B. Taylor (Surrey)
1957 M. J. Stewart (Surrey)
1958 A. C. D. Ingleby-Mackenzie (Hampshire)
1959 G. Pullar (Lancashire)
1960 D. A. Allen (Gloucestershire)
1961 P. H. Parfitt (Middlesex)
1962 P. J. Sharpe (Yorkshire)
1963 G. Boycott (Yorkshire)
1964 J. M. Brearley (Middlesex)
1965 A. P. E. Knott (Kent)
1966 D. L. Underwood (Kent)
1967 A. W. Greig (Sussex)
1968 R. M. H. Cottam (Hampshire)
1969 A. Ward (Derbyshire)
1970 C. M. Old (Yorkshire)
1971 J. Whitehouse (Warwickshire)
1972 D. R. Owen-Thomas (Surrey)
1973 M. Hendrick (Derbyshire)
1974 P. H. Edmonds (Middlesex)
1975 A. Kennedy (Lancashire)
1976 G. Miller (Derbyshire)
1977 I. T. Botham (Somerset)
1978 D. I. Gower (Leicestershire)
1979 P. W. G. Parker (Sussex)
1980 G. R. Dilley (Kent)*
1981 M. W. Gatting (Middlesex)
1982 N. G. Cowans (Middlesex)
1983 N. A. Foster (Essex)
1984 R. J. Bailey (Northamptonshire)
1985 D. V. Lawrence (Gloucestershire)
1986 A. A. Metcalfe (Yorkshire)
     J. J. Whitaker (Leicestershire)
1987 R. J. Blakey (Yorkshire)

*A special award was made to Bill Athey (then with Yorkshire) as the outstanding young batsman of the year.

Where a player has played for more than one county, the one listed was his club at the time of his selection by the CWC.

Given that some of the more recent selections still have time to develop, the list shows a fair measure of perspicacity on the part of the cricket writers in spotting the stars of the future. Those who have so far not gone on to play for England (taking 1983 as the dividing line) are Brian Taylor (1956), Colin Ingleby-Mackenzie (1958), John Whitehouse (1971), Dudley Owen-Thomas (1972) and Andrew Kennedy (1975).

All the other players in the list went on to play Test cricket, many of them with outstanding success, and eight of them captained England: May, Cowdrey, Greig, Brearley, Boycott, Botham, Gower and Gatting. In fact from the first year of the award up to 1982 (again we are allowing winners of the past four years an opportunity to develop further) the Cricket Writers' Club nominees have totalled more than 1,200 Test caps.

Glamorgan, Worcestershire and Nottinghamshire are the only counties not to have produced a Young Cricketer of the Year. There is a slightly higher percentage of batsmen than bowlers in the list; five all-rounders and three wicket-keepers. Fast bowlers have won the award far more frequently than spinners; right-hand batsmen outnumber the left-handers by three to one. If Geoff Miller (1976) is classed as an all-rounder (and few would argue with that) the last full-time spin bowler to be chosen was Phil Edmonds in 1974.

1950: Roy Tattersall (OB, LHB), tall, angular off-break bowler from Bolton (Lancs) who played 277 matches for Lancashire and 16 Tests for England. He took 1,369 wickets at 18.03 in his first-class career.

1951: The award was well timed to catch the early days of Peter May's (RHB) career at Cambridge and with Surrey. Possibly the most gifted of our post-war batsmen, he headed the average at Charterhouse when he was only 14 and made a polished 146 for Public Schools v Combined Services at Lord's when he was 17. He played 66 times for England, 41 as captain. He was captain of Surrey from 1957 to 1962 and since 1982 has been chairman of the English Test Selectors.

1952: Freddie Trueman (RF, RHB) was described by John Arlott as 'never simply a cricketer; he was purely, in mind, method and heart, a fast bowler.' His career ranged over 20 seasons of bowling with never less than 100 per cent hostility and it brought him 2,304 first-class wickets at 18.29, with 307 Test victims. He also scored 9,231 runs with three centuries and held 439 catches.

1953: Michael Colin Cowdrey (RHB) was destined to be an international cricketer from the moment he was given the initials M.C.C. and responded by playing in 114 Tests (27 of them as captain). At 13, he played at Lord's for his school (Tonbridge) and in his first-class career he accumulated 42,719 runs with 107 centuries. He also held 638 catches, mostly at slip, and his two sons followed him as Kent players.

1954: Peter Loader (RFM) was one of the spearheads of Surrey's great championship sequence in the 1950s with an outstanding return of nine Warwicks wickets for 17 in 1958. In all he claimed 1,320 first-class victims and had a Test hat-trick at Headingley in 1957.

1955: Ken Barrington (RHB, LBG) served a five-year apprenticeship on the Surrey staff before making his first-class debut in 1953 and, if being dropped from the Test side for slow batting is one of the blots on his escutcheon, there ought to be a separate entry in the record books of the number of times he saved England by his tenacious and courageous batting. He scored 31,714 first-class runs, took 273 wickets with his leg-breaks, and held 515 catches. Eighty-two Tests left him with an average for England of 44.82.

1956: Brian Taylor was Essex's wicket-keeper in 539 matches between 1949 and 1973 and was captain of the county from 1967 to 1973 when be became a Test Selector. He went on the MCC tour to South Africa in 1956–57.

1957: Mickey Stewart (RHB) was appointed England's first-ever full time team manager in 1986 after managing Surrey from 1979. Before that he played 498 matches for the county, scoring 26,492 runs in his first-class career which included eight Tests. A brilliant close-catcher, he claimed 634 victims and his son, Alec, followed him into the Surrey side as an accomplished batsman and fieldsman.

1958: Colin Ingleby-Mackenzie began his captaincy of Hampshire that season. He may well have owed his selection as Young Cricketer of the Year more to his bubbling, colourful personality than to the quality of his cricket, although he scored 1,613 runs in 1959. 'Dingle', as he was universally known throughout the game, was ever a popular figure with the cricketing press because he could always be relied upon for a good 'quote', and he was a noted raconteur as well as a stimulating companion on 'social' tours (e.g., E. W. Swanton's, Duke of Norfolk's, International Cavaliers).

1959: Geoff Pullar (LHB) was a natural middle-order batsman who moved up to the opener's position to meet England's needs in the late 1950s. He was solid and consistent, rather than spectacular, and completed 28 Tests with an average of 43.86. In all, he made 21,528 runs and after retiring at Old Trafford did much to help junior club cricketers.

1960: David Allen (OB, RHB) was one of a group of talented off-spinners all playing county cricket at the same time and thus had to work hard for his 39 Test caps. He was also a better-than-average batsman and did the double in 1961. His 1,209 first-class victims were claimed at a cost of 23.64 and he also scored nearly 10,000 runs.

1961: Peter Parfitt (LHB, OB) was born in Norfolk, Edrich country, and played much of his early cricket for Middlesex alongside Denis Compton. He hit seven centuries for England in the course of his 37 Tests and averaged 40.91. An excellent slip-catcher, he claimed 564 victims, many off his close friend, Fred Titmus, and he totalled just under 27,000 first-class runs as well as taking 277 wickets with his off-breaks.

1962: One of the outstanding slip-catchers of his day, Philip Sharpe (RHB) almost certainly owed his original Test selection to his ability in that department and in fact he held 17 catches in his 12 games for England. But he also averaged 46.23 with the bat and scored 22,530 runs (with three double centuries) in his first-class career, mostly with Yorkshire, but he played 40 matches for Derbyshire after leaving his native county. He held 617 catches in his career, almost all of them at slip.

1963: Geoffrey Boycott (RHB, RM) was the outstanding opening batsman for England from 1964 to 1974 and, after a period of self-imposed exile, from 1977 until 1981. He played 108 Tests and scored more runs (8,114) than anyone else in Test cricket except Sunil Gavaskar. In his first-class career, which ended in 1986, Boycott totalled 44,210 runs and is the only player to average more than 100 in a season twice.

1964: Mike Brearley (RHB) was an outstandingly successful England captain in 31 Tests largely because of tactical flair and an ability to get the best out of his players. As a batsman, he hit more than 1,000 runs in a season 11 times and reached 2,178 (average 44.44) in 1964. On his record as captain of Middlesex (1971–82) and England (1977–81) he has to rank in the forefront of post-war leaders.

1965: Alan Knott (WK, RHB) was third in line (after Leslie Ames and Godfrey Evans) in the remarkable dynasty of Kent and England wicket-keepers. While many judges rated Bob Taylor (Derbyshire) as highly as Knott behind the stumps, the Kent man's batting usually got him the Selectors' vote during most of their respective careers. Knott played 95 Tests, scoring 4,389 runs and claiming 269 dismissals. In his first-class career he scored 17,431 runs and claimed 1,260 wicket-keeping victims.

1966: Derek Underwood (LSM) was an original type of left-arm bowler, delivering his spinners at almost medium pace, and on rain-affected wickets he could be quite unplayable. In his first season for Kent he took more than 100 wickets, the youngest player to do so (he was 17 when the season began), and he had taken 1,000 wickets by the time he was 25. If he had not joined the Packer 'circus' in 1977 and then been banned from Test cricket for three years for playing in South Africa in 1982 he would almost certainly be the world's leading Test wicket-taker.

1967: Tony Greig (RHB/RMF/OB) was South African-born but qualified for Sussex in 1967 at the age of 20 and made a century in his first championship game. He became captain of the county in 1973 and of England in 1975 when he was the leading all-rounder in the country but was deposed, as we have seen, for his part in recruiting

players to join Kerry Packer. Since 1978 he has lived in Australia but his brother, Ian, who formerly played for Sussex, is now captain of Surrey.

1968: Bob Cottam's (RMF) outstanding season (130 wickets at 17.56) won him the YCY award and a trip to Sri Lanka and Pakistan the following winter. He took just over 1,000 wickets in a 264-match career, which covered 12 years with Hampshire and four at Northampton.

1969: Alan Ward (RF) was seen as England's best fast bowling prospect in the post-Trueman era, but injury dogged him during a ten-year career and his five Tests were spread over seven years. His best year by far was 1969.

1970: Chris Old (RMF) was another bowler who suffered more than his share of injuries, but he played in 46 Tests and bowled particularly well for England in certain matches, notably Christchurch (New Zealand) in 1978. During the following summer he took four wickets in five balls against Pakistan. In 1981 he was made captain of Yorkshire but, beset by the Boycott controversy, he left the following year and joined Warwicks.

1971: John Whitehouse was 22 when he won the award in his debut season with Warwickshire and impressed as much by the stylish way he made his runs as the number he recorded. Perhaps he did not *quite* fulfil all the hopes of those who first saw him play, but he became a consistent scorer with 1,543 runs at an average of 42.86 as his best season in 1977 and went on to captain his county in the two following seasons.

1972: Dudley Owen-Thomas won four Blues at Cambridge between 1969 and 1972 and his six-season career with Surrey straddled his university years.

1973: Mike Hendrick (RMF) became a particularly effective bowler in limited-overs cricket because of his great accuracy, allied to movement off the pitch. He played in 30 Tests but was frequently picked in a squad of 12, then became the man left out on the first morning. For a tall man, he was a good catcher at slip or gulley.

1974: Phillipe Edmonds (SLA), from his 1971 debut at Cambridge (and also for Middlesex), was a gifted bowler and a strong-willed character with highly individual views which brought him into conflict with two of his captains, Mike Brearley and Mike Gatting. His partnership with John Emburey was by far the outstanding spin-bowling pairing in England cricket from the mid-seventies until increasing business interests caused Edmonds to give up full-time cricket after 1987.

1975: Andrew Kennedy made his debut for Lancashire when he was 20 after establishing a reputation as a high-scoring left-hand bat in the Lancashire League. Just when his county career seemed to be in a decline after a promising start, he played a series of outstanding innings in the mid-seventies to win the Young Cricketer of the Year award.

1976: Geoff Miller (RHB/OB), a genuine all-rounder, played in 34 Tests between 1976 and 1984, and also became one of the country's outstanding slip-catchers. He captained Derbyshire in 1979, 1980 and 1981 and toured Australia on three occasions. He left for Essex in the mid-eighties.

1977: Ian Botham (RHB/RFM), an all-rounder of outstanding ability and one of the game's most colourful characters. His season of 1981, after being deprived of the England captaincy, will never be forgotten and, despite frequent brushes with authority on a variety of matters, he remains the game's top 'box office' personality. He moved from Somerset to Worcs in early 1987 and at the end of 1987 was the world's leading wicket-taker in Tests.

1978: David Gower (LHM), an elegant and polished left-hand batsman of great ability who captained England in 1984, 1985, and the beginning of 1986. An automatic selection for England when available (he opted out of Test cricket in the winter of 1987–88) and is nearing 100 Tests.

1979: Paul Parker (RHB), the new Sussex captain for 1988, has played only one Test (1981) which seems astonishing when one considers the immense potential he showed in his three years at Cambridge (1976–78). He scored 215 against Essex in his first season at University. An excellent fieldsman, especially in the covers.

1980: Graham Dilley (RF, LHB) is another fast bowler whose career has been interrupted by injuries and also by problems with his action. Nevertheless, he has looked one of England's outstanding fast bowling hopes for the past six or seven years. Moved from Kent to Worcs in 1987.

Bill Athey (now with Yorkshire — he moved to Gloucs in 1984) received a special award as the outstanding young batsman of the season in which he made his Test debut.

1981: Mike Gatting (RHB, RM) became captain of Middlesex in 1983 and of England in 1986 and quickly established himself as one of the tougher and more rugged type of leaders who set their own example. A good, hard-hitting batsman, he has little tolerance for anyone who does not give 100 per cent in any side he skippers. Achieved unfortunate, and unprecedented, publicity for his clashes with Pakistan umpire Shakoor Rana on the 1987 tour.

1982: Norman Cowans (RF), born in Jamaica but qualified for England, went on the England tour to Australia in 1982–83. He played an important part in Middlesex successes in the first half of the 1980s but appeared to lose some of his confidence after being dropped by England.

1983: Neil Foster (RFM), an accurate and penetrative bowler who moves the ball off the seam and in the air. Bowled exceptionally well against Pakistan at Headingley in 1987 but was on the losing side. A useful tail-end batsman, he has done well for England on a number of occasions and is a fine thrower from the deep.

1984: Robert Bailey (RHB/OB), Staffordshire-born as a number of Northants recruits have been over the years, has been highly regarded by observers of the game for the past three or four years. A very hard-hitting batsman who can expect a Test chance before long.

1985: David Lawrence (RF) is a genuinely quick bowler who formed a formidable opening partnership with the Jamaican, Courtney Walsh, for Gloucs in 1984. If he has not quite fulfilled the hopes of the England Selectors when they sent him to Sri Lanka with England 'B' in 1985–86, he is known to have the ability to bowl really fast.

1986: Ashley Metcalfe (RHB), one of the new generation of Yorkshire batsmen, scored 122 on his debut in 1983 at Bradford. He is a handsome stroke player of great confidence and a good fieldsman in the covers. Married to the younger daughter of Raymond Illingworth.

James Whitaker (RHB) is a Yorkshireman, too, but opted to play for Leics after leaving Uppingham School. An accomplished stroke-maker who was disappointed not to do better (though with only limited opportunities) on England's tour to Australia in the winter of 1986–87.

1987: Richard Blakey is a wicketkeeper-batsman from the Huddersfield League who gained a regular place at No. 3 for Yorkshire in 1987. He made his first double-century at Headingley on the day that Donald Carr went to inspect the wicket — criticised as sub-standard — on which England had lost to Pakistan two months earlier.

Photographic acknowledgement

The authors and publishers would like to thank the following photographers and agencies for permission to reproduce their copyright material:

Photoscource
Pages 13, 14, 18 (both, 19, 23, 25, 35 (below), 37, 41, 42, 46 (left), 47, 50, 52, 64, 67, 84, 85, 86, 91, 94 (left), 102 (above), 111.

Sport & General Press Agency
Pages 17, 27, 34, 38, 39, 55 (right), 56, 58, 59, 60, 63, 68, 71, 72, 79 (below), 80, 81, 89, 98, 99, 109, 114, 121, 126, 139, 174.

Times
Pages 18, 21, 33, 35 (above), 74, 95, 106, 131 (left).

Press Association
Pages 54, 75, 79 (above), 125, 140, 149 (right), 153 (both), 162 (below), 169, 177.

Patrick Eagar
Pages 51, 94 (right), 102 (both), 105, 109, 110, 113, 119, 127 (above), 134, 135, 138, 143, 144, 148 (right), 161, 175 (both), 180, 181, 189, 190 (above).

Ken Kelly
Pages 55 (left), 90, 118 (left), 130 (below), 131 (right), 133, 152.

Graham Morris
Pages 190 (below), 193.

All-Sport Photographic
Pages 148 (left), 165, 166, 192.

Colorsport
Pages 130 (left), 149 (left).

Sporting Pictures (UK)
Pages 118 (right), 158.

Bob Thomas Photography
Pages 88, 136.

Syndication International
Page 122.

Bill Smith
Page 127 (below).

Associated Sports Photography
Pages 99, 154, 162 (above), 186.

BBC Hulton Picture Library
Page 22.

Telepix
Page 29.

Peter Whyte
Page 191

Alan Cozzi
Page 171

Universal Pictorial
Page 185

Property of David Frith
Pages 12, 30.

All other photographs not credited come from private collections.

Index